The Medieval New

THE MIDDLE AGES SERIES

Ruth Mazo Karras, Series Editor

Edward Peters, Founding Editor

A complete list of books in the series
is available from the publisher.

THE
MEDIEVAL
NEW

Ambivalence
in an Age of Innovation

Patricia Clare Ingham

PENN

UNIVERSITY OF PENNSYLVANIA PRESS

PHILADELPHIA

Published by
University of Pennsylvania Press
Philadelphia, Pennsylvania 19104-4112
www.upenn.edu/pennpress

Printed in the United States of America on acid-free paper
1 3 5 7 9 10 8 6 4 2

Library of Congress Cataloging-in-Publication Data
ISBN 978-0-8122-4706-0

for Doug

Contents

Introduction

Newfangled Values

Le nouveau n'est pas une mode; c'est une valeur.
—Roland Barthes, *Le plaisir du texte*

Novelty-mongering does not necessarily reflect novelty, much less progress.
—David Edgerton, "Innovation, Technology, or History"

"The New is not a fashion," writes Roland Barthes, "it is a value."[1] Referring to novelty as a feature of the pleasure of the text, Barthes casts the new as discursive value rather than empirical fact. This seems both undeniable and counterintuitive. From the "New World" to the "latest iPhone," newness stakes its power on the side of the event, unpredicted and unlooked for—on surprise and discontinuity as empirical fact. Yet our attraction to gadgets, fashions, or breathtaking discoveries exceeds utility, as a variety of scholars have shown.[2] Take, for example, medieval historian Lynn White's controversial "stirrup thesis" (1962). White's ground-breaking account of the instrumentality of the lowly stirrup to the dramatic rise of feudalism was, of course, mostly wrong about feudalism; but this has not blunted the significance of his imaginative method to the History of Technology, a field still oriented around the inestimable value of small inventions. Yet if the full measure of our fascination with new things, new discoveries, or new events is on display in narratives like White's, the process by which the new affects the movements of history and culture is not adequately described by them. Whatever the new is or means at its broadest, it is not the stirrup (or any other single invention, discovery, or mode of thought), no matter how seductive or ingenious such arguments may be.[3]

The new, instead, finds meaning within a larger narrative arc. It is in *narrative* that the unusual, the anomalous, or capricious takes on innovation's dazzle and shine. The new appears, moreover, primarily in the backward glance, what Jacques Lacan and Slavoj Žižek call the *après-coup*. As Nicholas Taleb demonstrates (analyst of the unlooked-for event coded as *The Black Swan*), the contours of newness emerge only once the anomalous is elevated, retroactively, to the status of the transformative, rather than, say, relegated to the dustbin of history as irrelevant.[4] Narratives about the new mark the valuations through which scholars, scientists, historians, or marketers insist that something anomalous deserves our care—and our careful attention. This is precisely the benefit sought by Lynn White when he insisted that we care about a seemingly small invention like the stirrup and, by extension, look again at a host of historically undervalued breakthroughs.

Yet if the new is a value, it has persistently seemed *not* to be a medieval one. Even Barthes locates the emergence of the new in the post-medieval age: "the erotics of the New began in the eighteenth century: a long transformational process."[5] Scholars have long thought, as Barthes seems to, that medieval people could not have cared less about the new; Barthes emphasizes the distance crossed by that "transformational process" through which Western culture, once fascinated with conservation, became enamored of the new. Few doubt, of course, the astonishing inventiveness of the medieval era itself, a time of developments in a range of fields, from architecture to armaments, chemistry to clocks, from music to monasticism to mechanics, translation to toys. Despite this recognition, the Middle Ages continue to be understood as a time exclusively preoccupied with revivals of old forms, rather than an embrace of novelty or an active avant garde.[6] This, I argue throughout this study, misunderstands both the persistent problem of the new and the complex, fascinating, and equivocal treatment of that category regularly found in the medieval record. Such assumptions need to be rethought in the light of developments both within and beyond the field of Medieval Studies.

Few contemporary medievalists are likely to credit the opposition of a traditional Middle Ages against an innovating modernity. We know by now, in the much-cited words of Bruno Latour, that "we have never been modern." Critiques of periodization are well advanced, and diverse scholars have helped to dismantle models of historical difference dependent on an absolute rupture of then and now, medieval and modern. We have come to recognize the persistence of the past, thanks to work by Bruce Holsinger, Michelle Warren, Karma Lochrie, Jennifer Summit, Tom Prendergast and Stephanie Trigg,

David Wallace, and Aranye Fradenburg; and thanks to the work of William Kuskin, Elizabeth Scala, Jeffrey Jerome Cohen, John Ganim, Kathleen Davis, and Carolyn Dinshaw, among others, we mark the power of repetition, recovery, or return for historical attachments, literary production, and temporal change. Yet such insights have more often led to an account of the persistence of the medieval old in the modern new, rather than the kind of analysis I undertake here, a reading of the new ready to be discovered in the medieval archive. In some cases, this work has unintentionally obscured the problem of newness as such.

No one, least of all those critiquing an overemphasis on historical discontinuity, would argue that new events, eruptions, or shifts never occur; the notion that certain provocative differences mark, say, the transit from the twelfth century to the twentieth (or, for that matter, the fourteenth to the fifteenth) seems beyond doubt. Yet how are we to account for such alterations, for change *as* novelty, without relying on overblown versions of the new as opposed to the old? How to articulate changes in literary practice, in language, or genre, in modes of production or reading, without reinstalling the new as absolute break? How, to take an example in a different register, might we grasp the arresting nature of the claim that the voyaging Christopher Columbus encountered something "new," without overlooking the admiral's attachments to "old world" models, religious, navigational, or prophetic? An examination of what I am calling the medieval new can assist us here. This is in part because "old" and "new" did not signify in the same way in the Middle Ages as they do today. For one thing, and as we shall see, writers at that time did not regularly cast innovation as utterly distinct from the old. For this reason and others, certain subtle medieval versions of the new might harbor important creative and critical ambitions. This is a point of particular cogency in an age when "innovation" has become a nearly ubiquitous slogan for the twenty-first-century university, an institution which is also dedicated to the preservation and renewal of diverse cultures past and present, of histories of reading, of research, of artistic, musical, and literary production.

It is time, then, to consider the problem of the new anew. To be sure, the notion of *The Medieval New* still seems oxymoronic. This is precisely the point. Examining an archive of paradoxical representations of the new in the context of contemporaneous philosophical controversies over *novum* and its cognates, I argue, first, that widespread caution about the new was generated, not by the blind appeal of tradition in a religiously conservative age, but as a response to radical expansions of possibility in realms of art and science; and, second, that novelty—from Aquinas to Columbus—provoked ethical questions to which we might return. For unlike models of thought motivated by late capitalism—in which "new" and "innovation" are synonyms for the good—the medieval "new" served as a means to adjudicate the ethics of invention and eventful change, leveraging thorny problems of fate, creativity, and desire. The medieval discourse about the new engaged questions of value at every turn. When alchemists claimed that Art could accelerate the processes of Nature, they troubled stable distinctions between the counterfactual and the counterfeit. While poets cautioned against the seductions of the "newfangled" (the term, if not precisely coined by Chaucer, regularly used by him in novel ways), they nonetheless deployed such disruptive power as incitement to their own versification. When artisans invented gargoyles, or scribes designed fanciful marginalia, their compositions would be both praised and castigated as perverse, the latter famously, in Alain de Lille's *Complaint*, by the allegorical figure of Nature herself.

This book reconsiders the insights mined from the equivocal medieval rhetoric of novelty by analyzing select, influential signifiers of the "new" from the twelfth to the sixteenth centuries. Newness—linked to but not identical with innovation in this archive—emerges as a "problem-question,"[7] central to many of the era's most important debates. Scholastic taxonomies persistently engage the new, whether, as Aquinas does, by considering the newness of the world (*novitas mundi*), or, as Bonaventure would, by distinguishing new compositions (*novae compositiones*) made by humans from new metaphysical things (*novae res*) preserved for God alone; or, as in the writings of Duns Scotus, while pondering the sudden advent of new ideas. This preoccupation has not been fully recognized, and needs to be understood in relation to the extensive aesthetic, literary, technical, and religious vocabularies developing throughout the period: the descriptions of novel gadgets, the man-made marvels of romance; the rhetoric of novelty in hagiography, such as is found in the 1228 *Vita of St. Francis*; expressions of desire for youth and youthfulness whether in lyrics or in the loathly lady tradition; prophetic histories of a new age or of the longed-for New Jerusalem; Dante's neologisms and his *Vita Nuova*. Diverse treatments of the new shed light on the vicissitudes of epistemology, ethics, and desire.

Yet to reconsider the complex problem of the new, I must also engage some influential narratives of culture and human ingenuity through which the medieval new came to figure the impossible, the prohibited, or the oxymoronic. Thus my second aim, entwined with the first, involves attending to the ways in which the medieval era has long performed a kind of historiographic work in our understanding of the attractions of novelty, offering the ballast of tradition as a brake on the drive to make it new. Such a project requires a method of dialectical rereading rather than simple historicist recovery.[8]

If, as we have supposed, the medieval period is generally inhospitable to the notion of the new, why have so many of its thinkers, such as Aquinas, or Roger Bacon, or Dante, been crucial to popular and scholarly accounts of modern innovation and culture, as, for instance, in modernist writer and Harvard medievalist Henry Adams's *Mont-Saint-Michel and Chartres*; or in Ezra Pound's exhortation to make it new? And why have premodern categories related to novelty (*curiositas*; *ingenium*; ex nihilo) been instrumental in accounts of modernity, like Hans Blumenberg's, originality, like Kant's, or secular form, like Adorno's?[9] Rather than dismiss all such periodizing narratives as biased or blind, I take them as serious attempts to confront difficult questions of value and meaning that emerge in the complex historical relationships addressed by the category of the new.[10] What, after all, constitutes something new, and how can we be confident when it has influentially appeared? Thus, my study is aimed at two different sets of readers: at those interested in tracking the way novelty and tradition entwine at key moments in the culture of the high and late Middle Ages; and at those wishing to rethink current assumptions about newness from the vantage of the intellectual history that helped produce them.

Accounts of modernity as a period of secularization, or disenchantment, or rationalization have supported many of the familiar assumptions about the Middle Ages as uninterested in novelty—in standard readings of "disenchanted" modernity ascribed to Max Weber, or in Walter Benjamin's account of allegory, Jacob Burckhardt's *Kulturgeschichte*, or Hans Blumenberg's reading of medieval *curiositas* as a theoretical dead end.[11] Medievalists, too, have contributed: Richard Firth Green reads the alchemical project as "studiously regressive"; Hans Gumbrecht insists that transformative events in the Middle Ages were "detached from innovation"; Beryl Smalley views the oscillations in ecclesiastical attitudes toward novelty as regularly neutralized when "tradition confronted tradition"; Michael Camille claimed that medieval artisans—no matter how whimsical their compositions—were committed to what he called "secondariness."[12] Yet medievalists today also join colleagues in adjacent fields in questioning histories of "secularization" and "disenchantment," reconsidering the continuities as well as disjunctions among eras early and late. Historians of science now stress the instrumentality of the so-called "occult" medieval "sciences" to later disciplines of chemistry and astronomy; scholars more readily acknowledge the productivity of premodern imaginative literature for dreaming up whimsical (or crackpot) mechanics, to say nothing of the vernacular innovations of language and verse, produced by way of a culture of artistic copying.

Yet no one has yet explained why, particularly as a deeply innovating culture, the Middle Ages produced such an ethically charged, ambivalent account of the new. And no one has linked this ambivalence to certain equivocations legible in influential periodizing versions of modernity. We have instead read the cautions against the newfangled in the medieval record as a defense of tradition, wrongly assuming that a period committed to old *auctoritas* could not also be complexly preoccupied with the benefits and liabilities of novelty—or vice versa. Developments in critical and cultural theory can help us here. We now know, thanks to Gilles Deleuze, that repetition, a practice crucial to a medieval artistic culture of copying, plays a dynamic role in the production of new things and ideas[13]; we recognize, thanks to Jacques Lacan, on the one hand, and Nicholas Taleb, on the other, that the outlines of the new emerge mainly in retrospect; and the writings of Bruno Latour, Craig Calhoun, and David Edgerton have helped us better understand the dynamics of technological networks of change where tradition and repetition can serve as a means to promote rather than stymie new things and ideas.[14] A broad reconsideration of the medieval newfangled is now not only desirable, but also possible in a way it has not been before.

As the preceding suggests, I contend that our analytical tools need to be trained not simply on the cultural status of innovation, then or now, but on the broader category of the new as such. Only in this way can we track fully the desiring structures embedded in the conviction that innovation is easily recognized, and closely tied to productivity as the primary cultural work that matters. In the remainder of this introduction I reconsider some influential medieval key words so as to reoccupy "the new" as a category both of history and of value. Immanuel Kant's profound rethinking of *ingenium* (idiosyncratic whimsy) and Hans Blumenberg's influential account of *curiositas* (curiosity) are crucial to what follows. Each has played a particular role in the process by which the modern notion of the "new" has emerged as a purified category, torqued away from the fabrications of mere technology, on the one hand, and a medieval culture of copying, on the other. Attending to this broadened account of the new illuminates the process by which innovation has come to figure as that superior and far-reaching brand of newness privileged over and above the trivialities of mere novelty.

A History of Signifiers

While novelty and innovation have a common linguistic root ("novus"), the two are more and less than synonyms of one another. First, to the less: in contemporary parlance the two differ not only in degree, but also in kind. A novelty is not, after all, simply a miniature type of innovation; the word smacks instead of the cheap, the ephemeral, the trivial. Now to the more: both words gesture toward renewal and fresh-feeling, hinting at the intimacies of recreation with re-creation, or the links between play (novelties are toys, after all) and the most ambitious creative productions, technological, literary, philosophical, artistic, or scientific. In contemporary discourse, the trivialization and diminution of "mere" novelties serves to cast innovations as large and important. Innovation, in this mode, is thought to be best pursued through especially useful disciplines like the sciences, rather than through "traditional," that is, humanistic, ones, the latter increasingly understood as inessential, or expendable, no matter how edifying or enjoyable they may also be.

There is an important premodern discourse of ethics behind this confidence, yet it is one that today goes largely unacknowledged. The influential distinction between "use" and "enjoyment" originates with Augustine, but two other medieval key words pertain: *ingenium* and *curiositas*. Attending to the history of these two signifiers can help us.[15] Both converged on profoundly ethical questions. There was, for one thing, a large and interesting literature on pleasure and knowledge in ethics, touching on the place of the passions in medieval psychology.[16] Literary scholars analyzing poetry in the period of high scholasticism have emphasized the degree to which ethics and enjoyment— the relation of human happiness to virtue—preoccupied various intellectuals throughout the high Middle Ages, with established "points of contact between philosophy, poetry, theology, and law" well into the fourteenth century.[17]

Ingenium—one of the etymons embedded in Kant's account of Genius— was crucial to this history. A key category by which medieval writers considered the new, premodern *ingenium* traces its coinage to Cicero, in whose writing it figured inborn, though idiosyncratic, talent.[18] "The chief virtue of the orator is inborn *ingenium*, from which sharpness of mind arise sharpness in invention, richness in exposition and ornament, firm and long-lasting memory," he writes in *De oratore*.[19] During the medieval period, *ingenium* figured as whimsical cleverness, and was regularly cast in distinction to convention and things conventional (*usus* or *consuetudo*). This *ingenium* bridged what we today understand to be very different kinds of intellectual endeavors. As its etymological links to both ingenuity and engineer suggest, *ingenium* pertained to the technologies as well as to the arts, referring to invention in forms philosophic, aesthetic, and technical. Vernacular forms (*engin* in Old French, *gyn* or *engyn* in Middle English) refer to poems, to tapestries, to jeweled mausoleums, but also to narrative histories, mousetraps, automata, or flying buttresses. In its medieval usage, moreover, *ingenium* raised ethical questions: cleverness and wit were virtues; yet one could be too clever by half, deploying ingenuity in the service of deceit or fraud. And this was indeed its particular place in debates over the vicissitudes of human innovations.

The premodern tradition of *ingenium* turns out to have been useful to Immanuel Kant, and it serves as one of the two etymological strands at play in his unruly signifier for originality and innovation, Genius (German, *Genie* from the French, *génie*). In § 46 of his *Third Critique*, Kant offers *ingenium* as the first player in a doubled etymology of Genius: "Genius is the inborn predisposition of the mind (*ingenium*) through which nature gives rule to art."[20] Building on a key word through which, as we shall see, medieval thinkers regularly considered the new, Kant emphasizes genius as an inborn human capacity. But everything that follows this emphasis will depersonalize genius as something in excess of inborn talent; as is well known, the Latin *genius* (guardian spirit) is Kant's other etymological root. By the time Kant uses the latter term, much of its mythopoetic sense of "genie" (or "jinn") was diminished,[21] but he nonetheless points to the source of genius in nature, its workings hidden even from the person of such talent. Kant sets his treatment of genius against the tradition in another crucial way, one that has made appreciating the nuances of medieval accounts of the new especially difficult. His genius does not pertain to the scientist, and certainly not to the technician, but exclusively to the artist. Unlike the earlier tradition in which invention, human creativity, and idiosyncratic whimsy figured across the range of creative activity, Kant deploys *ingenium* in an account of the creation of new things reserved exclusively for the innovative artist. And in this way he also preserves the realm of science as free from idiosyncrasies or aesthetic influences.

Kant will also, in the context of this account of genius, distinguish the originality of genius from "original nonsense."[22] Gesturing toward problems of frivolity and triviality also crucial, as we shall shortly see, to the medieval case, he insists that few artistic idiosyncrasies rise to the level of the exemplary brand of originality that marks the art of genius. Thus, even as he strips the notion of *ingenium* of its premodern ethical resonances as a potentially deceitful kind of cleverness, Kant encodes pejorative features of apparently excessive creativity. These features are found in the medieval record by way of my second key word: *curiositas*, or specifically via *vitium curiositatis*, the vice of curiosity. As is well known, the trivial, the superfluous, the unimportant are explicitly raised, in medieval accounts of making, by way of this second term.

A neologism also first used by Cicero, the word *curiositas* was based on the adjective *curiosus*, which in turn derived from the substantive *cura*, or care. This derivation underwrote centuries of debate concerning the relation of the pursuit of knowledge to questions of value: what kinds of things, and what kinds of intellectual pursuits, are deserving of our care and our careful attention? Care extends from things therapeutic to things philosophical, from attachment and ministration to attentiveness and responsibility. By the twelfth century this was a fundamental and wide-ranging ethical question. Medieval Christian moralists writing on the topic regularly deploy the links between care and curiosity. And Hans Blumenberg will hang his account of the transition from medieval to modern epochs, in his *Legitimacy of the Modern Age*, on their use of this etymology.[23]

Augustinian and scholastic cautions against the dangers of *vitium curiositatis* (the vice of curiosity) are popularly thought to have placed near absolute limits on the moral pursuit of knowledge, limits particular to medieval thought. *Curiositas*, so Christian Zacher asserted in an influential but unfortunately overstated account, "diverts [our] spiritual sight from otherworldly goals, distracting [us] with the spectacle of worldly landscapes."[24] Such a statement oversimplifies a range of subtle and nuanced debates on this topic occurring throughout the medieval centuries. It was not, for example, true that *curiositas* was identical to *vitium curiositatis*, as both Zacher and Blumenberg assume. Nor is it true that medieval thinkers were uninterested in parsing the differences between *bona*, *media*, and *mala curiositas*, as did their ancestors and their posterity.[25] Efforts to distinguish "good" curiosity from "bad" curiosity postdated ancient times, as Richard Newhauser has established definitively, and neither term could be defined, as Zacher implies, by a phrase like "the eager desire to know." "This is because," as Newhauser points out, "the moralists never considered the desire to know as something evil in itself, certainly not after the recovery of Aristotle's *Metaphysics*."[26] We recall, of course, that the opening statement of the *Metaphysics* supports the claim for such a desire as morally neutral: "All men are, by nature, desirous to know things."

Augustine, Abelard, and Aquinas were all concerned with the role that the human desire for knowledge played in the pursuit of human happiness, if in slightly different ways. How, these thinkers ask, is *curiositas* related to those things on which our happiness depends, the pursuit of knowledge among them? By way of its etymological links to care, this brand of *curiositas* will influentially come to police the border that separates those essential things that deserve our care from those inessential, superfluous things that should properly lie outside it. In the particularly influential Thomistic tradition, important to Blumenberg, the pursuit of Aristotelian "scientific demonstration" will be legitimated by differentiating knowledge necessary to our happiness, what Aquinas terms *studiositas*, from human inquiry preoccupied with inconsequential things. It is important to note that, in its original context, such a distinction did not undermine "secular" intellectual endeavor so much as support it, or certain versions of it: scholastic inquiry could thus be defended as focused on matters of necessity, necessity being, in Aquinas's Aristotelian project, the proper object of reason.[27] Along the way questions of excess, waste, and superfluity gained further ethical resonance. *Vitium curiositatis*, Aquinas argues, wastes time: far from being necessary for human happiness, it draws us toward "restless activity" amid "the futility of trying to achieve under [our] own power the lost fullness of . . . existence."[28] In this Thomistic tradition, *vitium curiositatis* came to be characterized as "care" for superfluous matters.

That said, medieval categories of *curiositas* and *vitium curiositatis* ranged well beyond this influential Thomistic distinction, and evinced a surprising degree of conceptual flexibility. Far from shying away from questions about the nature of curiosity, a pursuit that might seem, in the wake of Thomas, itself a waste of time, medieval thinkers display persistent and flexible interest in the power and possibilities of *curiositas*, good, bad, or mixed, at a time when some (but not all) versions of it were understood to converge on "a state of the passions . . . entail[ing] both sensitive and intellective faults."[29] Qualifications regarding the vice of curiosity will be made with regard to the human senses, and descriptions of *vitium curiositatis* will converge on excesses of desire associated with many of the capital vices, the seven or eight (sometimes more) chief categories of sinfulness.

Premodern *curiositas* was, in this regard, an enormous category and a remarkably mobile one. It was linked, variously if also at times simultaneously, to pride, avarice, gluttony, and/or sloth. Moderation in intellectual pursuits

was regularly recommended, as when moralists like Peter of Limoges emphasized "how pernicious an *excessive* curiosity of the eyes can be"[30] (my emphasis). While Bacon's *Opus Majus* does not, as far as I am aware, engage the
discourse of *curiositas* directly, it does, like Peter's *The Moral Treatise on the Eye*,
link research findings we would recognize today as scientific to avowedly
moral pursuits, presumably at least in part to legitimate a research program
during the contentious times surrounding the scholastic condemnations of
1277.[31] If mention of these thirteenth-century condemnations of the University Masters at Paris or Oxford raises the specter of religious blindness, or
suggests unusual strictures on intellectual freedom, we might recognize, along
with Edward Peters, the degree to which intellectual freedom historically
emerges less as a discourse of "goods pursued and sustained for their own sake"
than as "a compromise between contending ideologies and powers,"[32] as it did,
Peters argues, in both Aquinas's Middle Ages and Max Weber's modernity.

Of course, the specificities of those ideologies and powers vary according
to circumstance. My point is not that there are no sharp distinctions between
the medieval concerns about *ingenium* or *curiositas* and modern theorizations
of the same. There were, for instance, limits placed on speculative knowledge
during the medieval period, and Blumenberg's account of that tradition is an
important one. And it is surely notable that the medieval discourse classified
certain ethical issues by way of curiosity (the point, for instance, that knowledge used for personal profit constitutes a species of *vitium curiositatis* via
greed), concerns raised today in alternative registers, but raised today nonetheless. My point is that the very mobility of this category suggests an abiding,
even obsessive, preoccupation with a wide range of ethical questions related to
human knowing. Avarice and gluttony make problems of appetite one of the
focal points of analysis and, accordingly, query the relation of the particular
individual to the larger society of which she is a part. Concerns about the intellective and libidinal appetites regularly drove, rather than arrested, creative
production in poetry as well as metaphysics. Curiosity, then, involved not
doubts about knowledge as worth pursuing, but the *kind* of knowledge worthy of such pursuit and the best ways of pursuing it. "What was important,"
writes Newhauser, "was not a question of knowing, but of misplaced *cura*, of
excessive care."[33] Care, that is, about what were understood to be self-serving
or inconsequential matters. Debates about which disciplines or topics deserve
our care remain crucial to the functioning of knowledge systems to this day.

The discourse of curiosity and care, deployed during the Middle Ages to
defend secular knowledge, will be redeployed in accounts of secularization like

Blumenberg's to bolster the very realm that Kant exempted from his account of artistic genius: theoretical science. In the wake of this work, novelty, precisely as a question of value, was split in two: the value of the work of art for its own sake was abstracted as an aesthetically radical brand of the new, on the one hand; on the other hand, the value of innovation was grounded in theoretical science, not ingenuity or technical whimsy, as the precinct for the pursuit of essential questions related to human care. Once these narratives of value for the new took hold, the earlier tradition, which conjoined fields of "art" and "sciences," and considered the new via a discourse linking technologies to art as well as to ethics, could only seem irrelevant to such questions.

Blumenberg's intellectual history maddeningly misreads key features of the larger medieval discourse of curiosity,[34] yet his work nonetheless remains insightful, particularly insofar as he links differences of thought and value to a continuing concern with questions of care. His account of these differences can, moreover, be leveraged for another account of the new, one that emphasizes, even more than Blumenberg himself, the *persistence* of the contrast between necessity and superfluity with distinctly premodern roots. Residual features of this distinction continue today in pragmatic debates about the nature of novelty and innovation both.

The Shock of the Old

The questions of value raised by the story of the medieval new that I am about to offer remain fully relevant today. If the new constituted a "problem-question" for the scholastics, it has, arguably, emerged again as a "problem-question," particularly for the Liberal Arts. Influenced by business models of "creative destruction,"[35] the achievement of innovation seems regularly predicated upon a systematic rejection of what is "established, traditional, familiar, and comfortable."[36] The current conversation, that is, regularly opposes conservation, tradition, even at times history itself, to all things new. But amid what Naomi Klein calls the "shock doctrine" of disaster capitalism, and given the force of "creative destruction," and its new partner "disruptive innovation," innovation emerges as an increasingly problematical category, a point that historian of technology David Edgerton has eloquently made. "It is a mistake to believe," Edgerton writes, "that [innovation] has been central to public policy (market liberalization has been much more significant) or that innovation has in fact increased."[37] Edgerton places the current preoccupation with innovation as part of a drive toward what he calls "novelty-mongering," a trend that, he argues, "does not necessarily reflect novelty, much less progress."[38] Such critiques urge us to question the current over-valuation of innovation however defined; and they astutely challenge the designation of "tradition" as trivial or superfluous, as well as the regular equation of innovation with neoliberal definitions of economic progress.[39] Deservedly so. This point is useful for medievalists, particularly as some influential accounts of premodern technological innovation, for instance, Joel Mokyr's *The Lever of Riches: Technological Creativity and Economic Progress*,[40] pursue neoliberal models of creativity tied to market expansion, with an accordingly limited picture of medieval novelty and innovation both.

In his larger body of work, Edgerton resituates the productive advances wrought by "traditional" methods and modes for an account of twentieth-century technology.[41] His *The Shock of the Old* (2007) highlights a host of related historiographical problems. Does innovation inhere primarily in shifts related to the creation of objects, or to their use? By what method can we assess the myriad ways in which procedures, tools, inventions, or their adoption engage with, repeat, or depart from tradition? And by what logic are such objects linked to, indeed crucial agents in, a discourse about progress ineluctably driving technological histories? Edgerton's work not only broadens our sense of the imprecision of current accounts, it also makes clear the perverse histories produced when the chronologies of technology are driven solely by a search for innovations. And his questions seem especially trenchant to those of us working with cultural materials that explicitly cast invention or change in terms other than old versus new.[42]

It may be too soon for Edgerton's work to have achieved its full effect, though today assumptions about "creative destruction" remain surprisingly pervasive—and are regularly bought on the slimmest of evidence. Even penetrating analyses of the ideologies of "creative destruction" aimed at Humanities researchers, as, for instance, in Alan Liu's *The Culture of Cool: Knowledge Work and the Culture of Information*,[43] overstate the case. Liu's investigation of the place of the literary and aesthetic in what has become, he argues, a "regime of systematic innovation"[44] attempts to fight notions of "creative destruction" by redeploying them to serve rather than hobble work in the arts and humanities: radical artistic creativity (the so-called "destructive creativity" of avant garde artists like Banksey) innovate even as they gum up the works of capitalist production; as such, Liu argues, they offer a model of art able to subvert the culture of information, offering another chapter in the long history of radical artistic originality.

Yet Liu's account of "Literature and Creative Destruction" gives up too
much ground regarding both creativity and new things.[45] For one thing, he
coordinates artistic acts of copying, artistic "appropriation" or "sampling,"
with "acts of destruction" deployed by "the most ambitious art" to "make history." When even "sampling" figures as a tool of "creative destruction"—rather
than, say, an innovative act of ambivalent *homage*, we have bought entirely the
notion that innovation lays waste to what has come before. The notion that
modern creative artistry aspires to a radical break with all that has come before
traces its history to Romantic-era notions of authorship and poetic genius,
indebted to Kantian accounts of the genius as radical innovator, both unique
and exemplary.

Given the current context and the intellectual history just rehearsed, the
category of technology will serve as a crucial hinge for my reoccupation of the
vicissitudes of the medieval new, and for a host of reasons. In the first place,
today's category of technology considers questions examined during the Middle Ages by way of the "sciences"[46] on the one hand and poetry on the other.
Furthermore, the modern demotion of technology away from "pure science"
means that technology is more closely aligned with novelty, with fabricators
and makers, than it is with innovative speculation in Blumenberg's sense. In
this way, modern technicians resemble medieval artisans, the latter a term that
included poets as well as stone masons. Today's understanding of technology,
I would argue, shows the residue of a wide range of features of the medieval
discourse of the new.[47] The modern category plays a key role as heir to the
premodern one: crossing artisanal technique with imaginative cleverness; mix-
ing tradition with novelty; prompting a series of ethical questions having to do
with the limitations of mechanization or the promise of freedom. Finally, in
both registers copying emerges as essential in a way not easily accommodated
either by theoretical science or by Kantian Genius.

A return to the medieval record can, as a result, shed light on features of
our current problem-question. The following chapters analyze a medieval alternative spanning the aesthetic and scientific registers, and combining tradition with originality. The premodern record does not rank innovation over
novelty; it crosses the "sciences" with the artistic and the technical. This is, in
fact, one of its virtues. And in this it foregrounds features of "innovation" recently emphasized by Bruno Latour.[48] Furthermore, if some medieval thinkers
worry over apparently superfluous things, others play with all manner of odd,
quirky, or whimsical monstrosities. My account of these traditions of invention attends to the equivocal evidence so as to think through the features of an

attraction to novelty both linked with, and in excess of, instrumental productivity.[49] What, I ask, might the ambivalent status of newness during the medieval centuries offer for a fuller version of the shape and history of the new than the one currently on display? This means, first and foremost, that we acknowledge the early discourse of newness as something more complex, and more ethically interesting, than has heretofore been recognized. For reasons that should be clear by now, this account will take the measure of a number of disparate fields, natural philosophy and poetry, book production and cosmology, romance and gadgetry. This book, then, synthesizes important specialist accounts of the history of philosophy and of technology, as well as the power of the object in literary romance as a genre.

Equivocally New

The history of medieval newness powerfully celebrates and queries the power and point of repetition. Precisely because the Middle Ages were home to a dynamic international culture of artistic, religious, and technical copying, medieval debates about the new can contribute to ongoing reassessments of the productive drive embraced by reworking, rereading, reshuffling, or "sampling" earlier work. Copying is a very old practice, one of the primary ways that early writers pursued their interest in the new (see Chapters 3 and 4), famously renewing the stories told by literary contemporaries and predecessors, "sampling" well-known plots and poetic set-pieces in fresh new ways. Poets offered ingeniously subtle examples, even as some, like Chaucer, regularly tease readers with fake sources and misattributions. Medieval artists and technicians reveled in the genuine pleasures of duplicating nature in culture, explicitly rearranging familiar figures and forms so as to prompt new accounts, and, perhaps surprisingly, producing some moving philosophical musings on the nature of the new along the way. And so, of course, did their Renaissance successors. Historians of art now more regularly blur period boundaries, and reconfigure the older Burckhardtian view of Renaissance artistic originality to stress continuities with habits long thought to be "medieval": as Ladis and Wood put it, "borrowing of another's style" and "even the conscious denial of an artist's individuality might serve as a creative stimulus" throughout the Renaissance, when an artist's willingness to "hide his personality . . . by adopting another's style" seemed proof of both "extraordinary self-awareness and singular manual skill."[50]

In general, today we readily recognize the productive power of repetition, in ways both cultural and theoretical. Thanks to Gilles Deleuze, we understand "bare" repetition as precisely the "historical conditions under which the new is produced."[51] Committed to the radical account of future possibility available through Nietzsche's notion of "eternal return," Deleuze resituates repetition, as found in Freud's theory of the drives, beyond a bounded, and internally conflictual, model. Yet at the same time, he preserves the importance of repetition itself, severing what he calls "bare repetition" from Freud's death instinct. Deleuze's work poignantly reminds us of the possibility—the hope—embedded in Nietzsche's "eternal return": enacting repetition, even under the sway of compulsion, harbors the desire for a different outcome, for a new future. It is, in this regard, a wager on possibilities as yet unseen.

While Deleuze's thinking is generally understood as a radical departure from Freudian theory, it nonetheless resonates with a range of psychoanalytic writings, both certain features of Lacanian theory, and clinical literature subsequent to Freud, equally concerned with various types of repetition, or with the interplay between repetition and newness. "The meaning and import of repetition in human life must be considered in all its diversity," wrote Freudian clinician and theorist Hans W. Loewald in 1971, since everything "depends on *how* [things] are repeated"—"to what extent they can be taken over . . . and made over into something new."[52] Lacan's revision of Freud's notion of sublimation took up the relation of repetition and innovation by way of medieval accounts of creation ex nihilo (examined in more detail in Chapter 1), redeploying an equivocal kind of repetition as crucial to all manner of creative productivity.

Thus, while it may seem surprising to some, a fully *equivocal* model of the new remains persistently legible in psychoanalytic work, with implications for a renewed understanding of history, as such theorists have long insisted.[53] If, as Freud opined in *The Question of Lay Analysis*, "every discovery is always only half as new as it appears to be at first,"[54] this suggests that newness might be a glass half empty *and* half full. Such remarks by Freud are redeployed by Jean Laplanche, who emphasizes "new" developments in psychoanalytic thinking in terms resonant with earlier discourses of the new studied here: as a *return* to the source. "We will see that to carry the new is not necessarily to innovate, and not necessarily to distance oneself from foundations," writes Laplanche. "Between the term new and the term foundations," he continues, "there is thus an oscillation: the fact of making a return to foundations in order to renew them. To get back to the source." This is because "Psychoanalysis shows

us that history proceeds not by continuous progress, not by accumulation, . . .not by a development without fail." Laplanche here synthesizes his
own body of work as a clarification of "what founds psychoanalysis"; his methodology of rereading and return is not unique, but is also fundamental to
Jacques Lacan's theoretical and therapeutic innovations explicitly cast as a "rereading" of Freud. My point here is that such psychoanalytic accounts do not
deny the possibility of new insights, practices, habits, or discoveries in favor of
an always-deadening form of compulsive repetition, but instead emphasize
the equivocal ways something is recognized, or named, as new. This is not the
new as *opposed* to what has gone before, but entwined with it.[55]

In the medieval record, too, much depends on how things are repeated.
Yet we have not always recognized this fact. Even highly theoretical accounts
of medieval poetry, such as Jacqueline Cerquiglini-Toulet's *A New History of
Medieval French Literature*, tend to regard medieval approaches to old and new
via "a dichotomy," with one pole or the other favored "depending on the time
period, mentalities, and temperaments."[56] Yet medieval commitments to the
antique and modern, foundation and renewal, regularly offer not dichoto-
mous but insightfully *equivocal* accounts of newness as such. This picture of
newness punctuates the account that follows. I pay special attention to those
incidents where repetition and novelty emerge relationally. Diverse figures
(natural philosopher and linguist Roger Bacon, Geoffrey Chaucer, or musi-
cian and poet Guillaume de Machaut) attend to the new by casting it in paradoxical terms. Machaut, to take an example examined in detail in Chapter 4,
will deploy "new" ("de nouvel") equivocally to mean both "once" and "again,"
casting the novel through the fundamental paradox of its repetition. The new
emerges in Machaut, and in Chaucer who follows him, within the space of
this fundamental contradiction: an incomparable thing, replicated; a rare
event, repeated. In the scholastic context, examined more fully in Chapters 1
and 2, return to foundations constitutes a primary route to new practices,
rubrics, or developments. While invested in religious discourses keyed to specific times and places, the Cistercians, in particular, justified new religious
practice as a return, even more a *reformatio*, of tradition, a point emerging in
the famous debates over innovation between Bernard of Clairvaux and Peter
Abelard. As the fact of that debate also suggests, not all such returns pursue
innovation forthrightly. Elsewhere in the medieval record, desire for newness
equivocates between repetition as sameness and repetition as change, as when
even the recursive Fortune's Wheel appears by way of the up-to-the-minute
gadgetry of tooth-edged gears, as it does in the beautiful illumination from

manuscript FR 1586 (an important manuscript of Machaut's *Remedy of Fortune* housed in the Bibliothèque Nationale de France) gracing the cover of this book.

Engaged with such rich evidence of novel repetitions, my account of the paradox of the new offers a counter-narrative to its standard history as radical break or stark originality. Directed equivocally toward both idiosyncratic whimsy and convention, toward delight and desire but also prohibition and submission, the medieval ambivalence about the new raised persistently ethical questions. Attending fully to this ambivalence, I rely on the notion of ambivalence in its psychoanalytic sense: the simultaneous existence of contradictory attitudes and feelings toward a single object. Such contradictory impulses can, moreover, help explain the particular features of obsessive thought legible in scholastic practice.[57] This history of medieval creative production, precisely as an obsessional culture of copying, sheds light on the novel productivity at stake in how old things are reread, retold, rewritten, or rethought. In this way, it also sheds light on the innovating methods and practices of humanities research. Rereading practices are crucial to the ways humanities researchers innovate in almost every instance.

The book is organized around three pivotal key words: "Ex Nihilo," "Ingenium," and "Curiositas," thus grounding the overarching argument in debates important both to the treatment of the new in the Middle Ages and to modernity's periodizing claims. I adopt a largely chronological arc. Part I, "Ex Nihilo," demonstrates the ways in which the scholastic metaphysics of creation worked around the qualifications and limitations that philosophical inquiry placed on human creativity. Chapter 1, "Scholastic Novelties," reads the new as a "problem-question" beginning in the twelfth century, central to many of that era's most important debates. Medieval debates about innovation rework the contrast of old to new in favor of the distinction between social use and custom (*usus; consuetudo*) on the one hand, and inborn cleverness (*ingenium*) on the other; such moves preserve routes to human invention in an ethical discourse of wide resonance. Chapter 2, "Conjuring Roger Bacon," revisits the longstanding fascination with questions of Roger Bacon's scientific precocity. Bacon worked at the cutting edge of available knowledge during his lifetime, but by his own testimony was no "novelty-mongerer." I read Bacon's development of specific classes of linguistic equivocation as crucial to his speculations on things as yet unseen, from flying machines to underwater boats. Assessing mechanical transformations, some counterfactual and others counterfeit, the friar endeavors to legitimize intellectual inquiry at the limits of the possible.

While Part I tracks medieval newness as a means to adjudicate the boundary between the new as an idea and newness as it pertains to objects and things, Part II "Ingenium," takes up the well-known debates over the distinctions between legitimate and perverse compositions. In many ways the heart of the book, Chapters 3 and 4 turn to romance literature as a location for the full consideration of the novel inventions of Art and Science, and the properties that pertain to novelty. In Chapter 3, "Youthful Ingenuity," representations of childhood take center stage. Utopian representations of youth shed light on romance as a genre, described by one scholar as a "toy box" and contemporaneous with an international mass market in toys. The internationally popular *enfans* tale *Floris and Blauncheflour* (*FB*) offers an unusually enthusiastic account of the power of youthful *ingenium*. Close consideration of the French and Middle English versions reveals the processes by which the new comes to figure as an abstract category in literature, an adjectival marker for wondrous objects. Examined in the context of the Schoolmen from Part I, *FB* translates the transactions of Christian and Islamic intellectuals into the charming love of children as, I argue, a means to tame the more violent, indeed dangerous, desires at stake in invention. Chapter 4, "Little Nothings," takes up the ethical questions posed by the ambition of gadgets, the whimsical medieval *drôleries* surviving mainly in romance. Chaucer's *Squire's Tale* follows Guillaume de Machaut's *Dit de l'alerion* in examining the new as a concept, an idea associated with the rare or unusual. Yet if Machaut explores the new as a rare specimen beyond price, Chaucer attends to such novel economies as potentially compassionate or heartless. Opening ethical questions that he ultimately refuses to settle, Chaucer stages the desire for new things amid international relations of gift and exchange.

In Part III, "Curiositas," problems of technical knowledge converge on questions of epochal history. Chapter 5, "Suspect Economies," revisits debates surrounding alchemy as a craft linked, by the late Middle English period, to the profit motive. Chaucer's *Canon's Yeoman's Tale* tracks the ethical economies of speculation as pertinent to critiques of fraud and the counterfeit. Yet the *Canon's Yeoman's Tale* also urges us to see the power of poetic fabrication as superior to alchemy's sketchy metaphysics. Chapter 6, "Old Worlds and New," offers a culminating consideration of the epochal shift sponsored by "New World" discovery. Here I revisit eventful claims surrounding the new world of 1492 to reconsider the problem of the epoch. 1492 stands first among the

markers of historical rupture, harbinger of a New Humanist Age enthusiastic
about novelty. According to this view, data mined from a "New World" revolutionized bookish, medieval geographies. This culminating chapter argues
instead that the persuasive power of Columbus's "new world" was itself a
bookish matter, a textual effect of the culture of copying productive of and for
early book history.

Throughout, I remain interested in both the difference of medieval and
modern and the interpenetration of traditions and terms. And modern writers, or modern books, make select appearances: Henry Adams's account of the
problems of history in *Mont-Saint-Michel and Chartres* inaugurates Chapter 1;
the early twentieth-century story of the Voynich manuscript, fraudulently ascribed to Roger Bacon just at the time Medieval Studies was emerging as a
professional field in the U.S., appears at the start of Chapter 2; Descartes's
meditations on wonder and novelty close Chapter 4; historiography concerning the modernity of childhood opens Chapter 3. Finally, while this study is
ambitious, I do not claim to offer here the final word on what is clearly an
enormous question. Rather than provide an exhaustive account of what now
seems to me an extraordinarily detailed, tricky, and rich medieval discourse of
the new, it is my hope to reopen the entire question of the status of the new in
medieval culture, a question long thought settled.

Attending to the specificity of medieval culture—one of novelty's "hard
cases"—will complicate our understanding of tradition and innovation both,
showing the continued relevance of humanistic inquiry in the so-called "traditional disciplines" for pursuit of a humane future. Linking "old" rules with
"new" enchantments, this is a story of the ways new things emerge even as old
patterns recur. It is a story of the complex associations of tradition with rather
than against innovation, of old alongside the new. Yet it is also at the same
time a story of the ways in which the rearrangements of tradition can nonetheless startle us—even enchant us—appearing with the sheen of the new. The
inverse is, of course, also true: the new may, as form and surface, constitute in
disguise the glamor of something very old.[58] On the one hand, this means that
what seems new can return us to the past inescapably; as the Real it can, in
fact, present the past as inescapable. On the other, we might well learn that
this oscillation between old and new—one with implications for past, present,
and future—can also point to the most precious part of the enchanting magic
of newness: its vital, even utopian ambition for keeping desire alive.

PART I

Ex Nihilo

Chapter 1

Scholastic Novelties

The perils of the heavy tower, of the restless vault, of the vagrant buttress; the uncertainty of logic, the inequalities of the syllogism; the irregularities of the mental mirror—all these haunting nightmares of the Church are expressed as strongly by the Gothic cathedral as though it had been the cry of human suffering, and as no emotion had ever been expressed before or is likely to find expression again. The delight of its aspirations is flung up to the sky. The pathos of its self-distrust and anguish of doubt is buried in the earth as its last secret.
—Henry Adams, *Mont-Saint-Michel and Chartres*

To the American layman of the nineteenth century, the subject of medieval philosophy and theology offered above all the opportunity to be ingloriously wrong—indeed one still feels the risk.
—Michael Colacurcio, "The Dynamo and the Angelic Doctor"

In the final paragraph of *Mont-Saint-Michel and Chartres*,[1] Henry Adams draws the complex oscillations of human history to a fine point. The book that begins, as John P. McIntyre points out, with the heights (its opening sentence, "The Archangel loved heights") ends buried in the earth. The Gothic cathedral, its soaring vaults now "restless," its ingenious buttresses now "vagrant," expresses, "as no emotion had ever been expressed before" or since, the "haunting nightmares of the Church" as a "cry of human suffering." Medieval philosophy's drive toward universal oneness is nobly undone: its logic uncertain, its syllogisms unequal, and its mental work irregular. For all the grand aspirations toward universality and truth, the "anguish of doubt" and the "pathos of self-distrust" persist.

Readers of *Chartres* (along with his famous essay "The Virgin and the Dynamo" from *The Education of Henry Adams*) often find Adams's turn to the Middle Ages as resolutely anti-technological as it is anti-modern. Yet this final paragraph suggests something else. Scholastic logic and the Gothic vault appear not as glorious remainders of a superior premodern unity so much as avatars of a persistent human problem: the conflict between universality and particularity, mind and matter, the one and the multiple. As is well known, Aquinas attempted to reconcile these: "The hive of Thomas Aquinas," writes Adams, "sheltered God and man, mind and matter, the one and the multiple, within the walls of a harmonious home."[2] *Chartres* ultimately casts medieval achievement with the ambivalences characteristic of modernism: ambition combines with irregularity; heights converge on depths; soaring faith confronts anguished doubt. Adams construes a Middle Ages that anticipates the dynamic discontents of modernity, as the problem of history itself. As Jennifer Fleissner puts it, "what [*Chartres*] shows most clearly is not the displacement of unity by multiplicity, but, rather, that 'The attempt to bridge the chasm between multiplicity and unity is the oldest problem of philosophy, religion, and science' ([*Chartres*,] 621)."[3]

This is not, of course, the usual way that Adams's medievalism has been understood. Conventional readings have instead insisted on an opposition between the Middle Ages and modernity. Thus, in an otherwise informative account of "the growth of Medieval Studies in North America, 1870–1930" (including Adams's years as professor of medieval history at Harvard), William Courtney unquestioningly asserts:

> It was in the artistic and intellectual achievements of the 12th and
> 13th centuries that Adams saw the value and essence of medieval
> society against which he judged the modern age and found it
> wanting. In contrast to the spirit of the Virgin to whom much of
> the artistic and intellectual products of the high Middle Ages
> seemed dedicated, the dynamo stood forth as a materialistic,
> dehumanizing symbol of greed and valueless technology.[4]

In Courtney's assessment—taken here as emblematic for an unfortunate consensus—Adams deploys the medieval as the spiritual foil to a modern dehumanizing materialism. This is Adams the reactionary, the nostalgic, the pietistic elitist.

Yet if the dynamo stands for valueless technology over against a medieval spiritual wholeness, why does Adams translate Aquinas's term *Primum Movens*, familiarly rendered as "prime mover," into the language of technology, as the Prime Motor? And why would he cast the problem of human freedom in Thomas's account of God in the language of modern mechanics? Consider: "The [Thomistic] scheme seems to differ little, and unwillingly, from a system of dynamics as modern as the dynamo. Even in the prime motor, from the moment of action, freedom of will vanished."[5] Or, "As it is used by Saint Thomas, the exact, literal meaning of Grace is 'a motion which the Prime Motor, as a supernatural cause, produces in the soul, perfecting free will.' It is reserved energy, which comes to aid and reinforce the normal energy of the battery."[6] Or, again, "To religious minds [my] scientific inversion of solemn truths seems, and is, sacrilege; but Thomas' numerous critics in the Church have always brought precisely this charge against his doctrine and are doing so still. They insist that he has reduced God to a mechanism and man to a passive conductor of force."

Adams plays with the specialized vocabularies of both ages, toggling between scholastic metaphysics and modern thermodynamics. Nor is this "very peculiar treatment"[7] of the Angelic Doctor much at odds with scholarly accounts of Thomistic thought. Adams acutely addresses the scholastic preoccupation with the problem of matter: "In the 13th century, mind did admit that matter was something—which it refuses to admit in the twentieth."[8] And he "sketched an historical view of the scholastic synthesis which agrees, to a remarkable extent, with that of an orthodox, professionally eminent philosopher like Étienne Gilson."[9] I would go even farther: there is evidence to suggest that Adams influenced Gilson, who cites his work approvingly.[10]

Complex temporalities are at play in Henry Adams's account of medieval philosophy. His is emphatically not the story of the fall from medieval grace and grandeur into a debased world of technological mechanization. His is not the story of an Age of Spiritual Tradition eclipsed by an Age of Technological Innovation. Using the vocabularies of scholastic philosophy and thermodynamics interchangeably, Adams emphasizes the continuities between the philosophical problems raised by modern technology and those erupting in the twelfth and thirteenth centuries. And his rhetoric renders Aquinas as a thinker on the cutting edge. Colacurcio even opines that in Aquinas, "Adams discovers . . . the father of modern scientific rationalism."[11] This claim may go too far, too fast. Nonetheless, Colacurcio recognizes the formative nature of Adams's temporal crossings: if the medieval would prove crucial to Adams's account of modernity, so, too, do modern models (the battery, the dynamo) inform, not oppose, Adams's reading of Aquinas. The Angelic doctor, Adams argues, finds his own dynamo in the theory of God as the energy and force that drives and sustains the universe.

From the vantage of Adams's work, early twentieth-century worries over human compulsions and mechanization replay questions about determinism that date back centuries. Again, in many ways he is not wrong. Medieval thinkers of the twelfth and thirteenth centuries faced these questions head on. Scholastic preoccupation with the problem of universals is well known. And with regard to determinism, twelfth-century condemnation of the Latin Averroists critiqued some commentators on Aristotle for their apparently deterministic views of the universe and of human activity in it. Strictures against potentially heretical implications of astrology, furthermore, were pointed at conjunctionism, that is, the belief that human fate was determined by astrological alignments. Scholastic masters like Aquinas proved to be absorbing to Adams because, considered alongside figures like Francis of Assisi, they emblematized the fundamental ambivalence of their age: as "haunting nightmares of the Church" expressed as "no emotion had ever been expressed before or is likely to find expression again."

Yet, when Adams renovates Aquinas's Aristotelian vocabulary, he does more than suggest that the old questions still resonate. He suggests that modern ambivalence about the new technologies, worries that such inventions might prompt compulsion, or mechanization, continue a longer debate—as yet unresolved—about matter, human agency, and innovative change. The signifiers shift—what was once a problem for scholastic philosophy is now a problem for physics—but the dilemma they circle repeats. Adams admires medieval culture not because it succeeds where modernism fails, but because medieval thinkers, in his view, faced up to the full complexity of the problem. Medieval culture constitutes Adams's intellectual ancestor not in pietistic fideism, but in a refusal to shrink from such complexities. Readings that see Adams as committed to the Virgin and not the Dynamo mistake this complex intellectual attachment for something more conventional. Such conventional readings assume things not in evidence: that Adams's Middle Ages offer only a refuge from modernist anxiety about new technologies. This view is predicated on an assumption Adams does not share, an assumption that the Middle Ages remain—resolutely—a time of the old, of conservation not innovation, of tradition rather than cutting edge. We might instead, and from the vantage of Adams's peculiar account, reconsider a more ambivalent reading of medieval accounts of the new.

A number of professional medievalists writing and working in the early part of the twentieth century similarly find avatars of modernity in the medieval record.[12] In this larger cultural context, Adams's account is all the more intriguing, particularly as he does not offer a teleological emergence of a recognizably modern form from an inchoate medieval development. For Adams, the long view of history offers no straightforward genealogy of evolution or devolution, but rather poses, repeatedly, a set of crucial human problems. I wish, at the start of this study, to suggest two things: first, the degree to which Adams, obsessed as he is with mechanics, energy, technology, remains ambivalent about, rather than disdainful of, scientific rationalism and modern technology; secondly, the extent to which this *ambivalence* underwrites an insightful account of medieval scholasticism. Adams turns to the medieval period because he finds there a clear articulation of the historical questions that preoccupied him: of human aspiration toward singular truth and of the limits posed to that aspiration; of human freedom and "scientific," or "mechanistic," necessity.

I begin with Adam's "peculiar" account because we need historical whimsy like his to reconsider the story of the new as it emerged during the high and late Middle Ages. Adams's playful translation of medieval scientific terminology—for example, the "Thomistic scheme" as "dynamo" or the Prime Mover as "Prime Motor"— has a doubled force. On the one hand, he urges upon us the shared dilemmas, uncanny repetitions, and recurring scholarly preoccupations that continue to perplex human thought. What are the limits of determinism, and what is the possibility for historical change? But Adams's rhetoric also suggests a self-conscious historicism that insists that we can understand something crucial about then and now by recasting the medieval record in terms resonant to our own moment. Although his readings are precise, his interest in the past strives for something other than strict historicist recovery. Something more than archival fascination or nostalgic piety propels him.

Such a deliberate turn, insisting that the past might be translated into terms usable in the present, propels my study, too. Like Adams, I also begin with a reconsideration of the questions that preoccupied scholastic thinkers. Rereading scholastic debates over *novum* and its cognates (*novitas mundi, novae compositiones, novae res*, to name the most obvious) in this chapter will help us see that widespread caution about the new during the long medieval period was generated not by the blind appeal of tradition in a religiously conservative age, but as a response to radical expansions of possibility in realms of art and science. On the one hand, scholastic precision organizes the dramatic, metaphysical power of new things (*res*) in beneficent terms, as a feature of God's generosity and part of the generative nature of divine freedom. On the other hand, discriminations about the new lead to taxonomies in which the conventional is distinguished from the cleverly unique, the deceptive from the self-evident, usage from reason, and custom from truth.

To be sure, parsing the finer points of Thomistic philosophy is no easy task. It still offers, as Colacurcio puts it, "the opportunity to be ingloriously wrong"; one does, indeed, "still feel the risk." Yet I am convinced that, far from viewing new things and new ideas as antithetical to intellectual, human life, the scholastics were obsessively interested in what to make of the dizzying array of new experiments in commentary, poetry, art, architecture, translation, rhetoric, mechanics, and alchemy emerging from the twelfth century onward. The new was, I argue here, a perplexing and absorbing "problem-question"[13] for the Schoolmen.

Scholastic Arts

By any reckoning, the period of the twelfth and thirteenth centuries, often described as a medieval "renaissance," was a remarkable time when cultures in Western Europe welcomed massive innovations: in architecture and engineering (the flying buttress), urbanization, vernacular literature (troubadour lyrics), history writing (both chronicle and romance), translation (the Schools of Toledo and St. Victor), and, of course, philosophy (the increasing circulation of texts and commentaries on the work of Aristotle). Such innovative vitality was linked, moreover, to considerable international and intercultural ferment, cross-cultural encounters violent (the Crusades, the Mongol invasion) and peaceful (as testified in the travelogues of William of Rubruck and Marco Polo); mercantile (the Silk Road, the creation of Cairo as a trading center); and intellectual. Scholars continue to debate the precise nature, politics, and variety of those encounters, but all would agree that their exacerbation was transformative for Europe.[14]

Arabic scientists, philosophers, and commentators were of course instrumental in making Greek texts, particularly the works of Aristotle, available in the West. From the late eleventh century on, medieval philosophy witnessed vital transactions among Jewish, Islamic, and Christian thinkers. In the nineteenth and early twentieth centuries, the story told about the introduction of Aristotle's works emphasized the dangers that the pagan philosopher's works posed to Christian theology, and to the doctrinal orthodoxy of the Catholic

Church, specifically, by way of scholasticism. The primary evidence adduced here was the condemnation of the teaching of the *Libri Naturalis*—the name under which Aristotle's *Physics* circulated during the Middle Ages—at the University of Paris in 1210 and 1215. Such prohibitions and bans would be repeated by Pope Gregory IX in 1231 and 1270; and in 1277 both Étienne Tempier, bishop of Paris, and Archbishop Robert Kilwardby in Oxford would publicly condemn certain interpretations of the *Physics*. (The Oxford ban would be renewed in 1284.)[15] Revisionary trends in the history of philosophy remind us, however, that the persistent repetition of these condemnations suggests something of the vitality of Aristotle's influence at the time: condemnations need to be repeated only when earlier bans have lapsed or been forgotten, only, in other words, at such time as earlier proscriptions seem to be having little effect. The Philosopher's work was widely read by the masters even during the years of proscription at Paris; just as Oxford did, the University of Toulouse made something of a reputation for itself by marketing its Aristotelian curriculum at precisely the time that Paris had suspended lectures. And while it is now accepted that an expurgated version of Aristotle's *Physics* was a crucial part of the university curriculum at Paris by at least 1250, Rega Wood has suggested that Franciscan Richard Rufus of Cornwall was lecturing there on the *Libri Naturalis* as early as 1238.[16] Even more profoundly, Alain de Libera argues, in contrast to the textbook view, that the so-called crisis of scholasticism began among Islamic intellectuals before wholly "being imported (with the model of the intellectual itself) to the West."[17]

Scholars, that is, continue to debate the meaning of the ways by which Aristotle and his commentators came to be so important to European intellectuals in the high Middle Ages. The Philosopher's writings on logic, on mimesis, on natural philosophy, or on metaphysics—alongside the work of Jewish scholar Moses Maimonides (1135–1204) and the Arab translators and commentators, Ibn Sina (973–1037), known in the West as Avicenna, and Ibn Rushd (1126–1198), known as Averroës—would radically energize a whole host of important questions about creation and thus about novelty. A measure of Aquinas's respect for Averroës can be seen in the fact that he regularly refers to him, alongside Aristotle "the Philosopher," as simply "the Commentator." Dante would, of course, count Ibn Rushd as especially esteemed among the virtuous pagans of his *Divine Comedy*.

The scholastic precept preserving radical creativity, creation ex nihilo, for God alone is well known. God—preeminent creator, artisan, maker—produces out of nothing; human making, in contrast, can only rearrange,

recompose, rework those things already in the world, just as Adam and Eve—
themselves divinely created from nothing but dust—fashioned coverings from
fig leaves found in Eden, the perfect garden already made by God. Their modesty, while certainly "new" in postlapsarian Eden, constitutes not an innovative push forward but that "fall" backward from which humankind has never
recovered, the exemplary definition of human degeneration. Franciscan theo-
logian Bonaventure (1221–74) offers what will become an especially influential
version of this view, writing that, while "the soul is able to make new compositions" of what it receives from the external world, it "cannot make new
things." ("Anima enim facit novas compositiones, licet non faciat novas res; et
secundum quod fingit interius, sic etiam depingit et sculpit exterius." III S. 37.
Dub 1.)[18] Hugh of St. Victor (1096–1141) makes a similar point, one that
Bonaventure will develop, delineating a hierarchy of creative agents: God
(who operates ex nihilo), nature (operating ens in potentia), and human artists
(who produce ens completum), following after nature.[19] Human artifice is, in
this view, a means of forming things "mechanical, that is adulterate," as Hugh
puts it.[20] In contrast to the mechanical, adulterated, inferior composite creations made by human artisans stands, of course, God's perfect, original, and
originating creation. Human creative capacity has limited access to newness,
constituted through synthesis, through the creative reworking of things already created. Human innovation is thus derivative rather than originary, a
humbler, second-order power able to rearrange preexisting creation in new
ways, but unable really to entirely *invent* new things.[21]

Yet, while the scholastics clearly subordinate human composition to
God's creative sublimity, the definitional care with which these questions are
treated nonetheless preserves the possibility for new human productions, depending of course on what we mean by "new." If Bonaventure understands the
innovative power of the human artisan as humbler than God's creative potency, he does so as part of an attempt to explain human artisanship, to articulate in the most precise terms possible the way that human artisanal
production also gains purchase on the new: even if they are not original, and
thus originating, in any absolute or, as we shall see, metaphysical sense, new
compositions (*novae compositiones*) are, after all and quite explicitly, still new.

While Bonaventure's presuppositions are Augustinian and Neoplatonic,
more influential writing on creation and "newness" will emerge in the context
of efforts to consider Aristotle's philosophical insights and their uses for the
West. The issues at stake are cosmological as much as scientific and technological, and to understand their complexities we need to further unravel the

notion of creation as ex nihilo. Averroës will present the religious notion of creation ex nihilo as incompatible with the method of philosophical demonstration offered by Aristotle.[22] Insisting on the unity of truth, as Richard C. Taylor puts it, that "the truth of religion and the truth of philosophy are one and the same,"[23] Averroës deploys philosophical demonstration to clarify what, according to Taylor, he saw as excesses in theological or scriptural interpretation. The religious notion of creation ex nihilo is an important example for Averroës because it became a case with which to display the superiority of philosophical demonstration, the formal structure of logical argument, for which geometry was a model, both to dialectical reasoning and to religious accounts of revelation; it was, moreover, one of three positions that Persian scholar al-Ghazali, in his treatise *On the Incoherence of the Philosophers*, used as evidence of the apostasy of philosophers as such. In his delightfully titled *The Incoherence of the Incoherence*, Averroës responds to al-Ghazali, pursuing, in Taylor's words, "the understanding of the metaphysical dependence of the world on God in accord with the account of God as creator by way of final causality. . . [who] draws [the world] from potentiality into the actuality of existence."[24] This view does not require a historical moment of origination, or a view of the radical "newness" of the creation of the world.[25] Averroës handles the question of the historical moment of creation, as recounted in religious texts, by implying that, in forming the world, God actualized it out of existing matter rather than out of nothing.[26]

Thomas Aquinas will disagree with Averroës on this point, yet addresses the question of creation ex nihilo in precisely the Aristotelian terms of demonstration (the "new logic") that Averroës promotes. He is not, however, exactly an Aristotelian on the question. Aquinas's delimitation of the meaning of creation will be crucial to his work: he will circumscribe the verb "to create" to mean nothing less than an act of God. Aquinas raises the issue of creation ex nihilo in the first, fifth, and eighth articles of Question 45, in part I of the *Summa*. The first article, "Whether to Create is to make something from nothing," takes up possible objections to this proposition and responds here by defining "creation" in absolute terms as "the emanation of all being from the universal cause, which is God" (I.45.a.1). Here, then, is the radically absolute definition of creation as God's exclusive power: "to create is, properly speaking, to cause or produce the being of things" (I.45.a.6), hence "to create is the proper action of God alone" (I.45.a.5).[27] The point here is not to render human cultural production impossible so much as to clarify and define God as the conserving, or sustaining, cause of the world, both unique and sublime;

indeed, Aquinas contrasts his technical definition of "to create" with Augustine's "equivocal" use of the term "as when we say a bishop is 'created'" (I.45.a.5). Aquinas's circumscribed notion of the act of creation preserves God's originating power as absolute; it thereby follows that no human being can create new things (*res*) in a metaphysical sense. And, as William Newman demonstrates, this point will be crucial to Aquinas's concerns about the claims made for technological transformation by the alchemists.

It's worth noting that, in referring to "the being of things," Aquinas seems engaged in a bit of sleight of hand.[28] On the one hand, "being" (*esse*) would be God's preserve; as responsible for the being of things, God would indeed be creative in a fashion distinct from every other kind of creativity. At the same time, and on the other hand, this does not mean that God necessarily creates the *things* as such, for whose being he is responsible and the creator. Aquinas's solution—distinguishing the being of things from the things themselves—manages the problem of new things by redirecting the question from particularity (the things themselves) to universal (being). This move preserves God's metaphysical monopoly on creativity; yet it also begs the question of the particularity of those objects. The human pursuit of new compositions—as a pursuit of new particulars—remains very much in play.

Furthermore, when he distinguishes God's power to create from the "equivocal" usage of the term in Augustine, Aquinas sharpens the difference between what we might call the metaphysics of Creation (the nature of being) and any particular newly made change (as when a bishop is created) or composition. "Equivocal" here is meant in a precise way, contrasting with "univocal" attributes of God and developing out of medieval theories of language, including the well-known complex theory of analogy, examined a bit more thoroughly in the next chapter.[29] This point, too, alludes to the problem of universals and particulars, an issue that runs through medieval language theory, with its diverse modes of analogy and allegory, one developed further in the work of the nominalists. My point here is that even as Aquinas delimits "to create" to the one God, human activity and human composite creations come into view, as diverse things produced in particular times and places. While Aquinas is primarily concerned with the unity of truth as distinct from questions of social or historical diversity, many from Hegel onward have pointed out the extent to which scholastic thought persistently responded to pressures coming from more immanent registers, such as the state, technological developments, economic patterns, or other material circumstance.[30]

A similar point concerns Aquinas's account of *novitas mundi*, the newness of the world. At this point, however, we can see that creation emerges for Aquinas an as implicitly cosmological issue—and, in that regard, we see here a kind of creationism,[31] though not anti-scientific in the scholastic definition of the latter term. Aquinas will next move to discuss the metaphysical nature of creation by distinguishing it from historical notions such as that of the newness of the world (*novitas mundi*). Question 46 ("On the beginning of the duration of creatures") pushes further, and in Article 2 ("Whether it is an article of faith that the world began"), *novitas mundi* emerges in his consideration of the question of the eternity of the world:

> The newness of the world cannot be demonstrated on the part of the world itself. For the principle of demonstration is the essence of a thing. Now everything according to its species is abstracted from "here" and "now"; whence it is said that universals are everywhere and always. Hence it cannot be demonstrated that man, or heaven, or a stone were not always. . . . Likewise neither can it be demonstrated on the part of the efficient cause, which acts by will. For the will of God cannot be investigated by reason, except as regards those things which God must will of necessity; and what He wills about creatures is not among these. . . . But the divine will can be manifested by revelation, on which faith rests. Hence that the world began to exist is an object of faith, but not of demonstration or science. (*ST* I.46.2)

Aquinas enters the debate on the eternity of the world by arguing that details about the duration of the world, whether either its past or its future might be finite or infinite, cannot be inferred from the nature of the observed world. In this he contests both Bonaventure's position, that the world is finite both as to its past and as to its future, and the position of Averroës, that the world is infinite in both directions, a position also held by Latin Averroists such as Siger of Brabant.[32] The *novitas mundi* (the "newness of the world," an idiom that implicitly contrasts with *aevitas mundi*) refers to the question of the world's duration and, thus, of temporality. His point, that issues of duration (whether the *novitas mundi* or, implicitly, the *aevitas mundi*) cannot be demonstrated by the world itself, is part of a larger Aristotelian question about the relation of eternity to necessity.[33]

In Aristotle's cosmology, the eternal and the necessary are coextensive. In this and related discussions, "necessary" (meaning, quite strictly, unable not to be) contrasts with "contingent" (meaning possible and dependent). In

contrast to Aristotle, Aquinas argues that it is prima facie possible that the
world could be both everlasting, since we can't tell anything about the duration of the world from its existence, and contingent. Severing Aristotle's link
of the necessary with the eternal, Aquinas argues that what looks to be a question about the duration of the world—its beginnings and/or endings—is, in
fact, a question about the nature of the world's existence. This is a crucial
move, in part because it insists that what looks to be a historical question, to
do with a particular moment in time is, in fact, a metaphysical one. Furthermore, the fact that *novitas mundi* cannot be demonstrated in itself means that
the historical newness of creation emerges here as a matter of contingency
rather than necessity, gesturing toward questions of God's power and ultimate
freedom:[34] if the "newness" of the world, or, for that matter, any question to
do with the world's duration, were capable of demonstration, then it would
have occurred necessarily. But if the newness of the world were a necessity,
then God could not have created the world freely, but only of necessity. Creation ex nihilo cannot be logically demonstrated precisely because such divine
creativity is understood to be an act of absolute freedom: God's radically contingent act.

Aquinas threads a very small needle here, not only with regard to the
definition of "creation" but also with regard to the notion of necessity. That
which is "necessary" is the proper object of reason for the scholastics, since that
which is necessary contains within itself sufficient grounds for its existence—
and thus can be logically demonstrated to be true. Insofar as scientific demonstration is understood to provide access to truth, it offers knowledge about
those things that, following necessarily, are unable not to be. For Aquinas, any
particular beginning of the world, and its according "newness," is not among
these. It is instead a contingent event: it could occur, or not occur, at any particular moment. Contingency is, in this case, the proper object of causation by
a will that could choose otherwise. On one hand, the issue of the *novitas
mundi* is a philosophically neutral point, standing for any attribute to do with
the world's duration. Contingency signifies the complex array of alternatives
to necessity at the limits of scientific demonstration; as in contemporary historicist method, contingency here sets the stage for complex considerations of
possibility, as well as for questions of freedom as distinct from, although related to, questions of necessity.[35] This complex of issues will develop further in
later nominalist thought as the problem of possible worlds—the distinction
between God's *potentia absoluta* and the *potentia ordinata.*

Aquinas's metaphysics of creation thus purposely sidesteps questions of creation in historical time,[36] except to note that such matters are contingent. It is here that Aquinas's *novitas mundi* might be surprisingly synthesized with Bonaventure's account of the *novae compositiones* made by the human artisan. Human agency is, in both, simultaneously free and limited: "second order," "equivocal" cultural productions differ in kind from those things (*res*) that God creates. If this closes one metaphysical question, it opens another ethical one. New compositions, entirely possible for human agents, are not vital emanations of nature but productions of art, "mechanical . . . that is, adulterate."[37] Art may perfect nature, but new compositions, whether in poetry or plastic arts, of alchemy or astrolabes, whether mechanical or monumental, cannot claim new metaphysical forms.[38] Indeed, the productions of art and natural philosophy will continue to demand definitional attention, and delimit improper kinds of artifice in ways that today seem inhospitable to the impulse of human innovation; yet these debates would both channel and unleash cultural productivity in all manner of technologies, propelling scientific and artistic practice in the thirteenth century and beyond, as scholars like Michael Camille, Sarah Kay, and William Newman have variously shown.[39]

Surveying some orthodox notions of creativity and creation, particularly as they relate to the danger of idols, Camille emphasizes the "secondariness" of the artist's creative power in medieval aesthetic theories.[40] But even he has not adequately assessed the full complexity of the problem of novelty in this case. Camille's account of the theological limits placed on medieval artists goes a long way toward explaining the difficulty of a category like the avant garde in and for the Middle Ages. It is certainly true that the work of art as revolutionary manifesto designed to scandalize, its newness an affront as much to the senses as to conventional sensibilities, was not an orthodox medieval value or philosophical habit of mind. Medieval art was hardly self-announcing in this way.[41] Yet Camille overemphasizes the impossibilities this poses to the recognition of new human creations:

> The restriction of representation to a second-order status explains
> not only the medieval artist's uncertainty with depicting certain
> forms that do not seem to pertain to God's creation (such as idols)
> but also the consistency with which he clung to archetypal models:
> copies of copies that forever secured him within a safe cycle of
> duplication and secondariness, adapting and altering compositions
> but rarely creating new ones.[42]

When he depicts the medieval artist as "clinging" to the "safe cycle" of duplication, Camille significantly underestimates the compelling nature of questions of newness at the time. He implies that copying or new composition is
always derivative and never new, an implication that is undermined by examples elsewhere in Camille's own work. A host of novelties—new ideas, new
texts, new things—on display at the time led to complex taxonomies of new
things, spread out over a diverse array of texts and thinkers. The resulting
account of the new carefully distinguished metaphysical newness from historical newness, and, accordingly, new metaphysical things (*res*) from new
composite creations, or compositions. But it is precisely in this way that the
question of novelties converged on problems of meaning, motive, ethics, and
truth.

Use and Ingenuity

In his treatment of creation, Aquinas has a particular aim in mind: to cope
with the problem that creation ex nihilo posed to Aristotelian notions of eternity and necessity. The resulting definition of the verb "to create" restricted
creation to its metaphysical limits, as a power for God alone. Aquinas solved
the problem of creation ex nihilo (although it should be noted that the first
thinker to imagine the possibility of such a solution was Moses Maimonides),
using the "new logic" to resituate a question of historical origins as a question
about the nature of the world and God's sustaining power and force. It is this
feature of Aquinas's thought that would inspire Henry Adams to render the
Primum Movens as the Prime Motor, God as divine Dynamo. Yet Aquinas's
solution to the problem of creation, for all its brilliance, did not fully untangle
the question of the new and its vicissitudes. This solution did not put an end
to the problem of the new in "adulterated" form. Accounts of the so-called
perversities of human creative endeavor accelerate from this time onwards. A
fuller taxonomy—one spread out across a range of important twelfth- and
thirteenth-century texts, (philosophical, historical, scientific, and literary) will
be required. Part of the reason it has been difficult to see the new as a "problem-
question" pertinent to the period concerns precisely the diffuse nature of this
archive.

     In the larger networks of philosophical signification, *novum* and its cog-
nates will continue to generate both definitional problems and categorical
distinctions. One of the most important of these is the clear difference

between notions of innovation and the idea of the new. Throughout the scholastic record, innovation and newness are not, despite a shared Latin root (*novum*), regularly placed side by side. The two were not interchangeable. Indeed, quite frequently, debates about innovation sidestep questions of old and new altogether in favor of ethical considerations of the use and abuse of making itself. As David Luscombe points out in his reading of Peter Abelard's rhetoric of innovation, quarrels over innovation in and around the twelfth century, "do not usually portray conflicts between what is old and what is new, but conflicts between *usus* or *consuetudo* on the one hand and *ingenium* on the other."[43]

The distinction between *usus* or *consuetudo* and *ingenium* can shed light on medieval concerns about innovation, as we shall see in a moment; but it also sets in fine relief the importance of texts of romance to the problem of novelty, one of the arguments of this book. The ethical problems of *ingenium* are regularly staged in romance—romance being the genre of *ingenium* par excellence—as Robert Hanning and others have taught us. *Ingenium* connotes the potential for deceit (more precisely, ambiguity of motive and purpose), thus drawing attention to the designs, in all senses of the term, harbored by particular human makers, whether charlatan, genius, crackpot, fraud, poet, or engineer. Tracing debates between Abelard and Bernard of Clairvaux over the primacy of intellection, Robert Hanning rightly insists that *ingenium* occupied "a middle ground of ambivalence, in which admiration for ingenuity mingled with worry at the amorality of this human faculty and even with cynical conviction that men will inevitably use their wits for mere self-aggrandizement, whatever their pious protestations to the contrary."[44] *Ingenium* implies the possibility of falseness and deceit—it alludes to the complex relation between fiction and the lie, and to the limits of what can be imagined, all questions to be addressed more fully in later chapters of this book. It is also one of the etymological ancestors to the notion of innovating "genius," that category crucially linked to artistic innovation from Kant onward.[45]

Yet, despite the common translation of the Latin *usus* with the modern English *use*, the contrast of *ingenium* to *usus* or *consuetudo* does not refer primarily to the distinction between the useful and the frivolous. The contrast between *usus* and *ingenium*, while implicitly ethical, is not reducible to such instrumentality. Terms originating in Roman law, *usus* and *consuetudo* imply instead the knowledge, practice, and habits of social and cultural groups: that which is commonly known, customary, and public. *Usus*, in particular, tended to signify social agreement, joint use, notions, habits, and practices held in common. *Consuetudo*, as readers of legal history well know, refers explicitly to custom law. It implies a set of practices and strictures so well known, so generally and openly agreed upon, as to be not particularly controversial, nor, accordingly, liable to solipsism or deception. (Of course, matters of law and custom were rarely as straightforward as this implies.)[46] But it could also mean education, training, and formal study. In his *Historia calamitatum*, Abelard defends his own decision to lecture in Paris on matters about which he had no formal training by opposing *ingenium* to *usus*: "*non esse meae consuetudinis per usum proficere sed per ingenium.*"[47] Here and elsewhere, Hanning argues, Abelard positions himself as an individual talent over against a larger intellectual system, referring to "the entire system of training . . . (under the term *usus*) and to his own impulse to control the system through the power of his mind . . . (under the heading *ingenium*)."[48]

Interestingly, even *usus* and *consuetudo* would be pressed into service to *defend* novelty, usually by insisting that a new practice or habit came from an unrecognized but nonetheless established custom. In this way the new could be justified as an explicit return to tradition, even a *reformatio* of the traditional. Responding to Bernard of Clairvaux's critique of the "new" usage of an unusual version of the Lord's Prayer among the nuns of the Paraclete convent, Abelard defends the practice through an analogy to observances introduced by the Cistercians, practices that Bernard himself categorized as new and as a renewal of earlier traditions. The preceding suggests that, in the period before Aquinas wrote, questions of the new emerged by way of diversities of practice, of history or culture: what was a customary usage at one time or in one culture might seem radically novel in another. New things might emerge historically or contextually, if not metaphysically; in the arguments of the Cistercians, new things were justified as a return to foundations, a rhetoric that entwines old and new rather than opposing them.

In defense of the new, *usus* and *consuetudo* also had limits. Luscombe notes that in this instance Abelard defends novel practices on the grounds of logic, reason, and truth, arguing that "usage should not have priority over reason nor custom over truth" (193).[49] And custom could indeed be seen as conflicting with reason. At the start of his *Opus Majus*, Roger Bacon lists the influence of custom (*consuetudinis diuturnitas*) as one of four major causes of error.[50] In these moments in the record, we can see the tensions between treatments of the new as an idea, and treatments of the new as a practice, object, or thing. The contrast between *ingenium* and *usus* evokes law and its prohibitions. It evokes the distinction of the whimsically idiosyncratic to the customary and conventional.[51] But it is also worth noting that defenses of novelty on the grounds of use and custom, sometimes over against authority and tradition, would implicitly counter the charge that something novel necessarily set the individual against the group, or amounted to a secret and ingenious deception, since use and custom referred to customary habits of groups or communities. The next generation of writers will exert significant pressure on such questions.

In particular, the problem of the experience of something radically new would require further commentary. In the next century Bonaventure's fellow Franciscan John Duns Scotus will offer a dramatic account of humanity's access to the new as particularly noticeable by way of the intellect. This is a remarkable turn, in part because Scotus approaches novelty through something other than the senses, after the manner of those new historical or cultural usages or compositions, and legible in the discourse of *vitium curiositatis* (the vice of curiosity), as in Peter of Limoges's *The Moral Treatise on the Eye*. According to Olivier Boulnois, Scotus raises the question of the emergence of a new *idea*—a different category from a new "thing" as such—in terms of the human experience of sudden insight. Boulnois reads Scotus to argue that, "Ideas are something radically new, a sudden production of novelty" ("La pensée est quelque chose de radicalement nouveau, une production soudaine de nouveauté.")[52] In the *Ordinatio* Scotus makes the point that an idea has being after nonbeing, "as we experience" ("intellectio actualis est aliquid in nobis non perpetuum sed habens 'esse' post 'non-esse,' sicut experimur. Istius oportet ponere aliquam causam activam, et aliquo modo in nobis"). The existence of an new idea, logically, occurs only after it had no existence.

The radical nature of this point is hard to overstate. For one thing, the terms here verge on the metaphysical ("esse," after all, signifies "being"), even as this description of the emergence of something new emphasizes a moment in time: the rupture of a novel idea (the break between "esse" and "non-esse") is experienced, emerging not *from* nonbeing, but *after* it (*post "non-esse"*). Scotus is interested in the human experience (*sicut experimur*) of what Boulnois calls "something radically new." As Boulnois points out, Scotus's interest in the advent of some new thing or event does not involve the kind of creative power that Aquinas reserves for God; metaphysically, here too, nothing can be fabricated that does not disrupt God's sustaining creativity. And yet Scotus applies a familiar scholastic distinction to suggest the difference between novelty as such (in itself: metaphysically impossible for human agents), and novelty in/ for human knowers (novelty of ideas and for us: "as we experience"). His emphasis on immediacy and discontinuity—that is, on a spontaneous experience of an idea that was not apprehended previously—is a crucial turn in thinking, as is the reliance not on logical demonstration so much as on experience. Indeed, the fact of our (unmediated) experience furthers the certainty of this for Scotus, even if the emergence of a new idea cannot be logically demonstrated. This seems to be a further development in assessments of human capacity with regard to the new: an ability to experience, recognize, or apprehend new ideas.[53]

It is perhaps an obvious point, but one that needs making nonetheless: these questions and the debates over definitional specificity that they generated were produced not by the caution of an inherently traditional or orthodox age, but as a response to radical and sudden expansions of possibility. Medieval diffidence on the question of new things and new ideas existed alongside radically new developments in nearly every cultural realm. The according emphasis on the limitations posed to human making, the respect for authority, both preceding and outlasting the period, arise less from a disinterest in the new than as a response to the challenge new things and new ideas posed epistemologically as well as ethically. Philosophical discourses surrounding creation ex nihilo or the distinction of *ingenium* from *usus* and *consuetudo* were both responses to the emergence of new texts (Aristotle and the Arab commentaries) and new practices (as in the case of alchemy or the nuns of the Paraclete). Interest in newness prompted a passion for classifying and defining, and not, as we might expect today, enthusiastic confidence. This is a real difference between then and now: today we readily assume that genuine innovation can be easily recognized, and newness perceived in real time. Medieval thinkers did not share those assumptions, and were absorbed instead by taxonomies that weighed the benefits as well as the limitations of new things. Adept at devising technical vocabularies to organize knowledge and experience, the scholastics devoted enormous time and energy to this work, analyzing or qualifying what kinds of newness might emerge under a variety of circumstances, and what kinds of claims for newness were, of necessity, impossible. Their answers are at times, as in the case of Abelard's debate with Bernard, explicitly defensive. At other moments, such taxonomies operate by way of disavowal: circumscribing and qualifying the reach of divine creativity, so as to preserve legitimate adventures in human productivity—delineating the new compositions that humans compose and, at times, enjoy. Or enjoy too much.

Yet, rhetorics of the new were not limited to scholastic taxonomies. A complex network of equivocal accounts of the new engaged a significant archive in and beyond the twelfth and thirteenth centuries: from critiques of the newfangled found in the pages of romance, to rhetorical set pieces on the freshness of spring; from descriptions of new gardens or young women in Middle English lyrics to Bonaventure's *novae compositiones*; from Dante's *Vita Nuova* to Aquinas's *novitas mundi*; from claims that Francis of Assisi was a "new" kind of saint to critiques of the "new apostles" (*novi apostoli*) that Peter Abelard, defending his own innovations, disdains in the *Historia Calamitatum*.[54]

Creativity—and the new things invented—may be good or ill, and qualifications like those just described are driven as much by a wish as by a worry. On the one hand, these definitions stake a claim to novelty in quite precise terms, affirming the ways that human creatures *can* experience and make new things. Far from averting human cultural productions, the preservation of creation ex nihilo for God alone would prove remarkably generative. On the other hand, respecting the metaphysical limits that creation ex nihilo imposes on human making attempts to guard against potentially dangerous, monstrous, or heretical deployments of creaturely power.

Guarding against such monstrous progeny turns out to be an impossible task. Out of *nihil* come hosts of little nothings, and an entire scaffolding of ethics developed as a means to deal with them. Creative agents during subsequent eras will aim directly at innovation, embracing originality self-consciously; it is my contention here that the work of medieval creative agents sheds light on a creativity of creatures, and the productive point of impossibility. Proscriptions on creaturely power may have constituted a response to the prolific inventions of its time; but such proscriptions would have a considerable afterlife. Jacques Lacan's account of creation ex nihilo helps us to understand how and why this was so. Scholastic accounts of creation ex nihilo are crucial to Lacan's *The Ethics of Psychoanalysis* (Seminar VII), specifically linked to his rereading of Freud's notion of sublimation, and Lacan reprises many of the issues important to the scholastics: freedom, contingency, necessity, the one and the many. Indeed, he resituates the brand of nothing offered by creation ex nihilo as the sine qua non of human creative work, coordinating the special features of godly creativity with the repetitious patternings of desire that have come to be called the discourse of Courtly Love.[55] Part of a psychoanalytic movement similarly preoccupied with questions of creativity, of freedom, of limitation, and of submission, Lacan emphasizes the power of impossibility coded in the prohibition against human creation ex nihilo, a force that, in psychoanalytic terms, propels innovative poetry, art, and techné.[56]

The One and the Many

Lacanian analyses of medieval culture are by now well established, and scholars such as Richard Glejzer, Alexandre Leupin, Alain de Libera, Sarah Kay, Aranye Fradenburg, Jessica Rosenfeld, and Erin Labbie all note Lacan's productive engagement with the scholastics.[57] The scholastics appeal to Lacan in part because their work registers explicitly the place that impossibility occupies for desire and creativity both. From this vantage, a Lacanian reading of scholastic accounts of creation suggest that it is *impossibility* rather than necessity that deserves to be recognized as the mother of invention. This can help us see how the scholastic proscriptions on human creativity approach the new in a roundabout way.

To understand the full import of this point, we must begin with what seems to be an unrelated one, and with one of Lacan's punning asides. In his much-discussed lecture, "Courtly Love as Anamorphosis," Lacan claims, with characteristic tongue in cheek, that the discourse of courtly love appeared ex nihilo. There is much at stake in this punning avowal. Firstly, Lacan plays on the problem of human making within medieval philosophy, reorienting the historical emergence of so-called courtly love as an impossibility: only God creates ex nihilo; such claims cannot be made for poetic or artisanal productions such as the poetry of courtly love. Lacan jumbles Aquinas's careful distinctions, but not as a result of fuzzy thinking; the former can be as admiringly or maddeningly precise in his definitions as the latter. Instead, Lacan's punning reference suggests that courtly love is, like scholastic restrictions on divine creation, organized around a *nihil*.

Medieval orthodoxies of creation will prove to be important throughout Seminar VII, particularly in the lecture "On creation ex nihilo," where "knowledge of the creature and of the creator" will be central to his thinking.[58] And here he turns forcefully to a metaphor of creativity that had long been important to Judeo-Christian tradition, the metaphor of the potter: "According to a fable handed down through the chain of generations, and that nothing prevents us from using, we are going to refer to what is the most primitive of artistic activities, that of the potter."[59] This example alludes to the biblical traditions from the books of Jeremiah and Isaiah, whereby the relation of potter to the clay he molds figures the relation of God to Israel, of Creator to creature: "Can I not deal with you, Israel, says the Lord, as this potter deals with his clay? You are clay in my hands, like the clay in his, O house of Israel."[60] Here, then, is a dominant metaphor for creation: the divine artisan molds dead matter into living creature. He is the potter; we are the clay, the work of his hands.

Reference to the potter simultaneously raises human creative acts and the orthodox view of human creatureliness, of God's preeminent position as Creator; it also, for Lacan, gestures to the emptiness at the heart of the Real, a place occupied by the Lady in the courtly love relation. But, as an artifact that physically encircles an empty space, the example of the potter's vase can also make clear that this "nothing" has a *positive* valence; it alludes to a structural emptiness—the emptiness around which the human potter forms the vase. "Nothing" is, on the one hand, simply nothing, gesturing toward the material impossibility at the heart of this belief, that matter, in other words, can neither be created nor destroyed. On the other hand, "Nothing" is more than nothing; recalling the *nihil* identified with God's creative extravagance, it is the emptiness at the heart of human creativity.

This view of creation ex nihilo is important to Lacan's understanding of the Thing (Freud's *Das Ding*) and to its place in his reading of courtly love. Playing with the echoes between "sublimation" and "sublime," as both Aranye Fradenburg and Nancy Frelick point out, Lacan argues that processes of sublimation impinge on the structures of social and cultural elevation and value alluded to in and through the category of the Sublime, particularly in its godlike capacity as the unrepresentable, the ineffable, the impossible.[61] Poetry thus shares with scholastic accounts of creation a crucially veiled secret: that prohibition, impossibility, sublime emptiness all unleash creative desire. This desiring structure motivates the amorous, arduous labor of making, remaking, composing, or creating.[62]

Even as blocks, prohibitions, impossibilities persist and recur, they do not preclude creative productions but are instead the *conditions of submission* under which new compositions can be created. Emphasizing submission may seem strange in this context, accustomed as we are to imagining human creativity and the resulting creative productions, at least from Kant onward, as a dynamic pursuit marked by a refusal to submit, by a certain kind of freedom. The coordination of submission and creation legible in scholastic accounts of the new seems overwhelmed by constraint, by rule, by dogmatic prohibitions. Yet Lacan's treatment of the debates of the twelfth century makes clear that it is precisely through submitting to creation ex nihilo as an impossible, sublime, ideal that a host of ingenious, creative, legitimate, perverse work-arounds are engendered.[63] From this creative submission, Aquinas forged not only his monumental *Summa*, but also genuinely new solutions to a set of thorny intellectual problems about creativity itself.

In a host of fields, medieval creative agents confronted, over and over, the human power to create as a perverse submission to this sublime impossibility. Precisely as a moral and ethical ideal, the doctrine of creation ex nihilo sets in motion the problems of morality about human making so well documented in the critical tradition.[64] Such problems range from the punning strictures against "unnatural" and "perverse" grammatical arrangements found in Alain de Lille's *De Planctu Naturae*, to the "monstrous" rearrangements of the natural world in gargoyles on Gothic cathedrals or manuscript marginalia, to the representations of the "Mounted Aristotle," noted in Chapter 3. The ethical charge of the medieval new would motivate concerns with the ethical problems of *ingenium* and the complex debates on *curiositas*. Submission to the ideal of divine creativity produced not only a rather astonishing array of "adulterated" new things, poems, tales, and images; but also a persistent return to problems of "adulteration": to deception and quackery, to desire and ethics, to "perverse" and "unnatural" texts, to selfishness and greed, and to the problems incurred by a proprietary attitude toward the world and its artifacts.

Sarah Kay argues that Lacan was attracted to the literature of courtly love because this poetry secularizes this brand of submission, translating submission to divine law into submission to the courtly lady. By the end of the great century of the scholastics, as she puts it, "an alternation between sublime and perverse structures" produced "an equivocation between commitment and disengagement."[65] Lacan also seems to have been attracted to the way the scholastics understood human making as dependent on ("secondary to") larger cultural structures. One of Lacan's primary insights—and he takes great pains to critique ego-psychologists on this point—has to do with the degree to which desire and signification occupy a cultural field, rather than a strictly individual one. He thus and unsurprisingly argues for an understanding of sublimation as something more than the libidinal satisfactions that particular artists derive from their creative activity. While these satisfactions are of interest, he wishes to stress that, as satisfactions, they depend first and foremost on the possibility that language might be able to form, as he puts it, "a structure within a social consensus": "What needs to be justified is not simply the *secondary* benefits that *individuals* might derive from their works, but the *originary* possibility of a function like the poetic function in the form of *a structure within a social consensus*" (my emphasis).[66] Sublimation, a "universal" structure, thus and nonetheless comes to depend on the particular ways that language functions at a given time, a shift in emphasis from the benefits that sublimation grants to particular artists, to sublimation as a function of signification itself. "It is," he continues, "precisely that kind of consensus we see born at a certain historical moment around the ideal of courtly love."[67] The importance of a (nonconscious) social consensus here is notable: as with the qualifications of Bonaventure, this account does not depict the artist as the solitary innovating genius who shatters aesthetic rules and flouts convention.

But that is not to say that either Bonaventure or Lacan renders human creative production *merely*, or condescendingly, derivative. Read closely, both Lacan and the scholastics disentangle the universal structure of human creativity from particular signifying technologies and particular historical contingencies. Throughout "Anamorphosis," a diverse array of cultural forms, each the object of a certain "social consensus" at a given historical moment, "represent a different relationship to the void of the real"[68]: the cave paintings at Lascaux, the potter's vase, the lyrics of courtly love, Cezanne's apples, Holbein's anamorphotic art. Each of these examples, but especially the lyrics of courtly love, occupies a doubled and paradoxical history in this account of creativity: productions of an *innovative* social consensus that emblematizes a universal structure of modern subjectivity.[69] Certain little nothings like the caves at Lascaux, or the lyrics of courtly love, will emerge as "breakaway moments"[70] in cultural history; yet, still functioning as the universal structure of creative productivity, they constitute a representative of the "existence of the emptiness at the center of the real that is called the Thing."[71] Like the scholastic taxonomies read above, this account combines the new with the universal,[72] and change with repetition.

Art has particular prominence in Lacan's account, offering a specifically productive relationship to the void of the real. Succinctly characterizing these diverse cultural registers in Lacan's thought, Luke Sunderland writes, "Whereas science forecloses the void, and religion avoids and respects it, art surrounds or encircles it."[73] The medieval record, however, suggests a slightly more complicated signifying circuit for the signifier *sublimation*, for "Art" was not so entirely distinct from "Science" at that time. A signifier deployed in psychoanalytic theory since 1916 to describe the transformations of desire into cultural

productions (poems, paintings, and the like), *sublimation* also has a chemical
and alchemical past, one that, beginning in the twelfth century, is freighted
with both scientific and metaphysical meaning. It would not, perhaps, go too
far to suggest that the medieval history of alchemy offers a deep history not
only of modern chemistry, as William Newman argues, but also of sublimation as a vector for human creativity.

According to the *OED*, the word *sublimation* was first used as a noun in
English in John Gower's *Confessio Amantis*, where it refers to the chemical
process of changing liquid to vapor form. In fourteenth-century alchemical
texts, sublimation, from the Latin *sublimare* (to raise or elevate), is used specifically with regard to demonstrable processes of transformation: liquid sub-
limated into air. The "sociolect" of medieval alchemy would venture far
beyond any "foreclosure" of scientific thought. We approach such difficulties
in the next chapter. For now, it is important to remember that the transformations and elevations of water into air became models for imagining even more
ambitious, impossible transformations; a model for conceiving processes that
would test the counterfactual limits of metaphysical possibility.

The registers change. What was once a name linked to novel alchemical
material transformations becomes the term for a novel understanding of the
material output of desire. What Aranye Fradenburg calls "the history of the
signifier" can help us to track historical recurrence and historical change, even
as we watch the signifiers involved jump their tracks: from "art" to "science"
and back again. And just as Lacan's medievalism enables us to consider such
convergence of continuity and change, Henry Adams's medievalism, with
which this chapter began, toggled back and forth between persistent problems
and changing signifiers. For Adams, as for Lacan, many of the artifacts of
medieval culture point simultaneously in two directions: to the irresolvable
problems of human desire and history; and to the material output at particularly creative historical moments. This doubled—ambivalent—view urges on
us attentive care with the ways that old and new entwine.

Other early twentieth-century fans of the Middle Ages would take a considerably more enthusiastic and forthright view of medieval innovation. At
about the time that Freud redefined sublimation for his own purposes and
Adams penned his praise of *Chartres*, American medievalists, amateur and
professional, were captivated by the evidence of innovation in an extraordinary manuscript ascribed to a precocious scientific thinker from the thirteenth century. The Voynich manuscript would catch the eye of Adams's

contemporaries and colleagues, many of them founding members of the Medieval Academy of America. Here they could identify, or so many of them thought, the work of an innovative thinker par excellence, a man who, in their view, could lay claim to having been the most radical scientific innovator of all time.

Who else but the irascible Roger Bacon?

Chapter 2

Conjuring Roger Bacon

I have not seen a flying machine, and I do not know any one who
has seen one; but I know a wise man who has thought out the
principle of the thing.
                —Roger Bacon, "Epistola de secretis operibus artis et naturae"

I had long been romantically interested in Roger Bacon and was
eager to believe . . . that he was the greatest scientific genius the
world had ever possessed.
                —John Matthews Manly, "Roger Bacon and the Voynich
                                                            Manuscript"

In the popular imagination Roger Bacon remains the romantic figure of scientific genius that he once was for John Matthews Manly. Readers today imagine the thirteenth-century scholar as a radical innovator, "one of the most significant and irreplaceable figures in the history of science";[1] he features prominently in Donald Sharpes's *Outlaws and Heretics: Profiles in Independent Thought and Courage* (2007); English editions of Bacon's *Secrets of Art and Nature* remain in print thanks to popular presses specializing in "Alchemy and Hermetica," or in the occult. Bacon continues to be, as William Newman puts it, "a name to conjure with."[2]

Yet, if Bacon has been regularly defended as an innovating virtuoso, he has just as regularly been ridiculed as a fraudulent necromancer, at least since the seventeenth century.[3] Only four of the friar's minor writings appeared in print during the three centuries subsequent to his death. Portions of his *Opus Majus* dealing with mathematics and with optics were published in 1614 at

Frankfurt; it would be another hundred and twenty years before much of the rest appeared in England (1733). Another century would pass before the publication of the *Opera Inedita* (1859).[4] As a harsh critic of his contemporaries who was often at odds with his superiors, Bacon's genius has at times seemed to rest on his irascibility, on the degree to which he resisted the putatively "backward" impulses of his era.

Why has Roger Bacon proved to be so controversial? What can Bacon's fluctuating reputation tell us about the circulation of the new in the medieval discourse of natural philosophy, as well as in its modern descendants? Addressing the major controversies of his time, Bacon worked across a range of historical texts in an impressive diversity of languages; he worked both as a member of the Order of Friars Minor and as a secular master, as a theoretician and a practitioner, at Oxford and Paris, and places in between. "A savant of very great scope, the one who taught Western Europe to think about light, force, and species,"[5] Bacon ranged widely. His writings regularly cross borders, combining natural philosophy with an interest in magic; Arabic astrology with European prophetic histories; craft practice with philosophical disputation; linguistic equivocation with alchemical matter. The hybridity of these interests contributes to Bacon's vacillating reception, even as they point to certain features of the altogether ambivalent medieval pursuit of novel ideas and inventions.

The current chapter takes Bacon's reputation as a starting point, arguing that the alternating historiographic and cultural valuations surrounding him encode features of the ambivalent view of new things and ideas legible in the medieval record. I wish to analyze, rather than to duplicate, this equivocal response to innovation as a particularly forceful, and ethically interesting, approach. The equivocations surrounding Bacon can help us to assess certain ethical ambiguities, just as Bacon's vacillating reputation symptomatizes the ambivalent way that intellectuals of the twelfth and thirteenth centuries approached novelty. John Matthews Manly (1865–1940)—the famous philologist, founder, along with Edith Rickert, of the Chaucer laboratory at the University of Chicago in 1924, and longtime editor of the journal *Modern Philology*—testified to the romantic attractions of Bacon's apparent innovations even as those innovations remained in doubt.

Romancing Bacon

Manly's "romantic" interest in Roger Bacon did not emerge from thin air. It was fueled by the 1912 discovery of an apparently medieval manuscript written in cipher, containing numerous illustrations as well as surprisingly accurate scientific diagrams. The Voynich manuscript, it was claimed, was inscribed with an anagram of Bacon's name[6]; and it conjured the friar as the precocious forebear of nineteenth-century scientific method. Prestigious academics took up the cause. William Newbold, Adam Seybert Professor of Intellectual and Moral Philosophy at the University of Pennsylvania, spent years deciphering the manuscript, and it was he who argued to great fanfare in April 1921 that the manuscript contained a complex and multilayered cipher which, when decoded and translated, attested to Bacon's thirteenth-century "invention" of the microscope and the telescope, and included accurate descriptions of microscopic observations of spermatozoa and even a drawing of the Andromeda Nebula as observed through a telescope.[7] Newbold's presentation before the American Philosophical Society and College of Physicians in Philadelphia was big news, announcing, as a headline in the *New York Times* would put it, "Bacon, 700 years Ahead in Science." Subheadings to the story suggest the enthusiasm that greeted Newbold's initial claims: "Medieval Friar had theories on the solar system and the microbe. / He anticipated Pasteur. / Persecuted as a Necromancer, he buried his discoveries in a puzzling cipher. / Dr. Newbold found the key."[8] Describing the history of these events, Lawrence and Nancy Goldstone note that, from this point on, "both Newbold and Bacon burst from the cloistered confines of medieval scholarship into the popular arena and became instant celebrities."[9]

Yet the confines of medieval scholarship were hardly cloistered at the time Newbold spoke. Key figures in this debate published in magazines like *Harper's* and *Scientific American*, and the audience was compendious, interdisciplinary, and public, numbering engineers, mathematicians, architects, and scientists as well as medievalists and historians of science. The excitement over the Voynich manuscript indicates not the rarefied air but the popular reach of medieval studies in the early twentieth century. Alongside the work of Henry Adams noted in Chapter 1, this episode corroborates accounts of the historical intimacies between academic medieval studies and popular medievalism.[10] Indeed, if embarrassed medievalists eventually came to wish for a more cloistered environ, this may have been because nearly all the grandiose claims made for Bacon's monumental achievements would soon be called into doubt.[11]

Manly was not the only scholar to express doubt about Newbold's claims, though his response would be definitive. It was all the more devastating, since it amounted to a retraction of an early public defense of his friend's project published in the pages of *Harper's* in 1921 and timed to accompany Newbold's initial announcement.[12] In 1931, ten years after that early endorsement, Manly would reverse himself, arguing instead that the claims for the Voynich manuscript were imaginative rather than accurate, and the evidence for Bacon's precocity was "the subconscious creation of Professor Newbold's enthusiasm and ingenuity."[13] The complex cipher and anagrammatic system Newbold had devised to translate the manuscript was, Manly asserted, "so vitiated by its flexibility and ambiguity that no confidence can be given to messages deciphered by it."[14] Manly's opinion was all the more authoritative, grounded as it was in cryptological expertise he had gained during his work with the British MI-8 during the First World War.

When Manly cautioned his readers about the enthusiasms—his own included—surrounding Newbold's big announcement, he ascribed them to a "romanti[c] interest" in Bacon's genius. Bacon's powerful seductions made even Manley swoon. Evidently illustrious "professionals" can get carried away, conjuring a set of findings to suit their yearnings. Such remarks remind us, first, that enthusiasm is not simply the mark of the amateur; it is internal to professional debates in academic fields and, in this case, a prompt for the professional medievalist, a point that Manly apparently wishes to disavow. And in his mode of lamentation, Manly casts such eagerness as soft-hearted as well as soft-headed, and an obstacle to the willing recognition of cold, hard fact. Over-excitement figures, thus, as an impediment to an apparently professionalizing rigor. This is arguably one result of an abiding romance with newness. But that is not to say that such romance, for all its grandiose dreams of astonishment, might not also have profoundly positive effects.

As we now know, Manly's remarks encode the kind of distinctions from which professional Medieval Studies emerged, where the romance of desire for the past comes under the disciplining rule of authority, or a credentializing rigor. If today scholars seem more willing to acknowledge the pleasures that must motivate scholarship, the opposition implied by Manly's confessional mode still exerts a certain force, particularly in the field of the History of Science, where the story of the Voynich manuscript amounts to something of a cautionary tale. Manly's apologetic account of himself as a reformed Voynich enthusiast can, by contrast, draw out the productive (if messy) nature of this kind of ambivalent back-and-forth. If Voynich did not, and in fact could not, establish Roger Bacon as "700 years ahead in Science," the early twentieth-century reception of this manuscript nonetheless made a variety of questions regarding Bacon's work, on light, perspective, and alchemy, both exciting and urgent. Bacon's popularity grew as a result, and debates over his accomplishments fueled a number of important projects, including an effort to establish scholarly editions of his work, many still in use today. But what does it mean that Roger Bacon has remained a lightning rod for the problem of medieval innovation in such extreme terms, a paradoxical touchstone for both exaggerated praise of early innovation and strident derision of it? It has been difficult to tell—and not only because of our "romance" with Roger—what to make of the various claims made on his behalf. Which are reliable and which are overblown?

There is more to this story. The early reception of the Voynich manuscript foregrounds the astonishing agency of the solitary man of genius, marking the innovator as brave (male) hero, a lone wolf willing to contest the biases and banalities of an otherwise constraining age. If the fascinating history of Bacon as an innovator of the first magnitude offers a view of the new as both desirable and valuable, it also suggests such values were, in the Middle Ages, impossible to admit openly. Even as it "conjured" a fraudulent history for Roger Bacon, the Voynich manuscript uncovered the agency of modernist speculation for the story of medieval newness as a covert operation. Novelty and its mysteries were imagined as a medieval anathema, necessarily rendered in secret cipher. Bacon's work emerges as a species of forbidden desire. In this way, Bacon is rendered out of joint with his own times, a precociously modern scientific seeker born in the wrong age. This romance with Roger Bacon is also, then, a romance with newness as the province of adventurous iconoclasts. Diligent drudges or whimsical dreamers need not apply.

Such fables cast long shadows in the public imaginary. Insofar as assessments of Bacon's thinking are tied to the notion of his exceptional precocity during an otherwise "backward" time, newness remains fundamentally at odds with the Middle Ages as such; and this despite the fact that, by any accounting of the evidence, the period during which the irascible friar lived and worked witnessed an exciting proliferation of new ideas, new methods, and new things in the West. Historians of medieval science have, in response, rightly and repeatedly insisted that the thirteenth-century Franciscan was, as Lynn Thorndike put it in 1923, a "man of his time,"[15] one, in Amanda Power's more recent assessment, "highly responsive to the burning issues of his day."[16] They are each exactly right. Yet insofar as such reminders continue to imply that the medieval era was inhospitable to—always harshly critical of—new ideas and things, even revised versions of this story prove disabling at least for a consideration of the diverse and ambivalent ways in which medieval thinkers regularly pursued, even romanced, newness themselves.

Assessing the advent of the new is no easy thing—now or then. Popular accounts of scientific and technological "firsts" imply that innovation is easily recognized, that newness is self-evident as a rupture in time, an obviously revolutionary moment of remarkable genius, or the product of dramatic change. Even as it claims Bacon's revolutionary agency, the full story of the Voynich manuscript suggests otherwise. Overdetermined reactions to the manuscript linger, symptomatizing the problem of the new as a feature of cultural and technical histories: a "now you see it, now you don't" index for discovery, change, or hope. Yet the advent of the new is not discovered or recognized so much as it is promoted, so Bruno Latour argues. Networks of writers, thinkers, institutions, and laboratories, quiet promoters or loud provocateurs, work to endorse, negotiate, react to, redefine, and gain adopters for the next best idea or thing. Innovation depends, that is, on groups of actors rather than on either individual genius, or the accuracy of any single invention or discovery.[17] And fractious disagreement is more the rule than the exception: "Doubt, trust, then gratitude and admiration, or, on the contrary suspicion, defiance, and even hate are at the heart of innovation."[18] The history of the Voynich manuscript is notable in part because it makes clear that claims made on behalf of scientific genius occur in excess of either historical fact or technological utility. From this perspective, what Manly denigrated as Newbold's "imaginative ingenuity" seems less an impediment to the recognition of Bacon's innovating reach than a promotion of it, all the more so on account of the public controversy that ensued.

Newbold's promotion of Bacon occurred at a time when both popular and scholarly audiences turned to the medieval archive for the deep story of secular modernity; some, like Henry Adams, emphasized the continued relevance and imitative power of medieval pursuits of all kinds. Others saw secular modernity as a uniquely innovating age. Yet the secularizing story of modernity remained throughout an equivocal one: we have, as Latour avers, never been entirely modern;[19] and even as an innovative aesthetic force, modernism's tie to newness was never entirely secure—as its persistent interest in things medieval, its persistent concern with what Fredric Jameson calls "the worn world of people and things" makes clear.[20] The Ezra Pound who charged modernist aesthetes to "make it new!" was a devoted reader, translator, and imitator

of Dante, the troubadour poets, and Anglo-Saxon heroic verse. The era of
high modernism was also an era of high medievalism, one that witnessed an
explosion—at once dismissive, nostalgic, scholarly, and erotic—of work on
medieval poetry, medieval architecture, medieval science, and medieval state-
making. In American academe, this was the moment of the founding of the
Medieval Academy and the journal *Speculum*, in which Manly's critique of
Newbold appeared—still a flagship venue for medieval historical work.

Bacon's "novelties"—real or imagined—span the gap between novel
claims as useful speculation and as error or fraud. And the controversies surrounding his work pertain to philosophical questions about art and nature
important to the history of science, as well as to the apocalyptic millenarianism associated with Bacon's confrere Joachim de Fiore (d. 1202). To be sure, in
Bacon's medieval context, unlike Newbold's modernist one, questions of innovation or speculation did not emerge via any clear opposition of old to new.
The notion of the new, as we shall see, equivocated throughout the record.
These equivocations can help us to consider the narratives of valuation for the
new from an oblique angle.

Authoritative Speculations

It is a delicious kind of irony that the man in whose name the Voynich manuscript was forged had, centuries before, railed against the fraudulent uses of
authorities in new books ("novos libros"). In his famous *Epistola de Secretis
Operibus Artis et Naturae,* or *Letter on the Secrets of Art and Nature* (hereafter
Secrets), Roger Bacon cautions against the fraudulent claims of certain magicians who use authority duplicitously:

> But as for all the things that are contained in the books of magi-
> cians, they are rightly to be rejected even though they contain some
> truth, because so many untruths abound that what is true and what
> is false cannot be distinguished. Thus whatever they say—it has to
> be denied that Solomon or other wise men composed this or that,
> since these kinds of books were neither accepted by ecclesiastical
> authority nor by learned men but by seducers who have deceived
> the world. And *they compose new books, and multiply new inventions,*
> as we know from experience. And then to allure men more thor-
> oughly, they give grand titles to their works, and shamelessly ascribe

them to famous authors; And not to omit anything touching these
things, they compose in a grandiloquent style and counterfeit a text
in the form of lies.[21] (emphasis mine)

[Sed quae in libris magicorum continentur omnia sunt jure arcenda
quamvis aliquid veri contineant; quia tot falsis abutuntur, quod non
potest discerni inter verum et falsum. Unde quicquid dicunt quod
Salomon composuit hoc vel illud, aut alii sapientes negandum est;
quia non recipiuntur hujusmodi libri auctoritate ecclesiae, nec a
sapientibus, sed a seductoribus, qui mundum decipiunt. Nam et *ipsi
novos libros componunt, et novas adinventiones multiplicant*, sicut
scimus per experientiam; et tunc ut vehementius homines alliciant,
præponunt titulos famosos suis operibus, et eos magnis auctoribus
ascribunt impudenter; ac ut nihil omittant de contingentibus,
stilum grandisonum faciunt, et sub forma textus mendacia
confingunt.[22]]

At first glance, this all seems unsurprising. When Bacon insists that some new
books and new inventions should be rejected because they deceive the world,
he offers a standard example of the "medieval" disapprobation for the new.
Yet, even as the critique leveled is familiar, the relation of true to false and old
to new is complexly drawn. For one thing, the new books of "magicians"
should "be rejected" because they seduce, so Bacon argues, not by way of innovation but by way of old authorities. And even though such books "contain
some truth," they cannot be trusted, since "so many untruths abound, that
what is true and what is false cannot be distinguished." Writers deceive by
grounding their claims in false accounts of authorities or other well-regarded
authors. As bad readers as well as duplicitous writers, such "magicians" ape an
impressively lofty style so as to allure, seduce, and deceive.

Yet more is at issue than the fraudulent, or intentionally duplicitous, use
of *auctoritas*. Questions of error also obtain. Bacon's first mention of those
truth-challenged magicians twice deploys the term "falsus" ("quia tot falsis
abutuntur, quod non potest discerni inter verum et falsum"), a word with a
semantic range that includes attestations of error or mistake. Not all deceptive
claims are designed to deceive; errors, mistakes in translation or spurious uses
of logic can misrepresent or misconstrue without any particularly duplicitous
intent. And indeed, attention to such subtlety seems warranted, given the
emphasis on the coexistence of truth with error. There were stronger words

Bacon could have used; and he will, in fact, prefer a stronger term with reference to the writings rather than the writers: errors and false attributions of
authority result in *textus mendacia*, counterfeit or fraudulent texts. Such writings can be dangerously alluring not only because they deploy authority falsely,
but also because in doing so they authorize future errors and proliferate future
mistakes. As such, "magicians" misuse authority and err in the textual letter;
yet they prove dangerous because they gussy up such errors with glorious titles
and famous names. This combination renders their texts, in Bacon's final judgment, mendacious.

Such remarks occur throughout Bacon's larger corpus. Attention to the
specificity of the letter is, in a manner of speaking, precisely the mode that he
adopts throughout his work. The friar's interventions into many of the major
debates of his time emphasize problems of translation and of language, and he
wrote passionately about the insufficiency of Latin for understanding a range
of authoritative texts originally penned in other languages. On the one hand,
he regularly rails against the corruptions introduced by linguistic error. "[I]t is
no small impropriety," he writes in a typical passage from his *Opus Majus*, "to
make mistakes in words; because as a consequence a man errs in his state-
ments, then in his arguments and at length in what he reckons as conclusions." Citing Aristotle and Boethius, Bacon stresses the importance of
linguistic accuracy for experimental science: "For the principal difficulty in a
science and its usefulness are found in knowing how to understand the words
employed in the science and to express them in a wise manner and without
error."[23] Language, from translation to etymology, remains crucial to all such
endeavors.

Interpretive accuracy and linguistic equivocation are two of the friar's
most persistent preoccupations. While a full exploration of Bacon's semiotics
lies outside the scope of the current study, a discussion of Bacon's quirky contributions to medieval theories of linguistic equivocation can shed considerable light on the writings that made him popularly famous as a forward-thinking
prophet of flying machines.[24] The nature of equivocation proves to be one of
the knottiest questions of his age; it had been a logical problem for medieval
thinkers in the wake of Aristotle's association of equivocation with deception
and logical fallacy. Equivocation was of interest to a host of writers, philosophers as well as poets, although Bacon was the only medieval thinker to define
it in ways that take into account "the complexities of linguistic signification"
itself.[25] Bacon's account of equivocation ventures beyond the dialectical vacil-
lation between contradictory poles: high vs. low; matter vs. form.[26] His

interest, as we shall see, lies less in the poles of apparent contradiction than in a complex and contextual middle ground, the space bounded by yet not accommodated in standard linguistic or logical limits. Pushing the definition of equivocation beyond these limits, the friar delineated a number of new linguistic subcategories or classes.

The majority opinion in Bacon's day held that the essential link between a sign and the thing it signified was unchanging. In contrast, Bacon stressed relational modes of signification.[27] Any sign, he emphasized, was related not only to the thing signified, but, and more important, to the interpreter to whom it was addressed. He stressed the importance of context as a key feature of a word's meaning. This required the development of a number of new classes of equivocation, all unique to Bacon's work. Most important for my purposes is the class he terms the "equivocation of appellation,"[28] a new subcategory resulting from the diversity of what were known as "impositions" of a word, that is, intentional usages of common and proper names. In this case, as we shall see, names for things equivocate whenever their linguistic contexts change.

By the thirteenth century, "impositions," or proper and common names, were understood as a type of *significacio ad placitum* (signification at [one's] pleasure) and, as such, thought to be a class of free and rational linguistic acts. Bacon pointed out, as Roger Mahoney notes, that in certain contexts "one is free to select a name that was originally imposed for one thing and reimpose it for anything else," and indeed "even [for] things that do not exist."[29] To take one of the friar's famous examples, the name "Caesar" need not be limited to the figure intended in its original imposition, the particular "Caesar" who first bore the name. Once the living man originally intended by that name was no longer living, the word could be freely reimposed to intend, variously, that particular but now deceased Caesar (as deceased, already a different referent from the living man), or any other future Caesar. As this example suggests, specific cases concern the function of words related to change over time and circumstance. With regard to temporal change, moreover, Bacon argued for a special circumstance by which common or proper terms are to be considered equivocal if they designate either (a) things that once existed but no longer do, or (b) things that will only exist in the future.[30] Indeed, Bacon pointed out that speakers regularly, and without much fanfare, revise the meaning of a word in situations where no appropriate word already exists, or when any particular thing referenced by it has ceased to exist.

These theories are pertinent, I argue, to Bacon's writings on the books of

the magicians, and they shed light on the often-cited lists of inventions taken
from that same text. Much of Bacon's popular reputation rests on a set of
speculative sentences in the *Secrets* describing an array of possible objects produced through a collaboration of "Art and Nature." With the constant refrain
"machines can be made" ("instrumenta possunt fieri"), Bacon adopts a condi-
tional form (and, for some of the verbs, the subjunctive mood) as he renders
an exciting list of new possibilities: "For machines for sailing without human
oarsmen can be made, to make the largest river and marine ships go with a
single steersman at the greatest speed as if they were full of people." ["Nam
instrumenta navigandi possunt fieri sine hominibus remigantibus, ut naves
maximae, fluviales et marinae ferantur unico homine regente, majori veloci-
tate quam si plenae essent hominibus."][31] "Chariots can be made to move with
a inestimable force without an animal." ["Item, currus possunt fieri ut sine
animali moveantur cum impetu inestimabili."] "Flying machines can be
made, . . . by which wings put together artificially would beat the air in the
manner of a flying bird." ["Item, possunt fieri instrumenta volandi, . . . per
quod alae artificialiter compositae aerem verberent, ad modum avis volan-
tis."][32] "Instruments could also be made for walking in the sea, or in rivers
even down to the bottom without bodily danger." ["Possunt etiam instrumenta fieri ambulandi in mari, vel fluminibus usque ad fundum absque peri-
culo corporali."][33] And there may even be remedies that may lead to "the
prolongation of human life" ["prolongatio vitae humanae"].[34] In summary,
"an almost infinite sort of things can be made, like bridges over rivers without
pillars or any kind of support, and instruments and unheard of engines." ["Et
infinita quasi talia fieri possunt; ut pontes ultra flumina sine columnas vel
aliquo sustentaculo, et machinationes, et ingenia inaudita."][35]

Recognizable terms take on diverse new meanings. Ships, chariots, wings,
bridges, are all reimposed in the direction of a novel context and use. The term
"instruments" equivocates repeatedly. Each usage intends a diverse object in at
least two ways, as regards to the specific instrument imagined (the newly envisioned chariot, ship, bridge, etc.), and as to the intention of something not
currently in existence, but something nonetheless capable of being made. The
possibilities seem infinite, even to the speaker: "And after I observed things
like these, when I consider well, nothing is difficult for me to believe, either
divine or human." ["Et postquam huiusmodi perspexi, nihil mihi est difficile
ad credendum, quando bene considero, nec in divinis, sicut nec in hu-
manis."][36] He names objects not currently in existence ("unheard of engines")
by way of unfamiliar versions of familiar things: ships unlike any ships

currently known; cars that move on their own; bridges that can operate in ways that seem impossible.

Bacon's own theory of the "equivocation of appellation" can help explain a burst of writing that otherwise seems uncharacteristically fanciful. Insofar as Bacon's writings attest to the existence of devices as yet unheard of, he deploys a type of equivocation that is both speculative and temporally multiple. These things, Bacon insists, have been done in classical times; they can be done now, freshly or again. His list, "clearly inspired by the marvels of romance,"[37] depends on a type of multitemporality familiar to readers of medieval fictions, where past descriptions of marvelous things converge on present and future ones. In this regard, his treatise adopts something of the awkward temporality often associated with romance, as when medieval retellings of classical tales update ancient figures in newer garb, as, for instance, when *romans antiques* depict Aeneas in the garb of a chivalric knight. Such moments were long considered evidence that the medieval period lacked a notion of history entirely, its thinkers and writers incapable of conceiving of historical difference or temporal particularity. We now know that such complexities of timing indicate not an absence of historical thinking, but a particular kind of asynchronous, even "untimely" temporal consciousness.

Yet, and particularly in the light of Bacon's own emphasis on such things as both traditional and new, this brand of anachronism insists on the possible "now-ness," and thus the *newness* of instruments or stories from times long since past. And while he does not seem interested in the paradoxical nature of such an account of the new (a point of surprising interest to poets like Machaut or Chaucer, as will be clear in later chapters), we might note the degree to which Bacon's larger work regularly marks new developments by reimposing older names for credible futures. Taken up in the timing of once and again, the has-been and the not-quite-yet, this is the agency of the object as both enduring and new, where tradition combines with ingenuity in a complex and strange kind of counterfactual futurity.

Furthermore, like the magicians he chastises, the friar ascribes his work to old authorities such as Pliny, Aristotle, and Galen, and he, too, uses the letter to "multiply new inventions." Authorities, when properly read, offer Bacon a kind of backstop to linguistic or philosophical speculation. Bacon's enlarged understanding of equivocation does not, that is, license unlimited modifications to words and their uses. As this treatise also demonstrates, he remained a linguistic taskmaster throughout his life, one with little patience for errors in etymological understanding or in translation. The fraudulent, or counterfeit, serves as a limiting case, one still pertinent to his brand of counterfactual thinking. And, as we shall see shortly, in the fractious years of the 1260s, Bacon would launch a strident critique of the "new" Masters at the University of Paris, also largely on the grounds of their linguistic limitations.

Contentious Networks

> Every new thing is an innovation, and every innovation is an error,
> and every error leads to hell.
> —proverbial, ascribed to Mohammad[38]

The list of instruments found in Roger Bacon's *Secrets* corroborates a point observed in the previous chapter: premodern discourses of innovation were pursued via the complex interpenetration of old and new in a discourse of ethical concern. In the disagreements between Abelard and Bernard of Clairvaux noted in Chapter 1, the contrast of the conventional (*consuetudo* or *usus*) to the whimsically idiosyncratic (*ingenium*) was crucial. Bacon, we might note in passing, deployed *ingenium* and its cognates throughout his treatise, emphasizing the legitimate power of creative whimsy. (And, indeed, *consuetudo*, or convention will rank high on Bacon's list of the causes of error.) The distinction between the conventional and the idiosyncratic had ethical implications, and these will be forcefully worked out in texts of poetry, particularly romance, as I will discuss in later chapters. Ethical concerns were also raised in religious discourse, precisely through the association of error with moral corruption.

Working near the end of the great Translation Movement (1140–1280), Friar Bacon knew the Islamic debates concerning the links between innovation and error, and the questions surrounding the virtue or vice of new pursuits. He lived during those decades when new ideas, methods, and questions were fueled by the intellectual and political agitation emerging in the wake of the "new Aristotelianism," and by wide-ranging reactions to it. Philosophical questions to do with the unity of truth, in debates over accounts of divine creation ex nihilo, emerged in the wake of Aristotle's introduction in the West. Bacon belonged to this generation of scholastics, those living and working in intellectual centers at Paris and Oxford in the decades after the West's disastrous Second Crusade and the fall of Jerusalem (the generation of Aquinas; the generation following Abelard, Bernard of Clairvaux, or Peter the Venerable).

Even before joining the Order of Friars Minor, Bacon had spent years admiring the Franciscan masters at Oxford. He rarely agreed with their Parisian counterparts, and was clearly irritated that many of those (Richard Rufus of Cornwall; or Bonaventure, fellow Franciscans both) were more famous than he. He preferred the work of Averroës to that of Avicenna.

As part of a larger defense of his absorption with Aristotle's commentators, particularly with the natural philosophers working on alchemy and astrological astronomy, Bacon held firm to the value of accuracy; in these writings as well as in his ground-breaking treatment of vision and perspective, linguistic accuracy was especially prized as a way to ensure scientific rigor. Linguistic accuracy would have been all the more crucial—and difficult—in the alchemical contexts also pertinent to the *Secrets*. Alchemy relied on a kind of doublespeak, on the use of linguistic enigmas and puzzles, a habit that Bacon not only clearly realized but also regularly adopted, as he does in latter portions of that treatise. Throughout his writings, the friar repeatedly insists that philosophical or scientific subtleties might only be accurately evaluated once they were accurately understood. This meant, among other things, reading these texts in their original languages, a program which, in his view, would enhance a coming age of (Christian) cosmological renewal and herald a worldwide Christendom: "mechanical inventions like flying machines and optical devices, astral and geographical influences, the correct ordering of law and society, the abolition of sexual (and moral) irregularity, and the reform of education were all necessary to defeat the Tartars, the Saracens, and the soon to appear antichrist."[39] His attention to the political and religious power of language and translation followed the model of Peter the Venerable, who had translated the Qur'an for similar reasons.

Bacon would seem, in this regard, more dogmatic than inquisitive. And to those who imagine innovation as a necessarily secularizing impulse, Bacon's religious fervor and triumphalist commitments may seem to compromise his reputation as an innovator. Yet his own relation to religious orthodoxy is itself complex, and the friar's contentious relationship with his superiors has also been used to justify the account of Bacon with which this chapter began, a solitary innovating seeker standing against the biases of his age. The primary evidence adduced here has been the friar's apparent condemnation and punishment, in 1278, on suspicion of the promulgation of so-called "novelties." According to the *Franciscan Chronicle*, the friar's writings were "condemned and reprobated . . . as containing some suspected novelties, on account of which the same Roger was condemned to prison." ["Fratris Rogerii Bachonis

Anglici, sacrae theologiae magistri, continens aliquas novitates suspectas."][40] This chronicle, written some hundred years after the event, is uncorroborated elsewhere in the record. By some accounts, the friar's censure by his superiors was an entirely quotidian affair to do with his failure to submit to the daily requirements of the fraternal life. Other readers situate Bacon's sentence within the larger condemnations of 1277, and thus very much within the intellectual trends of his time.[41] One thing seems clear: whatever trouble he found at the hands of his Franciscan superiors, Bacon did not set himself against them so much as fiercely engage their struggles and political disputes.

The times were contentious. Friar Bacon had a powerful ally in Pope Clement IV; his *Opus Majus* was composed at Clement's request. Clement sought Bacon's opinions regarding a host of matters, including the situation at Paris involving what Jeremiah Hackett calls "the wholesale warfare about Aristotle in the Arts faculty," as well as the apparent infighting between the friars and secular masters.[42] Certainly, insofar as it was known among Bacon's immediate circle, Clement's request would have gone some way toward legitimating his continued research. Yet it also placed Bacon in a difficult position within his order. In 1260, at the Council of Narbonne and in response to political pressures from both within and outside the order, Bonaventure and other superiors had promulgated a statute that forbade the publication of books or pamphlets without explicit permission from superiors. Clement's *mandatum* to Bacon was given only six years later; it commanded the friar to send to him a written account of his studies, "not withstanding any prohibitions of his Order,"[43] and, for whatever reason, recommended secrecy. Any number of circumstances may have suggested secrecy as the best course of action in such matters; after all, alchemical treatises were routinely written in enigmatic code.

Yet, if the pope commanded and thus endorsed Bacon's writing, he did not finance his research. Books were expensive.[44] The Franciscans, while still a relatively young order, offered institutional stability and resources, particularly libraries. A latecomer to the Franciscans, Bacon was a secular master for much of his early adulthood. In his youth, his extensive research program had been financed by a personal and quite substantial fortune. Financial losses, in the wake of political turmoil in England, meant that by 1263 Bacon's family money could no longer be relied on to underwrite his research costs. He had no doubt been attracted to the friars because of his admiration for the famous Franciscan circle of intellectuals he knew, in person or by reputation, during his time in Oxford. His appreciation of the extensive libraries that the friars owned throughout Europe surely contributed as well.

Bacon's Franciscan context is notable for one more reason. If Roger's love of "novelties" prompted the Franciscan authorities to condemn him, novelty also held a particularly arresting fascination within the hagiographic tradition associated with the order. Early hagiography surrounding the founder claimed St. Francis as a radically new kind of saint; the friars a radically new kind of order. The *Vita of St. Francis*, composed by Thomas of Celano in celebration of Francis's canonization in 1228, emphasized Francis as representing, in the words of William J. Short, "a new kind of holiness, breaking with, surpassing or transcending the tradition."[45] Throughout the Celano *Vita* newness emerges as "a leitmotif," with over forty references to the various ways in which Francis embodied a joyful "newness" or "renewal."[46] Francis's emergence as a new kind of saint in the order's own hagiography undoubtedly converged on the prophetic millenarianism associated with the Joachites, those admirers of Joachim de Fiore's (c. 1135–1202) complex concordance of new epochs—a real attraction for the group known as the "spiritual" Franciscans. Yet within the order, the Celano *Vita* endorsed newness as renovation, such that "novelty far from being a vice, [was] transformed into a virtue."[47] This rehabilitated brand of newness imagined the new as both immersed in tradition and extending beyond it, the virtue of Francis's newness heralding a renewed age of sanctity.

Within the Franciscan context, then, ascriptions of novelty equivocated rather dramatically. Novelty was both a vice worthy of censure and a saintly virtue justifying canonization. In the fifty-year interim between Thomas of Celano's 1228 *Vita* of Saint Francis and Roger Bacon's 1278 reprobation, new philosophical questions and answers proliferated, alongside prohibitions and their ensuing controversies. Condemnations of the teaching of Aristotle's *libri naturalis*, a ban originally promulgated in 1210 and 1215, had been repeated at Paris in 1231, just after the Celano *Vita* was penned; such prohibitions would be renewed in the years just before Bacon's censure, in 1270 and 1277. By the 1260s debates focused on the theology faculty raged specifically over questions of determinism, and many of the later condemnations aimed directly at a group known as the Latin Averroists, those preferring the commentaries of Averroës to those of Avicenna, for their arguably deterministic views of the universe and human activity in it.

The stakes in the controversies, already enormously high, were increasing in the late thirteenth century. In the condemnations of 1277, 219 propositions were placed under suspicion of heresy. Most of these "aimed at Aristotelian metaphysics and natural philosophy interpreted along astrological (Averroistic) lines."[48] By this time, Bacon had become something of an expert on Arabic writings on astronomy; his *Opus Majus* interprets aspects of Abu-Maʻshar's *On the Great Conjunctions*, a politicized account of the uses of astronomy for historical interpretation. "Conjunctionism," the astrological theory that certain conjunctions of planets could have a determining effect on human affairs, was condemned as antithetical to a belief in human freedom, and Bacon's interest in such theories has been one reason adduced to explain his condemnation.[49] Both Albertus Magnus and his student Thomas Aquinas had devised distinct solutions to the problem of determinism, and both sought to produce accounts of the new knowledge for legitimate use in the West.[50] Bacon adopted the solution on "conjunctionism" favored by Albertus Magnus.[51] Yet his position was not identical to either of these.

Probably in response to the renewal of the condemnations and to the developing antagonism between Oxford and Paris, Bacon's 1260s writings defend, Richard Lemay argues, an "older, Oxfordian strain of Arabist thought."[52] This is, Lemay writes,

> a marked characteristic of the Roger Bacon of the 1260's. He
> attempts to defend the role of Abu-Maʻshar, Pseudo-Ptolemaic and
> other "experimental" books, when the younger generation of
> University teachers were providing new and controversial interpreta-
> tions of Aristotle's texts, and when the younger theologians like
> Bonaventure among the Franciscans were highly critical of the
> deterministic tendencies in astrology and alchemy in the new
> translations of scientific works.[53]

Bacon's defense of the Oxfordian version was leveled on pointedly linguistic grounds; he "relentless[ly] disparag[ed]" the faulty translations on which the new accounts of Arabic studies were based. "Newer" translations, Bacon argued, erred, and thus misrepresented the "new" science; such faulty work cannot be trusted to offer accurate accounts of conjunctionism, which, accordingly, should not be judged by them. While he did, that is, critique the newer curriculum being established at Paris after 1260, Bacon's critique is no reactionary dismissal of the novel as such. The "new" functions contextually (that is, and according to Bacon's own theories, equivocally) here: it figures less as a singular innovative advance on knowledge than as one side of a competition over different versions of the "Arabic" record. This is a startling exception to Pierre Michaud-Quantin's claim that "from the thirteenth century, the term *novus* is likely to take on a positive value," since a "*translatio nova*" is a better translation than those that preceded it."[54] Not so, Bacon would insist. I wish to note two things: first, that Bacon's concern with accurate accounts of what were at the time cutting-edge versions of Arabic astrological astronomy engages questions that are at once "scientific" and religious. Yet he locates error neither in the philosophical questions of planetary motion nor in the (religious) question of determinism, but as a matter of language: in meaning as related to translation and change. Linguistic errors are a constant preoccupation and an issue directly related, as we have seen, to his other concerns.

Bacon's larger interest undoubtedly included the religious questions raised by Joachim de Fiore, whose work promoted a utopian typological vision of history, based on an elaborate concordance and a computation of eras and ages, and according to which the final new age, a peaceful thousand years that would usher in the apocalypse (and thus, the New Jerusalem) was at hand.[55] According to Hilary Carey, Bacon's account of astrological astronomy was "interpretive," "not prescriptive," and his writings persistently suggest that he was driven, as she argues, "not only by his faith in the analytical power of astrology, but [by] the moderate Joachimist [sic] sympathies of the Franciscan circles at Oxford and Paris in which he moved."[56] Where Aquinas refuted Joachite theories in his *Summa*, Bacon's *Opus Majus* cites Joachite prophecies explicitly as part of a defense of the scientific rectitude of "astronomers and astrologers who are philosophers,"[57] suggesting his interest in apocalyptic accounts of salvation history as a means to legitimate his work with astrological astronomy. The links between Joachite prophecy and the Arab astronomers that Bacon adopts will have an important afterlife, particularly for a story of the medieval new. These moments in his *Opus Majus* will circulate influentially in the *Imago Mundi* of Pierre d'Ailly; from there, they will influence Christopher Columbus as he envisions, and gains support for, his New World voyages, a point developed in my final chapter.[58]

For now we should note that Bacon's engagement of conjunctionism with Joachite prophecies seems to have been politically complex, although this, too, has been difficult to assess. Certainly Bacon's rhetoric regularly adopts triumphalist versions of Christian righteousness; and certainly Joachite prophecies deploy religious typology, offering a version of the perfection of history founded on Jewish supersessionism and leading straight to the apocalypse. Yet Bacon's response to his adversaries, near or far, was persistently language based: the "account of the sciences and philosophy in Bacon's later works is largely a polemic for the uses of the liberal arts in the reading of sacred scripture."[59] Moreover, throughout the *Opus Majus*, Bacon reserves some of his most withering condemnations for the violent Teutonic Knights and Knights Templar; he expresses special contempt for gruesome, and in his view scandalous uses of Christian militarism at the time. He disagreed with those, like Bernard of Clairvaux, who had earlier recommended military solutions to the problems he ascribed to pagan intransigence or heretical error.

Carey renders Bacon's politics in the starkest possible terms: as "tactical and strategic warfare," a "reprehensible" recommendation of the "medieval equivalent of biological and nuclear weapons."[60] I take her point. Yet it is difficult to reconcile this assessment entirely with his writings either on the subject of war, on language, or on the prophecies. The prophecies no doubt helped to legitimate his astronomy; but he never did produce a forthright endorsement of war, in terms of either strategy or tactics. The furthering of Christendom, Bacon writes to Clement, "requires rather the way of wisdom than the labor of war."[61] Clearly invested in Christian superiority, Bacon nonetheless contrasts his intellectual project to the militarism of crusading violence. He was, to be sure, dedicated to the supremacy of the West, but it is intellectual endeavor, and the rigorous study of languages, that will provide, he argues, a Christian minority's surest defense against its others.[62]

Writing after the fall of Jerusalem, Bacon ascribes Christianity's failure to the excesses of its militarism. Violent conquest exacerbates hatred toward Christians; whatever the putative righteousness of the cause, the strategy of war is destined to fail, not only on account of the bad actions of Christian warriors who bring "the Church to confusion" (Bacon has special contempt for the Templars and the Teutonic Knights on this score), but also because of the scandalous reputation Christians gain as a result. Such tactics are destined to fail, moreover, because Christians are a global minority: "For Christians are few, and the whole broad world is occupied by unbelievers."[63] In the debates over crusader strategy, then, Bacon's position is more in keeping with a type of project earlier advanced by Peter the Venerable than with the militarism associated with a figure like Bernard of Clairvaux.

In the wake of a century of debates and condemnations over the teaching of Aristotle and his Arabic commentators, Bacon deploys the "new" less as a marker of historical rupture or dramatic insight than as the figure for one side of a complex, ideological, ethical, and intellectual controversy. Precisely because of its importance to speculative endeavor both religious and scientific, Arabic erudition needs to be understood accurately, he argues; only then can it assist in a larger, Christianizing project.[64] Arab scientists were, in this regard, equally important intellectual and textual neighbors for Bacon[65] as his coreligionists. Their work inspired his own; debates over the conflicts between religious doctrine and Aristotelian science were first treated, and solved, by them. These thinkers became, as Alain de Libera argues, the model imitated by the scholastics, ultimately imported to the West in the figure of the intellectual.

The ambivalent nature of the relations between Christian and Muslim intellectuals suggests the vitality of those relations as well as their politics and power: the dynamic coexistence of affection with aggression, imitation, and competition prompts moments of change, peaceful as well as violent, admiration and condemnation in equal measure. Such slips and splits mark the contentious, contradictory, and vacillating networks in which the friar worked. Bacon's relation to all his various interlocutors makes it impossible to characterize his relations in singular or straightforward terms: as either, on the one hand, utopian relations of the type sometimes associated with the School of Toledo, where tolerance, respect, on the model of *convivencio* apparently held sway; or, on the other, crudely appropriative, racist, and reactionary. Even more: this view of Bacon's context suggests these two alternatives to be entirely insufficient for an understanding of the complicated network of intellectual exchange and the innovations wrought thereby. It was precisely the rapid, and fractious, succession of texts, readings, quodlibets, errors, translations, condemnations, agonisms, disagreements, and debates that together prompted diverse new responses: from reconsiderations of the new as a philosophical category, speculative descriptions of instruments old and new, articulations of new solutions to thorny dilemmas, novel commentaries, and fresh translations of influential texts. Far from limiting or disabling the consideration of radical concepts and fresh concerns, this fraught scene—by virtue of its vital controversies—promoted a host of innovations in thought, language, art, and natural philosophy.

Roger Bacon's reputed—even infamous—irascibility emblematizes this feature of his context. And this may be one reason why the cranky friar has so persistently seemed the poster child for controversies surrounding innovations. Yet his history offers an account of the new that is not opposed to the "old," at least not in the simple way that it has often been read. Bacon's linguistic usage of the "new" persistently emphasizes its contextual features: newer, "bad" translations have been allowed to "pass" for particular political reasons, even, as he puts it at one point, "for the peace of the Church."[66] Such remarks demonstrate the degree to which translation serves a host of masters, pragmatic and political as well as linguistic. It shows, as well, that Bacon's enlarged definition of equivocation cannot entirely curtail the debates, controversies, or disagreements about linguistic meaning even in context. Bacon's insistence on the importance of language study—as with his detailed attention to the "particular quality"[67] of specific languages, or the complications that linguistic diversities pose to naming, meaning, and interpretation—resonates with his critiques of those who use authority erroneously, whether Parisian masters promoting "new" translations, or magicians writing "new" books. Such writers are flawed because they are unwilling or unable to track texts with the linguistic precision required for such work, precision that he is sure he alone can master.

Bacon's critique of new translations takes on special importance given the friar's account of linguistic equivocation, as we have seen. And linguistic equivocation is important to his widely circulating writings related to alchemy. The *Epistola de Secretis Operibus Artis et Naturae* will circulate in a variety of manuscripts in Latin, French, German, and English translation, eventually by way of an early modern English printing as "An excellent discourse of the admirable force and efficacie of Art and Nature."[68] Bacon's scholarly output circulated widely, that is, not by way of his masterwork, his *Majus Opus*, but via this "Discourse of Art and Nature" printed as part of *The Mirror of Alchimy, Composed by the thrice-Famous and Learned Fryer, Roger Bachon* (1597). It would later be published in various versions as "The Secrets of Art and Nature" or "The Magical Letter of Roger Bacon." In this influential treatise the question of the new emerges explicitly, and signifies equivocally.

Bacon's Equivocations

As we have seen earlier, Bacon rejected the new books of the "magicians" because they seemed, as the 1597 early modern English translator will put it, "so stuffed with fables that the truth cannot be determined from falsehood."[69] Yet Bacon's treatise registers the incredible power of these new books equivocally, for they also "multiply new inventions, as we know from experience": "Nam et *ipsi novos libros componunt, et novas adinventiones multiplicant*, sicut scimus per experientiam." The dependent clause is ambiguous—what is it, precisely, that we know? That inventions multiply in novel forms, or that they circulate seductively by way of new books? What are we to make of the charge that it is the usage of old authority that proves to be so seductive? If, as we have seen, Bacon's critique of the magicians contrasts *auctoritas* with *textus*, his point is a complex one. For one thing, even these new books, as he admits, "contain something of the truth" ("aliquid veri contineant"). A little later, he will assert, "Yet we must consider, that many books ascribed to Magicians. . . contain the dignity of wisdom." ("Considerandum est tamen, quia multi libri reputantur inter magicos . . . continent sapientiae dignitatem.")[70] Nor are the books of the magicians the only such new inventions described.

Charges against the fraudulent uses of authority and language embed a larger concern with the effective power of language as such. Bacon turns shortly to consider the power of linguistic "charms, characters and their uses."[71] Translators have rendered his point variously. The Latin text reads, "Nam procul dubio omnia hujusmodi nunc temporis sunt falsa et dubia . . . ," literally "For, most certainly, now at this time all things of this sort are false and doubtful." Bacon's early modern translator emphasizes Bacon's particular authority, emphasizing an authorial "I" who "adjudge[s] these [charmes and characters] to bee all false and doubtful."[72] The point would have been important to that editor in his context, and he elaborates the continuing problem with charms by adding an emphatic subtitle concerning "such like trumperies that are used in these days."[73] Later translators render Bacon's comments on the false and doubtful in equally definitive terms, yet with precisely the opposite meaning. The modern English pamphlet, *The Magical Letter of Roger Bacon* (published in a list of titles in "Alchemy and Hermetica") offers: "For I doubt very much whether all things of this complexion are now false and dubious."[74]

Clearly Bacon remains, as Newman put it, "a name to conjure with." Yet some of this conjuring attends the fact that Bacon's larger point in this passage is an equivocal one. In the same paragraph, the friar notes that certain uses of these "charms and characters" can have a kind of placebo effect on the bodies of those who are ill. The point is delicate: while it is not as though such characters and charms are effective in and of themselves ("non quia ipsi characteres et carmina aliquid operentur"), the patient may nonetheless be affected by such words, and as a consequence "renew many things in his own body," recovering former health ("et animus patientis excitetur, et confidat uberius, et speret, et congaudeat; quoniam' anima excitata potest in corpore proprio multa renovare, ut de infirmitate ad sanitatem convalescat, ex gaudio et confidentia").[75] Such ministrations are "not to be abhorred" ("non est abhorrendum").[76] Under certain circumstances, that is to say, charms, words, and characters can have beneficial (even more, curative) effects and so should not be condemned entirely.[77]

In the larger context of his equivocations on the nature of charms and characters, Bacon's critique of "new books," occurring within this section of the epistle and before his list of speculative instruments, functions to distinguish the friar's own counterfactual speculations from the counterfeit claims made by less accomplished "magicians." In this way, he effectively wards off critiques of his own enthusiasms. Having already come upon the explicit critique of the excessive "magicians" who fraudulently compose new books, readers may be more ready than they otherwise might have been to consider Bacon's speculative list of inventions. In distinguishing the inaccurate accounts of the new associated with the "Magicians" from Bacon's own speculative but nonetheless "traditional" versions, the treatise makes way for legitimate speculations on the new, those accurately grounded in old *auctoritas*. Bacon's larger rhetorical moves help, that is, to differentiate his own futuristic musings from what he would have us see as a trivial kind of speculation, one unmoored from learnedness like his.

The question of the new is then both equivocally tied to claims of authority (to *auctoritas*) while also in excess of such categories (converging on *textus*). This excess alludes to the problem of speculation itself—that mode of thinking at the limit of what can be known. At that limit, it cannot help but raise questions of error or fraud, as indeed it does in the epistle. The relation of error (or fraud) to futurism depends on Bacon's equivocal imposition of the names of new things: it would be fraudulent or erroneous to claim the existence of something that is not; but not if the name of a thing is reimposed on a future eventuality. Bacon's distinctions hinge on this equivocal understanding: some "new" books and inventions are fraudulent tricks, superficially drawn, deploying authority erroneously. "New" is, in this context, a marker for error linked to his critiques of other kinds of errors, linguistic particularly. Yet other "new" inventions, like his own speculative list of marvelous things, are grounded in the proper use of traditional authorities and hint at possibilities still in the offing. "New" in the latter sense opens on a kind of object-oriented futurism.[78] This is an equivocation with ethical resonance; it raises the possibility of deceitful purpose or fraud, even as it disavows the fraudulent claims of those unlearned "magicians." In its own equivocal way, Bacon's counterfactual speculation sidesteps the dubious ethics of both error and deceit. Tradition occupies a key place: not opposed to innovation, but a fulcrum for adjudicating accurate speculations from lies, counterfeit versions, or errors.

Many of the friar's other counterfactual speculations in this, his most famous epistle, pertain to his alchemical work.[79] While I will reserve my fuller

examination of alchemy for Chapter 5, I wish to pause here to note that Bacon's position on the debates over the nature and power of human creativity
are similarly unique. Unwilling to privilege either the power of artifactual
labor over the processes of nature, or nature's processes over art, as Bonaventure or Hugh of Saint Victor do with their hierarchies of human creativity,
Bacon insists on the superior force and efficiency of the two working together.
In this he leverages a distinctive philosophical position, sidestepping the hierarchy of creative endeavor[80] and favoring the *collaborations* of Art with Nature.
This claim, that art need not be subservient to nature, but could "use Nature
as an instrument," Stanton Linden argues, constitutes one of Bacon's particular contributions to the debate over alchemy.[81] He argues for a powerful creative teamwork of human makers with nonhuman processes and things. The
shift was important. Bacon's "bold synthesis of alchemy and medicine, in
which both are subordinated to *scientia experimentalis,* was a significant novelty for its time . . . foreshadow[ing] the development of a medical alchemy in
the following century."[82]

Bacon's critique of the errors of the "magicians" served political as well as
rhetorical aims. While the picture of the magician as a figure of superstition
and harm had circulated among patristic writers, by the twelfth century and
after the figure was regularly associated with scientific practice. "The new
magic that entered Europe through Arabic sources carried with it the stamp of
great learning and authority. And the magician depicted in these works was a
man of great devotion, chastity, and pursuit of character."[83] Unlike other writers, Bacon does not oppose natural philosophy to magic; nor does he clearly
assert the contradictory relationship of one to the other. And, unlike others,
Bacon will never use the common term "natural magic," although that phrase
is regularly used in work that Bacon apparently knew, such as William of
Auvergne's.

"Magic" functions equivocally too. Not all brands of it are equal. Bacon
hoped to persuade his audience not so much of the utter illegitimacy of the
"magicians," but of the inferiority of their work to his.[84] Do not mistake, he
argues, entertaining tricks for cutting-edge developments in human understanding of, and collaborations with, nature.[85] Such distinctions have heirs in
today's narratives of value for the new, when mere "novelties" contrast with
far-reaching "innovations." And this opposition has itself contributed to the
longstanding impasse over the friar's originality: modern histories of science
and technology, dismissive generally of so-called "primitive magic," cannot
seem to accommodate Bacon's hybrid, equivocal network.[86] Bacon's work, in

its context and its aftermath, foregrounds instead the intimacies between "magic" and "science." The exact nature of the relationships between working alchemists and elite philosophers like Bacon, between alchemical theory and praxis, including the extent to which Bacon himself experimented, remains the subject of some debate. Newman argues (in contrast to longstanding views) that Bacon's interest in alchemy was practical as well as theoretical, and a particular alchemical cipher that circulated with the "Secrets" is likely to be authentically Baconian.[87]

Anxieties of fraud persist; questions of the counterfeit linger. Controversies surrounding the practice of alchemy—as natural philosophy but also, eventually, as a craft practice will cast long shadows. Particularly as a feature of a late medieval discourse of alchemy, such concerns will be taken up in a later chapter and in the context of medieval strictures against *vitium curiositatis*, or the vice of curiosity. But before attending to the ethics of those issues, we need to explore further the ethical implications of the category *ingenium*, a term important to the scholastics, but used most cannily and elaborately in the work of medieval poets.

The scholastic debates discussed in the first section of this study emerged contemporaneously with a vital scene of massive creative output in Latin and vernacular textuality, what Jacques LeGoff calls the age of a "parole nouvelle."[88] Vernacularity came to compete with, and be subordinated to, Latin *auctoritas*, a process well described by Rita Copeland.[89] One result of this "new and potentially transgressive pluralism" [90] was a heightened struggle over textual authority, and a longstanding discourse on reading and gender. Ethical questions were implicated, and not only in the problem of adjudicating "good" things from "bad," "natural" productions from "adulterated" ones. The relation of desire to enjoyment, and of pleasure to reason, would be debated over the next two centuries.

Romance was one genre in which such debates were staged. In recent years, scholars have revised our understanding of romance, shedding light on both innovation and novelty. Robert Stein reads the epic response to vernacular romance as an eruption of tradition designed to counterbalance the astonishing newness of the romance form.[91] Scott Lightsey stresses the relation of Middle English texts of romance to the fresh imagination of "man-made marvels." And we are only now beginning to understand, thanks to E. R. Truitt, the process by which the ingenious devices described in romances of Alexander or Charlemagne, or depicted in manuscript illuminations, led to new technological knowledge. It is to these iterations of the problem of the medieval new that we turn next.

PART II

Ingenium

Chapter 3

Ingenious Youth

"The world of the romances," writes Richard Kieckhefer, "seems at times a vast toy shop stocked with magical delights."[1] Kieckhefer's popular history of magic in the Middle Ages casts the enchanting pull of romances as a fantasy associated with childhood. The toy shop metaphor may seem odd for the medieval context, however. Following the work of Philippe Ariès,[2] social historians had long surmised that childhood did not properly exist during the Middle Ages, a hardscrabble time (apparently) when people were little able to afford the trifles of childhood play.[3]

This assumption has come again under revision, thanks in part to the discovery of large numbers of hollow pewter trinkets—many of them children's toys—preserved in the riverbed of the Thames. Hollow-cast figurines of knights datable to c. 1300 presumably for boys; miniature metal tableware ostensibly for girls; lead-alloy hollow heads—including one that may be a Christ figure, a grotesque, and two that resemble a "caricatured Jewish head" with pointed hat, all of which may have been puppet heads;[4] one remarkable hollow-metal miniature bird, originally with moving parts "that enabled the bird to bob and its tongue to go in and out";[5] and a mold that was clearly used to produce quantities of toys. Based on these findings, archeologists hypothesize the mass-production of lead-alloy playthings "produced more for a mass market than [as] the privileged treasures of a rich elite."[6] These artifacts suggest not only that childhood existed during the Middle Ages, but also that considerable technological skill was dedicated to its entertainments. They also make one wonder why social historians have been so quick to assume a Middle Ages absent children—an idea which is, relative to the evidence, "virtually baseless," as Geoff Egan puts it.[7] These and other little nothings of medieval cultural production have been catalogued in the work of scholars like Kieckhefer, Scott

Lightsey, or William Eamon;[8] yet they have only recently begun to feature in technological histories, a point of some concern to later chapters.

For the moment, we can note that while Kieckhefer's work helps us see the technological advances embedded in medieval accounts of magic, his metaphor of medieval romance as a vast toy shop also situates the adult delights of medieval fiction as ancestor to the novel playthings of modern childhood. Nor is he alone: various "medieval" romances were popularly marketed as "modern" children's literature during and after the eighteenth century; the attitudes of a medieval "age of faith" are regularly said to converge upon the habits of magical thinking apparently operative before the "age of reason," whether the latter applies to the putatively more secular period known as the Enlightenment, or to the age of a particular individual in the acquisition of seven years. To assume that medieval enchantment survives modernity via the delights of childhood casts Western history as a Bildungsroman, a narrative of maturation that marks the medieval era itself as the childhood of the West. Insofar as the Middle Ages constitutes the childhood of Western Europe, medieval children recede from view, no matter the contrary evidence. If modern childhood is defined by its preservation of an enchantment identified with the Middle Ages *tout court* (an enchantment that constitutes, that is, a structure of feeling for the medieval adult), whither the medieval child?

A Middle Ages without childhood can, of course, usefully serve the developmental-historical view of the rise of scientific calculation, one that relocates the future of medieval enchantment in the sensibilities of the modern child, a view that not incidentally seems to evacuate the complications of history and childhood both. And regarding those complications, consider the evidence just described: the toy as stereotypical Jewish head, the apparently gendered arrangements of domestic and military playthings, remind us that childhood, whatever its novel delights, also constitutes a training ground for later ideological beliefs.

Gadgets and children's toys were not the only ways that the medieval record testified to the pleasures and powers of youth. In the long wake of Ariès's provocative but ultimately unsatisfying work, scholars have analyzed the various ways that vernacular literatures address children, whether representationally as characters, or pedagogically as audience. A significant body of vernacular writing (romances as well as *chansons de geste*) recounts the "enfances" of famous historical figures: Alexander the Great, Godfrey of Bouillon, Virgil, or in the story cycle of *Guillaume d'Orange.* Knightly youths, moreover, make regular appearances as secondary characters in romance, heirs of heroic fathers often assisting in the violent exploits of their progenitors.[9] In the Middle English context, of course, the word "child" refers to "youth of noble birth, esp. an aspirant to knighthood; also, a knight or warrior."[10] It was regularly used as a name for a young knight, as, for example, "Childe Horn." By the time Chaucer's precocious child-adventurer, Sir Thopas, battled Sir Oliphant for the hand of his beloved Elf-Queen, an audience could recognize a wide range of French and native tales of youthful adventure satirized in the eponymous tale.

Fables and fictions explored childhood in part because many were used in educating children. Traditions of Aesop's fables, as Seth Lerer points out, appraised the value of *ingenium* with vulnerable animals using wit to outsmart stronger persecutors, enemies, or pursuers. They modeled a kind of cleverness desirable in any student of logic and grammar. Take, for instance, the crow, a "figure of invention or craft, . . . and model for a student similarly taxed to find grammatical or intellectual solutions," so as to "demonstrate that, in the words of a Vatican Library manuscript, *ingenium superat vires*: cleverness beats force."[11] Probing the limits of such cleverness, fables also recounted situations of "*ingenium* gone wrong—wit and instruction pressed into the service of cupidity or vice."[12] The genre weighed good and bad outcomes. In the wider literature, too, animals (as in *The Owl and the Nightingale*, or Chanticleer's dispute with the wily fox) tested *ingenium* as an ambivalent value, usually with high stakes for the animals involved.

Ingenium—whether deployed to invent poetry, to devise alchemical recipes, to dream up mousetraps or battlefield devices, to design mechanisms for toys, table fountains, or mechanical clocks—could have differential effects that were neither readily predictable, nor evident, especially to the unwary. Yet if the word's ambiguities are apparent throughout the literary record, it is in romance that the notion is most extensively entwined with new things and novel ideas, as a figure for idiosyncratic, whimsical creativity, or associated with what Lightsey calls "man-made marvels."

Ingenious Techniques

Consider the following scene from Chrétien de Troyes's *Yvain, or the Knight of the Lion*. Early in his adventures, Yvain pursues the mortally wounded Esclados back to the latter's castle; the portcullis has been defensively booby-trapped: it hides a spring and fulcrum, tripping a sharpened iron gate, ready to fall on any intruder. Chrétien's description of the contraption is surprising for its length as well as its detail.

Le porte fu mout haute et lee
Si avoit si estroite entree
Que .ii. chevaliers a cheval
Sans encombrier et sans grant mal
N'i porroient ensamble entrer,
Ne doi hommë entr'encontrer
Qu'ele estoit tot autresi fete
Come arbaleste qui aguete
Le rat tant qu'il vient au forfet;
Et l'espie est en son aguet
Desus, qui tret et fiert et prent;
Qu'ele eschape leus et destent
Que riens nule adoise a la clef,
Ja n'i touchera tant souef.
Ainsi dui trebuchet estoient
Sous la porte, qui soustenoient
Amont une porte a coulant
De fer, esmolue et trenchant.
Quant riens chel *engien* adesoit,
Le porte d'amont descendoit,
S'estoit pris ou detrenchiés tous
Cui la porte ataignoit desous.
Et tout entour a droit compas
Estoit si estrois li trespas
Com se che fust sentiers batus. (ll. 905–29, emphasis mine)[13]

[The gate was very high and wide, but had such a narrow entry-way that two men or two horses could not pass through together or meet one another in the gate without crowding or great difficulty; for it was built just like the crossbow that awaits the rat on its furtive scavenging: it had a blade poised above, ready to fall, strike, and pin, and triggered to be released and to fall at the slightest touch. Similarly, beneath the gate were two fulcrums connected to a portcullis above of sharp, cutting iron; if anything stepped on these devices, the portcullis overhead dropped and whoever was struck by the gate would be slashed entirely to pieces.][14]

The gate, modeled after a rattrap, endangers knights and horses alike. Yvain's horse is killed, as he nearly is himself when his horse trips the "beam that support[s] the iron portcullis."[15] It is a dramatically close call: the falling portcullis slices his horse and saddle in two, even shaving the spurs off Yvain's feet. His horse's death and Yvain's survival are accidental. But the gate's fall and near miss make clear the surprising difficulty of predicting the effects of some unforeseen thing. Furthermore, embedded in Yvain's *aventure* (from Latin *adventura*, meaning something still to come about), the occurrence at the gate gestures toward the future as well as toward the retrospective backward glance. This is the temporality of "the marvel breaching the limits of the thinkable,"[16] that brand of asynchronous thinking evident in Roger Bacon's list of flying machines and underwater boats.

This description marks the first attestation of a mechanical rattrap in the historical record. It is on account of such details that we can reason with some confidence that the twelfth century did, indeed, build a better mousetrap. Chrétien's verses give dramatic force to the dangers of the cutting edge, rendered here at their most literal. The resonance between this gateway gadget and the lethal innovations of the battlefield are not coincidental, as the description borrows from military innovations contemporaneous with it. The crossbow, for instance, was a new technology in the late twelfth century, a "Frankish novelty" from the time of the First Crusade; its use was prohibited "except . . . against the Infidels" in the canons of Lateran II (1139). The "trebuchet" (a stone slingshot mentioned here at line 919) was "refined in Europe c. 1200."[17] Even the metaphorical equivocation ("Qu'ele estoit tot autresi fete / Come arbaleste . . ." "For it was built just like a crossbow . . .") serves, rather than undermines, technical precision in a description striking in its realism. Chrétien's lines draw attention to the dramatic suspense of plot; they also suggest that an absorbed interest in the technical details of the gadget can extend the audience's enjoyment of its gruesome possibilities—and the deaths still to come.

Nor is the technical detail inconsequential either to the plot of *Yvain* or to a narrative of technical history. In its fascination with the details of how even new mechanics might kill unpredictably, the text evinces a worry as well as a wish. Yvain may seem to escape relatively unscathed, but we shouldn't underestimate his loss of horse, saddle, and spurs, all markers of knightly identity.[18] The effect of the contraption is entirely unpredictable. An *engin* crafted for defensive protection can prove lethal even to those it was designed to protect. The description emphasizes a lively, if sinister, mechanics, lending vitality to metal and wood in verbs active and rapid-fire: the crossbow-like mechanism "awaits" (*aguete*) the furtive rat, ready to "fall, strike, and pin" ("tret et fiert et prent," l. 915): a malevolent and hidden agency of things.

The century that produced the romance as a literary form was among the most inventive of the Middle Ages. The mechanized horizontal loom, the artesian well, percussion drilling (first used in 1126 by the Carthusian monks), tidal mills, glass mirrors, and windmills were all introduced during the twelfth century, either for the first time or for the first time in Europe. The post design for the windmill was an innovation brought to Europe by members of the Third Crusade.[19] Romance discourse becomes particularly notable in this context precisely because it regularly entwines the rhetoric of *ingenium* with the equivocal effects of these mechanical contrivances. Romance encodes an ethical ambivalence linked to its account of idiosyncratic creativity as well as to mechanical invention, the novel contraptions, gadgets, or tools that simultaneously excite and endanger.

Over thirty years ago, Robert Hanning's creative and subtle *The Individual in Twelfth-Century Romance* definitively established the importance of *ingenium* ("engin in Old French")[20] to individuality, of both character and author, in the French romances of the high Middle Ages. He, too, emphasized its equivocal nature: "*Engin . . . can deceive, improve, or educate, depending on the intent of the engigneor.*"[21] Hanning links *engin* to the intent of the individual maker, to "artistic self-consciousness, that is, fascination with the power of man to create and order his world, like a substitute God, making of reality as he finds it a new, artificial, sometimes illusory world."[22] And his comparison ("like a substitute God") is apposite, particularly given scholastic debates over creativity examined in the preceding section. Hanning establishes the relevance of early romances to disagreements between Abelard and Bernard of Clairvaux over innovative developments of the twelfth century; but he fixes these concerns to that time, arguing that the discourse of *ingenium* abated by the thirteenth, the later period apparently "inhospitable to the . . . excitement, rebellions, and discoveries" of the twelfth.[23]

From the vantage of romance novelties, however, the record suggests otherwise. *Ingenium* and its cognates (OF: *gin*, or *engin*; ME: *gyn* and *engyn*, all related to modern words from engine to ingenuity), continue as keywords in romance well into the fourteenth century, increasingly linked to mechanical contrivances and other idiosyncratic things. That said, Hanning is right to suggest a shift in the later tradition, when an ever greater ambivalence seems evident. Sometimes, as in developments in the story tradition of Floire and Blancheflor, the rhetoric of *engin* extends toward a more pragmatic, more measured, and less overtly enthusiastic, direction. Yet if later romances suggest a less excitable account of newness, they seem no less hospitable to parsing the complex implications of novel pleasures.

Tracing this shift is one of the reasons that *Floire and Blancheflor* (hereafter *FB*) marks the main subject of this chapter. There are others. If the range of translations, chronicle interpolations, and the variety of versions is anything to go by, the story tradition of these two young lovers was, by the thirteenth century, something of an international blockbuster.[24] Furthermore, the various redactions of *FB* associate the value of *ingenium* with the discourse of the new as it pertains to childhood, offering a powerfully optimistic representation of the ambitious cultural power of clever children. Geraldine Barnes has noted the somewhat unusual nature of this association; such cleverness would be "more commonly associated with the witty and complex personalities of chivalric romance."[25] What are we to make of the links between the vocabulary of cleverness and the productive force of youthful desire here?

The story tradition of *FB* details the myriad ways that the adulterations of human creativity can serve deceitful purposes. A false grave adorned with moving statues tries to tempt Floire to relinquish his love for Blancheflor; in pursuit of that love, a deceitful young Floire will take on the false identity of the architect and engineer. Such episodes mark *ingenium* as productive of tricks and traps. Yet, in the hands of children, and deployed in the service of young love, these counterfeit machinations gleam untarnished, their makers apparently above reproach. Particularly in its Middle English redaction, the poem contrasts charmingly cunning children with their equally clever, but far less winsome, adult adversaries. In this way, the poem preserves a certain innocent brand of novel making, one untainted by dangers like those that attend Yvain's rattrap, the castle gate within which Chrétien's hero, pursuing the wounded Esclados, was nearly killed.

Read as a story-tradition, *FB* takes the full measure of creative whimsy. In its attention to childhood, moreover, *FB* mitigates the apparent problems of cross-cultural collaborations occurring among the schoolmen. I wish, that is, to situate the thirteenth-century romance in the context of the intercultural collaborations associated with scholasticism. Recasting Christian / Islamic collaborations in terms of the delighted enchantments of childhood, the romance pursues the affective power of a cross-cultural schoolroom as a site of knowledge production and fresh-feeling both—a set of activities capable of

intervening in a world where commodification and enslavement do not have
the last word. Yet *FB* does not embrace such collaboration unequivocally. The
determined brand of youthful *ingenium* legible in *FB*, I argue, defuses potentially worrying effects of idiosyncratic cleverness, by mitigating, through the
earnestness of youth, the alarming possibilities of new texts and technologies,
or the dangers of invention's deceitful potential. Youth, here, emerges as a
particularly innocent and thus utopian brand of freshness, one capable of
counterbalancing the death-dealing impulses of powerfully clever adults.
Splitting the benefits of youthful *ingenium* from more murderous machinations, *FB* tries to reassure a society that is managing both the beneficial and
the lethal consequences of human invention. In this chapter, I will suggest
that the differences between the French and the ME redactions can illuminate
a process by which European culture tamed the wilder dangers of newness.

Disarming Pleasures

Accounts of the thirteenth-century ME *Floris and Blauncheflour*[26] have long
emphasized the story's considerable "charm." "One of the earliest and most
charming [in] English," writes Lillian Hornstein in a representative description, and a story in which "tender love and youthful innocence overcome all
obstacles," and "love conquers all."[27] A summary of the plot will be instructive:
Two children, Floris, son of the "heathen" king of Spain, and Blauncheflour, a
captive Christian maiden, love each other. Born on the same day and raised
side by side, their mutual childhood devotion is initially indicated by Floris's
insistence, at age seven, that he cannot be separated from his companion even
to attend school. The devotion of these two children continues to worry Floris's father the king, who now becomes especially insistent that the pair be
separated. Floris's parents devise a plan, conspiring first to kill the young girl,
and later deciding to send Floris away for a time, in the hopes that time and
distance will cool his youthful ardor. Of course, as anyone familiar with traditions of *fin' amor* might have told them, this separation only fuels the young
couple's love-longing. In hopes of a more permanent solution, the king and
queen trade Blauncheflour to Egyptian merchants, who in turn sell her to the
emir of Babylon, in whose harem she is kept as his prospective queen. When
Floris returns home, he sees a tomb bearing Blauncheflour's name, a tomb
erected by his parents to fool him into giving up a love now dead. Distraught,
and yearning to join his paramour, Floris attempts suicide. His horrified

mother now quickly reveals the truth, and Floris immediately goes off to find his beloved. He is aided in his journey by a number of figures—the wife of an innkeeper; a second innkeeper; a watchman at the bridge named Darys; and the porter who guards the gate to the emir's seraglio tower—astute guides who advise the youngster and help him in his quest. In Babylon, Floris learns that Blauncheflour is held with a number of other women in the emir's harem, and housed in an inaccessible tower. After successfully convincing the tower's porter to help him gain access, Floris is carried into the women's chamber disguised in a basket of flowers. The lovers are united, yet their trials are not over. Found sleeping together by the jealous emir, both are condemned to die. Despite their possession of a magic ring capable of keeping one of them alive, death for both seems inescapable. Neither is willing to use the ring to survive without the other. Yet their survival is not far to seek: in a final turn that demonstrates the power of their love, not to mention the romance relating it, the outraged emir softens as Floris tells his tale. He grants them pardon. Having escaped the nefarious designs of yet another sovereign, the two lovers marry and go off to rule their own country.

Alluding to the tale's deployment of various locales and ethnicities—Spanish Muslims and Christian captives, Egyptian merchants, the harem of an emir in Babylon—and echoing a sentiment first articulated by Laura Hibbard Loomis, Hornstein describes the tale as a perfect blend of "East" with "West," such that "the charm and mystery of the East complement the chivalry and sentimentality of the West."[28] Elsewhere scholars have emphasized the diverse sources and analogues of the tale—earlier episodes that encompass Byzantine, Greek, and Arabic love stories—while noting the excision of explicit references to the problems of religious difference in half of the Middle English versions. Unlike Chaucer's *Man of Law's Tale*, and unlike other redactions of the story in verse or chronicle, the marriage between a Christian woman and a "heathen" prince does not require a religious conversion here. Religious issues are, in the words of editor Jennifer Fellows, "conspicuous by their absence."[29] Fellows continues, "nothing is made . . . of the difference in creed between Floris and Blauncheflour, or of the thematic potential of that other virtuous pagan, the emir." Echoing the opinion of George Kane, she concludes, "*Floris and Blauncheflour* remains an enchanting but essentially amoral tale."[30]

To be sure, in light of recent "postcolonial" analyses of the intercultural politics of romance, Hornstein's characterization of Eastern "mystery" and Western "chivalry" would today be viewed with considerable skepticism.[31]

And the "charm" of the ME *FB* has, indeed, come under such scrutiny. Rejecting romantic musings on the text's "enchantments" in favor of a reading of the sexual politics of its traffic in women, Kathleen Kelly emphasizes a persistent concern with exchange, possession, and enslavement, arguing that the poem should be read "as a locus of tensions: tension between East and West, Christianity and Islam, women and men."[32] This opposition between pleasure and politics has, moreover and until recently, constituted the general view of popular romance in the larger medieval cultural scene, and has, accordingly, grounded much of our understanding of the contribution that the genre makes to relations between Christianity and Islam during the later Middle Ages.[33] That is, accounts of the enchantments of romance and accounts of medieval relations between Arab and European cultures have regularly foundered on a similar opposition: in both registers enchanted desire contrasts with the scholarly, the rational, and the analytical.[34]

When contemporary critics oppose the pleasures of desire to the analytical proclivities of scholar-critics, they deploy an opposition with a long history. "In man is found a continual hostility between lust and reason," claims the beautiful Natura in Alain de Lille's *Plaint of Nature*.[35] Potted versions of what has heretofore been seen as a straightforward medieval condemnation of desire as concupiscence have been undergoing revision for quite some time, and scholars continue to describe established "points of contact between philosophy, poetry, theology, and law" on these topics well into the fourteenth century.[36] Such crossings have led to new readings of the *Plaint* (Schibanoff, Bruneau, Scanlon, Guynn, Burgwinkle, Rollo[37]); Occitan poetry (Kay, Gaunt); and other influential texts such as the *Roman de la Rose* (Huot; Rosenfeld). In her recent study of the medieval ethics of enjoyment, Jessica Rosenfeld emphasizes the degree to which some medieval thinkers (as, for instance, Abelard) linked virtue and pleasure, reading Aristotle as "minimizing the differences between those who would pursue pleasure and those who would pursue virtue, arguing that they are basically the same."[38]

Yet, even as the pursuit of pleasure converges, in Abelard's work at least, on the pursuit of virtue, the mediating role of reason for both pursuits takes on a special importance. Tensions between pleasure and reason persist, with strong Aristotelian resonances as a consequence of the image, from the *Nicomachean Ethics*, of horse and rider as a sign for the rule of reason over the passions. The figure was widespread and various, and frequently appeared in "perverse" as well as orthodox guise. Versions of the "mounted Aristotle," or "Aristotle and Phyllis" related "how the philosopher Aristotle, wisest of men, was tricked by a beautiful woman into allowing her to ride him like a horse."[39] These figures, analyzed by feminist scholars beginning with Susan Smith,[40] may at first glance seem to be a simple case of anti-Aristotelianism. Yet considerably more was at stake, as both Smith and Marilynn Desmond point out.

Drawing out one strand of this archive in the context of the new Aristotelianism, Rosenfeld reminds us of the imbrication, not the opposition, of reason with desire. "The poets were drawn to dissect the assumption," she writes, "that human reason always functions as a check on desire."[41] The mounted Aristotle opens these questions further as versions variously imply the Philosopher as the "foolish wise man,"[42] or, conversely, "tricked because of his wisdom."[43] Certainly the tradition as a whole suggests, to borrow from Rosenfeld, that "intellectual pursuits cannot work as a prophylaxis against desire," since intellectual work "is all too easily transformed into erotic pursuit."[44] This debate propelled considerable artistic output, generating an impressive array of literary and visual inventions.

We can see here something of the vitality sparked by an artistic culture of copying, and Smith emphasizes the novelty thereby produced: "Every new deployment of the mounted Aristotle," she writes, "represents an opportunity seized by the artist to exercise his powers of invention by offering it up in a new visual environment, carrying the new interpretive thrust that the environment conferred."[45] The productive power of the trope of horse and rider ventured well beyond its intended limits, in versions high and low, authoritative and ironic. As was the case with the discourse regarding alchemy, novel creative output is here propelled, not stymied, by philosophical debates of significant ethical consequence. Diverse versions of the mounted Aristotle—copies of copies of copies—could, on the one hand, qualify as Bonaventure's *novae compositiones*, new compositions in all their adulterated glory. Yet they also show how rapidly the creative adulterations of poets and artists venture beyond the proscribed limits of art as *ens completum*;[46] "perverse" images rearrange fragments of nature to monstrous effect.

The insistence that human compositions constitute "adulterated" productions, a notion associated, we recall, with the "mechanical" in Hugh of St. Victor's topography of creative invention, enables as much as it limits. Alain's Natura, banging out natural things on her anvil, explicitly deplores such monstrous progeny. And yet, as recent readings of the intricacies of both the *Plaint* and the *Roman de la Rose* show (even, by some accounts, legible as a debate between these texts), no amount of contempt for perverse productions could stem the tide. Links between poetry and perversion were fundamental.[47] As

Schibanoff, writing about the *Plaint*, puts it, "A necessarily fine line divides the creative use of words and the illicit use of words, the poet and the pervert."[48]

The notion of poetry as an "adulterated" form, and the poet as potentially perverse, alludes to *ingenium* in yet another sense; the sexual logic of heterosexual reproduction informs the word's second etymon, *gignare*, to beget, to give birth. As a host of readers have shown, the *Plaint* deployed heterosexual "kinship relations as an allegory for narrative structure."[49] Alexandre Leupin notes the etymological links between Genius and this aspect of *ingenium*, a narrative logic by which Natura's hammer and anvil refer to the "genital organs."[50] Adulteration, in this context, emerges as an equivocal notion, referring both to the alterations that human makers enact upon the created world and the potentially transgressive nature of such acts as, in the case of the *Plaint*, but not only there, sodomical. Like modern notions of perversity, this implies perverse love as pleasure without function. As this admittedly too brief discussion suggests, medievalists working in these areas have helped to complicate older notions of the unrelentingly hierarchizing, static, and transcendent medieval worldview evinced even in those texts like de Lille's which seem, at first glance, unequivocal in denouncing love of like with like, whether sexual or grammatical. In fact, intellectuals at the time were, we now recognize, debating and refining the equivocal nature of the sign. Roger Bacon, as we have seen, devoted considerable attention to language in complex debates over the nature and uses of signs, in the tradition stretching from Augustine through Aquinas to Dante. Poets engaged such matters primarily, though not exclusively, through allegories like the *Plaint* or the *Roman de la Rose*. Scholars continue to debate the degree to which the paradoxes and equivocations evident in such texts accord entirely or even primarily with what David Rollo calls their "monitory tenor."[51]

Yet if scholars have astutely analyzed the ethics of enjoyment in these traditions, they have not as frequently emphasized the extent to which these debates were shot through with the influence of the Arabic *falasifa*.[52] They converged, that is, upon another contemporary intellectual problem: the indebtedness of Western intellectuals to that brand of "left-wing Aristotelianism"[53] debated among the Arabic philosophers and commenters on Aristotle. It is here, I think, that the story tradition of *FB* can prove particularly illuminating. *FB* imagines a Christian-Arabic schoolroom just after the time when the schoolmen were falling hard for the newly available Arabic commentaries on Aristotle. Particularly in its ME redaction, *FB* emphasizes the innocence of desire amid such interreligious intimacies.

While the Middle English redaction of *FB* is my primary textual object here, the readings that follow also engage the ME adapter's primary source, the French *roman idyllique*, also known as the "aristocratic" version.[54] This is for two reasons. First, the schoolroom is explored in the ME version in a way that it is not in the French. But secondly, and more importantly for my larger argument, the question of the "new" emerges explicitly in the more concise English version, and in a way that seems designed to defuse the threatening implications of *ingenium* legible in the French. Whereas the French source traces the story of these young lovers through a persistent debate between relevant allegorical figures such as *Amour* and *Savoir*, pursuing the tension between these two impulses throughout the tale, the Middle English adapter emphasizes dramatic action, eliminating all the more abstract narrative intrusions. It is through just such a redirection that the category of the new is explicitly introduced. It is to this displacement that I turn first.

Early in the French text, the poet elaborates the gorgeously decorated empty tomb devised by Floire's parents to hide the fact that their son's paramour is gone, sold off to merchants from the East. The description of Blancheflor's false grave is extraordinary, with over a hundred lines given to extolling its lavish excess, in some of the most beautiful lines in the romance. Perched atop an incomparable marble stone gleaming in the sun ("fin marbre estoit / Inde, jaune, noir et vermeill; Moult reluisoit contre soleill" [lines 553–55]) sit golden statues of the two young lovers fashioned with jewels. Side by side, the lovers exchange flowers. A golden Blancheflor offers a rose cast in gold to Floire, who passes her a "golden white lily" ("d'or une blanche flor de lis," line 573) in return. Magnificently rendered in precious metal, yet (and paradoxically) also lifelike, the mechanical lovers embrace and kiss, moving, bending, seeming, as if by magic ("par nigromance," line 586), to whisper to one another as wind blows through hollow pipes placed carefully around them.

This adorned mausoleum itself sits amid a magical garden filled with fragrant flowers, trees in perpetual bloom, and sweetly singing birds. The ekphrastic description emphasizes opulence, alluding to a wide array of artistic techniques. This is something never seen before.

Onques més por une pucele
Nu fu fete tumbe tante bele.
De riches listes est listee,
De bons esmaus avironnee.
Pierres i a qui vertuz ont

Et moult granz merveilles i font:
Jagonces, safirs, calcedoines,
Esmeraudes, bones sardoines
Et bons coraus et crisolites
Et diamanz et amacites.
Toute iert la tombe neelee
De l'or d'Arrabe bien letree.
Les letres de fin or estoient
Et en lisant ce recontoient:
"Ci gist la bele Blancheflor
Que Floires ama par amor." (ll. 638–53)

[Never was a tomb so beautiful made for a maiden. It was encircled
by a rich border of beautiful enamel and precious jewels, with
marvelous powers. Jacinth, sapphire, chalcedony, emerald, hand-
some sardonyx, and coral and crysolite, and diamonds and ame-
thysts. The entire tomb was inscribed in Arabic gold. The golden
letters recounted to any who would read them: 'Here lies the
beautiful Blancheflor whom Floire loved for love.']

This is an astonishing display of art and text (see lines 560–653 for the full
description), and readers are drawn into the extraordinary scene. Lively statues, gold-cast replicas, sit atop the tomb. In the context of the larger plot—
and amid the efforts of Floire's parents to rid themselves of the troublesome
maid—the scene combines vitality with deadliness, technical innovation and
murderous intent. If this is charm, it has, like Goldfinger, an uncanny cast.
The description nonetheless emphasizes the sweetness of the earthly lovers, their
gilded likenesses mirroring a mutual fidelity emblematized in their names, the
echoes explicit in the French. White flower gives Flower a rose; Flower gives a
golden white flower to White Flower: a stark image of mimetic desire at its most
alluring. The images themselves mark, or so the poet tells us, both a remarkable
resemblance ("faithful" and "true to life") and an unparalleled event, something
never seen before: "I have never seen anything like it," the poet interjects ("Plus
que riens nule qui ja soit" [565]). "Granz merveilles" (643) dazzle, sparkle and
shine in the sun.

Extravagant tombs like this one appear elsewhere in romance, as, for example, in the *Roman d'Eneas*. Analyzing the ekphrastic narrative commemora-
tions in that romance in the context of what he terms "Gothic innovations" in

a "new era of political incorporation,"[55] Noah D. Guynn emphasizes the ways tombs encode "erratic, improper, and unviable"[56] alternatives to the heteronormative and procreative rules of romance. In the *Eneas*, an extensive description of the mausoleums of Pallas and Camille freezes in time these two figures of sexual deviance. That romance, Guynn argues, "literally erects monuments to sexual deviance, immobilizing the threat of the impure body in marble and metal and signifying its enclosure and exclusion."[57] Such monuments undercut the drive of the romance plot to consolidate procreative, phallocentric power by way of state formation and the *translatio imperii* tradition.

The tomb in *FB* also registers a certain kind of deviance, though not obviously the same-sex eroticism legible in the *Eneas*. In the larger plot, and in the context of the Spanish setting, Blancheflor's Christian difference poses problems for Floire's parents, who see her as an inappropriate bride for their Muslim son: unlike the Middle English adaptation to which we will shortly turn, the difference in creed constitutes an obstacle only ultimately overcome by Floire's conversion. Yet the evidence from the tomb's description suggests something a bit more complicated. For one thing, it monumentalizes such cross-cultural love, rendering the lovers in perpetual three-dimension. With its letters in Arabic gold, and its gold-cast metal dolls of boy and girl, the tomb does not insist upon cultural difference, so much as testify to a beautiful union of Christian and Muslim. Freezing these two together, presumably for all time, the *engin,* for that is what it will shortly be termed, encourages us to reflect not on the differences but on the remarkably intense similarities between the lovers. This tomb literalizes the artistic and technical productivity prompted by the mutual affection of Muslim and Christian. Intercultural collaborations bring new artifacts into the world.

Indeed, if the tomb is any indication, difference seems less troubling than does similarity. And the sibling cast of Floire and Blancheflor's relationship may well be part of the problem: while neither identical nor even fraternal twins by birth, the two lovers were born on the same day and raised together by Blancheflor's mother. Their relationship, in other words, converges on questions of milk kinship, a type of relation codified in incest prohibitions in Islamic law.[58] The French poet is obviously well versed in such matters, and will go to the trouble to stipulate more than once that Blancheflor's mother did not nurse Floire, although the children shared every other kind of nourishment (see lines 176–82, 187–94). Such insistence on the part of the poet contributes to the listener's outrage at the actions taken by Floire's parents.

The golden lovers atop the tomb allude, if in a tentative way, to this kind of sibling closeness, the twin figures rendering their love a bit incestuous, and thus perverse. Certainly either problem complicates questions of inheritance and lineage; and in the larger plot Floire's love for Blancheflor constitutes a stubborn refusal of his parents' dynastic hopes for him.

In that sense it is all the more remarkable that this monument to love is built by Floire's parents, and, notably, as a defense against any potential future for the children's heterosexual procreativity. Intimations of deadliness linger. Precisely as a tomb, an *engin* of memorialization, the edifice has a mortifying effect on Floire, who cries out in anguish. Presumably this is his reaction to seeing Blancheflor's golden image, his beloved's form in cold metal. Readers have long assumed that the statues testify to the enduring power of young love, a contrivance that Floire's parents have devised as a way of recognizing their son's love even as they try to persuade him to move on. Yet if that is so, what compelled them to include the gold-cast figure of the son they hoped to save, and on the very tomb through which they hoped to save him? Just how deep do the murderous impulses of these parents run? This tomb—like their resistance to Blancheflor generally—may well bespeak a desire to keep their son forever young and for themselves, caught like a rare specimen in amber and frozen in the brilliance of his golden youth. Theirs seems a particularly deadly kind of parental affection.

Confronted with a gilded image of his own face and form, Floire can't help but see intimations of his own mortality, himself entombed, even if in gold. When he shrieks, we are also reminded that this extraordinary expenditure of treasure and talent is hollow at its core, all a magnificent ruse. We know that Blancheflor is not inside this tomb, and within three hundred lines Floire's mother will confess to the deception, proving to him that his beloved is not dead by showing him the tomb's empty insides:

"Biau Fiuz," fet ele, "par engien,
Par le ton pere et par le mien.
. . . . .
N'est pas morte, . . . (ll. 860–63)

["Dear son," said she, "this was a ruse / by your father and by me. / . . . / She is not dead.]

The tomb is a counterfeit adulteration. An empty *engin* (l. 860), and as such a perfect figure for sublimation—the artistic production that preserves, protects, and detours around the empty place of the Thing, as a figure doubly lacking here: Blancheflor is gone; and she is gone again, even her dead body absent from the tomb. This is the courtly woman imbricated within the structure of sublimation, and as a figure for the emptiness at the heart of the Lacanian Real—the female body as both occasion for art, and a sign of the lack, the emptiness that art circles and preserves. The fleshly Blancheflor haunts even as readers register the unparalleled nature of the art here crafted.

This is also a fabulous bit of both poetry and storytelling. And so it is somewhat astonishing when the Middle English adapter eliminates nearly all of it. Starkly modifying his source, his empty grave seems, in contrast, disappointingly modest. Yet I do not mean by this remark to return us to an earlier critical moment when readers regularly deplored the inferior nature of the ME version vis-à-vis the French. I am convinced that the ME adapter is up to something very interesting as well. His grave, still false, is rather unremarkable, utterly ordinary. It hardly seems worthy of the name *engin* at all. Except for one small, and I argue, telling, detail: a linguistic substitution that makes explicit the association of the rhetoric of *ingenium* with the new.

In place of the rich poetic description of marble and silver, in place of any description of the devoted children's images fashioned in gold, we read of a gravestone, with only the barest hint of the original:

They lete make in a chirchè
A swithe feire grave wyrche,
And lete ley ther uppon
A new feire peynted ston,
With letters al aboute wryte. (ll. 209–13, emphasis mine)

[They commanded to be made in a church / such a fair grave worked, / and commanded to be laid thereupon / *a new beautifully painted stone* / written all about with letters.]

The poet replaces the lengthy description of a man-made marvel with a linguistic marker. And in place of the extended description we are provided a categorical adjective: the gravestone, beautifully painted, is new. The poet neither describes nor explains, but merely stipulates the point, keyed to the dramatic action of the plot. The new stands here as abstract category, not wondrous object, a classification quite literally displacing the fascinating detail and grippingly affective power of the original image. On the one hand, this alteration corroborates Barnes's reading of the ME poet's general tendency to emphasize plot and action "at the expense of the descriptive."[59] Yet, by so radically eliminating the extraordinary, marvelous, outlandish features of the description, the ME adapter also moderates its poetic effect.

Gone is the uncanny shimmer—gone are the startling links between vital metal and dead reckoning. Floire, like his French readers, paused before the arresting pleasures of Blancheflor's grave. The English version offers, instead, the briefest mention, slackening the versifying tension at the very moment that his source text had been building it. In the place of the grave as a marvel as yet unseen, there is, simply, a stone new and newly placed. We cannot tell if its beauty is in any way unusual. Replacing an extensive and palpable description with a categorical adjective, the adapter tamps down the energy and excitement of the source. If the ME version is charming, as critics claim, such work suggests that its charms are actively pursued and hard-won: the ME adapter's lighter, more pragmatic, touch works to disarm the arresting, and alarming, novel pleasures of the monumental mausoleum. In the process, the new emerges as less deadly than as simply straightforward, functional, and instrumental.

This is one of the only explicit references to the new in the story tradition of *FB*, yet it is far from the only example of the ME poet's moderating pen. As I will now go on to suggest, the poet's repeated use of charm, of moderation, and of the modest sufficiency of youthful ingenuity works to establish a defanged, domesticated version of *ingenium*. The fresh face of youth moderates novelty's dangerous potential. Such youthful ingenuity, that is, disciplines newness; it eases the troubling potential of the new by eliminating its more death-dealing possibilities. As far as the two children are concerned, such an association, as we shall eventually see, serves its own disciplining function.

To be sure, the ME *Floris and Blauncheflour* also depicts an amorousness with real power: this is charm to considerable, and forceful, effect. Floris's desire for and devotion to Blauncheflour enables his persistent ingenuity, one that allows both young lovers to overcome the powers and principalities, and not coincidentally, parental demand, organized against them. Furthermore, the "charm" of this narrative suggests not only or mainly, *pace* Kelly, Europe's desire to commodify or colonize "exotic" Eastern cultures, but a rather more delicate, if more fantasmatic, one: the hope that Europe's admiration for the cosmopolitan Arabic world of learning is mirrored back, returned in complementary degrees. It is a feature especially emphasized, and thus legible, in the Middle English version. This emphasis on the schoolroom found in all of the Middle English versions also draws out the importance of childhood here. In his expansions of the scene, the ME poet emphasizes the innocence of new learning. Floris's yearnings signify in the sweet ardor of a child.

Scholastic Passions

On its face, and for all its modesty, *FB* incessantly emphasizes the power of these children in surmounting impossibility: at every turn, Floris overcomes the familial, geographic, and even geopolitical obstacles stacked against him. Unlike much of the courtly love tradition, desire demolishes impossibility, even as the challenges the lovers face heighten the narrative power of their mutual affection. The ME versions excise the more philosophical meditations on love that are found in the French, omitting, for example, the extended dialogue between *Amour* and *Savoir*, or the concern with dynastic lineage evinced in the Spanish chronicle tradition. This shorter redaction focuses upon the two crucial aspects of Floris's success: the good counsel he receives from his various guides along the way, and his own creative ingenuity in managing his difficult circumstances. Yet the ME versions also draw out the meaning of the schoolroom that marks the opening scene in all of the Middle English manuscripts. As we shall see, passion and reason are coextensive, serving one another with startling force.

The opening episode reveals the extent of this association when Floris's fervent bond to Blauncheflour emerges, tellingly, as the necessary condition for the boy's learning. Readers have not yet noticed the complexity with which these issues are drawn out in the Middle English redaction. When the young Muslim prince (Floris) refuses to attend school without his Christian companion (Blaucheflour), he sets the stage for the conflict narrated in the remainder of the tale: his faithfulness to her alarms his father, the king of Spain, who shortly determines that the two youngsters must be separated at all costs. Their separation drives all subsequent action in this romance.

By the eighth line, the king determines that the boy, now age seven, should go to school, "as men don, both hye and lowe" ["as men, both high and low, do"].[60] The poet describes the king's interest in the benefits of such learning on his son's behalf, and the Middle English version, in contrast to its source, details the king's motivations explicitly:

The King behelde his sone dere,
And seyde to him on this manere:

That harme it were muche more
But his sone were sette to lore,
On the book letters to know,
As men done both hye and lowe.
"Feire sone," he seide, "thou shalt lerne:
Lo that thou do ful yerne!"[61]

[The King beheld his dear son / And said to him in this manner: /
That it were much greater harm / unless his son would be set to
learning / on book letters to know / as men, both high and low, do.
/ "Fair son," he said, "you shall learn: / that is what you do desire
entirely!"]

Invoking the greater harm that might come from neglecting the schoolroom,
the poet first notes the king's motivation indirectly, and emphasizes the benefits that accrue to learned men. The use of indirect speech seems notable, as
critics have long pointed out this poet's typically lively use of dialogue. Further, when the poet actually quotes the king's words in the final two lines of
this passage (a quotation not found in his source), the emphasis shifts from the
cultural benefits of schooling to Floris's particular desire for it. The king's direct address thus translates the concerns of paternal duty for princely education into the father's verbal imperative about his son's desire. On one hand, the
father's words draw attention to the importance of desire to the habits of erudition, linking longing to instruction, yearning to learning. Indeed, the final
rhyming couplet of "lerne" with "yerne" condenses and intensifies the association of knowledge with desire here.

On the other hand, the sovereign's command is also explicit ("thou shalt
lerne"), forcefully rendered in the imperative mood. What does it mean that
the king's direct statement of his command comes to us in the process of its
translation as the prince's desire? Such a rapid oscillation between paternal
demand and filial desire suggests the problematic uses to which preemptive
accounts of yearning might be put. For the king's words also enact a displacement that Floris's response to him will eventually make clear: positioning
knowledge as that for which his son "do ful yerne," the father reorients the
son's desire away from childhood longings that predate the classroom. School
emerges, in the king's address, as a substitute for and an advance upon his son's
passion for his playmate, Blauncheflour, as well as for her mother, the "Cristen
woman," described four lines earlier, who nourished ("fedde") these two

children she "lovyd" "ful wel" (ll. 3–4). In a structure resonant with Lacanian versions of the relation of desire in language to the Symbolic order, the poet here depicts linguistic knowledge, by way of the paternal demand, as displacing and compensating for a willingness to relinquish the body of the woman, or, in this case, the bodies of two women, mature and juvenile, the current maternal object and the future beloved. The ME poem rehearses this standard account of male heterosexual desire in its first fourteen lines.

Floris demurs, utterly unwilling to relinquish anything at all. The son's immediate response stops the king in his developmentalist tracks, and the dialogue here draws the reader into the sweetness and energy of the boy's youthful ardor. Quick to grasp the gendered implication of his father's plan, and horrified at the thought of having to give up any time with Blaunchefflour, Floris tearfully fights back:

> As he stood byfore the Kyng;
> Al wepyng seide he:
> "Ne shal not Blaunchefflour[62] lerne with me?
> Ne can y noght to scole goon
> Without Blaunchefflour," he seide than;
> "Ne can y in no scole syng ne rede
> Without Blaunchefflour," he seyde.
> The king seide to his soon,
> "She shall lerne, for thy love." (ll. 15–24)

[As he stood before the King; / he said, weeping fully: / "Shall not Blaunchefflour learn with me? / I cannot go to school / without Blaunchefflour," he said then. / "Nor can I neither sing nor read in any school / without Blaunchefflour," he said. / The King said to his son, / "She shall learn, because of your love."]

It is this kind of lively dialogue that has earned the Middle English adapter well-deserved praise; one can almost hear the boy stomp his foot in frustration at his father's cluelessness. The son's wailing repetition of Blaunchefflour's name (three times in the space of five short lines) offers a dramatic alternative to the account of desire that the king has just delivered, particularly as Floris's speech is significantly amplified from the source.[63] Even more significantly, his insistent repetition keeps Blaunchefflour at the center of the scene—linguistically as well as typographically.

In light of this impassioned display, the father's confident imperative seems at best condescending and at worst manipulative. The king's words identify schooling as the true object of the boy's longing; Floris's disconsolate weeping responds with an object lesson in his father's misreading. Not only does the king's command threaten to deny Floris his most esteemed companion, it misrepresents this decision as motivated by paternal commitment to his son's own yearning. Moreover, Floris's remarks constitute a formal refusal of, and resistance to, the paternal law, here also the sovereign's wish. Deflecting the redirection of his desire away from his youthful companion, Floris makes her presence central, as the very condition of his ability to learn. That centrality is legible only in the context of her absence, each line emphasizing Blauncheflour's value to him by imagining him without her. The terms are absolute. He can "in no scole syng ne rede" if Blauncheflour shall not "lerne with" him. There can be no learning at all—not any yearning for it either—without his dearest love.

We are offered, in the first twenty-five lines of the Middle English version, two models of the relation of desire to knowledge, together a more extensive consideration of the point than that found in any of the sources. As I will eventually suggest, this emphasis resonates with some innovations in English education at the time. For the moment, however, I wish to note that the king's command joins desire and knowledge in the standard structure of sublimation, whereby the absence of the beloved reorients desire toward new objects of study, the energy of childish passions redirected toward reason. An all-male space, the schoolroom imagined by the king is a site of desire unencumbered by females as either knowing subjects or beloved objects. This is a version of all-male study familiar to us from the long history of misogynistic complaints about the distracting powers of women, including some versions of the "mounted Aristotle." It is not, as we shall see, one that much matches what we know about schooling in England during the time that the Middle English poet was working on this text. Floris's response, in contrast, reimagines the schoolroom as an extension of the companionability of the nursery, here rendered in utopian terms. Coordinating knowledge with desire in a passionate display of his attachment to Blauncheflour, Floris insists that the girl, not only as an object of his desire but also as a fellow student, is the necessary condition for his learning. Rather than worry that an overabundance of passions might distract from learning, the Middle English redaction elaborates their enabling intellectual function.

The force of such desire is undeniable. And thus, in a fantasy resonant with the hopes of children everywhere, the sovereign father immediately reverses his position and willingly accedes to the wishes of his son. Yet, even in relenting, he seems to miss Floris's larger point; for one thing, his words strangely reverse the relation of love and learning that his son has just described. Floris insists that it is his learning that is dependent on Blaunche-flour's companionship; the king's reply stresses the opposite, Blauncheflour's learning will be allowed "for [Floris's] love." In fact, multiple loves converge confusingly at this point: the king's love for Floris, Floris's love of learning, Floris's devotion to Blaunceflour, and her devotion for him, all circle and propel the action. The passions of the children sit at the center, in reciprocal relation and wholly complete: Floris gains access to his desire for learning only if she is present; Blauncheflour gains access to schooling only on account of his desire for her presence. Rather than oppose knowledge-seeking to desire, this opening dynamically engages its multiple erotics.

Thus, when, in the next few lines, "the scole" stages the mutuality of the children's intelligence and scholarly accomplishments, it does so with an over-determined force. The poet does not equivocate. "Their learning was wonderful," he writes, "and their love even more so."

To scole they were put;
Both they were good of wytte.
Wonder it was of hur lore,
And of her love wel the more:
The children lovyd togeder soo,
They might never parte atwoo.
When they had five yere to scoole goon,
So wel they had lerned thoo,
Inowgh they couth of Latyne,
And wel wryte on parchemyn. (ll. 25–34)

[To school they were sent. / They were both quite smart. / Wonderful was their learning / and their love even more so. / The children so loved being together / that they might never part from each other. / When they had been to school for five years / they had learned so well / that they knew enough Latin / and wrote well on parchment.]

Highlighting linguistic modalities—education is, after all, first depicted in line 11 as knowledge of "book letters"—the poet grants special status to words, letters, and books, the stuff, not coincidentally, of poetic adaptations. And the two children are now virtually indistinguishable from one another, recast by way of the third person plural: their talent ("Bothe they were good of witte"), their learning and love ("hur lore . . . hur love"), mark the classroom as an extraordinary site of plenitude where even the Latin they learn is judged to be "enough."

The specificity of the youngsters' facility with Latin marks the one detail that the Middle English poet preserves from the longer description of their scholarly activities in the French. In that version, the pair's linguistic knowledge explicitly outstrips the abilities of everyone around them. Their facility with Latin functions as a kind of secret language, a foreign excess unintelligible to the wider community of students in which they learn:

> Furent andeus si bien apris
> que bien sorent parler latin
> et bien escrivre en parchemin,
> et conseillier oiant la gent,
> en Latin, que nus ne l'entent. (ll. 268–72)[64]

> [They learned so well that they could speak Latin and knew how to write on parchment. They spoke Latin to each other when in the hearing of others, so that no one could understand them.]

Noting that this moment draws attention to the foreignness of Latin at a presumably Arabic-speaking Spanish court, Kinoshita links this representation of Latin to relations between Latin and vernacular textualities in the era of the European emergence of Arabic learning. She writes, "The children's precocious use of Latin as a kind of private code may signal its foreignness. . . . It may allude to the cultural difference between vernacular-speaking nobles and Latin-speaking clergy (the very gap that occasioned the rise of romance in the first place) and the children's ability to bridge it."[65]

Romance encodes its own version of the tension of reason to passion in the tradition of an excessive erotic desire figured as ecstatic, irrational lovesickness. The lovers' secret language may tentatively gesture to that tradition; moreover, in placing the schoolroom adjacent to the king's pleasure garden in which the children play together, the poet may allude to earlier representations of student lovers, such as that found in the early Persian poem, *Layla and Majnun*, where mad love is made explicit.[66] In *Layla and Majnun* two young lovers from different families, though not of different creeds, meet and fall in love at school; their families succeed in keeping the two apart, and Majnun's desire for his unattainable Layla transforms him into a holy man, poet and mystic both. Majnun, the lovesick madman, poet, and lover, casts a long shadow, inspiring not only Europe's troubadours and the larger traditions of courtly lovesickness, but twentieth-century composers as well.[67] In the context of this larger tradition of excessive love, the French poet of *Floire et Blaunchflor* stresses the intellectual productivity, even if excessive, when schoolroom lovers are allowed their time together.

If the Middle English poet follows this general impulse, he seems utterly disinterested in any kind of schoolroom excess, whether of love or of language. He offers instead an uncomplicated fantasy of completeness, sufficiency, and wholeness. There is no dangerous excess here, as this more concise version explicitly clarifies the children's knowledge of Latin as "inowgh." In that move, the ME redactor demonstrates his own perturbed reading of the French, where knowledge of Latin—particularly as foreign—seems by contrast to be potentially excessive, arcane, or self-indulgent. He implicitly defends the abilities of the children and the role of Latin as modest, and sufficient to their circumstance. Furthermore, Latin is not a language of privatized amorous intellectualism; it is not impenetrable to non-lovers, non-children, or non-specialists.

In that subtle revision, the Middle English adapter sidesteps altogether any concern with the potential dangers posed by the private delights—linguistic or not—of too much passionate togetherness. From that view, it is also no coincidence that the ME poet eliminates specific mention of the children's study of Ovid, whose *Ars Amatoria* was a standard of the elementary Latin curriculum. Thus circumscribing the problems that excessive passion might pose to reason, the poem emphasizes instead the sufficient—indeed, pragmatic—usefulness of the two together. Just as the ME poet has mediated the libidinal energy of the poetic description of the false grave, he here tempers any intimations of linguistic excess in the French, displaying instead the benefit of a pragmatic version of wit and ingenuity.[68] When he does so, the ME story of the childhood lovers stages a particular kind of linkage between desire and discipline: it shows not a desire *for* discipline, nor a disciplining *of* desire, but instead the very impossibility that discipline could ever be entirely segregated from desire at all.

The sufficiency of Latin may also gesture toward the history of competition between Latinate scholasticism and vernacular poetics; and it resonates as well with English schooling at the time. In his incisive revision to the history

of children's education in medieval Britain, Nicholas Orme has redrawn the
picture of the medieval English classroom. Thanks to his work, we now know
that girls were regularly educated, in wealthy houses as well as in nunneries;
that provincial schools existed alongside monastic *scolae* and university grammar schools; that particular attention to the education of children developed
in the thirteenth century, when writers such as Bartholomew Glanville, Vin-
cent of Beauvais, and Giles of Rome directed attention toward "the physical
characteristics of children, the methods of bringing them up, and the matters
they needed to learn."[69] More to the point, and as Ranulf Higden notes in his
Polychronicon,[70] by the early fourteenth century, Latin was taught in schools by
way of instruction in French; soon French and English grammars appeared,
written to be used in the grammar schools.[71] Translating the extraordinary
representation of Floris's and Blauncheflour's special facility with Latin into a
description of the sufficient measure of this knowledge seems particularly notable at a time when diverse grammars and languages compete for space in the
trilingual classroom.

The opening scene of the Middle English poem, I have been arguing,
resituates the opposition of passion to reason in favor of a view of their mutual, even pragmatic, usefulness. This twinning of desire with knowledge, one
that, as we saw at the beginning of this chapter, serves as an ethical prompt to
both poetry and philosophy from the time of the *parole nouvelle*, will continue in the remainder of the plot, though it is almost immediately set off by
its inverse. The schoolroom as a locus for wholeness, completeness, and sufficiency is short-lived. In the very next episode, Floris's parents trick their son
into leaving home for a second classroom, this time at the home of his aunt.
Before sending him off, they entice him with the deceitful promise that
Blauncheflour will join him shortly. Yet, lacking his beloved in this new locale, Floris makes good on his earlier prediction: now he really cannot learn.
His lovesick sighing, in explicit contrast with his learning, is now described
as "inowgh":

> His aunt set him to lore
> There as other children wore,
> Both maydons and grome.
> To lerne mony theder come.
> Inowgh he sykes, but not he lernes;
> For Blauncheflour ever he mornes.

Yf eny man to him speke
Love is on his hert steke.
Love is at his hert roote. (ll. 109–17)

[His aunt set him to learn / where other children were, / both girls
and boys. / Many came there to learn. / Enough he sighs, but he
does not learn; / he mourns always for Blaunchflour. / If any one
speaks to him / love is at his heart's base. / Love is at his heart's
root.]

In the new classroom, also, notably, coeducational, in a detailed specificity
that seems again to call up the English context, Floris loses linguistic capacity
to the degree that he lacks Blauncheflour: totally. Mournful sighs replace his
former competencies. The echo seems intentional, a means of intensifying the
contrast between one schoolroom and the other. It suggests, yet again, the
productive nature of his childhood attachment. But the shift also raises questions as to the meaning of "enough" in both contexts: the semantic range of
the Middle English word includes both sufficiency and overabundance. What,
after all, constitutes sufficient learning, or language, or love? How are we to
tell? This is, in fact, one way to construe the ethical debates about desire and
intellectualism summarized earlier. Given the full description of Floris's lovesick state in this second schoolroom, the word seems to slide from sufficiency
to overabundance. For what quantity of mournful sighs could ever be sufficient to Floris's desolation?

    The question of how much—difference, sameness, love, ingenuity, new-
ness, cunning, deceit, knowledge—is enough continues. In the French version, the vectors are less scholastic, more explicitly erotic. There is, for instance,
no explicit mention of any second schoolroom. Shortly after his arrival, a
mournful Floire is led into the new city, where his hosts tempt him to replace
Blancheflor with a new love object: "Aprendre le maine Sebile / O les puceles
de sa vile, / Savoir se il oublieroit / Blancheflor et autre ameroit, / Més riens oïr
ne riens veoir / Ne li puet joie fere avoir" (ll. 369–74). ["Sybil led him to learn
with the maidens of the city to know whether he could forget Blancheflor and
would love another. But nothing he heard or saw could give him joy"].
Blancheflor, the lover of his former days, remains irreplaceable, set apart.
Floire will not be tempted by these newfangled attractions. But the freshness
of young love is nonetheless also urged upon us, as this version elaborates

Floire's love as the urges of a boy of a certain age. The conventional metaphors of sexual blossoming or budding fruit seem here a paean to youthful—perhaps even virginal—sexuality at the moment of its ripening.

> Le fruit de cele ente atendoit,
> Més li terms lons li estoit,
> Ce li est vis, du fruit coillir.
> Quant Blancheflor verra gesir
> Jouste soi et la beissera,
> Le fruit de l'ente lors queudra. (ll. 382–87)

> [He awaited the fruit of the graft, but it seemed to him that he had to wait a long time to gather the ripe fruit. When he saw Blanche-flor lying near to him and he kissed her, then he will gather the fruit of the graft.]

While not exactly pornographic, the description is sweetly erotic, an eleven-year-old boy imagining future *jouissance* with his beloved by his side. Count-ing the ways that Floire yearns to know Blancheflor, the French poet evokes not a second schoolroom so much as the pleasure garden of delights adjacent to it. In the context of this description, the ME redactor, with his compara-tively stolid emphasis upon book learning, seems something of a killjoy, pur-suing the less flowery, more pedantic associations of knowledge with love.

By displacing the erotic, fleshly tenor of his source with a schoolroom version of love-for-learning, the ME redactor quite determinedly gestures to-ward the pragmatics of education. This mediated association of love with books is one that he has been pursuing from the start. But here we also can sense hints of the anxiety embedded in the adapter's repetition of "inowgh": even as the poem twins love and learning, the ME redaction seems insistent upon claiming love *for* education, taming its libidinal energy by avoiding mention of the lovers' burgeoning sexuality. The ME poet, moreover, disarms even hints of *future* passion. He avoids the shattering implications of impend-ing *jouissance* in favor of the apparently more modest pleasures, the charming affections and playful yearnings of childhood infatuation.

In stark contrast to its French source, the ME romance lays its libidinal wager on puppy love, on childhood as a charming period of sexual latency. Modest accounts of youthful longings may here function to discipline intima-tions of *jouissance*, implying youthful sexuality as a problem solved by, not raised in, the coeducational classroom. Implications of sexual latency also function to downplay or hide away the potential excitement of new objects, libidinal as well as sexual, or the capacity of novel things to get our juices going. It was Freud who noted the specific relation of novelty to adult sexuality: "In the adult, novelty always constitutes the condition for orgasm", a remark that will later inspire Roland Barthes's account of the new as a "value" for the *Pleasure of the Text*. It is clear by now that the ME version of *FB* deploys its childhood charms as a means to cordon off what Barthes will term *plaisir*— with its easier pleasures—from *jouissance*, that orgasmic, destabilizing, and potentially traumatizing type of enjoyment available by way of new loves.[72]

Yet there are wider implications here, other ways in which the apparent toyshop "charms" of romance mediate the possible dangers of desire and creativity. Even Kieckhefer's account with which this chapter began partakes of such a mediating logic, associating the magic of romance technologies with the apparently safer pursuits of childhood. And yet, the novel mechanisms described in the French romances—Yvain's rattrap, or the moving statues atop Blancheflor's false grave—are both starker and more serious than this metaphor can account for. These objects are beguiling and disturbing, and while Kieckhefer's rhetorical finesse endeavors to capture this feature of romance attraction, his toyshop metaphor, like the condensations of the ME poet, tamps down the danger of contrivances or traps in favor of the cuteness of toys.

Even a toy, however, can be too charming. Such excessive charm turn toys into traps; if toys captivate too much, they may hold us captive. Elsewhere in the Middle English record, comic and ribald accounts of sexualized puberty also linked to a rhetoric of the new suggest a more ambivalent view. In a ME lyric found in an early fifteenth-century "minstrel song-book"[73] rife with sexual innuendo, a fruit tree in a "new garden" illustrates male adolescent sexuality to less idealized effect.

> I have a newe garden,
>   and newe is begunne;
> Swych another garden
>   know I not under sunne.
>
> In the middes of my garden
>   is a perer set,
> And it wil non pere bern
>   but a pere-jonet.

The fairest mayde of this toun
    prayed me
For to griffen her a gryf
of myn pery-tre.

When I hadde hem griffed
    alle at here wille,
The wyn and the ale
    she did in fille.

And I griffed here
    right up in here home,
And be that day twenty wekes
    it was quik in here womb.

That day twelve month
    that mayde I met
She said it was a pere Robert
    but non pere Jonet.[74]

[I have a new garden / and newly is begun; / such another garden / I
do not know under the sun. / In the middle of my garden / a
pear-tree is set, / and it will no pear bear / but an early pear (pere-
Jonet). / The fairest maiden of this town / prayed me / to give her a
graft / from my pear tree. / When I had grafted her / all at her will,
/ The wine and the ale / she in did fill. / And I grafted her / right up
in her home / and on that day by twenty weeks / it was quick in her
womb. / That day twelve months [after] / I met that maid / She said
it was a pere/pear Robert / and not an early pear (pere Jonet).]

The speaker casts his newfound sexual potency through the metaphor of the
early pear tree, or "pere jonet," the latter a pun on the speaker's name, presumably John, as well as on his recently flowered phallic "pear," the apparent object
of some enthusiasm on the part of the fairest maid in town. The central image
suggests youthful sexuality; as the editor puts it, "the poet's unique new garden
and its pear tree are suggestive of various signs of puberty."[75] Ultimately, the
somewhat inexperienced speaker here overestimates his own sexual control; he
is too confident of the exclusive nature of his "gift" to the young lady "right up

in her home." There was, it turns out, more than one newly fruiting tree in her garden. The joke, of course, is on John, as the lyric's punch line makes clear: the maid's newly born "pear" is père Robert's and not his. The sexual trick—a fifteenth-century riff on what will come to be known as "Mama's baby, Papa's maybe"—shows the limits of masculine knowledge and patriarchal control in ways that resonate with the tradition of the "mounted Aristotle." It was "pere Jonet," not this lovely maid, who got played.[76]

Furthermore, with its Frenchified punning, this lyric is precisely the kind of text that would reward a type of macaronic reading practice made possible by the polyglot classroom described earlier. For one thing, the central verb here (griffen; griffed), meaning "to graft," echoes the metaphor for sexual union noted in the French text. For another, the joke hinges on the fact that the (male) pear of "pere-jonet" puns "père," the French word for father. Throughout most of the poem, the language of nature codes emerging male desire as youthful virility: the boy "grafts" the maiden, and her womb quickens; "pere jonet" signifies both the boy's sexual flowering and the male phallus. When the final stanza turns his pear to "père" Robert, it negates John's virility alongside his paternity, in language now decidedly French ("non Pere Jonet"). Female sexual desire, in contrast, extends multiply, if also duplicitously; this duplicity may mean to reveal the darker side of feminine charms, combining pleasure and deception. Yet the speaker, his tone comic, seems to delight nonetheless.

The sexual innuendo of "Pere Jonet" may seem too bawdily explicit for the aristocratic children of the ME *FB*; but it also suggests the complications of both novel desire and desire for novel objects in a more ambivalent way than the ME romance seems to do. To be sure, "Pere Jonet" covers over the complex sexual politics of illegitimate pregnancy, but it also delights, like fabliaux, in the power and pleasure of youthful sexuality, here for girls as much as boys. Such versions of sexual fresh-feeling and newness appear regularly in the English literary record—as, for instance, in Chaucer's descriptions of Alisoun's vital attractions from the "Miller's Tale"—where they regularly mark the greater, funnier, and more spontaneous, sexual freedom to be found outside courtly confines.

For our young prince in the ME *FB*, in contrast, the ardor of new love is an entirely serious matter. Even as the two youngsters suffer separation, Floris and Blauncheflour remain children, the sexual implications of their desire stripped away, at least for most of the romance. Floris will persist in his efforts to be reunited with Blauncheflour, and the opening ME emphasis upon the schoolroom will give way to an account of the prince's ingenuity and canniness as he follows her. The ME poet's emphasis on Floris's wit, as Barnes shows, is regularly evoked through the rhetoric of ingenuity, in the range of variants on the Middle English term "gyn." When the Middle English poet evokes this vocabulary in the service of Floris's love, he recuperates wit and acuity—even when used to deceive—for earnest young love. In the second part of the romance, Floris's canny cleverness, and not coincidentally his storytelling ability, will save both children from death.

Ethical Deceits

Floris's motives throughout his journey to find Blauncheflour emerge in a sympathetic light and as superior to the more provincial wishes of the sovereigns he confronts, first his parents and later the emir of Babylon. This is true despite the young man's use of deceit in gaining his purpose. If the discourse of *ingenium* was, as Hanning and Lerer demonstrate, regularly deployed as a means to judge intent, and pointed toward distinguishing deceitful chicanery from righteous cleverness, in *FB* the desired ends apparently justify the duplicitous means, or at least some of them.

Just as the ME poet eliminates the descriptive battle between *Amour* and *Savoir* that guides much of the action in the French, he draws out, as Barnes points out, a proportionally more extensive account of the importance of ingenious cleverness (and good counsel) to Floris's success. The innkeepers, Darys, and the porter at the emir's tower who guards the way to the place where Blauncheflour is held, all assist the young lover. Before Floris can benefit from the porter's canny plan, he must win his trust, and he does so in part by masquerading as an architect, a description drawn out in the ME version. Darys instructs the young lover on how to dupe the "felonious" porter,

> Wende tomorn to the toure,
> As thou were a good gynoure.
> Take on thy honed squyer and scantlon,
> As thou were a free mason;
> Behold the tour up and doun.
> The porter is cruel and feloun;
> Wel sone he wil come to the,
> And aske what maner man thou be,

. . . .
Sey thou art a gynoure,
To beholde that feire toure
For to loke, and for to fonde,
To make such another in thy londe. (ll. 655–59, 667–70)

[Go tomorrow to the tower / as though you were a good engineer. /
Take in your hand a T-square and measure / as though you were a
free mason. / Look the tower up and down. / The porter is cruel
and felonious. / Very soon he will come to you / and ask what
manner of man you are. / Say you are an engineer / (come) to see
that fine tower / in order to look and to find out / how to make
such a tower in your land.]

Floris's disguise as "gynoure," puns the double meaning of "gyn": the boy
deceitfully apes the part of engineer, fully equipped with the tools of the
trade, square and measure. Used against a porter who cannot himself be
trusted, Floris fights fire with fire, and in that regard, is more admirable than
his deceit might otherwise suggest. In contrast to the ME redactor's pattern
of condensing his French source, Floris's specific conversations with both
Darys and the porter are amplified here, the technical details of his disguise
emphasized.

Throughout the remainder of the ME romance, the poet clearly delights
in the cleverness of the devices deployed in love's service. Floris resembles his
parents in this regard. They too, as we have seen, deployed ingenious disguises
to achieve their ends. They were unsuccessful, and unlike Floris, the effect of
their ruse seemed altogether more sinister. In Floris's case, the porter will ultimately agree to assist the boy. He helps him to devise the most delightful, and
delightfully eponymous, *gyn* found in the story, arranging to smuggle Floris
into the emir's tower, ingeniously disguised in a basket of flowers. In the English version, this is the moment of the linguistic joke on the lovers' names
that was explicit in the empty tomb in the French: flower hides in a basket of
flowers. The basket motif constitutes another gesture to Arabic literary traditions, occurring several times in the Arabian Nights.[77]

The gains wrought though such deceits are inestimable. They reunite the
separated pair, incomplete one without the other. When Floris jumps from the
basket, the scene of the lovers' reunion, witnessed by Blaunchflour's friend
Claris, emphasizes the couple as sharers in a solitary delight:

Ayther of hem other knewe:
Withoute speche togeder they lepe;
And klippt and kyst wonder swete.
Clarys beheld al this—
Her countenaunce and her blysse—
. . . .
Now Blauncheflour and Florys,
Both these swete thinges, ywys
Cryen her mercy, al wepyng. (ll. 804–8, 813–15)

[Either of them the other knew: / without speaking they leaped
together; / and hugged and kissed wonderfully sweetly. / Clarys saw
all this— / [Blancheflour's] face and her bliss— / Now Blancheflour
and Floris / both these sweet things, certainly / cried mercy to her,
weeping together.]

As the language of the text makes clear, just as they were in the classroom, the
two youngsters are in this "togeder." The phrase "ayther hem other knew," according to the *MED*, emphasizes a simultaneous reflection of the two together,
rendered elsewhere in the Middle English corpus as "either in other," or "mu-
tually." Their names have been signaling this mutuality all along: Flower and
White Flower mirror and double each other, and the combined power of their
passion surmounts the demands, the laws, the wishes of rulers in Europe and
"the East," in Spain and Egypt. Following exactly his beloved's journey to
Cairo, Floris also mirrors Blauncheflour's distress along the route, a fact that
proves crucial to the lovers' eventual reunion: those who meet the young
prince remark that his mournfulness reminds them of the young Blauncheflour they had seen just days before. Claris, Blauncheflour's best friend, will
protect their secret as best she can. When the lovers are at last discovered, in
violation of the emir's decrees, their story charms the emir, ultimately saving
the two from death. The emir's reaction literalizes the beneficial effects that the
charming stories told by loving children (and romancers) can have upon powerful adults. Charm saves lives.

If the reunion culminates with the lovers' kiss in both versions, the description of that event is distinct in each. The emphasis on the simultaneity of
Floris and Blauncheflour's togetherness in the Middle English is qualified in
the French. In that text, the lovers' recognition alternates from one to the
other: "Blancheflor l'a bien conneü/ Et il ra bien li conneüe" (ll. 2205–6). This

shift from "she knew / he knew" to "either knew the other" may seem a small difference, but it is a telling one. It is, of course, a feature of the ME poet's general tendency toward condensing his source. But it also underscores what seems a rather more enmeshed and oceanic union between the two, who seem not only mimetically linked but toy-like versions of one another.

In its final insistence upon these reciprocal identities, the twinned kiss and mutual delight, the ME poem comes close to the golden and idealized image of lovers from the French version, the pair of moving lovers atop the empty grave. Here, the two together lie "nebbe to nebbe / nebbe to nebbe and mouth to mouth" (ll. 889–90), a final mirroring repetition (face to face / face to face and mouth to mouth) drawing the reader into the lovers' intimate touch. When it does so, the ME verse evokes and displaces the earlier French mise-en-scène: two once golden lovers, now grafted in the "little death," and poised for a kiss or a whisper. Yet it is also here, for the first time in the ME version, that death beckons most dramatically. Discovering them in such repose, the emir draws his sword, threatening to kill them as they are.

The juxtaposition of the lovers' charming tableau and the emir's sovereign sword evokes an oscillation between love and deadliness that is legible earlier in the plot, rendered specifically in the willful sale of Blauncheflour to the emir in the first place. For if Floris's love for Blauncheflour justifies, late in the romance, the deceitful adulterations deployed on her behalf, other deceits do not seem so laudable. The ruses used by Floris's parents are not justifiable, even though these, too, are motivated by a certain kind of love. These *gyns* are not the same, and the differences between them engage the issue of intent long associated with the discourse of *ingenium*. Those ethical ambivalences are here adjudicated via the differences of youth and age. Youngsters, idealized and innocent, are touchstones for the utopian power of new things, for passionate ingenuity that saves rather than destroys. Elders are ascribed more murderous impulses.

And young love conquers all. By the end of the romance, the emir agrees to "foryeve that trespass" of the two "yif Florys told how it was," that is, if Floris would relate the story of their love. This may be the fantasy that the romance has been offering all along: a case study in the enchanting power of charming stories of youthful passion to overcome the limitations that parental law, region, creed, or custom place upon it. The history of romance traditions suggests a range of intercultural textual exchanges that cross exactly those oppositions. Although there has long been interest in delineating "Eastern" from "Western" traditions of romance, Floris and Blauncheflour can help us to reconsider what it means that such discriminations are so notoriously tricky.[78]

Viewed in the context of the complexity of debates over knowledge and pleasure, the story tradition of *FB* suggests that romance charm has its own ethical, even salvific, ambitions for the world. In this context the opening schoolroom scene in *Floris and Blauncheflour* seems entirely pertinent to the long intercultural history of the collaborations of scholasticism: knowledge production quite literally both required and produced Europe's desire for the sophisticated learning of the Arabic world. From this vantage, the mutual love between Floris and Blaunchefour encodes Europe's fantasy that its love of the Arabic world is returned in complementary degrees, as satisfyingly mutual: in this fantasy schoolroom, the "heathen" scholar Floris cannot learn without his Christian companion Blaunchefour. This, perhaps, is Europe's fervent wish: a wish for the mutual enchantment of Christian and Muslim as a catalyst to significant accomplishments. The pertinence of this structure to the tale is furthered when we recall that collaborations among European and Arabic scholars required the bi- and trilingualism of the culture in which this schoolroom is set: Spain, "an advanced civilization that would decisively change the face of European literary and intellectual culture."[79]

Yet the relations between the French and Middle English versions of *FB* have also suggested something of the way that idealized accounts of youth serve to manage the problem of the new, particularly as it relates to the rhetoric of *ingenium*. The Middle English *Floris and Blauncheflour* delights unequivocally in the charm of *ingenium* by channeling a version of newness via the fresh innocence of childhood. Along the way, the poem qualifies, condenses, and moderates the links between innovation and deadliness legible in the French, defending human ingenuity as propelled by innocent ambition and love without ambivalence or aggression. This is how *Floris and Blaunchefour* mitigates the aversive character of the new as traumatic rupture, as *jouissance*, as destructive, disruptive desire. The poem operates, to this degree, as a disarmingly defensive and disciplining text, protecting the gentle pleasures of novel attractions while circumscribing more horrific or murderous brands of novelty.

The view of childhood as a time of gentler enchantments—a time when our fresh eyes and innocent hearts thrill at the wonders of the world, a time when gadgets and toys instruct and edify, or when clever talking animals teach us, in fables, how to hone our grammatical and logical capacities—is based upon similar hopes. It, too, has considerable cultural power, then as now. This structure of feeling is part of what propels the view with which this chapter began, of romance as toyshop stuffed with magical delights. Raymond

Williams famously made the point: his evocative description of the "feeling of childhood" has long been imagined as the time before the commodification of people and things.[80] In this account of history it is important that the ingenious gadgetry of toys remain cordoned off from harsher mechanics of traps or tombs. Keeping the materialism of the former imbued with life-giving excitement and wonder requires us to divorce it completely from the latter.

There are worse things to defend against. When the medieval new appears in the guise of charming stories of young lovers, it channels one of the primary attractions of romance: the delectation of fresh-feeling powerful enough to keep desire alive. Just so did demand for the "charming" story of these two young lovers continue well beyond early scenes of writing or rewriting. Romance newness, in such guises, functions in utopian mode, as a means to insist on a world in which commodification, exploitation, aggressivity, or murderous intent do not have the last word. This is an entirely ethical aim. Yet we might, and at the same time, recognize that separating toys from traps may not be as easy as it sounds: Chrétien's audience delighted at the death-dealing rattrap that sliced Yvain's spurs right off his feet; the toy as Jewish head found in the riverbed of the Thames taught a good deal more than wonder. This is not to say that such enchantments are only deadly, or death-dealing; it is instead to imply that enthusiasm for the wonder of childhood invites thought as well as feeling, opening analytic opportunities in considering how, when, and why such associations are freshly repeated.

Chaucer's *Squire's Tale*, the subject of my next chapter, continues the association of novelty and youth. Yet whereas the ME *FB* dealt with the ambivalent discourse of *ingenium* by repressing the more traumatic aspects of the new, Chaucer's tale will draw out in astonishing detail the ethical complexities that inhabit our enchantment with the newfangled, in a complex account of novelty's double-face. Relations across religious and cultural difference in the *Squire's Tale* render the new as an exciting lure to desire; yet precisely as such, the new opens toward the unpredictable—casting novelty as peril as well as promise.

Chapter 4

Little Nothings

Long before the advent of modern aeronautics, crackpot inventors, artists, romancers, mythologists, and philosophers envisioned the possibilities of taking flight. Horses with wings, like Pegasus, and with pins, like Cambyuskan's magical horse in Chaucer's *The Squire's Tale*; ornithopters, or mechanical hybrids described in the works of Roger Bacon; the glider tested by Spanish Arab scientist Abbas Ibn Firnas (c. 875); and the bird-man experiments of Eilmer, as told by William of Malmesbury (c. 1140), all constitute a medieval prehistory for the modern glider, helicopter, and airplane. Throughout the early periods, flying machines delighted speculative thinkers, natural philosophers, and readers of literature: as marvels in classical and Vedic texts, as signs for wonder in medieval romance, as equivocal speculations in Bacon's *Secrets of Art and Nature* examined in Chapter 2, or in the experimental gadget-love of Leonardo's fifteenth-century Sketch Book. Leonardo has, of course, garnered most of the credit for the idea in the West; his sketches and rather terse writings "On Flying Machines" frequently figure as first examples of the philosopher-artist's fantastical, anticipatory genius, signifying the "modern" originality of a great Renaissance mind.[1]

Of course, as the preceding makes clear, we should know better. Despite a long tradition testifying to the immense power of premodern innovations, the Renaissance still gets more credit for "new" thinking and making than it deserves.[2] At least since 1940, when Lynn White's essay "Technology and Invention in the Middle Ages" appeared in *Speculum*, building on the work of European historians of the Annales school and revivifying the study of technology, medievalists have documented and debated the meaning of medieval invention. Bacon, among others, features prominently for his writings on flying machines and optics, and for his fascination with firecrackers and gunpowder.[3] On the question of Leonardo's originality, moreover, Frances and Joseph Gies remind us, "The historic value of Leonardo's 'notebooks'—actually an immense scattering of sketches and jottings—lies less in their author's own contribution to engineering than in their incomparable illustration of the atmosphere in which he lived, a time in which dreamers, tinkerers, and artist-inventors were applying themselves on the frontiers of technology opened by the discoveries of their medieval predecessors."[4] Scholars of technology, architecture, or philosophy; of economics, natural science, translation studies, or poetry have persistently stressed the many inventions and innovations emerging during the long period designated as medieval, and the variety of novel things imagined, described, or produced by its dreamers and tinkerers.

Previous chapters in this book attend to the philosophical and ethical questions prompted by medieval developments in human invention, intellection, and creativity. Part I, "Ex Nihilo," outlined their pertinence to the pursuit of the new as an idea, and to the equivocal tracking of the new as it pertained to things. Thinkers like Aquinas, Bonaventure, or Bacon devised intellectual systems that were flexible enough both to accommodate and to work around the limitations placed on human making at the time. The current Part II, "Ingenium," attends to the resulting ethical discourse dogging novel compositions and the humans who wonder in them. The story tradition of *Floire and Blauncheflor*, examined in the preceding chapter, renders the new not only as marvelous artifact but also as categorical marker. Such shifts, legible in the differences of the Middle English version from its French source, worked to tame the potential dangers of new things, grand or miniature. In its emphasis on the moderate charms of juvenile affections, the ME *Floris and Blauncheflour* splits the cleverness of ingenuity from more murderous deceits and impulses. This is the new as fresh-faced ingenuity rather than as mature genius.

The current chapter continues to explore the status of the new in romance texts. And here, I engage the new as related to, but not simply coincident with, the gadgets, mechanisms, gears, or man-made marvels, the rare or magical things found in romance as a genre. The romance discourse of novelty positions novel objects within an interlinked set of concerns related to ethics, metaphysics, exchange, and proprietary relations, all with institutional and philosophical points of contact. While Chaucer's *Squire's Tale* does not resolve these issues, his poem makes the stakes of such thinking clear.

Poetic Substance

Roger Bacon's futuristic list of marvels ("machines for sailing with human oarsmen"; "flying machines"; instruments for walking "on the bottom of the sea") was influenced by the texts of romance. And medieval romance abounds in an archive of little nothings[5]—the talking heads of brass or gold, moving statues, fountains, magical rings, or gardens of delights. The contributions that the genre has made to developments in the history of technology are increasingly well documented, if also surprising: scholars such as Scott Lightsey and E. R. Truitt, developing further the groundbreaking work of Lorraine Daston and Katharine Park, direct our attention to the productive preoccupation of romance with the mechanical arts, wherein wonderful objects and wondrous accounts of matter are both dreamt and dreamed-up.[6]

This romance economy of things has recently come under special scrutiny, particularly as a marker for the material power of imagination in the real world. The turn to things has claimed—and many intuitively feel the claim to be a fair one—that attention to what Lightsey calls the "thereness of objects" gets us closer to material substance and, thus, to things that matter.[7] Yet recent accounts of medieval household economies (Smith), visual object-love (Stanbury), or technological histories (Truitt) persistently stress the medieval object as shot through with philosophical, institutional, and ethical concerns. Nor is "matter" as straightforwardly "there" (in or out of poetry) as Lightsey implies. In other disciplinary corners—manuscript studies, for instance, or the history and philosophy of science—questions regarding of the nature of matter persist. In the twentieth century, and in material sciences like physics, the word "matter" is the name of a problem.[8] As literary critic and science-studies scholar Daniel Tiffany has recently put it, "it is only in philosophy or in some humanistic disciplines increasingly dependent on the authority of historical evidence, that one finds stable and functional definitions of materiality."[9]

Tiffany takes aim at poetic materialism; he argues that poetic forms of representation—particularly those founded on analogical and allegorical thinking—have a purchase on materiality, although not in ways we might expect. Analogical representational modes—those often thought to be least "realist," or most at odds with materialist concerns—best face up to the problem of matter and, accordingly, share much with scientific accounts of its substance. Poetry can offer a surprising place to reconsider matter in terms of what Tiffany calls "lyric substance," "a consistent and perhaps even systematic doctrine of corporeality proper to the devices of poetry."[10]

Tiffany's reorientation of materialism comes from at least two directions: from natural philosophy of the seventeenth century, which assessed the substance of bodies and poetry by comparing both to ingenious toys; and from current models for understanding the substance of matter developed in the physical sciences, particularly in theoretical physics. Protons, electrons, and neutrons (to say nothing of elementary particles like quarks), are known only by way of representational, analogical models. Our knowledge of the material facts of matter, that is, depends on imaginative representation and analogical models. Tiffany's work, like the work of Bruno Latour on which it draws, makes clear that imaginary modeling and analogical strategies of representation constitute, not the opposite of corporeality, but the epistemological *requirements* for understanding its substantial material form. And it is this confluence of corporeality with analogy that Tiffany also finds in poetry. Poetry pursues its own "doctrine of corporeality," he argues, by way of analogy and allegory. These modes, not realism, are most attuned to the facts of matter as substance.

Medieval romances, as we saw in Chapter 3, can revel in toy-like descriptions of certain corporeal things. Yet these features of romance description regularly suture such matter to ethical and philosophical concerns. This is a feature, not a flaw. The medieval case regularly heightens the ethical questions. Gilded statues of moving children atop mausoleums sparkle as aggressive parental deceptions; magical cups or life-saving rings raise both the pleasures and the problems of captivation. The *gyns* of romance, that is, converge on philosophical concerns, the ambiguities harbored by the discourse of *ingenium*. This means that efforts to isolate the "thingy-ness" of romance—to take, as it were, the *gyn* out of *ingenium*—will necessarily, if counterintuitively, blunt the material force of romance precisely as a poetic form. Romance may well sing hosannas to the magic of objects; but its own "doctrine of corporeality" embeds such things in a range of ethical relations.

Nor did every mechanical object described in poetry represent something that was already "there" in culture. As the account of Bacon's speculations in Chapter 2 suggests, romance mechanics laid claim to technology by way of a future still in the offing. When E. R. Truitt tracks the figures that she calls "metal people" described in romance verse, she shows us that these marvels were depicted with precision at a time well before Western Europeans had the requisite technology ("the invention of the mechanical escapement," or the "widespread use of toothed gears")[11] to build them. This was because, she explains, such things served as a means to engage the nature of poetic making as such:

The creation of fictional human automata was a kind of interroga-
tion by poets of the legitimacy of their own enterprise. As creators
of imaginary, mimetic worlds, intended to surpass in splendor,
wealth, wonder, and courtliness the world that the poets and their
audiences inhabited, the fictional automata become an instrument
of self-fashioning on the part of the poets.[12]

This materiality of human making aspired to a self-conscious kind of creativity. Truitt's work adds to our understanding of the complex sense of artistic
and artisanal productivity as converging on philosophical questions about the
legitimacy of human imagination and creative activity. But it also suggests that
the history of medieval mechanics cannot isolate the artifacts thereby represented from their metaphysical or aesthetic contexts.

Undoubtedly, the genre of romance contributed to the development of
gadgets, from gears to metal people; but it also, as Truitt's words above suggest,
trafficked in sumptuous matter, the "splendor, wealth, wonder, and courtliness" valued by poets and their audiences. Whole worlds were made mechanical: the famous Park at Hesdin, the setting for Guillaume de Machaut's
masterpiece, the *Remède de fortune*, was influenced by even as it influenced
literary representations of gardens.[13] Luxury items like table fountains or moving dolls led to mechanics of greater utility, as "the steps toward the invention
of the weight-driven clock . . . were motivated as much by the need for motion
in such automata as by more scientific concerns."[14] Such projects made wealth
conspicuous, and posed, in this regard, yet another ethical problem. Insofar as
romance materialism contributed to an account of the world as luxurious sen-
sorium, it raised questions of desire and appetite both in content and in form.
In the Middle English tradition, as D. Vance Smith demonstrates, "romaunce"
is "as often an economic designation as it is a formalist generic description"[15];
the genre thus serves "as a luxurious object itself," as well as "a symbolic good
that is part of the symbolizing repertoire of aristocratic luxury."[16] Sarah Stanbury notes that "the tension between the longed-for place of spirit and the
consolation of objects" was powerfully "at stake in late-medieval polemic
against images."[17] Such tensions would only increase as a "new market for
images . . . invite[d] further participation in the exchange of goods."[18]

Moderation was thought to be key to the ethical navigation of such appetites. And, not coincidentally although for different reasons, premodern aesthetics also emphasized the elegance of moderation by way of proportion.[19]
But how to judge when enough was enough? In the story of *Floris and*

Blaunchefiour, questions of sufficiency (of love, learning, closeness, or wonder) were hard to pin down: as we saw in the last chapter, "enough" all too easily converged on "too much." The late medieval era witnessed increasing efforts to parse such calculations, obsessive attempts to quantify the matter of things and the things that mattered: from usury or the limits that should be placed on mercantile profits to more transcendental and "seemingly immeasurable qualities such as the strength of Christian charity . . . or the quality of grace."[20] Excess constituted an ethical limit in these economies, and applied not only to things themselves, but also to the human impulses—sensory, intellectual, and spiritual—that such things inspired.

Excess emerges regularly in debates over romance in all its thingy-ness. In Geoffrey Chaucer's *Squire's Tale* formal, narrative, libidinal, and epistemological excesses are at issue. And here excess converges directly on the category of the new, rendered in that text in Chaucer's own novel usage: newfangledness. Chaucer's work has been important to this project overall, in part because words for newness and novelty pepper his poetry.[21] He explicitly casts intellectual endeavor as a metaphorical harvesting of "new corn" out of "old fields"; and he turns, in persistently equivocal ways, to the meaning and reception of news or new things. Among the motherly advice given at the end of the *Manciple's Tale*, for instance, is the admonition to stay away from the dangers of new tidings, whether false or true. Yet the poet will also, in counterpoint to the Manciple's admonition, evocatively explore not just the dangers but the reach and power of "New Tidings" in his dream vision, *The House of Fame*. Readers of Chaucer increasingly emphasize that the poet's detailed attention to things emerges out of a larger interest in natural philosophy and literary making.

In this larger corpus, the *Squire's Tale* is well known for its excess. When the Squire takes his turn at the Canterbury pilgrims' storytelling game, his tale impresses the audience as very much *too* much, on which account he is interrupted from finishing it; some readers see the tale, another of Chaucer's experiments in poetic composition and rhetoric, as a satire of just such excess. Nor is it coincidental that the plot of the *Squire's Tale* scrutinizes other kinds of excesses, via engaging descriptions of royal wealth and luxury. Furthermore, critics have long noted the tale's critical edge, with some reading it as a critique of the naïveté of simple wonderment in luxurious things.[22] Lightsey finds here a disenchanted version of an earlier romance admiration for *mirabilia*.[23] Yet such readings do not account for the tale's own considerable absorption with newness and fresh-feeling: as John Fyler points out, the tale's array of gifts, which include a magical ring, a mirror, and a sword, as well as a mechanical horse, offer together a kind of cosmological renewal, "a means of reintegration, of recapturing a lost world of freshness, transparency, and clarity."[24] Linking the tale even more directly with innovation, Alan Ambrisco emphasizes Chaucer's investment in the new immediacy of the English language, as a fantasy, he argues, of "flawless" communication.[25]

As this all suggests, the new has regularly emerged as a useful category for understanding the work accomplished by the *Squire's Tale*. Yet if the category of newness has been crucial to a number of important readings of the tale, Chaucer's own account of newness in it has more often been assumed than examined closely. A closer look reveals the significance of the function and meaning of novelty here. Part 1 of the tale seems at first glance to offer an unmediated account of the problems and pleasure of new things, describing the series of fabulous birthday gifts given to Cambyuskan (Genghis Khan) and to his daughter Canacee. A mechanical brass horse that can, with the turn of a pin, transport its rider beyond the bounds of the natural world takes prominence. Imaginary pictures of matter abound in Part 1, and those given the most sustained attention—Cambyuskan's horse, for example—cross the visible with the invisible, the intelligible with the puzzling and strange. Yet, and notably, the poet explicitly associates the newfangled not, as we might expect, with Cambyuskan's magical horse, nor with either the Squire's linguistic eloquence or his rhetorical failures, but instead with a traumatic experience of love. Whereas the first part details the court's delight in and debate over the fascinations of this innovative gadget, the tale's second part tells what seems only tangentially related, the story of a brokenhearted falcon, abandoned by her beloved tercelet for the newfangled attractions of a common kite.[26] Why, after all, does the poet link failed love with a flying mechanical contrivance? And why does the former, rather than the latter, occasion an elaboration of the problems and pleasures of newfangledness?

Locating the idea of the newfangled amid the repetitious patternings of what has come to be called the discourse of courtly love, Chaucer's Squire toggles between objects and subjects, oscillating from things to structures of desire. This is because, I will argue here, he wishes to consider an ethical dilemma lying at the heart of our desires for newness as such. Linking failed love with innovative mechanics enables Chaucer to consider the new as a lure, one as liable to motivate compassion as disdain, and an attraction that, under certain circumstances, works to propel problematic claims of ownership. We meet Chaucer's brokenhearted peregrine falcon, as does Canacee, just after she has been abandoned by her beloved tercelet. The bird speaks the problem of the new from the vantage of the formerly beloved, a love-object lately discarded as old; she occupies the place of the once-new, once-admired object at the moment it has been ignored, abandoned, and replaced. Now superseded, and crying out in pain at her rejection, Chaucer's peregrine sheds considerable light on the delicate economies of the newfangled for love, for household, and for poetry.

In considering the new from the position of the obsolete, Chaucer's poem works over the conceptual features of the category. He considers, via the peregrine, just what it is that constitutes the new as an attribute, a kind of nature. "Men loven novelries of propre kynde," laments the heartbroken bird, bemoaning the loss of an abandoning lover who has flown off in pursuit of a new love. While this phrase has long been read to imply that humans have a natural tendency (a nature, or "kynde") to yearn after new objects, I argue instead that Chaucer here refers primarily to the nature not of men but of novelty itself. Explicitly deploring newness, the peregrine vividly laments a disloyal lover's attraction to "novelries." From her perspective, the circulation of the newfangled emerges as, of "propre kynde," terribly unkind.

Chaucer's attention to the properties of novelty, furthermore and as I will demonstrate, builds on an intriguing consideration of the concept in a work written by one of his greatest influences, Guillaume de Machaut. Machaut's narrative poem the *Dit de l'alerion* (*The Tale of the Alerion*) offers its own intriguing meditation on the complex nature of novelty in the rare or the unusual; and Chaucer's *Squire's Tale's*, as we shall see, plays with the ethical limits of the new in ways that both echo and shift Machaut's treatment. When it does so, the *Squire's Tale* links properties of the new to the problems of appetite central to romance as a form.

Canacee's Novelties

Juxtaposed with the intriguing novelties given both to Cambyuskan and to Canacee in Part 1 of the tale is the starker, darker story of the self-mutilating peregrine told in Part 2. Thanks to the gift of a magical ring, Canacee can cross the linguistic gulf between humans and birds, gaining access to the bird's sad tale. This is certainly a new, and stunning, linguistic medium. Canacee's excited interest in her gifts—"swich a joye she in hir herte took / Bothe of hir queynte ryng and hire mirour, / That twenty tyme she changed hir colour" (5.368–70)—awakens her early, leading her to the garden ramble during which she encounters the peregrine in the first place. Yet this gadget enables a very old story of infidelity and pain: the lovesick, self-mutilating falcon has been abandoned by her tercelet, who, too easily seduced by newfangledness, turned to the love of a scavenger kite. From the point of view of the peregrine, desire for the new comes bearing marks of deadliness.

Such pain is literalized in the bird's body. As the falcon tells her tale, she has "Ybeten . . . hirself so pitously" that "the rede blood / Ran endelong the tree ther-as she stood" [Beaten herself so piteously that red blood ran down along the tree in which she stood] (5.414–16). The scene is dramatic, with the wetness of the peregrine's red blood running down along the branches and bark of the dry, white tree in which she sits (5.409). Against this backdrop, the peregrine opines that men and birds unhappily share a powerful attraction to certain properties of the new, superficial features that distract them from loves of real value.

> Men loven of propre kynde newfangelnesse,
> As briddes doon that men in cages fede.
> For though thou nyght and day take of hem hede
> And strawe hir cage faire and softe as silk,
> And yeve hem sugre, hony, breed and milk,
> Yet right anon as that his dore is uppe
> He with his feet wol spurne adoun his cuppe,
> And to the wode he wole and wormes ete;
> So newfangel been they of hire mete,
> And loven novelries of propre kynde,
> No gentleness of blood ne may hem bynde. (5.610–20)

[Men love newfangledness, of [its] own nature / as do birds that men feed in cages. / For though you attend to them night and day / and strew their cages with straw as soft as silk / and give them sugar, honey, bread, and milk / yet just as soon as his door is left up / He will with his feet kick down his cup / and go to the woods and eat worms; / So newfangled are they about their food / and love the nature of novelties / that no nobility of blood may restrain them.]

The suffering bird laments an indiscriminate love of the new: men, and birds, "loven novelries of proper kynde." The formulation, twice repeated, marks novelties "of propre kynde," literally of a characteristic nature; and the syntax has been read to suggest that it is the special, and deplorable, characteristic of men to "loven novelries," an attribute of humankind that is frequently noted in both medieval and early modern literature. Here, the familiar image registers pain and discontent in ways that converge on social class: just as birds like the tercelet spurn their rare cup, slumming after the ignobility of common worms, so is she, noble raptor, thrown over for a common kite.[27] Rather than signify value, newfangledness emerges as the stuff of smoke and mirrors, empty attraction to newness for its own sake.

Chaucer has used this image of the captive bird before, and to somewhat different ends. In book 3 of his *Boece*, a caged songbird (not, notably, a "noble" tercelet) similarly fouls food with dirty feet, yearning to return to the freedom of the woods. In that context, the bird's desire serves as an example of the natural order, the fact that all things in this world (like lions, saplings, and birds) adhere to their natural place, their "proper kynde."[28] Importing this image to the *Squire's Tale*, Chaucer changes the gender of the captive bird, a she, in *Boece*, twittering "with swete voys." He also shifts the emphasis from the caged bird's desire for freedom (she "seith the / agreables schadwes of the wodes, sche defouleth / with hir feet hir metes ischad, and seketh / mornynge oonly the wode" [3, m. 2, ll. 27–30]) to the male bird's appetite for worms. By changing the caged bird's gender Chaucer emblematizes the love of the new as, on the one hand, a particularly masculine propensity; the "men" of line 610 now seems gender specific. Yet the representation of desire shifts, too: desire for a life in the natural woods, a desire for life beyond the constraining limits of the cage, is recast as a desire to possess whatever is lacking, whether the object in question is worthy or not. The notion that woodland songbirds naturally long for freedom translates into the propensity of men to yearn after new (that is, formerly unavailable) things. Chaucer recasts yearning for a specific kind of liberation into an account of desire in which contextual and relational features prove determining: it is the unavailability of objects, rather than their inherent worth, that renders them desirable. By associating this form of desire with men's love of newfangledness, Chaucer underscores both the contextual and the ambivalent features in this account of novelty.

There is still more to be said about this odd passage, particularly about the special emphasis here on the caged bird's desire for worms. For one thing, raptors like the tercelet are birds of prey; unlike the caged songbirds of the metaphor, they do not "of propre kynde" desire worms at all. And even from a songbird's perspective, worms are hardly newfangled; here, they emerge as new insofar as they have been so long unavailable or deferred. The old

becomes the new under certain circumstances—and repetition prevails, func-
tionally as well as rhetorically (this is, after all, a reused image), a point to
which we will return.

As in her own self-mutilating acts, moreover, the peregrine's remarks display the sacrificial impulse embedded in the entire structure: just as she forfeits
safety and bodily ease for the self-abuse she heaps upon her now bloody breast,
so do the men and birds who "loven novelries" give up elevated circumstance—
sumptuous silks, cups filled with milk and honey—rejecting the elegant cage
and cup in favor of dirt and worms. Associating the love of newfangledness
with a desire to eat worms, the peregrine both registers her contempt for the
tercelet's bad taste and undermines the usual association of the new with glit-
tery attraction: rather than a fondness for frivolity, the love of novelty can
debase, motivating not the acquisition of luxury but its sacrifice. This means
that if the peregrine, by extension, deplores the tercelet's choice, she also and
at the same time makes it clear that the pull of the newfangled is powerful
enough to lure one to sacrifice easy pleasure for it.

Here, then, we see that desire for the new can prompt the sacrifice of
pleasure in favor of what Slavoj Žižek calls enjoyment, or pleasure in unplea-
sure. With regard to sacrifice as a form of desire, Aranye Fradenburg points
out that sacrificial discipline "enhances *jouissance*; it multiplies and extends its
possibilities."[29] In refusing elevated objects, the tercelet extends desire in all its
forms, eventuating in the peregrine's story and Canacee's creative response to
it. The desire of the peregrine, still directed toward her tercelet but now barred
from its fulfillment, erupts in self-mutilation and poetry both, and she tells
her moving story in lovely lines of verse. The tercelet's flirtation with the new
keeps the peregrine's satisfaction deferred, her desire engaged even more now
on its newly impossible object. As absent love object, what Lacan will call a
"cruel" as well as "inhuman partner," the tercelet constitutes the emptiness
that propels the peregrine's poetic activity.[30] This suggests that a desire for
novelty prompts sacrifice precisely because sacrifice multiplies and extends
possibility: the tercelet's desire for the new reverberates outward, generating all
kinds of creative productions.

The absent tercelet, that is, constitutes the emptiness around which the
peregrine's story detours, and it produces the falcon's self-mutilation as well as
her poetic refrain. By adopting a central narrative of loss in love, the tale's
second part keeps us mindful not only of the complex simultaneity of novelty
with painful repetition, but of the ways this contradictory structure makes
legible, to borrow Sarah Kay's formulation, "the emergence of the literary

object."[31] Indeed, the peregrine references a long tradition: faithless lovers fawn after new loves, leaving their former partners with nothing; this is, of course, old news, as those references make clear. These are also stories that Chaucer has himself told before, repeatedly: in the *Legend of Good Women*, in *Anelida and Arcite*,[32] and in the *Troilus*, most forcefully, of course, from the point of view of Troilus's love for the ultimately faithless Criseyde. If, as Ambrisco argues, the *Squire's Tale* is Chaucer's reflection on the linguistic innovations of literary English, at moments like these the tale remains interested in the ways in which even "new" languages fall back on older forms, nearly automatic in their force.[33]

Here, as elsewhere in Chaucer's corpus, relations between birds channel the complications of human sociality in terms related to gender as well as class. Even more curiously, Chaucer uses the particular phrase ("propre kynde") only four times throughout his entire corpus; the *Squire's Tale* and the analogous passage from the *Boece* account for three of these. What, precisely, is "propre kynde" where novelty is concerned? How are we to understand that nature proper to the newfangled? Viewed in the context of scholastic debates on matter and creativity examined in the first section of this book, and considered as part of an ethical discourse of the new that I have been examining, the question seems particularly pointed. To answer it, we need to consider a likely source for Chaucer's reflections on the newfangled, Guillaume de Machaut's *Tale of the Alerion*.

Rara Avis

A bird as rare upon the earth as a black swan.

—Juvenal, *Satires*[34]

Innovative poets—like the peregrine, Chaucer, and Guillaume de Machaut—traffic in well-worn phrases, regularly returning us to arresting images or familiar plots. Yet this hardly compromises the freshness of their verses. Chaucer's consideration of the new, as we have seen, reworked an image that he had used before. But Chaucer's poem was not the first to bring together the rhetoric of the new with avian love objects. His account of the peregrine's lament shows debts to Guillaume de Machaut's *Tale of the Alerion*, the latter an influence on the *Parliament of Fowls* as well. James Wimsatt suggests that, "it seems certain that Chaucer has some acquaintance with *Dit de l'alerion*, though he makes little specific use of it."[35] I will argue that Chaucer makes more use of it than we have heretofore recognized.[36] The consideration of novelty, by both poets, converges on the aesthetics of new poetic work.[37]

Noted for his innovations in poetry as well as in music, Machaut was a master of the "Ars Nova," the new style and form of musical production and performance (musical notation, polyphony) named after the treatise of the same name by Phillipe de Vitry (1291–1361).[38] Vernacular song emerged in the twelfth century, but it was in the early thirteenth that "a process of gathering together and writing down secular French and Occitan songs" began, from which point, as Ardis Butterfield puts it, "song became an increasingly literate art."[39] Machaut's work was important to this process, and recent critics have pointed to the poet's "glittering display of literary and musical collaboration," where "poetry and music forge together the sound of the page and the silence of imagination."[40]

While his 4800-line narrative poem, *Dit de l'alerion*, is not among Machaut's most innovative work (it does not, for instance, include songs, as does the *Remède de fortune*), it does include a somewhat surprising extended meditation on the new. The plot, rendered in alternating episodes devoted to falconry and to courtship, details a falconer's relationship with each of four birds, a sparrowhawk, a mythical alerion, an eagle, and a gyrfalcon. Throughout the poem, the narrative voice muses over the vagaries of courtship in a repeated pattern of "desire-possession-loss."[41] A didactic allegory, the *alerion* persistently emphasizes aristocratic virtues, and is usually understood to offer an account of proper thinking, speaking, and acting via its extended metaphor of men and birds. Machaut takes up questions of the new amid its treatment of the legendary alerion. The result is a fascinating account of novelty as, paradoxically, both linked to the rare and entwined with repetition. This overall theme is clearly cited by Chaucer's peregrine, and, as we shall see, Machaut's treatment of novelty informs Chaucer's meaning as well.

Machaut raises the falconer's desire as related to novelty on more than one occasion. In Part 1, the narrator emphasizes his attraction to the youth and wildness of his first bird, a sparrowhawk. Young and "newly caught," she beckons with the promise of vernal happiness: "Lors m'acorday je de venue / A l'esprivier pris de nouvel, / pour avoir son juene revel" ["I quickly found that I was drawn / to such a new-caught sparrowhawk, / that I might share her youthful joy"].[42] Yet, despite her promise as a "pris de nouvel," the sparrowhawk will ultimately disappoint. And so will two of the other birds that the falconer eventually possesses, the eagle and the gyrfalcon.

Machaut develops the features of the new most fully in Part 2 of the poem. Although the moment has been noted, it has yet to receive a full treatment of its dynamics.[43] The object of fascination at issue is not the once wild, still youthful sparrowhawk, but the poem's titular rare bird, the alerion. In the bestiary tradition, the legendary alerion figured as the scarcest of scarce creatures; the species was thought to survive, a single pair at a time, somewhere in India, a view perhaps founded on Pliny. Machaut's alerion is the rare female of this unique pair: a literal *rara avis* and as such an exquisite exemplum for an utterly uncommon thing. Possessing her is nearly impossible. This legendary bird will explicitly signify a specimen of that species of thing known as the new and strange.

Having lost his sparrowhawk in an unfortunate moulting episode, the falconer awaits his next falcon while musing on his desire to possess the alerion, a particularly rare species, "qui est uns oiseaus gentillès, / Gais, gens, jolis, joins et quillès" (1569–70) ("A very noble race of birds, / lovely, amiable, and gay"). She is "d'une estrangeté nompareille" (1579), an interesting phrase that editors Gaudet and Hieatt translate as "of a surpassing novelty." The narrator continues:

> Car ce n'est pas chose commune,
> Eins es trés tout aussi comme une
> Chose des autres separée,
> Dont elle est assez mieus parée
> De plaisir en audition
> Pour l'estrange condition
> Qui est ditte nouvelleté. (ll. 1583–89)

[They're not at all like common things, / but are very much like creatures / of a very different kind; / thus their praises are more likely / to be pleasurably heard, / since their condition is the strange one / that is known as novelty.][44]

Novelty, cast here both as a strange condition and as a condition of strangeness, defines the legendary species of bird through its fundamental difference from all that is common. This emphasis on the bird's uncommonness emerges in wordplay evident in the original, as the "chose commune" of line 1583 equivocates with "comme une / Chose" enjambed in lines 1584–85. The description plays like with, and against, unlike. This alerion is no common thing ("ce n'est pas chose commune"); if the bird is like anything ("comme une / chose"), it is completely like ("trés tout aussi comme") a thing that is like nothing else ("chose des autres separée"). With conscious repetition, the text renders the yet-to-be-seen alerion in equivocating degrees of sameness and difference. If she can be compared to anything, she can only be compared to something that is comparable to nothing; her similarity to something like nothing else is total, complete. Whereas Chaucer's mournful peregrine, a noble raptor, not a legendary bird, stipulates her value through a contrast to that utterly "common" species of bird, the kite, Machaut's alerion engages an even larger, and more conceptual, species: the very idea of something uncommon. As mythical bird, moreover, the alerion's uncommonness coordinates with her value as a rarity.

The poetic line amplifies this point in a fluctuation of similarity with difference, something with nothing. All comes together as a gloss on "novelty," the final word in this poetic sentence. Such wordplay, obvious in the original but lost in the standard translation, amplifies rhetorically through equivocation. In this way, the abstract category of the common (the familiar, conventional, or run-of-the-mill) reproduces the sense of its opposite, that category of no thing—and, not coincidentally, no species—like any other. Furthermore, Machaut's description of the strange bird doubles specimen with species, as the alerion incarnates a strange metaphysics of novelty. She is an unparalleled on two counts: both a unique specimen and a rare species of bird. Along the way, strangeness in its adjectival form converges on strangeness as an essential attribute, named here as a "condition." Thus, even as the repeated noun in this passage ("chose") is singular, the general effect redounds to an idea or categorical descriptor, translated by Gaudet and Hieatt by the plural. This is novelty as "estrangeté nompareille," incomparable strangeness. Most notably, the incomparable thing, the one-off, takes conceptual shape through acts of linguistic repetition.

Yet novelty, related to similarity as well as to strangeness, remains a complex condition in excess of either category. In the very next line, the narrator continues to explore its features:

Mais je l'appelle estrangeté,
Pour ce qu'elle genroit plaisance
De nouvel en ma congnoissance.
Car aucune chose nouvelle,
Ou cas qu'elle soit bonne et belle,

Et il avient qu'on en parole,
Il est certeins que la parole
En est moult volentiers oÿe
Des entendens, et conjoÿe. (ll. 1590–98)

[But strangeness is the term I use / because this state could certainly
/engender pleasure new to me. / For with anything that's new, / if it
be good and beautiful / and thus the subject of great praise, / most
surely what one has to say / about it will be gladly heard / and
welcomed by the listeners.]

Despite the claim of novelty as a "condition" just one line earlier, the meaning
and function of the "new" now shifts. Newness figures as a relational transaction capable of eliciting a wondrous response. Yet the precise distinction between the new and the strange seems a bit abstruse, and Gaudet and Hieatt's
modern English translation does not particularly help us here.

Attending more closely to the linguistic equivocations can, however.
While "de nouvel" would, particularly in this context, retain strong connotations of "the new," its most direct meaning in line 1592 would be "again," an
idiomatic usage that is also common in modern French. The narrator calls
these things "strange," rather than "new," to suggest that the pleasures associated with newness might nonetheless be familiar; that is, not utterly strange at
all. Or, better, the pleasures associated with newness remind the speaker of the
familiar pleasures that attend strangeness: "Mais je l'appelle estrangeté, / Pour
ce qu'elle genroit plaisance / De nouvel en ma congnoissance." The literal
translation then becomes, "But I call it strangeness / because it engenders
pleasure / again in my mind." As with the earlier relation between like and
unlike, the doubleness of "de nouvel" (both "again" and "new"), equivocates
between novelty and repetition, the one-off and the series: the new as singu-
larly strange recapitulates past pleasures of singular strangeness. As it has in the
plot of the poem as well: this doubled "de nouvel" recalls the earlier description of the wild sparrowhawk as "pris de nouvel" (l. 313).

The point seems to be that what the narrator calls "the strange condition"
known as novelty produces serial pleasures in the one-off, a familiar response
to uncommonness, one that has been experienced before, as, arguably, it will
be again. Novelty, as a condition and an idea, attends this central paradox: it
signifies that which is singular, the unique specimen; yet it can only exist as a
category (a species) once recognized as a something in excess of the utterly

unique specimen or singular thing, as part of a set containing more than a single example. The new, as species, occupies the space of this fundamental contradiction: an incomparable thing replicated, a rare experience, repeated.

Machaut's complex equivocation, however, also marks novelty as linguistically productive, and this is precisely what his passage will go on to suggest: any new thing, particularly a beautiful one, will be much talked about; news about novelties will be gladly heard. Novelty, the strange, but paradoxically repeatable, experience, increases the appreciation of things and creatures, enhancing the good and the beautiful.[45] The discursive singularity of the new repeats in a passage that accordingly emphasizes not only the paradoxical status of novelty, but the paradoxical status of repetition, too.[46] Repetition emerges both as the means by which we understand the force of novelty and as a way to extend novelty's attractions, an account of the new that is both phenomenological and aesthetic.

This analytical account of the new resonates in obvious ways with the ambitions of an innovative medieval poet. Drawing out the equivocal force of the newfangled via the power of signification, Machaut offers a view of novelty tied, that is, to a brand of copying still invested in uniqueness. And indeed, one might describe Machaut's own work with the bestiary tradition here in just such terms.[47] In its larger context, moreover, this paradoxical description converges on what Philip Fisher, writing about a much later period, calls, in the register of art, the "aesthetics of rare experiences."[48] Yet this is also a philosophically informed version of newness keyed to the medieval case, where novelty was rendered not in opposition to tradition, nor as opposed to the old. In considering novelty through a combination of poetic repetition and equivocation, Machaut seems to have anticipated a point well known today from the work of Gilles Deleuze: "repetition is the historical condition under which something new is produced."[49] Yet Deleuze's work arguably begs a question that Machaut takes up explicitly: it is not just that, but how, something is repeated. It is not only *repetition* that counts here: repetition remains entwined with the uncommon, the strange, the one-off.

In the poem before us, Machaut highlights the complexity of novelty in poetical as well as ethical terms; the new propels creativity as well as virtue. And just as the alerion is the perfect metaphor for rarity, she also occasions the narrator's ethical betterment. She is the priceless lady who elicits the falconer's best self; it is she who teaches him the limits of exchange as it pertains to value. When, at the end of the poem, the alerion returns to him, she grants the "astonished" narrator, now "wild with joy" (l. 4579), that delighted state he had been seeking all along. We eagerly await such a *rara avis* ourselves, on the lookout for unexpected experiences that might enhance our virtue; like the proverbial black swan, this rare bird propels our wildest dreams. Even as it lies beyond such possibilities, the alerion raises a hope for ethical perfection.

Machaut's rare bird renders novelty as itself a complex question that may redound to the ethical good. We should recall at this point that the *rara avis* to which Juvenal referred was also complexly keyed to ethics: his *rara avis* was the good wife. Such a rare figure has a darker, more obviously satiric, relation to impossibility than Machaut's legendary bird. The rarity of the good wife in the *Satires* is meant to indict Juvenal's larger culture, which should, presumably, give rise to many such creatures.[50] If Machaut seems to soften Juvenal's cynicism, he nonetheless shares something of the satirist's didactic impulse. The *Dit de l'alerion* regularly reflects on the virtues of labor in pursuit of valuable beloveds. Furthermore, Machaut's poem muses on questions of possession and loss, experimenting with various modes and means of acquisition. Should the falconer, having lost his sparrowhawk, simply buy another bird? Should he seek a new falcon from his fellow falconers, begging to be given one of theirs? Or should he placidly await their generosity? At the end of the poem, when his beloved alerion returns to him, she is revealed as beyond economies of exchange, barter, or even gift. She is her falconer's pearl of great price.[51] And such, as Leupin argues, redounds to the poem itself: Machaut's poem figures the symbolic object that "is not of the nature of property (l'avoir) nor even that of restitution," thus highlighting the collocation between incomparable bird and the work of the poet.[52] This is the novel work of art fundamentally in excess of the economies of exchange and beyond the logics of property.

In contrast to Machaut's use of novelty as that rarity located beyond economic calculation, Chaucer's consideration of newness and birds takes on novelty's role in just such dark economies. When the Middle English poet relocates the narrative of novelty's attraction to the mouth of an abandoned female raptor, he urges readers to attend to its cruelty. Chaucer's peregrine bemoans the logic of substitution by which a bird such as she can be so easily displaced, so willingly replaced, by someone or something new and altogether common. If Machaut's treatment of newness locates the new outside the "logics of property," Chaucer's tale of the lamenting peregrine self-consciously resituates "novelty" as a "general equivalent" in the relations of exchange prompted by courtly love: the peregrine laments the function of the newfangled as a currency against which all other libidinal objects are measured.[53]

This contrast with Machaut helps us to see that Chaucer's evocative phrase, "novelries of propre kynde," may deploy the Middle English word "kynde" in both of its senses. Crossing categories that are not obviously held together, "kynde" alludes both to the natural (kynde as kin, or nature) and the moral (kynde as generous or free-hearted). Such Middle English puns were not uncommon. "Exploring the *double-entendre* . . . of 'kyndenesse' must rank among the favorite verbal games" of late Middle English writers, claims Andrew Galloway.[54] The Middle English words "kynde / unkynde," as Galloway shows, were the vernacular words most frequently used to translate Latin *gratus* and *ingratus*; this prompted multiple puns, with texts exploiting the doubled meaning of "kynde" as early as the thirteenth century.[55] The lexical range of "kynde," in true deconstructive fashion, alludes to hierarchy, those natural places, as in Chaucer's *Boece*, that belong properly to birds, or lions, or saplings, as well as to what Galloway calls affinity: "By blending nature with reciprocation, Middle English 'kyndenesse' shifts religious and social bonds away from hierarchy and towards affinity, and the exploitation of these lexical possibilities may easily be aligned with the many distinctive late medieval forms of community or corporate identity in which reciprocation and close affinity or ideas of such affinity cohere."[56] In punning "kynde," Chaucer's peregrine deploys the word as pertaining to species as well as to ethics, and casts the economy of newness in harsh and ungenerous terms. The peregrine's critique of the newfangled, then, strikes at the heart of novelty's heartless nature.

In Chaucer's tale, the question of the new is equivocally rendered. Relations of generosity and affinity will shortly reemerge as equally productive for new things. It is not at all coincidental that, as we carry on in Part 2 of the *Squire's Tale*, the old, repetitive problems engendered by novel loves remain entirely productive for newfangled things. Even the peregrine who disdains love for the new cannot reject the new entirely: she requires new salves to heal her wounds.

> But Canacee hom bereth hire in hir lappe
> And softely in plasters gan hire wrappe,
> Ther as she with hire beek hadde hurt hirselve.
> Now kan nat Canacee but herbes delve
> Out of the ground, and make salves newe
> Of herbes preciouse and fine of hewe
> To heelen with this hauk. (5.635–41)

[But Canacee bore her home in her lap / And began to wrap her gently in bandages / where she had hurt herself with her beak. /

Now Canacee must dig for herbes / out of the ground, and make
new salves / from precious herbs of fine colors / to heal this hawk.]

Despite the sacrifice of luxury that the pursuit of the new has previously motivated, the new here registers as an ingenuity that is capable of refashioning
common things to healing ends. Base matter—roots dug out of the same dirt
as carries the common worm—offers up elevated treasures: precious herbs,
beautifully fine. This is, of course, a conventionally Bonaventuran example of
human artifice. Desire now multiplies and extends toward Canacee, whose
healing ministrations absorb her completely ("Fro day to nyght / she dooth
hire bisynesse and al hire might" [5. 641–42]). Even sumptuousness returns in
an elegant "mewe" that Canacee fashions as a sanctuary, adorned with blue
velvet and painted ornamentation, the mark of a generosity designed to heal,
protect, and console her newfound friend.[57]
    And if the peregrine's pain is produced by the other's captivation by nov-
elty (the tercelet's faithlessness), the other's captivation with new things (Canacee's enthusiasms with magic) also structures the very possibility that her
lamentable story will get either a hearing or a reparative response. Magic
makes possible a heretofore impossible intercourse. And insofar as Canacee's
excitement over her newfound little nothings impels her walk, readying her
ear for "every thyng / That any fowel may in his leden seyn" (5.434–35) and
that she will newly hear, the tale links the new to a creative ability to extend
oneself for another, to what Elaine Scarry calls the world-creating capacity of
the imagination, here specifically in the care of the suffering and injured. Here
we see, that is, a hint of the utopian hope that surrounds all new technologies
of communication. Human ears and lips, touched as if by magic, are rendered
more fully capable of hearing and responding to the sufferings of others, however "fremde," strange, they may be. Canacee can respond to the peregrine's
piteous cry because her senses are newly transfigured; she knows what remedy
to supply because her acquaintance with the natural world has been expanded
and enlivened.
    Of course, the tercelet's hope in newfangledness is utopian, too, particu-
larly insofar as the newfangled serves as a screen for those desires, like utopia,
impossible to fulfill. This is to say that this triangulation brings Canacee together with the tercelet through and across the body of the peregrine, thus
revealing the deeply, even madly, ambivalent nature of Chaucer's *ethical* relation to newness here: the absorption that motivates the smiling face of empa-
thy is the other side of novelty's lascivious grin. While these complications are

less obviously at stake in the tale's Part 1, there, too, we see the way desire and compulsion—rupture and repetition—might be twinned. If in Part 2 the living creature threatens death and deadliness, in Part 1 dead metal takes on the appearance of the living thing.

Something of Nothing

While productive of startling experiences, the little nothings of Chaucer's exotic romance would have been quite well known to any medieval audience. The magic ring, the flying horse, the speaking bird would not, that is, register as utterly "new"; they would be recognized as things that are valued for their strangeness. (Chaucer's mention of such things would, in other words, do precisely what Machaut's narrator described: conjure pleasures of the strange and new again in a reader's mind.) Cambyuskan's mechanical horse ranks high among Chaucer's fascinating objects, owing in part to its identity as such a recognizable and novel rarity. Chaucer's description of the horse partakes of "lyric substance," deploying analogy in the service of something in excess of matter.

In Part 1 of the tale, moreover, the horse seems to constitute something of a breakaway moment in the history of Cambyuskan's court:

> For it so heigh was, and so brood and long,
> So wel proporcioned for to been strong,
> Right as it were a steede of Lumbardye
> Therwith so horsly, and so quyk of ye,
> As it a gentil Poilleys courser were.
> For certes, fro his tayl unto his ere
> *Nature ne art ne koude him nat amende*
> *In no degree, as al the peple wende.*
> But everemoore hir mooste wonder was
> How that it koude gon, and was of bras. (5.191–200; my emphasis)

[For it was so high, and so broad and long / So well-proportioned to be strong, / exactly as [if] it were a Lombard steed. / So horsly, and so quick of eye, / as though it were a noble Apulian courser. / For certainly, from his tail to his ear / *Neither nature nor art could amend him* / *to no degree, as all the people knew.* / But always their greatest wonder was / how it could go, and yet be made of brass.]

Combining liveliness with mechanization, the horse apes nature ("so horsly . . . As it a gentil Poilleys courser were") even as it breaks natural bonds ("how that it koude gon, and was of bras"). Chaucer's neologism, "horsly," charmingly encodes the novel effect of the artifact come to life: the toy, as horsey as ever nature made, communicates a quickness of intelligence even while it stands mute before the court's gaze. As an artifact whose form can be amended neither by nature nor by artisanal skill, the horse outstrips medieval categories of those types of production available to humanity: repudiating the possibility of Nature or Art, the Squire excludes the two second-order creative powers that, according to medieval scholastics, follow after God's creative force. For all its mechanization, the gadget alludes to a power of creation beyond nature or the human. An extravagant gift from places unseen, this little nothing appears as if ex nihilo.

In describing the mechanical gadget as "quyk of ye," Chaucer emphasizes the doubleness of its "social life":[58] on the one hand, the descriptor refers to the court's visual consumption of the horse—its liveliness seems to them lifelike; on the other—as a phrase regularly used to signify vigor and vitality—it raises an impossible possibility, a metal horse with vibrant "health." The description joins stunning life with inert metal. An impossible mechanical display of the vital life force, the bent metal and mechanized gears encircle a liveliness that is essentially empty: there is nothing vital inside. Mechanics appear as sentience, and thus the automaton beckons with a vitality on which it can deliver only as illusion.

Or better, the horse's liveliness is analogical for a mechanized type of sentience: a subject in the invisible thrall of the death drive. From the point of view of Lacanian theory, this combination of living vitality and empty metal offers an example of what Rosalind Krauss calls the "optical unconscious," automaton as screen object, both concealing and revealing the subjectivization of the subject before the power of invisible forces, like the real or the unconscious. In his own discussions of automata, Lacan refers to Aristotle, where the term is normally translated as "chance"; he pairs it with *tuché*, or fate, a term that Lacan elsewhere glosses as "the encounter with the real." The automaton emerges as a figure harboring a specter of the Real, the mechanized features of the living thing under the deadening sway of compulsion:[59] life figured in dead metal.[60]

This is also, of course, dead metal turned to the semblance of life.[61] If we are offered here a paradoxical account of liveliness, we are also offered a similarly paradoxical account of materiality. And here we might extend further the view of materialism that is at stake in Chaucer's account of the epistemological force of the new. For if the horse of brass alludes, as a material object, to the power of human making, its description as "quik of ye" also extends a certain vitality to matter, the brass *gyn* inhabited by invisible energies always at the ready, poised for potential flight.

This brass marvel is artifact and aesthetic object, giving us an eye for form and image, for the visual splendor of the thing itself. As toys, automata frequently constitute our first aesthetic objects, as Tiffany notes. He cites Baudelaire: "The toy is the child's earliest initiation into art, or rather it is the first concrete example of art."[62] In this regard—in view of these links between artifact and art—we might recall that fables of "Virgil, the Necromancer," those stories of the magical, mechanical ingenuities that Virgil was purported to have made, flourished particularly in the late fourteenth century, and at the time of Chaucer's writing.[63] They rendered the poetic maker as both magician and as engineer. That is, if romance helped materially to produce gadgets, as Lightsey compellingly argues, it might itself be figured as a gadget encoding the very same ambiguities of meaning and purpose, with its own fine array of gadgets, bells, and whistles.

Scholars have long linked Cambyuskan's horse directly to the matter of poetry. Reading the classical sources to which Chaucer's poem alludes, Craig Berry describes the automaton as "an amazing piece of technology, and as a model of poetic inspiration which elides the difference between engineering and artistry," and "a model well-suited to a poet who served as Clerk of the Works and wrote *The Treatise on the Astrolabe.*"[64] Particularly as a paradoxical representation of the artifact as simultaneously living and dead, the horse is analogical to the poem itself: both the horse of brass and Chaucer's poetic rendition of him are simultaneously lively and inert; inhabited by vital energies yet mute before their audience. The poem serves as a screen for visible models rife with invisible things.

As in Part 2 of the tale, such specters of deadliness motivate newfangled poetry. But the mechanical horse also—here again the ambivalence—offers the utopian promise of absolute freedom, an ability to break through the physical limits of the natural world:

> This steede of bras, that esily and weel
> Kan in the space of o day natureel—
> This is to sayn, in foure and twenty houres—
> Wher-so yow lyst, in droghte or elles shoures,
> Beren youre body into every place

To which youre herte wilneth for to pace,
Withouten wem of yow, thurgh foul or fair;
Or, if yow lyst to fleen as hyein the air
As dooth an egle whan hym list to soore,
This same steede shal bere yow evere moore,
Withouten harm, til ye be ther yow leste,
Though that ye slepen on his bak or reste,
And turne ayeyn with writhing of a pyn. (5.115–27)

[This steed of brass that easily and well / Can, in the space of a
natural day / that is to say, in four and twenty hours / wherever you
desire, in drought or in rain / bear your body to every place / to
which your heart desires to go, / without harm to you, though it be
foul or fair; / even if you wish to fly as high in air / as an eagle does
when he desires to soar / this same steed shall bear you always /
without harm, until you are where you want to be / even if you
sleep or rest on his back / And turn back with the turning of his
pin.]

This description, spoken by the visiting knight who brings the gift to court,
simultaneously foregrounds safety and liminality: even a sleeping rider is safe,
as he flies between earth and sky, on the brink of danger and excitement,
breaking the bounds of time and space. The description certainly alludes to
the hyperexcitement, and transgressive power, of experimentation, the fantasy
of safely overcoming the impossible, breaking the physical limits of daily life
and of the natural body.

     As a *gyn*, the horse is of ambiguous character. As many have noted, the tale
emphasizes the energetic efforts of court sophisticates to sort through the meaning and workings of the impossible thing before them: "It was a fairye"; "They
murmureden as dooth a swarm of been, / And maden skiles after hir fantasies"
(5.201, 204–5). It is true, as many have argued, that Chaucer's Squire disdains the
enthusiasms of Cambyuskan's courtiers; their debate and "jangle," he implies,
shows a fuzzyheaded enchantment with magic, leading many to read the tale as
demystifying romance *miribilia* in favor of the rationality of science. Yet, whatever the dramatic features of Chaucer's Squire's attitude, the description of the
court's response emphasizes not the special stupidity of this particular group, but
the commonness of puzzlement before such subtle things: "As lewed peple de-
meth comunly / Of thynges that been maad moore subtilly / Than they kan in

hir lewednesse comprehende; / They demen gladly to the badder ende" (5.221–24). If we can read here the Squire's self-satisfied superiority, we can also read the courtiers' predicament in trying to recover from the fascination produced by this radically anomalous event, in trying to make sense of the (as yet) nonsensical, or to assimilate the radically new. And if the courtiers are ignorant of the automaton's mechanics, they are certainly not unlearned. The text repeatedly emphasizes the array of authorities referenced in their debate from the widest range of the Liberal Arts: poetry (stories of Pegasus and of the Trojan horse), philosophy (Aristotle), and the science of optics and perspective (Alhacen and Witello), all authorities known in the West. Taken as a whole, the scene repeatedly draws attention not to the insufficiency of this particular audience of knowers but to an experience of epistemological poverty as such, of the difficulty, altogether common, of knowing what to make of something novel or rare. Chaucer's mechanical horse redeploys Machaut's rare flying thing in a mechanism that prompts such epistemological problems.

Criticism, too, evinces its share in such problems. Many critics have seemed to embrace this flying horse as an imaginative enigma, despite evidence to the contrary. In a fascinating but largely overlooked essay, Marijane Osborne argues that the Squire's steed of brass is, in fact, an astrolabe, one equipped with a governing horse's head, operated by the turning of a pin, at its top.[65] Osborne persuasively links the description here to identical phrases in Chaucer's *A Treatise on the Astrolabe*, patiently explaining the precise workings of the mechanical contraption.[66] The fact that even recent analyses of the tale's manmade marvels continue to overlook the horse as astrolabe suggests the critical afterlife of the very epistemological difficulty that troubles Cambyuskan's courtiers. From the larger vantage of Chaucer's corpus, then, even this new, unassimilated, uncategorizable thing is not so new after all; a literal repetition, the Squire's "steed of brass" is a well-wrought urn that Chaucer has wrought before. As a technological artifact with cosmological implications—a "little nothing" prompted by very big ideas—the astrolabe seems altogether appropriate in this context.

The problem of the court's "lewedness" alludes, I argue, not to the failings of a particularly unsubtle, or easily fascinated, audience before the transformative power of novelty—even if that is the Squire's own unsubtle conclusion—but to the arresting power of fascination, and to the problem, both epistemological and ethical, of what to make of, and what to do with, new things. Will an enchantment with novelties help us to reimagine our relation to the world and one another—will we be, like Machaut's falconer, all the better for it? Or will we stand stock still, dazzled, updated, but stupefied?

Confronted with the incredible, the courtiers bring all of their best learning to the problem. Certainly their energetic response—like Canacee's—shows a renewed engagement in the material details of the world before them. That said, their activity has different effects from hers. Despite precise instruction as to how one might use it, the horse is taken to Cambyuskan's tower, stockpiled "among his jueles leeve and deere" (l.341), while this king, who is earlier described as "hardy" and "wys" as well as "riche" (l.19), "repeireth to his revel as biforn" (l.339). Despite the clearly disruptive nature of the event, nothing much changes at Cambyuskan's court. Contrasting Cambyuskan's courtiers with Canacee, Chaucer opens a central question concerning the ethics of new things. Later thinkers will attempt to regularize the question by calculating the particular kinds of wonder focused on the new.

Calculating Wonder

In linking wonder with novelty, Chaucer anticipates an association best known by way of the writings of René Descartes. Descartes's influential narrative of the new offered early modern thinkers a means to calculate the appropriate limits, the power, and the excesses of wonder in the new. While not the first to treat wonder as a passion, Descartes specifically regards it as a response to an encounter with novelty:

> Wonder: When our first encounter with some object surprises us
> and we find it novel, or very different from what we formerly knew
> or from what we supposed it ought to be, this causes us to wonder
> and to be astonished at it. Since all this may happen before we
> know whether or not the object is beneficial to us, I regard wonder
> as the first of all the passions. It has no opposite, for, if the object
> before us has no characteristics that surprise us, we are not moved
> by it at all and we consider it without passion.[67]

For Descartes, novelty both depends on the materiality of the object and exceeds it. We know something is novel when, exceeding either our expectations or our experience, it generates wonder, even astonishment, in us.

In the long tradition that Descartes inherited, the cognitive passions produced by novelties converge on other potentially excessive, potentially dangerous intellective prompts "such as horror and curiosity."[68] Building on a premodern tradition that managed the excesses of wonderment by separating it into types good and bad, Descartes also distinguishes "serviceable 'wonder' (*admiration*)," from its apparently stupefying twin, "astonishment" (*estonnement*)." As Daston and Park note, Descartes approaches wonder in the new by "acknowledging its utility as lure, but warning against its excesses."[69] Wonder can drive toward stupefaction, Descartes cautions; this is, in fact, that brand of wonder most associated with novelty. Yet, and unlike Chaucer, Descartes judges its diverse "cognitive effects" to be "diametrically opposed,"[70] novelty's power particularly devastating insofar as wonder in the new motivates the suspension of judgment entirely. Blindness and stupefaction close down thinking, stopping us in our cognitive tracks. In a move consonant with the medieval tradition on *vitium curiositatis*, Descartes associates this negative type of wonder with "blind curiosity": "the malady of those who are blindly curious, that is to say, who seek out rarities only to wonder at them, and not to understand them."[71]

Chaucer's Squire, critiquing the "lewedness" of Cambyuskan's courtiers, deploys a version of the distinction later offered in Descartes's account of wonder, whereby the "serviceable" wonder of admiration is differentiated from the "stupefied" wonder of astonishment. Yet the Squire's courtiers are not simply "blindly curious"; they, too, are trying to understand the horse of brass, the rarity placed before them. Rather than offer a brand of wonder safe from the vicissitudes of novelty's attraction, Chaucer himself figures wonder in the new by way of an ethical ambivalence that remains here unsettled. The new, as in Machaut, combines repetition with rarity, oscillating between familiar patterns and startling ruptures. Chaucer's tale renders "newefangelnesse" as inherently paradoxical, a feature of creative production that can produce breakaway moments, even as it partakes of older, repetitive forms. In his indebtedness to Machaut's reflections on the paradox of newness, and in his treatment of diverse newfangled gifts, abilities, loves, or healing salves, Chaucer demonstrates instead that wonder in the new, precisely as something both unique and repeatable, can incline in at least two directions, sometimes simultaneously: it can create the conditions of possibility for new realizations, new relations, new poems, or new inventions (Deleuze's "bare repetition"); or it can converge on the same-old, same-old, inspiring the consolidating satisfactions of mere accumulation, of a deadening kind of hoarding.[72]

Taken as a whole, Chaucer's account of the ethics of the new offers no easy resolution or consolation. Both Canacee's remarkable discovery of a talking bird and the court's equally remarkable experience of a flying mechanical horse rely on the wondrous powers of the newfangled; both suggest the possibility for a fundamental restructuring of perception and expectation offered by an encounter with something new. Yet, when the poem plays Cambyuskan's response to the flying horse against Canacee's actions, it suggests that novelty in itself proves insufficient to guarantee transformations of any kind. As far as we can tell, Cambyuskan trades the stupefaction of the new thing for the stupefaction of drunkenness. Canacee and the peregrine, in contrast, engage their initial scene of fascination by crafting lines of poetry, thinking, planning, even digging in the dirt so as to craft new things used to compassionate ends. Yet even the peregrine's future is left open: will the magical bird in her sumptuous enclosure become one of Canacee's collectibles, on a par with Cambyuskan's tower filled with jewels and gadgets? The tale's incompletion offers no answer.

In avoiding an answer, the *Squire's Tale* also implies that the ethics of the new demands, to some degree, a willingness to entertain, rather than immediately to resolve, this double-face of newness. This is a demand that authorizes pleasure in the wonder of the world even as it refuses to give up thinking about them, committed to repeated consideration of the problem of the various kinds of relationships—compassionate or consumptive—that such pleasures might produce. The technological know-how with which the tale is fascinated depends on an attachment to a creative rationality from which enchanted desire can never entirely divorce itself. In its elaboration of such an ambivalent view of novelty, romance verses can offer a kind of double helix entwining old with new, an engine driven by and driving the desire to feel afresh, to begin again.

Insisting on this doubleness, Chaucer invites us to consider the new as problem and opportunity both, drawing us into an ethical uncertainty that he refuses to settle. This ambivalent account of novelty refuses to wholly celebrate wonder in new objects as capable of curing our ills, or to wholly disdain the new as one more wondrous return of the repressed. It is, in other words, an ambivalence that carries its own ethical charge. Or to put this another way, the account of the new offered by the *Squire's Tale* reminds us that the fascination with body and matter that motivates conquest or consumption can never entirely be divorced from that version of delight that marks the beginning of human invention, and inhabits our attachments to one another.

In our own day, Nicholas Taleb has revived the figure of the Black Swan, Juvenal's image of the *rara avis,* as a metaphor for a capricious thing or unpredictable event with a massive impact. If such occurrences are, he argues, regular in human history, they are often granted a "retrospective predictability."[73] Narratives attempt to make sense of such random events, recasting things unexpected in narratives of value: looking back, the unlooked-for event now makes sense. In retrospect, we might even have seen it coming.

In the medieval case, as we have seen, the new figured less as a narrative solution to the problem of the unexpected, than as the term for an ambivalent, and equivocal, ethical problem all its own. It was not the opposite of repetition, or copying, but something emerging in relation to both. Chaucer and Machaut suggest the cultural power of textual repetition for the creation of new verses, figures, or poetic modes, as well as for an understanding of the new as such. When they deploy tradition and repetition in fresh and lively ways, these two poets do more than simply fail to celebrate the new as a radical advance, or aesthetic rupture. They do more than simply cast the new as a danger to be avoided. Read together, these two poets offer an account of fiction writing that takes the full ethical measure of the powers as well as the pains wrought by economies of the newfangled.

Such economies were equally at stake in the ethical discourse surrounding *curiositas*. Assessing the limits of curiosity—as it pertains to proprietary knowledge and claims to the things of this world—takes center stage in that medieval discourse most directly engaged with distinguishing those necessary pursuits from those judged to be superfluous. Sustained attention to these concerns marks the final section of this study.

PART III

Curiositas

Chapter 5

Suspect Economies

Traditional accounts of technological innovation privilege productive economies, often in explicit contrast to markets for luxury items like those recounted
in the *Squire's Tale*. Weberian sociology generally reserves technological advance for those things associated with production, not leisure, for usable, not
"frivolous," items.[1] Histories of medieval technology have accordingly stressed
the innovative power of flying buttresses, windmills, or cannons, and until
quite recently ignored the drôleries associated with medieval romance, the
automata or mechanical gadgets known from accounts of the garden at Hesdin, or the flying horses described in verse. Such luxuries, like the delicate ce-
ramic glazes or Ming vases fashioned by Asian artists, have seemed trivial or
superfluous and implicitly opposed to more purposeful technological
artifacts.

It is on just such grounds that the familiar economies of newness hierar-
chize value: innovations serve necessary and productive ends in contrast to
mere novelties, the latter either trivially worthless or decadent luxuries we can
ill afford. Medieval romances counter such instrumentalist histories, demonstrating something that strictly utilitarian accounts of newness miss: that the
exceptional, the set apart, the luxurious, the new-as-rare open questions not
only about the nature of productivity itself, but also about those suspect economies that oppose the necessary and the superfluous.[2]

I have argued throughout this book that medieval thinkers and writers
considered the category of the new in a more nuanced way than we have ap-
preciated. The oscillation of tradition and innovation marks literature as an
engine for both artistic and technological productivity.[3] In the genre of romance, old stories regularly got new ornaments: tales of emperors like Alexander or Charlemagne, stories of famous lovers like Floire and Blancheflor or

Lancelot are retold, in verses newly replete with ingenious contrivances, with statues that move, figures of knights or ladies made out of copper or gold, mechanical marvels that delight and entertain. Much of the cultural power of romance attends this kind of whimsical, idiosyncratic output, best understood "by recourse to study of the cultural and economic function of the crafts fairs, frivolous objects, crackpot inventions, pretty little nothings, clever contrivances, and the like, that were produced by, and circulated through, all ranks of medieval society."[4]

Through such creative acts "the obsolete takes on a new luminosity,"[5] to borrow the words of Alexandre Leupin. Leupin's remark defamiliarizes a medieval artistic culture of copying by suggestively recasting what has been called a "dichotomy" of old and new,[6] or an artist's "safe cycle of duplication and secondariness,"[7] as an act of glorious, even avant garde, illumination. The new of much medieval poetry marks its glamor with this kind of blaze: a resplendent re-creation of worlds dreamt before, now reworked to even higher polish. The process upends old and new, then and now, and to stunning anachronistic effect.[8] Chaucer's luminous description of Criseyde in widow's weeds, from Book I of his *Troilus and Criseyde*, may get the details of obsolete Trojan costumes exactly wrong,[9] but it does so to state-of-the-art aesthetic and poetic effect. Classical figures are regularly altered, which is to say updated, in medieval narrative, as when Aeneas casts a high chivalric shadow, or Theseus gains compassion after the manner of a late medieval prince. Once read as signs of a poetic consciousness that didn't, or worse, couldn't, register historical difference at all, such poetic gestures are now more readily acknowledged for the ways that they imaginatively refresh otherwise outmoded details with the fashion and power of the moment. This is a brand of newness as now-ness: the old becomes resplendently hip, freshly translated and elegantly adorned.

In updating earlier works, medieval poets were self-consciously dedicated to the obsolete, but not as part of some salvage operation.[10] This technique, argues Leupin, was itself radically new, rendered influentially in Geoffrey of Vinsauf's *Poetria Nova*, the handbook for medieval poets beholden to the old rhetorical masters Cicero and Horace. The *Poetria Nova* says precious little about invention but a great deal about amplification, repetition, or the workings of metaphorical elaboration, stressing the need to avoid rhetorical excesses and identifying excessive alliteration, or overly long passages, as stylistic faults. Skillfully reworking older figures or forms could prove doubly illuminating: poets could make worn metaphors newly radiant (that is, radiant once again) while bathing in a master's reflected glory. A layered "metaphorical use of words," to quote Vinsauf, "serves you like a mirror, for you can see yourself in it."[11]

Sidestepping oppositions of old versus new, medieval literary practice models this sort of radiant poetic sustainability, repurposing words, tropes, or story-traditions, so as to cultivate, as Chaucer puts it, new corn from old fields. Instead of tracking the new with single-minded purpose, the moderating pens of poets came at the new from this oblique angle, even as they also regularly described a massive array of innovative things. Even recycled traditions could be rather outrageously adorned. And medieval romances explicitly interested in this kind of newness regularly describe households filled with surplus goods. The poems examined in Chapters 3 and 4 are committed to the ethical questions raised by just such overabundance, though not perhaps precisely in the ways we might expect. Ethical matters emerge in each; yet neither romance marshals a simple critique of waste, obsolescence, or unproductivity.[12] Floris's parents, from the story of Floris and Blancheflor, deploy marvelously excessive new objects as part of their ingenious stratagems to keep Floris from ever leaving home, although their deceits are hardly admirable. At Cambyuskan's court, as rendered in Chaucer's *Squire's Tale,* the acquisition of marvelous objects proves both enabling and disabling, offering occasion for a larger reflection on the open ethics of commodity as well as kindness.

Oscillating patterns of moderation and surplus engage what Smith calls the "arts of possession," and by the late Middle Ages, questions of possession or proprietary calculations emerge with special force, as we saw in the texts examined in Chapter 4. Machaut's *Dit de l'Alerion* (a source, I argued, for Chaucer's musings on the newfangled) took up questions of possession explicitly by way of values beyond measure: the rarity of the narrator's legendary alerion became an occasion to ponder priceless things, including poetry itself. Measureless value seems less evident in Chaucer's *Squire's Tale,* where the newfangled emerges as the general equivalent in a troubling economy of exchange. In Chaucer's text love for the new displaced the old when the beloved peregrine falcon, a former lover now rejected and discarded, is heartlessly thrown over for the newfound attractions of a common bird.

We recognize even more today the implications of possession for debates over the proper uses of new things or new ideas. Proprietary rights, a legal category now used most regularly with regard to copyright, patents, or new inventions, accrue to artists or inventors insofar as they legally own their own ingenious novelties. This chapter considers the prehistory of such economies of the proprietary in the age before legal categories of intellectual property were fully established. Perhaps surprisingly, certain proprietary questions emerge as moral ones in the Middle Ages, illuminated by attending to the larger discourse of curiosity. We are ultimately headed toward an account of the ethical abuses of specialized knowledge in the "elvish" and experimental science committed to transforming matter: alchemy. Chaucer's *Canon's Yeoman's Tale* (*CYT*) interrogates calculations of value and profit for alchemists and poets both. In that tale, an apprentice alchemist recounts the devious nature of those greedy alchemical schemers using the products of their curiosity for personal profit. Yet I begin with a brief account of the location of moral concerns over such potential misuse of knowledge by way of the discourse of *vitium curiositatis*, the vice of curiosity.

Calculating Curiosity

Consider the following from Isidore of Seville: "Take calculation from the world and all is enveloped in dark ignorance, nor can he who does not know the way to reckon be distinguished from the rest of the animals."[13] Philosophical debates of the twelfth century—the dialectics of scholasticism in the quarrel over universals, for instance—suggest a deep propensity for questioning and reckoning, and much of this was brought to bear on the medieval understanding of curiosity, as associated with the capital vices. While medieval curiosity is best known as the category through which theoreticians placed limits on speculative thought, the discourse on curiosity was neither identical to nor subsumed by such features. Even in the work of Augustine, whose association of *curiositas* with pride would be important to later monastic descriptions of the vice, the vice of curiosity did not amount to an a priori rejection of knowledge or science as such. Far from simply disdaining or dismissing *curiositas*, medieval moralists and intellectuals thought and rethought the concept, insistently reworking, categorizing, recategorizing, and nuancing the topic.[14]

The etymological links between curiosity and *cura*, or care, grounded this wide-ranging debate, in which the vice of curiosity emerged as a misplaced kind of caring. "Both the zeal with which knowledge is sought and the areas being investigated to achieve knowledge lie within the purview of curiosity."[15] Cautions were raised against taking too great an interest in relatively inconsequential matters, or devoting too much time to unworthy or self-serving pursuits. Whether as a quantitative question of excessive interest or a qualitative question concerning a fascination with trivial things, the problem involved an error in relations of care. Medieval thinkers marked excesses by way of gradations of curiosity, assessing the difference between *bona, mala,* or *media curiositas.*[16] We might note in passing that debates of this kind can be found in a range of post-medieval texts as well. They continue today in the ethical debates over animal research, or space exploration. And, in the early modern period, they turn up in a tradition usually understood to emblematize "modern" intellectual freedom at its most expansive, the story of Faustus. As late as the late sixteenth century, Faust figures explicitly as one who perverts "his gifts . . . through his long study of philosophy and theology," a study that "led him to *curiositas.*"[17]

Calculating curiosity helped Aquinas (following Augustine, the first great "theoretician of curiosity"[18]) distinguish *curiositas* from *studiositas,* the latter a temperate attention to matters of consequence. In Aquinas's context, the question emerged out of a need to legitimate, in the wake of Aristotle's *Physics* and worries about it, the pursuit of certain kinds of secular knowledge. Yet we can see the same phenomenon in a more avowedly moral text, such as Peter of Limoges's[19] *The Moral Treatise on the Eye,* which emphasizes the moral features and limits of curiosity even as it reports on the findings of a rigorous research program concerning perspective and ocular function. Thus, the moral problem of curiosity rested in part in a potential for excess, a potential shared by other kinds of appetites. In the monastic tradition, curiosity could be critiqued as an excessive kind of caring, manifest through its association with various sins, pride, lust, greed, or gluttony.[20]

Given the diversity and range of examples, calculating curiosity seems to have been no easy task. By the late medieval era, precise methods of calculation preoccupied scholastic thinkers, and were important to economies both material and transcendent. Joel Kaye links scholastic moral preoccupations, as with charity or grace, to parallel developments in economic thought and practice. Questions of profit in all its meanings take center stage: "From the middle of the thirteenth century, philosophers weighed the difficult question of the legitimacy of mercantile profit" alongside quantitative treatment of moral categories like grace.[21] C. D. Blanton argues that shifts surrounding speculative thought in the wake of the nominalists depend quite literally on a development of new assessments of quantity, on differing "currencies."[22] The Oxford "calculators"—a group of fourteenth-century thinkers that included Thomas Bradwardine—approached philosophical questions from a mathematical perspective. Many of its key thinkers were administrators or bureaucrats whose "secular" involvements and institutional power urged an interest in calculation that would influence their intellectual work. Across Europe, developments in wage labor, double-entry accounting, and debt-structuring informed, as Kaye has shown, the late-medieval scholastic preoccupation with taking the measure of things spiritual (like grace) and secular (like profit from usury): ethical questions required increasingly quantitative answers.

The turn to quantitative methods meant an increase in tools for measuring excess, and built upon longstanding critiques of excessive desire and appetites. Medieval accounts of newness, as we have seen, regularly converged on worries about the frailties of human intellection or the human senses, and in some contexts accusations of the sin of curiosity could function as attempts to discredit scholars at the medieval university, alchemists included.[23] Proprietary uses of knowledge came in for full-throated critique when some moralists linked curiosity to the sin of avarice, accusing university professors of wanting to make money from their own knowledge. This critique emerges in monastic contexts as early as the twelfth century, and the point is explicitly cited by influential moralists like fourteenth-century Dominican John Bromyard, whose monumental *Summa Predicantium* would be mined as a source for sermons and cited well into the seventeenth century. Bromyard mentions the scholar "unwilling to share his own knowledge"[24] freely as an case of avarice.

Chaucer's *Canon's Yeoman's Tale* engages these issues in its account of the greed of alchemists. Alchemical work had its own moral problems quite apart from exploitative uses, and it could be associated with pride, greed, or gluttony on other grounds as well. By the fourteenth century, and in the late Middle English period, the equivocal power of alchemy reemerges in imaginative texts where the person of the alchemist converges on the figure of the elf. "Elvishness" hearkens, as we shall see, toward speculative fiction as well as technical transformation. Its appellation—in Chaucer's *CYT* but not only there—as an "Elvish" discipline suggests these limits. Taken together, this discourse can help us to reconsider why alchemy continues to occupy a pressure point in the history of legitimate scientific inquiry as a utopian pursuit: one rich with possibility if also fraught with ethical concerns.

As experimental thinkers, alchemists were liable for critique particularly insofar as their efforts seemed self-serving. The possibilities for fraudulent activity, the potential for overblown, counterfeit claims, haunted the figure of the alchemist well into the early modern period. Yet alchemy was not universally understood as a fraudulent, or even a "superfluous," science. Like most cutting-edge theorists, alchemists had broad and important ambitions, setting their sights on future improvements. Most of the various types of

alchemy—theoretical, practical, medicinal, or metallic—harbored, as Sheila
Delany has pointed out, a significant utopian impulse.[25] Roger Bacon's interest
in alchemy, for example, was directed at the prolongation of human life, as he
would put it, the "cure of old age." Aiming for the transmutation of common
substances into distinctly new matter of greater value, alchemists sometimes
claimed—against or despite the careful scholastic definitions circumscribing
human creativity—the possibility of producing new metaphysical things; yet
they would more conventionally cast their claims as aimed at the "perfection"
of nature through art.

Disentangling medieval alchemy from a longstanding erroneous identifi-
cation with "the occult sciences," William Newman reminds us that it was a
legitimate, if controversial, area of elite intellectual inquiry in the West from
the twelfth century onward. Alchemists strove to perfect nature either by rearranging, accelerating, or slowing nature's processes; in this project they engaged debates on art and nature inherited from classical accounts of mimesis.
Bonaventure's trifold theory of fabrication, creation ex nihilo, *ens in potentia*,
and *ens completum*, considered in the first part of this study, can, in fact, be
read as a *response* to such developments, an attempt to answer problems that
theories of the transmutation of species raised to Aristotelian notions of substantial form. It was in this larger context, moreover, that the discourse of
necromancy grew up around alchemy. Alchemical science and magic were
linked, as Newman compellingly shows, because the metaphysical questions
raised by alchemy were limit cases for human power over matter and nature:
"the theologians of the thirteenth century initiated a tradition of discussing
alchemy in the context of demonic power," he writes, "not because alchemy
was a form of magic, but because it represented the apex of the arts in its relation to nature."[26] As "the ultimate assertion of human power in the natural
world," alchemy would, by the thirteenth century, serve as "the benchmark
against which other arts . . . must be measured."[27] The alchemist's claims
pushed the perfection of nature to its outer limits, mining the edges of the
possible, endeavoring to harness the troubling vitality of matter for ennobling
purposes.[28]

Ennobled or not, the vitality of matter also posed ethical problems. It
was not regularly clear that the material strivings of alchemists were focused
on things of value. Recent analyses of medieval object-love stress the power,
vitality—and moral danger—of premodern accounts of matter, a notion inherited from Byzantine iconoclasts and Gnostic devotees.[29] Alchemy was implicated in these debates both because it represented matter as particularly

vital, and because alchemy had persistent links to Gnostic traditions emphasizing secret knowledge. While we should be wary of histories that cast medieval alchemy as a brand of esoteric religion (much of this is a nineteenth-century
invention),[30] scholars have yet to work out the precise degree to which particular alchemical practices or theories were indeed influenced, as some treatises
claimed, by Greek and Egyptian wisdom traditions. Christian Gnosticism—in
particular the brand inaugurated by Marcion—would of course reemerge in
the association of matter with evil deployed against the so-called Cathars,
also in the early thirteenth century.[31] As this brief overview suggests, the controversies associated with alchemy were as complex and as acrimonious as
today's debates over our genetically engineered food supply or stem cell
research.[32]

Yet even as a controversial endeavor alchemy was not understood as excessive simply on the grounds of the powerful claims of its "science." As in the
tradition associated with curiosity, critiques of alchemy would calculate particular features of the endeavor deemed to be fundamentally excessive in either
object or method. Chaucer does not directly associate alchemy with the discourse of curiosity and, given his approving mention of "curiosity" in his *Treatise on the Astrolabe*, it is unlikely that he would critique alchemists for an
interest in natural philosophy, however controversial.[33] Nonetheless, Chaucer's account of the fraudulent alchemist clarifies some of the stakes in the
moralists' concerns over excessive curiosity as it pertains to alchemical practice. Elsewhere in his corpus, Chaucer makes clear links between gluttony and
curiosity when, in the Parson's moral treatise, "curiositee" (or fastidiousness)
about food is marked as one of the types of gluttony (I.829); and earlier in the
Parson's treatise, the speaker critiques the greed of the merchant who idolizes
every coin in his coffer (l.749), subsequently evoking the tradition whereby
the crime of simony (the buying and selling of spiritual things) is named for
Simon Magus (l.782). In the Middle Ages, Simon, whose confrontation with
St. Peter is recounted in the book of Acts, was an equivocal figure, understood
variously as fraudulent necromancer, or wise man.

In Chaucer's *Canon's Yeoman's Tale*, alchemy is both a "cursed craft" and,
more ambiguously, an "elvysshe" one. But the tale takes clearest aim at the
alchemist by way of the economies of his work. Along the way, it alludes to a
problem that may well have bothered Roger Bacon, consciously or not: that
our interest and absorption in the agency of matter may fuel a materialism
ready to capture our love of new things for a greedy, proprietary worldliness.
Chaucer's fourteenth-century text will emphasize the profit motive by way of

craft alchemy, an endeavor pursued not only by elite university intellectuals, but also by middling canons and their somewhat vulgar yeomen.

Elvish Innovation

For out of olde feldes, as men seyth,
Cometh al this newe corn from yer to yere,
And out of olde bokes, in good feyth,
Cometh al this newe science that men lere.
   (*Parliament of Fowls*, ll. 22–25) [34]

[For out of old fields, as men say / Come all this new corn from year to year, / And out of old books, in good faith, / Comes all this new science that men learn.]

Geoffrey Chaucer shared Roger Bacon's interest in old books and new science. Like Bacon he linked *auctoritas* to *textus*, as "old" fields sprout "new" shoots. And like Bacon, Chaucer was a polymath of astonishing range, whose work with cutting-edge natural philosophy—not only in the *CYT*, but also via accounts of matter and perspective found in the *House of Fame*, or his *Treatise on the Astrolabe*—placed him in elite company. At the time of Chaucer's interest in alchemy, its value remained unsettled, its future inconclusive. It was unclear whether alchemy would eventually deliver on its utopian promise; yet neither was alchemy understood to be an utterly failed pursuit. Reputable scholars, up to and including Isaac Newton, would pursue it as a legitimate scientific practice.

In the *Canon's Yeoman's Tale*, Chaucer turns to the alchemical laboratory as a location from which to assess the promises and problems of the "corn" of this new field. But he also, and this is a crucial point, takes up questionable uses of the discipline in the context of craft knowledge and the profit motive. As many critics have pointed out, the multilayered narrative draws attention to the craft not only of alchemy but also of story-telling, a homology important to critical accounts of the tale. A summary will be helpful here: with the Canterbury pilgrims a mere five miles from their destination, a Canon-alchemist and his Yeoman-assistant surprisingly overtake the group, eagerly asking to join them. The loquacious Yeoman identifies himself and his Canon as alchemists who profit financially through alchemical "illusioun."

Overhearing his Yeoman's too-revealing confession, the Canon orders his assistant to pipe down, insisting that he keep their secrets. When the Yeoman
refuses to be silent, the disturbed Canon flees the company entirely, riding off
as suddenly as he appeared. Newly released from any obligation to his master,
the Yeoman now rather gleefully tells all, describing his difficult years as apprentice to the "slidynge science." His harsh account of his years of labor—
managing laboratory experiments or cleaning up after explosions—emphasizes
both backbreaking physical activity and a solid command of alchemical technique. Turning next to tell his fictional tale, the Canon's Yeoman recounts the
story of a "false Canon" (not, he is quick to insist, his former master) who,
through the use of tricks and schemes, swindles a priest out of his money. It is
easy, the Canon's Yeoman concludes, for men to take the gold they have and
transform it—into nothing. Alchemy marks just such a suspect economy.

Assessing the central point of the *CYT* has been difficult in part because
the text offers such a wide array of easy targets. Critics, that is, have disagreed
as to where, precisely, Chaucer wishes to take his aim: at the excessive and
fraudulent uses of knowledge, or at the harsh conditions of the Yeoman's wage
labor in the context of emerging mercantile capitalism? At the excesses of a
greedy alchemist who cares too much about his own financial profit, or at the
impassioned resentment of his blowhard assistant? Does a critique of mis-
guided knowledge here refer to exploitative laboratory practice, or to the keeping of (false) secrets as a means to trick the unwary? Does the tale critique the
"blind materialism" of science (Muscatine), or alchemy as itself "regressive"
(Green)? Or, does it offer a view of a "progressive" impulse through its account
of the "modernizing" effects of ideological demystification (Patterson)?[35] Does
the Yeoman's alienated labor anticipate Marx's collocation of alchemy with
capital (Knapp, Harwood)?[36] Or does the Yeoman's version of alchemical
fraud amount to an "idealized nostalgia" for yesteryear, longing for a purer
time when alchemists were learned philosophers worthy of respect (Sisk)?[37]
Literary critics persistently frame the point in polarized terms—regressive vs.
progressive; fraudulent vs. truthful; magic vs. science; intellectual vs. social;
historical decline vs. modern progress.[38] The equivocations associated with the
practice of alchemy or the figure of the alchemist have not, that is, registered
in readings of the tale.

Emphasizing such polarized terms, the reception of the tale duplicates
rather than analyzes medieval ambivalence about alchemical novelties. And
yet whatever the polarized terms employed, critics also consistently emphasize
Chaucer's inventiveness in crafting this tale, for which there is no surviving

source or analogue. As far as we can tell, the tale originates with Chaucer, although, as Carolyn Collette reminds us, it shows debts to the complex "sociolect" on alchemy that was available to him.[39] If critics have been divided on the politics of the *Canon's Yeoman's Tale*, that is, they have repeatedly returned to the ways that this most urgent and dramatic interruption in the narrative trajectory of the Canterbury project alludes to an innovative future. In such a context, Chaucer's authorial innovations appear forcefully against a backdrop of the apparently empty promises of alchemy itself. Such readings gain a purchase on Chaucer's innovations by relying on longstanding accounts of the "backward" nature of a so-called "occult" science.

I wish instead to read the tale as an equivocal treatment of the novel promises of alchemy, with particular resonance for the innovations of poetic fictions. Reapproaching the *CYT* with a broadened view of the tale's exploration of novelty and innovative transformations helps us to see Chaucer as a poet both absorbed with detailed knowledge about the theory and practice of alchemical science, yet also concerned with developments in the use of that knowledge, and perhaps unconvinced that alchemy's utopian future is unambiguous. Chaucer's *CYT*, I argue, associates the poet (and fabulist) with the alchemist so as to suggest the poet's superiority over the alchemist as artisan-craftsman on moral as well as epistemological grounds. Questions of language are at issue throughout Chaucer's tale.[40] This is unsurprising, since alchemy shared its regular practices of double-speak, cryptic uses of language, puzzling charms, tricks, or wordplay with poetry. Yet the tale urges us to look toward alchemists, not poets, as those profiting unjustly from a tricky use of language.

And yet, the tale emerges early on as itself something of a trick played on Chaucer's own Canterbury pilgrims. Certainly from its start, the *CYT* performs the surprising emergence of something "new." The dramatic advent of the Canon and his Yeoman interrupts the community of pilgrims on their journey, seeking to join the Canterbury group. They represent, in other words, a strikingly new occurrence for the stable, if contentious, band. Arriving suddenly, the two emerge out of nowhere and nothing—in the terms of the Canterbury project, they are pilgrims ex nihilo. Such poetic alchemy (numerous critics have argued the links between poet and alchemist[41]) toys experimentally with novel effects: What will a new element produce among the already highly reactive mixture of Canterbury folk?

Their arrival ex nihilo seems to involve arduous labor: the Canon and his horse work up quite a sweat. It is also enormous fun, and their profuse sweating "joye for to see" (l. 579). From the vantage of philosophical accounts of creativity, the moment may register Chaucer's joke on first-order, divine, creation as ex nihilo, out of nothing: the eruption of something so utterly new causes extraordinary exertion both in the narrative and presumably outside of it. Creation ex nihilo makes sweaty work for horses, canons, or poets. In narrative terms, moreover, this is a literal "multiplication" of pilgrims. "Multiplication" is the Middle English term for alchemical transformation, itself pregnant (to use another loaded word) with multiple meanings. An idiosyncratic and original poetic computation leavens the band of pilgrims: add two potential pilgrims; subtract one, a little prodding from the Host—et voilà, a newly original tale. Immediately, Chaucer links such multiplication to problems of literary interpretation: Where did these two come from and why? Who are they? Why are they riding so hard? And, eventually: Is the Canon who turns tail and runs the same "false Canon" described in the Yeoman's tale? The questions are difficult to resolve; and concerns with the use and reliability of knowledge are everywhere apparent.

In relating the Yeoman's realistic account of his dangerous laboratory work, the *prima pars* of the *CYT* urges upon us the reliability of first-hand knowledge and experience. We learn of the Yeoman's bodily injury, of the debilitating and exploitative effects of his work as a wage laborer. By his report, the laboratory in which he works is the site of an excessive, even inhumane, brand of *curiositatis*: this is experimental science focused too entirely on baldly material ends. The laboratory emerges as a locale for the exploitation of the laboring body, whether in the service of new alchemical knowledge or of some imagined future financial pay-off. The alchemist Canon who ran away may have done so, in fact, as a defense against just such critique: his excessive pursuit of knowledge or practice, to hear the Yeoman tell it, is marked by too little concern with questions of value, and with who or what might be lost in the process. Such activity could devolve from the sins of pride as well as greed, but the Yeoman emphasizes the latter, ending the autobiographical part of his tale by musing on faulty economies of value, on something and nothing. What seems valuable turn out to be empty, or worse:

> But al thyng which that shineth as the gold
> Nis nat gold, as that I have herd told;
> Ne every appul that is fair at eye
> Ne is nat good, what so men clappe or crye.
> Right so, lo, fareth it amonges us:

He that semeth the wiseste, by Jhesus,
Is moost fool, whan it cometh to the preef;
And he that semeth trewest is a theef. (8.961–69)

[But every thing that shines like gold / Is not gold, as I have heard
said; / Nor every apple that is fair to the eye / Is not good, whatever
men may chatter or cry. / Right so, lo, it fares among us: / He who
seems the wisest, by Jesus, / Is the greatest fool, when it comes to
the proof; / And he that seems truest is a thief.]

Coming at the end of the autobiographical portion of his tale, these remarks
comment on the vagaries of judgment, epistemological or ethical. As his experience has demonstrated, those who seem most knowledgeable are often fools;
the thief is the one who seems the truest. On its face, the comment glosses the
bare truth of the Yeoman's own wisdom as a reflection on the events just narrated. This is wisdom born of experience.

Of course, the *pars secunda* immediately undercuts this apparent reliance
on the evidence of experience, reminding us instead that eyewitness reporting
guarantees neither accuracy nor wisdom: we should not, as the false Canon's
alchemical tricks will eventually also suggest, too readily believe either our eyes
or our ears, a caution is equally useful for scientists, radical skeptics, or readers
of poetry. The larger point is made neither via eyewitness testimony, firsthand
experience, nor ethical aphorism. It is made by a poem that announces itself
as fictional, indeed, as a poem drawing attention to the multiplicities of fiction, and to layers of metaphor: a fable within a fictionalized storytelling competition taken up on a fictionalized pilgrimage. It is, moreover, in this context
that alchemy is, so the Yeoman asserts, "oure elvysshe craft" ["our elvish craft"]
(l. 751), a "slidynge [wavering] science" (l. 733) fraught with epistemological
difficulty.

And yet the critique of the false promise of this elvish craft sparkles by
way of Chaucer's own elvish poetry. In fact, the disturbing "multiplications" of
alchemical labor are most powerfully rendered in the descriptions of the harsh
transformations of the Yeoman's own body: his once ruddy complexion is now
"wan and of a leden hewe" [wan and of the color of lead] (8.728), his eye "yet
blered" [bleary] (8.730). Alchemical work enacts change, but it turns complex-
ions to lead, not gold. It blears rather than sharpens the eye. Nor is the specialized knowledge that alchemy promises rendered in unequivocally appealing
terms. The Yeoman insists, "In lernyng of this elvysshe nyce (var. wise)[42] loore,

/ Al is in veyn" ["In learning of this elvish foolish (var. wise) lore, / all is in vain." 8.841-42.]

Authoritative treatises can sometimes package vanity as learning. Ascriptions of the vanity of learning correspond to moments in the larger "sociolect" of both alchemy and "natural magic." This critique—that putatively learned texts do not always deliver real knowledge—telegraphs a point that Roger Bacon (himself both theoretician and practical alchemist) made in the preceding century, and regarding the equivocal nature of "magic" as speculative science. In his *Secrets of Art and Nature*, Bacon describes the problems of "new books" wherein some authors gussy up fraudulent facts by ascribing them to well-known authorities. Such texts, Bacon argues, proliferate errors and authorize future mistakes. Yet they are not to be entirely deplored, Bacon equivocates, since even here, one finds gems of wisdom worth further scrutiny. The textual variations in the manuscript traditions of Chaucer's tale, rendering the elvish science alternately "foolish" ["nyce"] or "wise," equivocate to the same effect: elvish science oscillates between wisdom and foolishness. Curious alchemical seekers, beware!

Chaucer's association of alchemy with elvishness is not unique. In a fifteenth-century Middle English verse dialogue, the Queen of the Elves schools the philosopher Albertus Magnus on practical matters related to alchemical work. That text, too, raises issues pertinent both to epistemological and to ethical rectitude: the "right" way. Trinity College, Cambridge MS. R. 14.44, entitled "The Right Path Albertus Bears Witness" or *Semita Recta Albertus peribet testimoniam* (hereafter *Right Path*),[43] followed Chaucer's poem by some decades, dating from the second half of the fifteenth century. The short dialogue of 64 lines stages a conversation between the prominent figure of philosophical authority and a figure of female sovereignty, the Queen of the Elves. These two authorities meet on a "somerys morwenyng" (summer's morning) in the "weldernesse" (l. 10), just outside the city of Damascus, a place with longstanding alchemical associations. Elchyzel, Queen of the Elves, schools Albert the Great in the recipe for an elixir capable of turning mercury into silver or gold. Sitting under a tree, she offers her help to the learned philosopher: "I am kome sche seyde in this morwenyng / to helpe the in thin stodying" (I have come, she said, on this morning, / to help you in your studying [ll. 19–20]). The illustrious philosopher "knew here ful wel . . . / for oftyn beforn he had here sene" (knew her well . . . / as he has often seen her before [ll. 14–15]).

Editor Peter Grund reads the inclusion of Albertus and the reference to

Damascus as part of an effort to lend credibility to an already discredited alchemical science. But if this is so, why bother including the Elvish queen in the first place? Albert's alchemical associations were well known; presumably he could have consulted a more respectable informant. Furthermore, plenty of alchemical treatises avoid hints at fraudulent figures in favor of strictly philosophical disputations between adepts as illustrious authorities. And why position Elchyzel as Albertus's tutor, rather than his student? Such a relation may well imply the admiration of a serious scholar for an alchemist elf; but it might also playfully suggest the alchemist's ability to cross cultures: elite and popular, philosophical and craft.[44] And even if Grund is correct in his assumption that the Elf queen represents the less admirable or rigorous elements associated with alchemical practice, the text does not recount Albertus's rehabilitation of her work, but her assistance of his. Not, it seems, for the first time. In this dialogue Albertus and Elchyzel are good friends; earlier collaborations predate this particular episode. With regard to the secrets of art and nature, the Queen of the Elves seems to have special standing; at any rate, she evinces greater wisdom, particularly as to the details of this recipe, than does Albertus. Most of the dialogue attends to their collaborative experimentation, via specific instructions for chemical multiplications written, as one might expect, in coded language.

Linguistic codes draw out the associations between alchemy and linguistic equivocation. Roger Bacon's work emphasizes alchemy as a collaboration of nature and art. *Right Path* depicts this kind of collaboration too, and the dialogic structure of the short verse emblematizes teamwork in form as well as content. Like master chefs perfecting a tricky recipe, Elchyzel and Albertus consult rather than debate or disagree. Their collaboration, joining an illustrious natural philosopher with a Queen of the Elves, emerges emphatically as the "right path": "Off all the weys that I knowe be est or be weste / Evere holde I this path for on of the beste" (Of all the ways that I know, from east to west / I always understand this path for one of the best [lines 2–3]). Given the unusual nature of this particular dialogue, the path in question refers not only to alchemy, but also to the kind of friendly collaborations in which Albertus and Elchyzel are engaged. When the dialogue of Albert the Great with the Queen of the Elves crosses the specificities of experimentation with occult matters, it suggests a complex interrelation between the "rational" and the "magical," two spheres not necessarily understood as starkly demarcated.[45]

Cited by the laboring Yeoman, the figure of the alchemical Elf gestures toward less harmonious collaborations. He emphasizes the dangerous limits of

natural magic used for personal profit, a kind of speculative thought associated with the negative type of curiosity. Drawing our attention to the "loaded"
discourse of elvishness throughout Chaucer's alchemical tale, Richard Firth
Green has emphasized the variety of things that alchemists and elves share: a
tradition of secrecy; the promise of ephemeral rewards; a persistent concern
with transformation; and a liminal cultural status. Both alchemists and elves,
Green writes, "hovered at the very edges of orthodox thought."[46] On that
edge, too, teeter questions of innovation of interest to poets: the limits of the
possible, the nature of equivocation, and debates on art's use of nature's power.

Unlike Green, I read the ascription of elvishness in Chaucer's tale as
equivocal rather than negative. For one thing, the descriptive language of the
tale is persistently doubled; for another, as we have seen, magic and alchemy
were close associates because both mined the limits and the horizon of what
might be possible—for good or ill. Chaucer's description of alchemical practice seems to want to have it both ways. The Canon's Yeoman is, on the one
hand, a whistle-blower. He testifies to the ethical and epistemological problems of alchemy as a practice founded on exploitation, illusion, and deception. Yet Chaucer's tale also, on the other hand and as Edgar Duncan pointed
out long ago, seems to open up the possibility for a genuine alchemy. We
might thus pause over any apparent opposition of rigorous science to frivolous
magic, and look instead to the intimacies between philosophical gravitas and
experimental recipes rendered here.

Elsewhere in Chaucer's corpus, elvishness figures as a locus of desire, and
not unsympathetically. In the prologue and tale of Sir Thopas, for instance,
Chaucer describes his "pilgrim" self as "elvish" just as this figure embarks on
his satirical tale. The Wife of Bath juxtaposes a late fourteenth-century mercantile "now" with the longed-for "then" of the Elf queen's "joly compaigne,"
a time when loathly ladies can become again forever young. From its very start
the *Canterbury Tales* takes desires for transformation seriously—desires for
healing and repair inaugurate the entire Canterbury project. In alchemy, as in
poetry, desires for transformation are sharpened to a fine edge, and pointed,
variously, toward skill and ingenuity, craft, deceit, or imaginative possibility.
This, too, is a fact that the *CYT* regularly registers.

Yet if the *CYT* renders alchemy an "elvish" science, it does not depict it as
a productive collaborative venture. Relations among alchemists and adepts
seem, that is, a good deal less effective in Chaucer's tale than they do in the
dialogue of Albert and the Queen of the Elves. Workers in the Canon's laboratory certainly collaborate, but there is little evidence that they follow a path

one could call "right." In fact, the only experiment the Yeoman describes goes
rather seriously wrong when the iron pot dangerously explodes. None of the
assistants seem certain of how or why the pot exploded. And yet, if the tale
persistently shows the destructive power of one elvish craft (alchemy), it uses
another elvish language (poetry) to render the point as vividly as possible. As
poetry, *CYT* also plays with the specific materials of experimentation to offer
a vibrant picture of substances transformed. It presents, for one thing, list
upon rhyming list of chemical reagents: sale ammoniac (ammonium chlo-
ride), sulfur, arsenic, saltpeter (potassium nitrate), cream of tartar, lime, brewer's yeast. For another, the tale both deploys and equivocates the technical
vocabulary of experimental processes: sublimation, purification, amalgama-
tion, calcination, distillation, fermentation, mollification, incorporation, ce-
menting, imbibing, to say nothing of chemical bodily changes like sweating,
foaming, faces turning red, or wan, or the color of lead. One can track the
persistent fascination with transformation in a number of places: in the precise
description of the swindler alchemist and his tricks; in the oscillation between
arcane techno-jargon and ideological skepticism; in the regular moments of
near-realist clarity.

In that last category we find the oft-cited description of the laboratory
explosion found in the *prima pars* of the tale, the section devoted to the Yeoman's first-person account of his experience in the laboratory:

Ful ofte it happeth so
The pot tobreketh, and farewel, al is go!
Thise metals been of so greet violence
Oure walles mowe nat make hem resistence,
But if they weren wroght of lym and stoon;
They percen so, and thurgh the wal they goon.
And somme of hem synken into the ground—
. . . .
And somme are scatered al the floor aboute;
Somme lepe into the roof. Withouten doute,
Though that the feend noght in oure sighte hym shewe,
I trowe he with us be, that ilke shrewe! (8.906-17)

[Fully often it happens thusly / The pot shatters and, good-bye!, all
is destroyed! / These metals are of such great violence / Our walls
may not resist them, / Unless they are made of limestone; / They

pierce fiercely and through the walls they go. / And some of them
bore into the ground. / . . . / And some are scattered all about the
floor; / some leap into the roof. Without doubt, / although the
fiend does not show himself in our sight, / I believe he is with us,
that wicked thing.]

Critics have mined this moment to support a view of Chaucer's critique of
either exploitative labor or alchemical quackery. Yet we see here, too, a fascination with matter to rival any alchemist. Material things—pots, metals,
walls—shatter, pierce, penetrate, scatter, and leap. All a little elvish, these
things are active agents—the event seems radical and unexpected, surprising
despite the Yeoman's stipulation that, "Ful ofte, it happeth so." This vivid
image of dynamic movement emphasizes matter come to life; the description
seems to be nearly incantatory in its use of repetition. This is great poetry,
depicting a pot at the precise moment of its shattering—metal bits flying in
every direction—in such vital terms. Even the immovable walls seem dynamically alive. They might, under certain circumstances, "make resistance" to alchemical shrapnel. The formulation foregrounds the *active* resilience of stone
and mortar, and the verbal form, "maken resistence," notably refers, in every
other instance listed in the *MED*, to sentient beings;[47] it regularly accompa-
nies the first- and second-person nominative, "you," "I" to "we," also used
with "mankind" or with personified figures like Fortune or the Church. This
particular usage, the *MED* claims, often carries moral or political connotations: Are we, then, to understand these walls as holding virtuously firm
against an evil, violently shattering pot?

The concise representation of dangerous matter depicts a problem at the
heart of alchemy's major ambition: the transformations produced to matter or
to bodies may not follow the efforts, intentions, or impositions of the alchemist. Even worse, as the rest of the tale makes clear, the promise of transformation may itself provide an alibi for the economic machinations of quacks
and charlatans. This is the promise of fraudulent science used in the service of
the bald profit motive. And in this regard it is particularly interesting to note
the tale's emphasis on describing late-medieval alchemy as a "craft." The semantic range of the Middle English term "craft" includes features of formal
science, skill, dexterity, learnedness, or ingenuity. It also refers to the organiza-
tion of craftsmen in a guild.

The Yeoman persistently emphasizes alchemy as this kind of practice.
While he alludes to some major aspects of its philosophical underpinnings, the

term "philosopher" occurs only six times throughout the text. In contrast, Chaucer deploys "craft" and its cognates 19 times, over three times more frequently: in the Prologue (three times, "his craft," [8.619, 621], and "craftily" [8.655], all referring to his Canon); throughout the description of the Canon's Yeoman's laboratory (nine instances: "elvissh craft" [8.751]; "oure craft" [8.785, 803, 866, 952]; "cursed craft" [8.830]; "that craft" [8.838]; "this craft" [8.882]; and "craftily" (8.903, referring to his Canon]); and throughout the tale of the (other) false Canon, where it occurs seven times: ("nobil craft" [8.1247] spoken by the duped priest; "false craft" [8.1320]; "sory craft" [var. "wikked craft" 8.1349]; "my craft" [8.1369], spoken by the false canon; "this craft" [8.1394], and "crafty" [8.1290]; "crafty science" [8.1253]). As practiced in Chaucer's tale, alchemy is less the elite intellectual pursuit that it was for Albertus Magnus, or Aquinas, or even Roger Bacon; it is a craft practice, apparently debased (or so the Yeoman seems to suggest) by the grimy corruptions deriving from the profit motive.

The emphasis is extraordinary, particularly in context. Competitions among practitioners of alchemy within Europe are pertinent here, particularly the relation of elite intellectual inquiry to craft production, the latter on the rise by the time Chaucer was writing. Operating outside the universities, artisans and craft practitioners also experimented with alchemical procedures; it was in these craft contexts that the tradition of alchemical secrecy came to serve as an extension of "ordinary craft procedures," as "practitioners turned their professions into closely guarded 'mysteries' and handed down trade secrets orally from master to apprentice."[48] Indeed, as Pamela O. Long has shown, "craft secrecy" developed early in alchemical circles, functioning as one feature of an increasingly proprietary attitude toward the operations and methods used by urban guilds from the thirteenth century onward. Secrecy concerning craft procedures developed alongside "the privilege or patent as a limited monopoly on inventions and craft processes." As she puts it, "In the medieval urban context, both knowledge of craft processes and mechanical inventions came to be considered intangible property separate from craft products and from the labor required to produce them."[49] What will eventually come to be recognized as intellectual property—also frequently guarded as secret—may start to emerge in these circumstances. In Chaucer's medieval urban context, then, alchemy was associated with developments in proprietary knowledge and trade secrets; by the later fourteenth century, proprietary practice and even the rights of patent in the field of alchemy meant that it was increasingly a guild and artisanal practice, deploying secret techniques for mercantile ends.

In this context, it may not be entirely surprising that the problem with alchemical ethics in the *CYT* tale involves not the attraction of the newfangled, but the love of money. The Canon's Yeoman explicates his larger point by way of the problem of "lucre." In a final passage that merges "philosophy" and "craft," the speaker orients his larger point with reference to issues of money and class:

> Considereth, sires, how that, in ech estaat,
> Bitwixe men and gold ther is debaat
> So ferforth that unnethes is ther noon.
> This multiplying blent so many oon
> That in good feith I trowe that it bee
> The caus grettest of swich scarsetee.
> Philosophres speken so mystily
> In this craft that men kan nat come therby,
> For any wit that men han now-a-dayes.
> They mowe wel chiteren as doon jayes,
> And in hir termes sette hir lust and peyne.
> But to hir purpose shul they nevere atteyne. (8.1388-99)

[Consider, sirs, how in each class, / between men and gold there is conflict / so widespread that there is hardly any gold left. / This multiplying blinds so many a one / that in good faith I believe it is the greatest cause of such scarcity. / Philosophers speak so mystically / in this craft that men can not understand those things, / for any knowledge that men have nowadays / they may as well chatter as do jays / and in their language set their desire and effort. / But their purpose they will never attain.]

Greed is a problem that crosses elite and mercantile cultures. The ethical question is economic as well as philosophical. Yet it is also a problem of the current moment, a trouble with things "now-a-days." Attention to the here and now motivates Sisk to read the alchemist's disillusion with alchemy as "motivated by nostalgic idealism and contextualized within a model of historical decline."[50] This is, she argues, "an understanding of history as a process of decline offer[ing] no theoretical space for the concept of progress."[51] Yet such remarks place in opposition concepts that were regularly understood equivocally. I will make more of alchemy's equivocal status as a "cutting-edge" science developed by way of proprietary artisanal alchemy crucial to both scientific practice and Chaucer's tale. For the moment, however, we might note that men "in ech estaat" struggle with gold, and such struggles impoverish us all; the pursuit of gold is the cause, not of greater wealth, but of scarcity. This is true no matter the estate of the person involved. Sisk reads the later lines in this passage as key evidence for the Yeoman's nostalgia for a "better past that was richer in learning."[52] Alchemists these days, her reading suggests, jape and chatter because they cannot pierce the secrets of authoritative philosophers of tradition, masters from the old days of real learning.

Yet the overall emphasis here seems to me less on what we might call the qualitative problem of the lost riches of learning than on the quantitative problem of literal riches, of scarcity and plenty. These were, moreover, the kinds of qualitative calculations important in the days of the calculators, as Joel Kaye demonstrates.[53] If Sisk sheds some light on the Yeoman's utterly conservative critique of alchemy as an artisanal craft, her reading cannot fully account for what Chaucer would have us see as the problem with the use of alchemy to multiply profit. And if the Yeoman describes his haggard body in ways that demystify the alienation of his own labor, he also offers in its place a mystified account of the power of the elite philosopher. As a story-teller who had earlier worked to reveal the power dynamics at issue in craft alchemy's own use of "privetee," the Yeoman does not now urge the secrets of natural philosophy upon us, at least not unequivocally. As far as secrets are concerned, the Yeoman has persistently indicated his wish to divulge them. If there is nostalgia here it seems to be motivated less by the longing for an earlier time of "pure" science or learning, than by a wish that what we might call the medieval "information economy" were contained, controlled, and directed by elite culture.

The problem of filthy "lucre" remains. The ethical question at stake pertains to those particular critiques of *vitium curiositatis* related to greed: the use of scholarly learning to grasp after gold. In Chaucer's account of craft alchemy, questions of quackery combine with caveat emptor: beware of duplicitous alchemists and all such hucksters. There was, as Chaucer well knows and as the tale repeatedly shows, much more to alchemy than the pursuit of precious metals. And precisely as a science concerned with vital matter, alchemy seems to offer attractions that Chaucer, the poet, cannot resist. In his hands, the prodigious details of chemical and material transformations do not, that is, add up to either an "antimatter" or "antiscience" screed. Instead, they show how poetry can depict, even more vividly than alchemy, the compelling details, the promises and problems, of material things.

By the end of the *Canon's Yeoman's Tale,* readers know a bit more about the complexities of matter transformed; and we can apprehend the gaps between desire and reality, or design and execution. We know this not only because we have been let in on some secrets—whether trade or philosophical—but also because of the representational finesse of this original fictional tale, a tale jammed full of rhyming lists of chemical processes, of alterations, sublimations, and multiplications of its own. Combining the power and problems of alchemical speculation with scientific specificity, Chaucer's equivocations clarify our understanding of creativity both as a hope "in the possibility of success" and a process engaged with texts and authorities, via productive repetitions, of "trial and error."[54] The poet, himself an experimental fabulist, offers both a wider view and a deeper analysis of alchemy's promise and risk than the craft alchemist can. For the poet is no mere entertainer, engaging in tricks and illusions so as to stash away a fistful of gold. He has other ambitions: to show us that his particularly precise fictions about swindlers, and alchemists, dreamers, laborers, and canons may well treat the equivocations of innovation, the problem of matter and morality, more profoundly than either the scientist or the metaphysician can.[55] Invention serves poetry as well as alchemy, an account of the human attraction to the new reaching from medieval sciences to medieval fictions.

In Chaucer's hands, this ambivalence is a deeply materialist project to which the fabulist is particularly suited. As noted, a number of readers of Chaucer's *CYT* have made the case for the implicit homology between the alchemist and the fabulist. Alchemy, like medieval poetry, trades in doublespeak, in enigmas and puzzles. It is, perhaps, a technical field as pointedly dependent on linguistic equivocation as is poetry. Positioned across the boundary of *auctoritas* and *textus,* alchemy resonates with poetry as a method of invention. But alchemy at this time was also emerging as a field of proprietary knowledge and trade secrets. Lisa Cooper has demonstrated Chaucer's particular preoccupation with artisans and craft knowledge. Throughout the *Canterbury Tales,* Chaucer stages a competition between poetic and artisanal making: "Chaucer is able repeatedly to acknowledge and make use of the parallels between the making of things and the making of poetry," she writes, "yet simultaneously stake a claim for the fundamental differences between literary making and literal making, between poets on the one hand and artisans on the other."[56]

It will be some centuries before notions of intellectual property come to accrue to the role of poet or author; it will be some centuries, too, before the image of the author as originating inventor, a solitary producer of uniquely original texts, will dominate.[57] Only after the eighteenth century, after sculpture, painting, and literature become subject to the laws of patent, after such items are recognized as things to be commodified and consumed by the general public, will notions of the work of art as such develop fully. By that time, moreover, the technical craftsman will have converged on the fabricator as laborer, the artisan whose handwork suffers in comparison to the grand innovations of either art or speculative science. The *Canon's Yeoman's Tale* illuminates one step in that long process. The questions raised, the competitions depicted, in Chaucer's account of elvishness, fraudulent making, and duplicitous secrets demonstrate the tensions produced via critiques of such profit-making. Considering the similarities of poet and alchemist, Chaucer deploys a notion of inventive fraud and duplicity that marks the problem of proprietary and commodified knowledge in explicitly ethical terms.

Moreover, Chaucer's attention to alchemy also demonstrates the degree to which an absorption with matter can fuel a materialism ready to capture our desire for fresh feeling so as to multiply profit. In later centuries, and under the conditions of capitalist production, this kind of materialism will prove powerful enough to underwrite the valued position of the new in an age of perpetual "innovation." Written during an earlier age of innovation, the *CYT* marks such developments with an ethical edge. Alluding to a complex of knowledge with gullibility, experimentation with problems of verifiability, utopian futurism with deluded quackery, it tracks the ways in which alchemy mines the limits and the horizon of the new: imagining in equivocal fashion a future set of possibilities—as well as their ethical afterlives in the capitalist paradox of novelty as a permanent feature of consumption.

Such ambivalence also extends well beyond the medieval era; both alchemy and printing would be persistently linked to necromancy in the post-medieval centuries.[58] The ethical questions I have been tracking also outlast the period. Proprietary uses of knowledge are again a subject of some concern—and today more than a few observers worry about whether and how the profit motive might compromise the common good, or damage the pursuit of specialized research. What are the limits of intellectual property as it pertains to human genes? Shall we grant proprietary license for "new" uses of rain-forest medicinals? How might research programs exclusively managed by for-profit entities, or defined primarily through the pursuit of patents or technological profit-making, compromise attention to enduring questions of science, art, knowledge, or value?

Despite the fact that such ethical concerns persist, accounts of the epochal break between medieval and modern regularly turn on the fiction that the Renaissance, for all its famed interest in returning to the sources, ushered in an era unequivocally committed to the new. Such accounts of epochal shift emphasize the power of the so-called "discovery" of the "new world" as changing everything. A limitless curiosity, a newfound fever for empiricism, we are told, shattered the geographies of a "bookish" medieval worldview. In the culminating chapter, I turn, finally, to reconsider the meaning of 1492, and the problem of the epoch. The process by which Christopher Columbus's geographic accident came to signify a new era engaged the medieval discourse of curiosity in surprising ways. The innovating admiral would be buried, at his own request, in Franciscan habit. His subsequent fame depended less on an unequivocal embrace of new things than it did on a renewed culture of copying, of reading and writing, via the recursive technologies of early print.

Chapter 6

Old Worlds and New

> Novelty became the sign not of an idea's radicalism but of its validity.
>
> —Anthony Grafton, *New Worlds, Ancient Texts*

The year 1492 stands first among the liminal markers of historical rupture, popularly understood as the harbinger of a new Humanist age enthusiastic about novelty, a new time of technological interest and advancement. According to the persuasive narrative advanced most famously by Anthony Grafton, data mined from Columbus's "New World" shattered medieval strictures against the impiety of *vitium curiositatis* (the sin of curiosity), and revolutionized bookish medieval geographies, granting empirical force to a Christianity driving toward the Ends of the Earth. A new empiricism, with its attendant possibilities for human achievement, apparently inspired Europeans to embrace novelty as an unquestioned value.

In this now standard version of the Columbus story, the new of "New World" signals as an event, as a decisive moment of epoch-making change. The year 1492 witnessed a formidable tear in the normal fabric of time.[1] In the historiography surrounding this event, moreover, 1492 signifies not only at the level of empirical fact as a date marked and memorized, but also as the eruption of empiricism itself. Yet, when we cast the "new world" event as a singular occasion, we misrepresent the long process by which a narrative of "before 1492" and "after 1492" emerged historically. A plurality of moments—spread out over centuries—would be needed before Columbus's voyages could register in such an eventful way.

Surprising discoveries, inventions, or happenings strike us first as anomalous. They disorient and confound. As we gain our bearings, capricious incidents may be cast aside as frivolous, dismissed as inconsequential, or discarded as irrelevant. Or they might, by way of retroactive interpretive value and judgment, be granted a prestigious status, valued as radically important, and in the process, granted the luster of the new. As all this suggests, anomalous events do not appear as new in real time. Such adjudications, instead, take place in the retroactive moment of the backward glance, the *après-coup*. And no single event, sufficient in itself, can enact the breathtaking claims so often made for newness as epochal break or revolution. Epochal breaks require reassessment, rereading, rewriting, and reinterpretation.

All of this clearly applies to Christopher Columbus's arrival on the island of Hispaniola. Fraught with epistemological and navigational complications, Columbus's adventure marked a mistaken landing in a misrecognized hemisphere. The capricious nature of the admiral's original circumstance has not, of course, compromised the narrative power of the new in the story now told about Columbus's New World. A remarkably persistent account of remarkable change accommodates the accidental nature of the Admiral's landing, even as it renders New World discovery the harbinger of a New Epoch. In this larger historiographical context, Columbus's new emerges, paradoxically, as both a monumental accident and that moment when the recognition of a secularized reality principle changed everything.

Narratives of affect and value are sedimented in such New World histories, as even those accounts of the Columbus event that are tied to the eruption of empiricism admit. When Grafton highlights Columbus's power as an effect of the "new" Renaissance value for empiricism, he links epochal shifts to an appreciation of the value of the value of novelty. The new emerges not only as a particular occurrence or invention of obvious value: newness figures as itself a legitimating property in an implicitly circular logic through which we recognize that the new has value when newness validates new ideas.[2] If, as Roland Barthes suggests, "The New is not a fashion, it is a value,"[3] this is the new as an altogether fashionable value.

Yet Grafton's narrative of value nonetheless, and from the vantage of my study, defends a particularly problematic association: the medieval value of the old, and of tradition, as residual, nonempirical, and in opposition to the new. Throughout this book, I have demonstrated the various ways in which medieval treatments of the new—as a concept as well as a categorical descriptor— trouble such a dichotomy. In the medieval discourses pertinent to innovation, the opposition of old to new was, in some crucial ways, beside the main point.

The pursuit of innovation in other terms, through an artistic culture of copying, and by way of the distinction of the whimsical to the conventional, marked the subject of previous chapters. This study has accordingly worked to deepen our understanding of the prehistory of that narrative through which the new is valued, simply, as a legitimating good. I have argued thus far that, from as early as the twelfth century, ethical questions pertaining to discourses of invention, innovation, and eventful change cultivated newness ambivalently and complexly, often by way of recognizably ethical categories: *curiositas* on the one hand, and *ingenium* on the other. Ethical discourses about the newfangled (discourses that would, *pace* Grafton, continue well into the Renaissance and beyond) developed as a means to adjudicate problems of fate and freedom, engaging the difficulties surrounding creativity and desire. Medieval writers questioned both the destructive and the creative powers as they related to change and innovation; and rather than opposing "innovation" to "tradition" (as in today's widespread understanding of innovation as "creative destruction"),[4] these thinkers entwined the new with the old in complex ethical debates over the extent and limits of human creativity and history.

Yet even as this is so, medieval writers also deployed the distinction of old to new in prestigious scriptural contexts and via a providential temporality of epoch-making consequence. The current chapter takes on this aspect of the medieval new, approaching the problem of the epoch—the role of the new as historical rupture—by way of Columbus's New World story. Following scholars of Columban texts, I address Columbus's activity in the context of religious prophecies and ethical concerns over possession that date back centuries. Situated within the late sixteenth-century moment, "new world" figures, on the one hand, a prospective narrative of prophetic futurism, what Jonathan Goldberg has called, "a history that will be,"[5] with ethical resonance; yet as a feature of today's periodizing histories, the Columbus event is also a retroactive narrative, an *après-coup* of epoch-making proportions. I hope, here, to disentangle the narratives of value and desire that are embedded in this paradoxical temporality.

Epochal Repetitions

Europe's longing for newness, as Mary Baine Campbell puts it, "seems to have been a real pressure" on the pursuits and voyages enacted both in advance and in the wake of 1492.[6] Yet what we understand today as the New World was not

immediately identified in such terms. As Campbell has shown, the discovery
of unknown continents in the wake of 1492 was only gradually taken as evidence that a "new world" existed. The unity of the globe, and its according
separability into old and new worlds, were not, she argues, self-evident. Early
encounters with previously unknown places and peoples seemed to be at first
a discovery of so many different "islands." Not until the seventeenth century
did what Campbell calls "the 'one-world' paradigm" gather steam; its advance
would, accordingly, signal "the decline of the trope of the island, or at least of
the island as 'little world.'"[7] It took, in other words, some two centuries for a
binary model of old world and new world to replace a plural account of islands: a plurality of "worlds"—and of islands as worlds—would constitute the
middle position of both scientific and geographic thought throughout the
fifteenth and sixteenth centuries.

Nonetheless, 1492 has been regularly and retroactively coded not as a
swarm of new information, not an array of multiple, plural, various particulars, but as a break on a cosmological scale. This has less to do with "new
world" empiricism than it does with "old world" prophetic and apocalyptic
histories that regularly deploy the "new" to describe providential worlds yet to
be. Cosmologies of the new as violent rupture were very much a part of Columbus's personal and cultural contexts; citations of the "new heavens and the
new earth" taken from chapter 21 of the Apocalypse of St. John echo in many
of his writings. Typological versions of the new are embedded in the account
of the New Jerusalem in this authoritative text, a use of the category of newness with significant cultural prestige in the Middle Ages and after. The admiral, who would write his own book of prophecies,[8] had been long preoccupied
with prophetic geographies and histories, and he would come to claim his own
importance in the context of a brand of apocalyptic thinking that had been
circulating in Europe for centuries. Columbus had "a providential conception
of history, according to which the discovery . . . was ordained at a propitious
moment," and he was "divinely elected as the instrument of it."[9] And his views
on time and navigation were influenced especially by the fourteenth-century
university master and encyclopedist, Pierre d'Ailly,[10] and, through d'Ailly's
work, by Roger Bacon and Joachim de Fiore. Columbus annotated his own
copy of d'Ailly's *Imago Mundi*. In the twelfth and thirteenth centuries, Joachim's theory of historical ages and Joachite prophecies concerning the end
times would circulate widely; such apocalyptic thinking, linked to astral determinism, would repeatedly be condemned by Church authorities as inimical to
a belief in human freedom. The Admiral's commitment to providential

histories was, in other words, consistent with the wide circulation of ideas that had been both popular and controversial as far back as Roger Bacon's day.

Like Bacon, Columbus lived at a moment when apocalyptic thinking was on the rise. In the textual imaginaries that supported his voyaging ambitions, the newness of "New World" borrowed the affective power of the image of the New Jerusalem, a figure for world renewal, in future tense: "And I saw a new heavens and a new earth, for the first heaven and the first earth had passed away" (Rev. 21:1). Keyed to place as well as time, imagined as both a city and an age, the New Jerusalem promises release from a worn and weary world of pain and death and loss to a temporal and spatial elsewhere. This is the ideal city that is nowhere yet on earth, location of a satisfaction still to be realized, a time when every tear shall be wiped away: "and death shall be no more, neither shall there be mourning nor crying nor pain any more, for the former things have passed away" (Rev. 21:4). A powerful and poignant image of rescue, the scene of the New Jerusalem blends the particular with the universal; the longed-for future is both a moment of intimate consolation and an era of renewal. Its novelty is cosmological: "See," the voice from the throne announces, "I make all things new!" This version of the new—linked to the familiar modes of Christian supersessionism found in accounts of salvation history both medieval and modern—cites the simultaneity of *telos* and *novum*.[11] In God's own brand of "creative destruction," paradise converges on the end times.

If we can track the continuities between Columbus's apocalyptic account of the new world and the texts and traditions of his medieval predecessors, the questions of epoch surrounding his circumstance persist.[12] Apocalyptic texts, moreover, beckon with the promise of epoch, offering a particularly influential model of historical rupture as cosmological severing of present from future. We know by now that such periodizing accounts always depend upon older texts, traditions, and temporal imaginaries. Columbus figures this doubleness of old and new in ways both pertinent to the problem of the epoch and in excess of it: motivated by cosmological descriptions of a providential future world, Columbus nonetheless happened upon an unexpected locale of great consequence. And his example urges epochal questions: When do material, intellectual, and cultural mechanisms of change rise to a level of general significance? Does the way that change entwines with continuity corroborate, or undermine, any history of difference in epochal terms? Acknowledging the degree to which Columbus was inspired by images and texts already old in Roger Bacon's youth does not fully undermine the sense that something was different after the Admiral's voyages.

Recently scholars have returned to the problems of epochal difference, raising again the debate between Karl Löwith and Hans Blumenberg over the status of the "modern" as a legitimately new epoch. The issues at stake are especially pertinent to the status of the new in the case of Columbus, and so we turn briefly to them. In *Meaning in History* (1949), Löwith persuasively argues that modern notions of world "progress" constitute the secularization of the older ("medieval") Judeo-Christian eschatology—a utopian New Jerusalem beyond the faults and frailties of the present day. Engaging Joachite prophecies as well as other texts also important to my study, Löwith casts secularization as less the achievement of modernity than its alibi, religious content secreted beneath a secular veneer. This thesis has had much to recommend it, not the least because of Löwith's penetrating analysis of apocalyptic histories and their continuing influence.[13] Following Löwith, scholars such as Julia Lupton and Kathleen Biddick have pointed to the persistence of typological thinking in notions of modern periodization. Typological thinking, Lupton writes, is "one of the foundational principles of modern periodization *per se*" which should "be dialectically engaged rather than simply rejected or replaced."[14] Biddick links typology to modernity to argue that, "supersessionary thinking and notions of modernity are closely bound."[15] These responses to the claims of modern periodization have helped to deepen our sense of the problems of value embedded in acts that define eras and epochs. Such work, particularly when considered in fully global terms, has usefully severed the links between claims of the "new" and accounts of historical progress.[16]

Defending the legitimacy of epochal claims for modernity, Hans Blumenberg's *Die Legitimität der Neuzeit* or *The Legitimacy of the Modern Age*, first printed in 1966,[17] rewrote Löwith's central terms. Metaphysical notions of progress claimed for modernity, Blumenberg argues, constitute not a secularization of Christian eschatology, but a *reoccupation* of Christianity's unsolved problems.[18] Arguing against the strong version of the "secularization" thesis in favor of what some have called its weaker twin,[19] Blumenberg depicts modern borrowings of premodern religiosity in functional rather than substantial terms: it is, he argues, the world-historical futurism central to Christian belief, not the content of its eschatological promise, that persisted beyond its necessary uses. Arguably, Blumenberg's own intellectual history proceeds dialectically. It certainly offers an unusually generous account of the dependence of some features of modernity on premodern thought: he repeatedly critiques the Enlightenment opposition between a modern "rational" age and a premodern "superstitious" or extra-rational one.[20] This is notable, again, when considered alongside projects appearing at about the same time, such as Kuhn's 1961 *Structure of Scientific Revolutions* and Foucault's 1966 *Les Mots et les choses.* [21]

Engaging the function of periodization dialectically, as Lupton recommends, can help us here; simultaneous attention to residual as well as emergent practices is at the heart of my own dialectical interest in assessing not only what the new meant in the time before modernity, but also what the medieval new means for the legacies of thinking that we have inherited. Blumenberg's work is implicated in this project as much for his story of modernity as on account of his reading of the medieval heritage. Blumenberg will err, as we will shortly see, in his account of premodern thinking on the topic of *curiositas.* Yet his account of modernity nonetheless proves illuminating for understanding crucial features of the legacies of thought that have produced the medieval new as an impossible association.

Crucial to Blumenberg's account is the particularly influential Thomistic context, whereby *curiositas* guards the border separating the necessary things that deserve our care from those superfluous things that should properly lie outside it. Modernity "reoccupied" this distinction, Blumenberg argues, severing the association of curiosity with superfluous things, and inaugurating a newly "theoretical curiosity," as a scientific use of abstraction, "freeing [curiosity] of its characterization as 'caring' about superfluous matters . . . [bringing it instead] into the central precinct of human care." [22] Modern scientific speculation redirected the uses of necessity and, accordingly, "rehabilitated" curiosity as the central precinct for modern care. This is the fundamental shift, he argues, whereby science became a primary register for the pursuit of human care, i.e., for the improvement of human happiness by way of scientific speculation. While I find Blumenberg's account of medieval debates over *curiositas* overly compressed, I do think he has a point when he suggests that the modern afterlife of the philosophical (and Aristotelian) understanding of necessity took a crucial turn in the modern age, as theoretical science became the location for the speculations on human questions judged to be of greatest consequence.

This emphasis on claims made by modern adventures in scientific speculation illuminates some of the processes by which such inquiry has come to stand, often in contrast to other pursuits, as crucially necessary for solutions to the most pressing human problems. Furthermore, given the implications of this association for a view of technological advance, it is not surprising that Blumenberg's *Legitimacy* was widely critiqued at the time of its appearance. His account would not have been particularly convincing to historians of technology working at the time, a group that included medievalist Lynn White, the founder of the Society for the History of Technology (SHOT) and author of the famous "stirrup thesis." Blumenberg and White were both working on the historical meaning of the innovation at a time when the uses of scientific inquiry for the general advancement of human care were being debated. By the 1960s some were arguing that advances in epidemiology or the agricultural "Green Revolution" could ameliorate life on the planet in ways heretofore unimagined, a brand of utopianism arguably supported by Blumenberg's account.[23] Yet this was only one strain of a complicated set of intellectual reactions to the problems raised by technology in the wake of the horrifying events of World War II. My point here is that the questions raised by discourses of historical and technological newness remain fundamentally questions of value. I would argue, moreover, that for all its limitations, Blumenberg's account of the legitimacy of modernity can assist us in understanding the narrative of the new—even Modernity as *Neuzeit*, the New Age—precisely *as* a discourse of value.

What seems both notable and as yet unremarked in this influential debate is the differing status of repetition in Löwith's or Blumenberg's work. Where Löwith sees repetition as a return to persistent and problematic tropes, or beliefs, Blumenberg reads "reoccupation" as a redirection of persistent questions for a different future. If these two share an interest in marking the power of historical repetition, they differ as to the meaning of such persistent returns. Blumenberg's Nietzschean commitment to human "self-assertion" emphasizes repetition and return in a larger story of increasing human freedom[24]; Löwith, on the other hand, reminds us of the degree to which claims of newness can occlude repetition as fate, the difficulties of getting beyond older structures of thought and desire.

The outline of Blumenberg's story of modernity as an enterprising advance is certainly, to borrow from Freud, history as "day-dream or phantasy" where "past, present, and future are strung together . . . on the thread of the wish that runs through them."[25] But precisely as such, it offers significant explanatory power regarding fantasies about the new that persist, particularly the longstanding opposition between "novelty" (as superfluous) and "innovation" (as necessary), but also regarding the notion of literature, particularly old literature, as irrelevant, in contrast to science, still viewed, arguably, as the "central precinct for human care." The narrative value of the new *for* modernity—a claim that, even more than secularization, constitutes the ultimate payoff for Blumenberg's study—circulates thus as a story of legitimation, but legitimation not only of an epoch, but of a certain tight association of innovation with the pursuit of those new things crucial to our happiness. And it is precisely this discourse of legitimacy that underwrites Grafton's confidence that the early moderns valued novelty in epoch-making ways, the new serving, at that time, as a means to legitimate, rather than invalidate, an idea.

Even when pursued dialectically, epochal claims remain controversial; such narratives signify in excess of their evidentiary claims, as the case of Columbus makes clear. Furthermore, this debate—between repetition as "reoccupation" inclined toward freedom and repetition as fraught with the limitations of fate—repeats a set of questions also crucial to medieval accounts of the new. Concerns over fate and freedom—over determinism or human agency—were crucial to scholastic controversies in the twelfth and thirteenth centuries.[26] Such concerns recurred in the careful efforts to distinguish the stupefying effects of wonder in the new from the cognitive passions that prompt fresh intellectual enquiry. The Löwith / Blumenberg controversy suggests the degree to which accounts of epochal change embed these same issues of fate and freedom. We should not be surprised when epochal narratives thus exceed their evidentiary limits. As C. D. Blanton puts it, "Whether grasped through lapsarian slippages of secularization or reckoned dialectically, medievalism in theory points only secondarily to the problem of the past at all."[27] Rather than dismiss such accounts as biased or blind, we might consider the values various stories of human fate or human freedom promote.

The Genoese Admiral who was, at his own request, buried in full Franciscan habit would be rehabilitated as the secular champion of epochal transformation. This account of Columbus, agent of a new epoch, points only secondarily to the historical man. The voyager whose search for Asia was prompted by a providential view of world history was "ill-equipped to play the role of epoch-marker."[28] Humanist writers of the sixteenth and seventeenth centuries would nonetheless claim him as such, and in the process translate a devout millenialist into a committed empiricist.[29] Repetition would be crucial here, too: a print-based culture of copying helped transform Columbus's apocalyptic new earth into a New World discovery.

The Mediated New World, I

The complex controversies surrounding Columbus's own historical moment remind us that epochal shifts, like the new itself, occupy a retrospective timing. In the context of both Columbus's activity and Blumenberg's epochal claims, a fuller account of the medieval "*curiositas* complex"[30] can help us to appreciate the ethical equivocations at issue throughout. Blumenberg will hang his account of the transition from medieval to modern epochs on the association of *curiositas* with care. Medieval Christian moralists writing on the topic deploy the links between care and curiosity. And the etymon prompted centuries of debate concerning the pursuit of knowledge and questions of value: what kinds of things, and what kinds of intellectual pursuits, are deserving of our care or our careful attention?

Columbus's interest in voyaging, his pursuit of seafaring knowledge, were grounded in a wide range of Christian texts,[31] a body of writings engaging *curiositas* in ways pertinent to travel and knowledge both. Travel was largely endorsed throughout the Judeo-Christian tradition, as Edward Peters points out, although it would from time to time register negatively as "restlessness and dissatisfaction with the self and the consequent capacity to become distracted by trivial objects of interest."[32] The ethical pursuit of knowledge involved a discourse first encountered in the work of Roger Bacon: the desire to know the secrets of the world. There were complex questions at stake, and these ventured across a range of disciplines—artistic, exploratory, philosophical, and moral. From this larger vantage, Blumenberg's account of premodern *curiositas* seems entirely "too narrow";[33] in the premodern tradition the term "can neither be applied mechanically to entire classes of experience and disposition, nor . . . be restricted to an exiguous model of the history of experimental science without considering its connotations in palaeopsychology, moral philosophy, and theology."[34]

Christian moralists engaged *curiositas* equivocally, and by way of any number of fictional, experimental, or philosophical, texts. Such debates were related, but not identical, to the debates about desire and intellectual work pursued through the discourse of *ingenium* and examined in Part II. Here, I wish to note the ambivalence with which curiosity was treated in the material that Columbus inherited: it could be recognized as a laudable ethical pursuit, particularly when undertaken so as to know more about Christianity, or to pursue Christian evangelism to the "ends of the earth";[35] yet curiosity might also be tainted with sin, of pride, as in Gregory the Great; or gluttony, as in Peter of Limoges; or lust or *acedia*, as in Augustine.[36] This is the kind of moral impulse, and moral ambivalence, that eventuated in Roger Bacon's defensive claims throughout his *Opus Majus*, as when he grounded his experimental and linguistic knowledge by way of Christendom's ambition for the whole world.[37]

Furthermore, and of central importance in the current context, critiques of *vitium curiositatis* regularly converged on narratives not only of superfluity but also of conquest, particularly by way of critiques of overweening territorial greed—as they did in the traditions surrounding Alexander the Great. Conquering sovereigns, both historical figures like Henry II, Roger II of Sicily, or Pedro III of Aragon;[38] and literary figures like Arthur,[39] were associated with Alexander the Great, as a historical model and one of the Nine Worthies. The medieval Alexander tradition engages *curiositas* by way of ethical questions related to ownership; in that context we can locate cautions against the proprietary treatment of knowledge, on the one hand, and claims to territory, on the other.[40]

Walter of Châtillon's twelfth-century *Alexandreis* offers a compelling example of such ethical cautions. In that widely read poem, Alexander's apparently unquenchable desire for conquest comes under regular critique, most notably in this case by the Indian Brahmins,[41] whose address to Alexander emphasizes the conqueror's gargantuan, and thus immodest, appetites: "If your body suited / your soul and mind, which grasp after enormities, / if your tremendous frame matched what you covet, / the whole vast world could never give you space."[42] Alexander's possessiveness, rendered in excessive terms, converges on a kind of covetousness that would, at the time, be well recognized as greed. Moreover, when Peter of Limoges wishes to argue, in his *Moral Treatise on the Eye,* in favor of sharing knowledge freely, he critiques any proprietary hoarding of knowledge, citing the *Letters of Alexander* in support. As in the first *Letter of Alexander to Dindimus, King of the Brahmins,* one reads this: "When it is communicated, knowledge is a source of abundance to which the suffering of loss is unknown, since knowledge is passed on as a bequest when it is shared with someone else. . . . Indeed, it has the capability of shining more brightly whenever it finds opportunities to offer more to others."[43] Not only is knowledge meant to be freely shared, but one who refuses to do so is guilty of the sin of greed, and should be "considered to have robbed his neighbor."[44]

Alexander proved to be a useful figure in such debates, both because of his place as a model for imperial sovereignty, and because of his link to the author of the *Nicomachean Ethics,* Alexander's famous tutor Aristotle. Aristotle's work was, as we have seen, important both to the philosophical questions concerning creation ex nihilo (examined in Chapter 1) and to the concerns with reason and pleasure (noted in Chapter 3). In the Alexander tradition, Aristotle was identified as the source for several pseudonymous texts in the Advice to Princes genre, most prominently the *Secreta secretorum* (Book of the Secret of Secrets), and a tradition important to both Roger Bacon and, in the later Middle Ages, to John Gower's *Confessio Amantis*.[45] Nor are the beneficial aspects of curiosity, via knowledge of the created world, illegible in the *Alexandreis*. The famous ekphrastic description of Darius's ancestral tomb from Book VII emphasizes the beauty of the world ("clearer than glass, purer than placid streams / a crystal image of the turning sky, / a hollow shell of balanced weight, on which / the tri-part world lay beautifully described"[46]) in a description that resonates, as editor David Townsend notes, with the contemporaneous *mappa mundi*.[47] Columbus himself will identify his voyaging ambition with Alexander's empire, calling the lands of his discovery "another world which the Romans, and Alexander, and the Greeks had striven to conquer."[48]

Such diverse evidence suggests the complexities of the ethical issues at stake: the created world was beautiful and knowledge of it could be edifying; but overly proprietary aims, immoderate grasping after either its territories or its secrets, should rightly come in for moral censure. Such concerns continue to the present day, although in different guises: in critiques over the proprietary greed of globalized transnational capital; or in calls for an end to excessive surveillance of what we would understand today as "private" information. My point is not that the discourse of curiosity continued into the modern age unchanged; it is instead that ethical issues continue to cling to the types of vices (greed, for instance) that were associated with curiosity in the Middle Ages.

Nor did the ethical resonances of conquest disappear with modernity, as contemporary work on Columbus's activity make clear. As a motivating force, the combination of utopia and apocalypse would overshadow the Admiral himself, inspiring a train of voyages and voyagers, motivating accounts of salvation, fate, plenitude, glory, pillage, and disaster. Djelel Kadir has helped us to recognize the exploitative effect that this prophetic impulse had and continues to have on the "worlds"—"new world" or "developing world"—that are its object.[49] And feminized images of America as a paradisic "virgin territory" were deployed as "chaotic and intimidating projections" that "legitimized conquest and subjugation."[50] Yet we can also hear in the biblical text an impulse that resonates with that "real pressure" for newness, the affective power of the desire to begin again, to regain fresh feeling, with the longing to be enchanted with the beautiful, to see a sparkling world, a place and a time beyond the "worn world of people and things," or a release from the crushing weariness of suffering.

If Columbus's motivations were ambitious in affective as well as cosmo-logical terms, his actions were hardly unique. European travelers had been seafaring since practically forever. By the early Middle Ages, Christian Euro-pean sailors had covered a "vast network of rivers that ran to the Baltic and North Seas, the Atlantic, and the Mediterranean," tracing "the most indented coastline in the world, . . . [one] laced with islands located along increasingly well-known sea lanes."[51] They appear, moreover, to have "discovered" the Western Hemisphere more than once: European settlements in North Amer-ica date from as early as the tenth century; Norse saga material—the *Saga of the Greenlanders* and the *Saga of Erik the Red*—report European settlements by the year 1000 on what is today the Labrador coast, stories that have lately been corroborated by archaeological discoveries at L'Anse aux Meadows, New-foundland, Canada. Old Norse sagas would not, however, gain widespread traction in Europe until the early seventeenth century: the first printed edition of *Greenlandia* appeared in 1605 in a Latin translation; such texts would not circulate widely until the nineteenth century.[52]

This absence of printed media stands in stark contrast to that other scene of printing, the one crucial to the reception of Columbus's voyage in 1492.[53] The importance of Columban texts has long been recognized as part of the retrospective narrative through which the new came to signify as an excite-ment about data and about writing. Campbell links new world narratives to developments in fiction writing and the epistemologies of science;[54] Latin Americanist José Rabasa attributes them to Columbus's own interest in writ-ing the world, a distinctly Renaissance activity, he argues, one that contrasts with a "medieval" interest in reading the world, not writing it. Relying, like Grafton, on the longstanding association of the Renaissance with novelty, Rabasa reads Columbus as "reflect[ing] on the new" by narrating the natural world, that is, the things, plants, and animals that he saw; nature became, Rabasa argues, a "locus to be inscribed on a blank page."[55] But this goes too far: for the pages through which the claims of new world discovery circulated were not, in fact, blank—the biblical signifiers and moral discourses on which they regularly depended were very old indeed. I want to reverse this story, of-fering in what follows an account of the new world less through the agency of a single writer or act of writing, than via a repetitious process of reading and publishing, of textual circulation; always, then, of rereading, imprinting, and reprinting.[56]

The Mediated New World, 1492, II

Both Rabasa and Campbell recall Columbus's famous reference to a "New Heavens and New Earth." Yet this reference did not circulate in a tidy chronology originating with the Admiral's pen, the Columbus event, or eyewitness testimony followed by a reader's reception of it. As we shall see, accounts of "new" lands with biblical overtones did not follow the Admiral's writing. They preceded it. Columbus's own citation of the biblical "New Heavens and the New Earth" dates from 1498, some four years after the publication of editions of Columbus's first letter, and right about the time those printed editions were being reissued, freshly translated in a host of vernacular languages.

The citation dates from the period of Columbus's third voyage, and occurs in a letter sent to Juana de la Torre, nurse to Don Juan of Castile, Ferdinand and Isabella's only son. Here, Columbus raises the image of divine newness as a vision given specifically to him. He writes,

> I came with such earnest love to serve these Princes, and I have
> served with a service that has never been heard or seen. Of the new
> heaven and of the new earth, which Our Lord made, as St. John
> writes in the Apocalypse, after he had spoken of it by the mouth
> of Isaiah, He made me the messenger and He showed me where
> to go.[57]

We recognize, in the latter half of this quote, the familiar apocalyptic citation of the new. The devout Columbus claims to be God's messenger, the herald of God's new world, his activity well placed within the context of the Christian prophets, and as the typological fulfillment of the word of the prophet Isaiah.[58] Yet newness emerges here in another way, too. Columbus emphasizes his superlative sovereign service as a radically new kind of political devotion, or so he claims, one that has "never been heard or seen." His newness was apocalyptic; it was, at the same time, *au courant*, a politically savvy response to the scene at the Aragon court.

Columbus's exploratory activity was controversial, as is well known. While Ferdinand and particularly Isabella continued to support his endeavors financially and philosophically,[59] others in and around their court openly derided him, actively working behind the scenes to cause him trouble. His increasing religious polemicism responds to the political machinations of the scene of his financing and support. As Fernández-Armesto puts it, Columbus's

"sense of divine purpose grew gradually and fitfully and was born and nourished in adversity."[60] But this also suggests that the Genoese admiral had
plenty of reason to want renewal, plenty of reason for cloaking his ambition in
the grandiose and legitimizing tropes of the biblical prophets. This is, of
course, a citation of the New that readers would well recognize as something
very old indeed.

The "new world" theory was aided by such citations. Yet Columbus's own
usage occurred rather late in the game;[61] the "new world" project was already
well advanced by the time this 1498 letter was penned. Another letter, one
claimed to have come from Columbus's own hand, was translated, printed,
and widely circulated as early as 1493, in the immediate aftermath of the admiral's first voyage. If, as Rabasa argues, the "new world" theory was aided by
Columbus's own writerly ambitions, it was advanced at least four years earlier
by way of the publication and wide circulation of another set of letters. The
textual situation of these documents is quite complex, and I do not have the
space to review it fully here. I recommend Margarita Zamora's groundbreaking analysis of that textual scene surrounding their publication, on which I
rely.[62]

The relation of the published letters to the admiral himself is far from
clear. The published letters were based on a group of texts known as the Santageal and Sanchez letters, addressed to two Aragonese court officials by those
names and published under the date February 15, 1493. Thanks to Zamora's
philological work, we now recognize the Santageal letters as texts themselves
created for wide circulation by someone other than Columbus. They are based
on a letter that Columbus did indeed send to Ferdinand and Isabella, but a
letter dated March 4, 1493, that is, seventeen days after the February date. The
February 15 letters, those that will be published and widely circulated, seem to
be redactions, indeed, particular readings of this March 4 letter. They follow
the prose of the March 4 letter in some crucial ways, but they also change its
overall rhetorical force, suppressing specific features of the original. Details
that might raise controversy to Columbus's venture, or couch that journey in
the pragmatic terms of business (that is, standard clauses in a contract between
a sailor and a patron, or specific financial requests) are excised. On the other
hand, passages that emphasize the honor and glory of the Europeans, in the
description of the reception given by native peoples to the Spanish on their
arrival, are intensified. The redacted Santageal letters, produced after March 4
but backdated to February 15, were presumably used to establish a version of
Columbus's report with an earlier claim than the Admiral's own. This

redaction, created in old Europe as temporally prior to the one penned on the voyage itself, was long thought to have historical primacy. And it is this letter—at least two steps removed from the Admiral himself—that would, nonetheless, be translated into Latin, Italian, Spanish, and Italian verse form, and would circulate in published books throughout Europe as early as 1493. Translated versions of the Santageal letters appear variously between April of 1493 and 1497 with an astounding total of seventeen editions, published in Barcelona, Rome, Basel, Paris, Antwerp, Florence, and Strasbourg.

As particular readings of Columbus's activity rendered in Europe in the aftermath of the first voyage, the Santageal letters are not as clearly tied to historicist, anthropological, or geographic accuracy as one might wish; these texts offer only the pretense of spontaneity or eyewitness reportage. These letters, moreover, endeavor to establish the geographic detail of an eyewitness report as prior to any mercenary or political concerns, concerns that would be only subsequently raised, these texts suggest, seventeen days later, in Columbus's March 4 text. This is not description but promotion, a process of international marketing, designed to create a particular image of both the Admiral and his work, spinning new world discovery as an eruption of data, an experience untainted by self-interest, or any such apparently craven motivations. This is, in other words, a discourse of value that elevates aspects of the capricious arrival on Hispaniola to a grander set of implications and meanings. Zamora puts it this way: "For almost five hundred years our sense of the Discovery has been the product of a reading that appears to have been little concerned with the objective representation of the geographical or anthropological aspects of the lands in question, or with historical accuracy. The Santageal version was much more interested in its own reception; that is, it was fashioned for the readers it hoped to engage, and the reactions it hoped to elicit."[63]

This may well be, as Rabasa claims, evidence of an agency of writing. But it is also an agency of editing, among other things. Nor is this only Columbus's writing, or an agency that can, in any way, be severed from those readerly acts that Rabasa associates with medieval habits of mind.[64] Furthermore, the circulation of the Santageal "reading" in one particular edition further aided the "new world" claim. I am particularly interested in the Latin translation of the Santageal letter that circulated in a 1494 Basel edition—an important and well-known version beautifully adorned with woodcuts. This codex includes a dramatic text, mostly in prose, ascribed to Carolus Verardus, written in praise of Ferdinand's 1469 conquest of Granada; it thus implicitly links the *Reconquista*, the putative triumph of Old World Spain over Islam, with the New

World discovery of "islands of the orient." Both are rendered so as to testify to the glory of Spain under Ferdinand.[65] The woodblock prints included are extraordinarily fine, and the final page contains one such print that purports to be a representation of ship in full sail, bearing the inscription "Oceanica Classis" (see Figure 1). A copy at Indiana University's Lilly Library bears an inscription, probably dating from the sixteenth century, attesting to the long tradition of identifying this woodcut as a faithful rendering of Columbus's ship: "a facsimile of the ship of Columbus as here represented," the English writer notes, "is considered by the editor [of a later text] as a faithful picture of the original" (see Figure 2).

We might, just for starters, note that "facsimile" is precisely the word to use in this case, although, while this image is indeed a "faithful picture" of the original from which it is copied, that original is not any particular caravel on which Columbus ever sailed. The wonderfully detailed image of "the admiral's own caravel" is now recognized as a detail taken from a woodcut in Bernhard von Breydenbach's lavishly illustrated *Peregrinatio in Terram Sanctam* ("Voyage to the Holy Land"), published in Mainz in 1486, best known for its amazing map of the City of Jerusalem. Breydenbach's illustrated text would be published in eight separate editions, all predating the 1494 edition of Columbus's letters. The original image of the caravel appears in a landscape sketch of the harbor at Modon, a Mediterranean port on the Peloponnese, and an important way station for pilgrimages to Jerusalem (see Figure 3).

The Basel edition of the letter of Columbus recirculates this image—now reversed, reframed, and remounted. Breydenbach's book, a fifteenth-century bestseller, features gorgeous woodcuts attributed to Revwich of Utrecht; those woodcuts were important to the book's popularity. Other ships taken from Revwich's woodcuts would be used to illustrate the Basel edition of Columbus's letter,[66] such as the image taken from the harbor at Rhodes. By 1498, some four years after the Basel publication of Columbus's letter in Latin, Dutch, and Spanish, editions of Breydenbach's work would also appear.[67]

These visuals, like the blend of *Reconquista* with New World, write new events on old stories, casting the reality of discovery through images of Old Europe. To be sure, these woodcuts were useful in part because they depicted the kind of sailing vessels in use at the time Columbus sailed. But their use also corroborates the degree to which early print offered a doubled culture of copying, both in the design of books and in the production of print runs.[68] My point is that one way that the Basel edition makes Columbus's voyage seem real, seem empirically forceful, is by way of the realistic detail evident in the

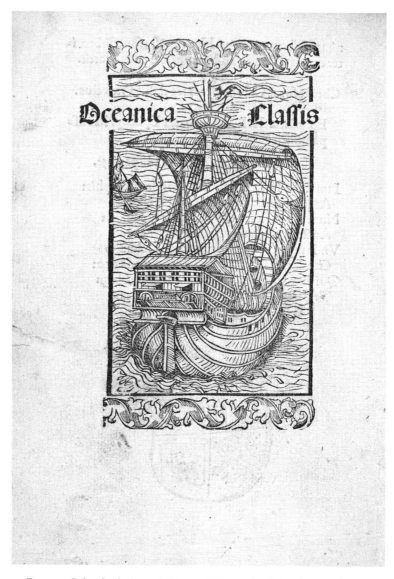

Figure 1. Columbus's Caravel, *Letter of Christopher Columbus*, Basel 1494.
Courtesy The Lilly Library, Indiana University, Bloomington, Indiana.

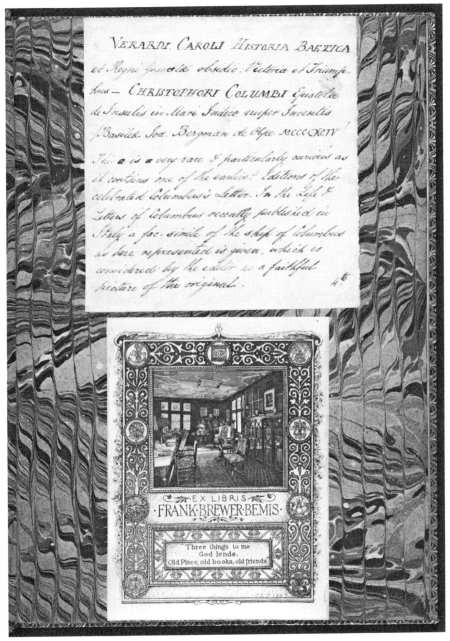

Figure 2. *Letter of Christopher Columbus*, Basel, 1494, inscription inside
back cover. Courtesy The Lilly Library, Indiana University,
Bloomington, Indiana.

Figure 3. Detail from the Harbor at Modon, Bernard von Breydenbach.
Peregrinatio in Terram Sanctam, Mainz, 1486. Courtesy The Lilly Library,
Indiana University, Bloomington, Indiana.

Revwich woodcuts. These are images, moreover, with their own purchase on
innovation: according to Elizabeth Eisenstein, the Revwich woodcuts exem-
plify an "increasingly precise and detailed" visual form as a new feature of late
fifteenth-century printing technology.[69]

The Basel edition installs such newness in relation to Columbus's act. This
is also a clear example of what William Kuskin terms "the printer's ability to
construct authority from pre-existing models."[70] And there is still another
kind of textual circulation at issue. An epigram added at the end of the Latin
text of Columbus's letter is included in this edition, and ascribed to the pen of
the bishop of Monte Peloso. This brief paragraph endorses the "discovery" in
political and religious terms even as it adopts language that is resonant with

biblical newness. Monte Peloso addresses "the most invincible King of Spain," but of course his intended audience is much wider:

> No region now can add to Spain's great deeds: to such men all the world is yet too small. An Orient land, found far beyond the waves, will add . . . to thy renown. Then to Columbus, the true finder, give due thanks; but greater still to God on high; who makes new kingdoms (nova regna) for himself and thee.

Columbus may have found new kingdoms, but God on high makes them. The epigram associates the new of God's dramatic creativity (the tradition of creation ex nihilo, examined in Chapter 1) with new discovery. The new "world" is not far to seek; it is a new creation, and a new kingdom made by God for "himself and thee." Thanks are due to Columbus as finder, and to God as maker, in a parallel structure that toggles from the first to the second. The use of a plural "new kingdoms" writes a plurality of diversity on the tradition of creation as divine innovation; it hints at the new world break, mapping territorial acquisition onto typological history, indeed, nearly conflating the two. It is not a far stretch, syntactically, semantically, and grammatically from "new kingdom" to "new world."

We should pause here to note that, far from being a completely new idea, this is an account of the new that is entirely consonant with medieval theological orthodoxies of creation.[71] God's claim to creative power—his creation ex nihilo of a new place—has been appropriated for Spain's territorial claims. God's new kingdom is Spain's own. The epigram coordinates conquest with innovation on a cosmological scale. New Creation converges on Columbus's new discovery: God, like the voice from the throne in the scene of the New Jerusalem, makes new; Columbus, human agent, is a "true finder" of God's creative extravagance. Even amid the territorial impulse in evidence here, geographic accuracy seems beside the point: the "orient land" found "far beyond the waves" was in the West, not the East. Within such a powerfully desirous history, errors of fact seem barely noticeable.

The "discovery" of America is not usually associated with a disdain for facts. Yet, instead of empiricism, the circulation of these Columban texts produced a consequential "reality effect," one that obtains in our persistent sense of the factual rupture between medieval and modern. Such an effect, we are ready to note at this point, depends upon multiple and unsettled temporalities: from Columbus's landing to the March 4 letter, to the redaction predated to February 15, to a publication in 1493, back to Breydenbach's 1486 edition with Revwich's innovative woodcuts, to the 1494 Basel edition, to the later translations and editions in 1498, these emerging just around the time Columbus himself describes the "new heavens and the new earth" in the letter to Juana de la Torre. Where in this amazing circuit can we locate the eruption of the new? With the landing? The genuine letter? The redacted letter? The initial edition of the redacted letter? With Columbus? With Breydenbach? With Revwich? Or with those anonymous redactors?

In terms of time and narrative, all of this suggests that the new world's link to the "new heavens and the new earth" circulated not only as prophecy, not only as typology, and not only as a retroactive backward glance by which anomalous details are recast as a fresh beginning. It circulated as all three. We have something more paradoxical, and a timing fractured by desire: for if the fear of and desire for apocalypse motivated Columbus's voyaging, then the history of that occasion is marked by what Deleuze calls a "reverse causality,"[72] a desire for the future that motivates action in the present. Yet insofar as the new world break also occupies the retroactive coding of the *après coup*, prophetic futurism is recycled retrospectively as something utterly new. It was in this way, too, that New World voyages, Columbus's as well as those who came after, made the knowledge of the world inherited in writings ascribed to Plutarch and Mandeville seem freshly plausible, even likely.[73]

This is a story in excess of the Admiral's writerly agency; but, even as such, it is a story that tracks the affective power of the new. Walter of Châtillon, who opens his twelfth-century *Alexandreis* with worries about the audience reception that will greet his work, recognized the affective power of the new. Another medieval writer, one long since disassociated from geographic verisimilitude, and known to us as John Mandeville, similarly observes the affective power of the new. In both instances, the new emerges as a textual feature, an attribute of narrative, and as a question of value, broadly conceived. And so I turn finally to a "medieval" travel narrative read by Columbus and those voyagers[74] who followed in his wake, from a writer who was, by some accounts, nothing more than an armchair tourist. These unlikely recapitulations remind us of the affective edge of the value for the new, of a repetitive longing for the epochal.

Mandeville's Elsewhere

When anything new is recited in the ears of the multitude, the mob
as a matter of time-honoured custom breaks up into various
passions.[75]

The wryly humorous Walter of Châtillon inaugurates his new verses on
the old story of Alexander with an observation about the "time-honored" custom of the audience as a mob. Passionate disagreements, he argues, greet new
work, and inflame the audience's passions:

> One applauds and proclaims that what he's heard is praiseworthy.
> Another, led on by ignorance, or else perverted by the goad of
> malice or hatred's tinder, judges harshly even what is well spoken
> and so deems that well-turned verses must be returned to the anvil.
> One might marvel that the human race has been so distorted from
> its original nature—that nature by which all things that God had
> created were very good. (Thus it is more inclined to damn than to
> forgive and finds it easier to distort what seems dubious than to put
> the better construction on such things.) Long fearing this, I
> intended to suppress you forever, O my *Alexandreis*.

Audience reactions disclose ethical frailties: the seductions of ignorance, the
"goad of malice," or "hatred's tinder." Walter's prologue makes a preemptive
move aimed at the ethics of stingy readers, inveighing against those "more
inclined to damn than to forgive." And his work expresses a host of ethical
concerns that we have seen in earlier chapters: the new as generative for comment and commentary was noted in Machaut's account of novelty from
Chapter 4; God's new creation was a crucial concern for the scholastics, as seen
in Chapter 1; the relation of new verses to Nature's anvil features in the debates
over pleasure and virtue noted in Chapter 3. The ethical problem for Walter
resides not in the newness of his text but in the "distortions" of his critics
whose reactions devolve from a fallen human nature. Envious readers, denying
the better angels of their character, read ungenerously; an innovating if defensive poet, accordingly, threatens to suppress his own work. It may well be his
best protection. Walter's preemptive rhetorical strike certainly hobbles his potential critics, ingeniously linking their churlishness to original sin. The legitimacy of new work prevails, and Walter will shortly rank himself within a

virtuous brotherhood of poets and church fathers, from Virgil to Jerome. As elsewhere in the tradition, the new embeds a narrative of moral value, emerging here as a feature of textuality that is arguably on the side of the angels.

The *Book of John Mandeville*,[76] the popular travel narrative that survives in a complex range of manuscript redactions, similarly legitimates the new as a feature of the created world. Where Walter depicts the new as a stumbling block for an audience of ignorant, envious, or malicious readers, the author we call Mandeville emphasizes the productive power of novelty for building an audience in the first place. Following his descriptions of the Lands of Prester John, and attendant upon his inability to describe the Earthly Paradise, "Mandeville" brings his travel narrative of marvels to a precipitous end:

> I do not want to say any more about marvels that there are there [sic], so that other men who go there can find new things to speak of which I have not heard mentioned. For many men have great delight and desire in the hearing of new things; and so I shall cease telling of the different things I saw in those countries, so that those who desire to visit those countries may find enough new things to speak of for the solace and recreation of those whom it pleases to hear them.[77]

New things, found not made, give "great delight," providing both spiritual "solace" and entertaining "recreation." To be sure, and as expected, Mandeville casts the new as human discovery, not creation, whereby things already made are now newly seen for their attractive power.[78] It is crucial, however, that the power of new things extends beyond the lands where they can be found to the narrators and writers who describe them. The magic of newness extends, that is, from the ultimate source of the creative Word to wordsmiths, particular writers "who can find new things to speak of." Those who *describe* the new things give "many men . . . great delight," not merely in the new things themselves, but in the *telling* of them. Thanks to a medieval writerly activity, marvels can be refashioned in language made freshly available for human desire. And thanks to the speaker's own modest restraint and self-confessed humility, those who come after might "find enough new things to speak of." This writerly devotion to newness will recur in later texts, as, for example, in the Prologue to Thomas More's *Utopia*.[79]

Mandeville's *Book* combines knowledge of new things with ethical concerns as "lessons to be learned elsewhere,"[80] making clear the links between enchantment and writing, between the creative Word and mere words. Yet he also evinces a desire to preserve the new as undiscovered, to keep its secrets fresh, available for other writers, readers, romancers. Moreover, at the very moment that he alludes to them, Mandeville—in perhaps a brilliant move of self-promotion—sets up obstacles for his readers, frustrating their desire for news about new things. He promises that the new will enchant while simultaneously withholding descriptive access to those enchantments. Obstacles to the new will, as a host of theorists from the psychoanalytic to the anthropological have noted, only heighten our sense of the value of its pursuit.[81]

Of course, Mandeville's words also—if quietly—evince a worry that newness might be, even as a feature of things created by God, in short supply. The new feels scarce; it might therefore someday be exhausted, depleted, tapped out. Mandeville's restraint thus hopes to preserve an archive of enchanting novelty elsewhere. This "elsewhere" lies nowhere else than on some future page; bounded by a description yet to be, it is pure creative potential. And if it is true, as some have argued, that the author of *The Book* never ventured further than his library—compiling his account of the marvelous world from a rich array of classical and contemporary sources—here we find moving testimony to the power of the signifier to energize desire and engage the imagination, to make us look again, see freshly. Set in new frames, reorganized in unpredictable arrangements, old books gain a fresh rereading: their enchanting features emerge anew, (re)circulated, (re)arranged, (re)made.

If Walter of Châtillon threatens to withhold his new work on account of the envious and aggressive desire of his potential readers, Mandeville lingers over newness as a textual effect, a circuit of desire in infinite regress binding an author to his audience. Between the two of them they map the equivocal, ambivalent range of the new as a medieval problem, and a question dependent upon relations of writers and readers. In Mandeville's terms, new productions by human writers borrow power from the world as a site for God's creative extravagance. In Walter's view, fallen human readers point their critiques at new creative endeavors, endangering their emergence by forgetting the goodness of all things.

As a structure of desire, in both of these cases, newness claims an *affective* register. Mandeville's fondest wish: that "those who *desire* to visit those countries may find enough new things to speak of for the solace and recreation of those whom it pleases to hear them" (emphasis mine). Imaginary visits, apparently, will do. The desire Mandeville describes will, as Columbus's letters make clear, lead to actual travel but does not require it. Mandeville makes clear that

newness occupies a magnificently recursive feedback loop, as writing and reading double back on a perpetual hope for freshness in other places. Desire is
everywhere (else), its ambitious appetite driving the search for new things,
prompting travel, or flights of fancy, and producing (if also paradoxically
withholding) new combinations of words now capable of making people,
places, and things palpably real to an ("old") audience already predisposed to
their pleasures.

If this seems an extraordinary version of newness as a kind of freedom, the
problem of fate, of typology, and of apocalypse, remains, of course. Those
difficulties were present in Mandeville, whose book displays ample aggression
toward certain of its "others." Despite the diversity of its manuscript and linguistic history or its moments of avowed admiration for the faithfulness of
Islam, Mandeville's fantasy of worldwide Christendom, like Columbus's marketers, or Roger Bacon's *Opus*, wagers on the universalizing appropriation of
all creation for "new" Christian uses. It is not at all coincidental that, whatever
"magnanimity" might be optimistically ascribed to Mandeville's text, Jewish
communities are not among those cultures that were either admired or sanctioned, as, for instance, in the horrifying representation of Gog and Magog,
the "Jews of the Ten Lost Tribes" closed forever in the hills leading to the Vale
Perilous, "which some men call the Vale of Enchantment."[82] Mandeville's clear
delight in newness sits alongside his use of the conventional tropes of medieval
anti-Semitism. God's preeminent claim to novelty means, on the one hand,
that medieval artists must disavow metaphysical types of innovation as a
means to the (material) pursuit of the freshness of novelty; it means, on the
other, that the incarnation of Christ constitutes a divine kind of magic, a newness powerful enough to repudiate the Hebrew traditions from which Jesus
came as the, now outmoded, "old" Law of Moses.

This "typological" use of the medieval new constitutes the darker narrative of its history. It is one face of the ethical limits to our enchantment with
novelty. Typology calls to mind those features of our attraction to the new that
psychoanalysis has also noted: when old structures reappear before us, they
can sometimes come decked in the sheen of the new. As Columbus's brand of
newness suggests, we do not always accurately recognize the new when it happens; but those misrecognitions do not dissuade us from continuing to look
for it. The Real—those traumas that structure our subjectivity, from which we
may not escape—returns. Yet the reemergence of old patterns doesn't always
look like repetition, at least not at first.

Such a material account of the new does not, however, mean that we should dismiss "newness" and our desire for it as all ideology, or as mere illu-sion. Everything depends on how the old is repeated. For amid this important reminder of the tragic way that history can echo, chime, or recur, there re-mains another wager altogether, and a hope in the different futures that might still and nonetheless come to be. We yearn, I think, for the transformation of our world and our lives; and such hopes are necessary not only for imagining the future but for keeping us interested in life. Like the Europeans who took to the sea, we too feel this as a real pressure. The possibility of change, the hope for rescue and consolation, the persistent desire for a way of seeing the world as fresh and lively remain a serious drive to human endeavor: this is the hope embedded in Nietzsche's Eternal Return; this is the possibility encoded in Deleuze's "bare repetition." In this regard, our enchantment with newness, for all its fits and starts, might help to keep us interested in planning for a future once again.

An Age of Innovation

> The announcement of decline is only the obverse of the insatiable
> hunger for the new at any price.
> —Jean Laplanche, *Nouveaux fondements pour la psychoanalyse*

In the breathtaking illumination of Fortune's Wheel found in BN manuscript
FR 1586 (an early manuscript of Guillaume de Machaut's *Remedy of Fortune*),
blind Fortuna turns her majestic wheel as figures clamber up, topple down, or
rest briefly on the heights in the usual cycles of ascent and decline (see Figure 4).
Familiar as a traditional, even standard, example of "medieval" iconography,
Fortune's Wheel is usually taken as evidence for the old, outmoded, medieval
notion of time. More a throwback than a view of history pertinent to the current century, Fortune's Wheel may seem an odd choice for the cover of a book
on the status of the new in and for the intellectual and literary culture of the
Western Middle Ages.

But look again. At some distance from her Wheel, Fortuna ratchets the
handle of a crank, assisted by state-of-the-art technology presumably designed
to make her labors less taxing. Tooth-edged gears dominate the frame, and if this
is a "standard" of medieval iconography, it is an altogether remarkable one, not
least for its depiction of cutting-edge mechanics. The illustration was likely composed before such mechanisms were in widespread use; yet, in its realism and
detail, the image evokes the technical specificity of a blueprint, a visual rendering in advance of actual cranks or gears like these. This is the repetitive Fortune's
Wheel rendered in the timing of the not-yet: a futuristic version of time's recursive movement. New combines with tradition, innovation with repetition in the
image par excellence for what I have been calling the Medieval New.

Figure 4. Detail, Machaut, *Remède de Fortune*, FR 1586, folio 30 V.
Courtesy Bibliothèque Nationale de France.

Whether as particular image or iconographic tradition, Fortune's Wheel raises enduring questions of fate and freedom. If the mechanized wheel is Fortune's own, then what hope have we for a future different from the past? What does it mean that even our most innovative technical inventions can end up cranking the same old wheel? Such worries have an old history. Or perhaps it might be better to say that medieval worries like these will have a long future, one persistently associated with the vicissitudes of technological advance. A spin of fortune's wheel might harbor the chance for a new day; yet even as the day seems new, it may return us to that fated place that we have been too many times before. Jacques Lacan stresses the links between chance and fate, the two operating together as a figure for "the encounter with the real."[1] Entwined with the compulsive repetitions that mark what Freud called the death drive, the real renders the very possibility of newness as both potentially traumatic and persuasively suspect.

Yet if Fortune's Wheel prompts serious debates over worldly change and mutability, the medieval figure also, as Andrea Denny-Brown has shown, tracks the changing aesthetics of sartorial fashion.[2] And so, too, does the image of Fortuna in Figure 4, dressed à la mode, fashionable tippets hanging from her sleeves and sporting a sophisticated pointed shoe. Change, then or now, marks crucial aesthetic features, even as we recognize the new, to evoke again the words of Roland Barthes with which this book began, as more "a value" than "a fashion." Analysts of the oscillations of repetition with newness, theorists such as Lacan or Deleuze, but also, it turns out, medieval poets Guillaume de Machaut and Geoffrey Chaucer, or the anonymous artist who wrought this image, urge the point upon us: everything depends on how things are repeated. This image of an utterly fashionable Fortune's Wheel illustrates a time when even the repetitions of timeworn things might be driven by or toward a new kind of power, poised toward a different aesthetic, technical, or human future.

This stunning illumination of fashionable Fortuna and her unrelenting Wheel dazzles as art by offering a radiant new version of an old iconographic tradition. As paradox, as equivocation, the image grants fashionable Fortune a "new luminosity."[3] Rendering earlier figures in resplendent array, medieval artists of all kinds self-consciously reworked the old, the apparently obsolete, in brilliant new style. Irreducible to either figural tradition or artistic originality, their practice offers one model for today, an art and culture devoted to repurposing, and a brand of cultural sustainability. Such insights can also prompt usefully equivocal histories or futures of newness, but only if we can still imagine the kind of analysis, the kind of study, that made this book possible; only if we still have access to the texts and contexts that offer the opportunity to consider ethical encounters with newness in various ages of innovation—then or now.

This seems a point of particular cogency, institutionally as well as intellectually, at a time when "innovation" has become a nearly ubiquitous slogan for the twenty-first-century university, also a time when the humanities are said to be in great "decline." An "insatiable" hunger for the new "at any price" fuels accounts of decline, as Laplanche notes. And so it seems no coincidence that our contemporary moment bemoans the decline of the Liberal Arts, while rushing toward a version of the new from which the "traditional" disciplines are almost always excluded. The future that beckons for the innovating University remains unclear, but we might remember that the University has long been the site for both edges of the medieval new, for experiments in new possibilities as well as for the conservation and renewal of diversities from long ago or far away. But for how much longer?

The defense of the University increasingly emphasizes its capacity to foster innovation; yet we often take for granted just *what* the new entails. This study has endeavored to reopen this question and, in this way, to add to the current conversation. A medieval brand of the new might dislodge prevailing assumptions (perhaps even our own) about the meaning of "innovation" or "novelty"; reorient an approach to newness that still too often depends on an untenable opposition to the old; complicate and deepen an understanding of tradition as ripe for repurposing; and continue to inspire our own uncommon rereadings or radiant rewritings. Attending to medieval culture—one of novelty's "hard cases"—has enlivened an equivocal new able to ground humanistic inquiry in all the so-called "traditional disciplines" for our own brand of luminous obsolescence.

Notes

INTRODUCTION. NEWFANGLED VALUES

Epigraphs: Roland Barthes, *Le plaisir du texte* (Paris: Éditions du Seuil, 1973), 65. David Edgerton, "Innovation, Technology, or History: What Is the Historiography of Technology About?" *Technology and Culture* 51, 3 (July 2010): 680–97, 681.

1. Roland Barthes, *The Pleasure of the Text*, trans. Richard Miller (New York: Hill and Wang, 1975), 40.

2. On the uses of apparently superfluous pursuits, see particularly Aranye Fradenburg, "Simply Marvelous," *Studies in the Age of Chaucer* 26 (2004): 1–26. The point pertains to all manner of business pursuits as well, and we might remember that even business sectors committed to the next great idea traffic in copies and knock-offs: as Johanna Blakley has argued, the fashion industry's traditional lack of copyright protection creates "a culture of copy" that, in fact, promotes "an open and creative ecology of innovation." The lack of copyright protection in diverse industries—from food (recipes) to entertainment (neither jokes, games, nor magic tricks can be copyrighted) to home décor (furniture design has no copyright protection)—has helped, not hurt, the bottom line. As Blakley's work makes clear, copying and sampling can propel rather than stymie creative innovation. The culture of copying that Blakely identifies with the nonproprietary, and materially productive, economy of contemporary fashion is not unique to the present moment. And it has recently changed rather dramatically. See Johanna Blakley, "Lessons from Fashion's Free Culture," 2010, http://www.ted.com/talks/johanna_blakley_lessons_from_fashion's_free_culture.html.

3. Thanks to Jonathan Elmer for this utterly useful conceptualization.

4. Nicholas N. Taleb, *The Black Swan: The Impact of the Highly Improbable* (New York: Random House, 2007).

5. Barthes, *Pleasure of the Text*, 40. Matei Calinescu reads Barthes's view as "an apparent Manichean struggle" between old and new, and (on those very grounds) argues that Barthes's "emerging temporal scheme has a sort of medieval quality about it: it cannot help but remind one of the hoary antiquus/modernus opposition." "Postmodernism and Some Paradoxes of Periodization," in *Approaching Postmodernism*, ed. Douwe Fokkema and Hans

Bertens (Utrecht: John Benjamins B.V, 1986), 239–54, 241. This seems wrong on both counts.

6. As Bruce Holsinger has shown, the innovations of the theoretical avant garde of the latter half of the twentieth century, including Lacan, Derrida, Bourdieu, all indebted to the ground-breaking work of professional medievalist Georges Bataille, harbor a resolutely medieval "archeology." *The Premodern Condition: Medievalism and the Making of Theory* (Chicago: University of Chicago Press, 2005).

7. The term is meant to emphasize the productive rather than limiting nature of certain kinds of problems. Gilles Deleuze, *Difference and Repetition*, trans. Paul Patton (New York: Columbia University Press, 1984), 154.

8. This is particularly true insofar as such discourses impinge on questions of religious belief. My own explications of religious notions of newness offer an account deployed for present uses. About the methodological problem, Stephen Justice writes, "modern scholarly accounts of medieval belief, which try to explain belief from the outside, cannot actually explain it. One reason they cannot is that medieval belief already incorporates their possibility as part of its skeptical self-affliction: naturalizing or demystifying accounts of belief not only are available to medieval sources, but are internal to their acts of belief." "Did the Middle Ages Believe in Their Miracles?' *Representations* 103, 1 (Summer 2008): 1–29, 17. This does not, of course, mean that we cannot understand aspects of the knowledge systems therein produced in ways that they might not have been understood at the time.

9. From Adorno's *Aesthetic Theory* (143–44): "Form secularizes the theological model of the world as an image made in God's likeness, though not as an act of creation but as the objectivation of the human comportment that imitates creation; not *creation ex nihilo* but creation out of the created. The metaphorical expression is irresistible, that form in artworks is everything on which the hand has left its trace, everything over which it has passed. Form is the seal of social labor, fundamentally different from the empirical process of making." This has been an important point for medievalists, especially via the work of Fredric Jameson, whose influence continues. For an interesting account of Adorno's use of the medieval, see Maura Nolan, "Making the Aesthetic Turn: Adorno, the Medieval, and the Future of the Past," *JMEMS* 34, 3 (2004): 549–75. Nolan emphasizes Adorno's account of secularization as paradoxical: "At no moment in *Aesthetic Theory* does Adorno allow [a] singular thesis of secularization to stand. [Secularization] takes its place, along with other historical and aesthetic theses, as part of an endless and contradictory process of development and change" (570). The place of the "medieval" in Adorno's thinking remains, she argues, "*multiple* and inconsistent" (555, original emphasis). On Adorno's nominalism as it pertains to art, see C. D. Blanton's brilliant essay, "Medieval Currencies," in *The Legitimacy of the Middle Ages: On the Unwritten History of Theory*, ed. Andrew Cole and D. Vance Smith (Durham, N.C.: Duke University Press, 2010), 194–232.

10. On the importance of engaging periodization dialectically, see Julia Lupton, *Afterlives of the Saints: Hagiography, Typology, and Renaissance Literature* (Stanford, Calif.: Stanford University Press, 1996) and Chapter 6.

11. Max Weber, *The Sociology of Religion*, trans. Ephraim Fischoff (Boston: Beacon

Press, 1963; repr. 1993). On Weber's use of the phrase "disenchantment of the world," see H. H. Gerth and C. Wright Mills, "Bureaucracy and Charisma: A Philosophy of History," in *Charisma, History, and Social Structure*, ed. Ronald Glassman and William H. Swatos (New York: Greenwood, 1986), 11; Jacob Burckhardt, *The Civilization of the Renaissance in Italy*, ed. Peter Murray, trans. S. C. G. Middlemore (London: Penguin, 1990); Hans Blumenberg, *The Legitimacy of the Modern Age*, trans. R. M. Wallace (Cambridge, Mass.: MIT Press, 1983).

12. Richard Firth Green, "Changing Chaucer," *Studies in the Age of Chaucer* 25 (2003): 27–52; Michael Camille, *The Gothic Idol: Ideology and Image-Making in Medieval Art* (Cambridge: Cambridge University Press, 1989); Hans Ulrich Gumbrecht, *The Production of Presence: What Meaning Cannot Convey* (Stanford, Calif.: Stanford University Press, 2004); Beryl Smalley, "Ecclesiastical Attitudes to Novelty, c. 1100–1250," in *Church Society and Politics*, ed. Derek Baker (Oxford: Oxford University Press, 1975), 113–31.

13. Deleuze, *Difference and Repetition*, 90.

14. Craig Calhoun, "The Radicalism of Tradition: Community Strength or Venerable Disguise and Borrowed Language?" *American Journal of Sociology* 88, 5 (1989): 886–914; David Edgerton, *The Shock of the Old: Technology and Global Culture Since 1900* (New York: Oxford University Press, 2007).

15. Fradenburg has articulated a means of considering the continuities and discontinuities of history by way of the signifier. I follow her methodological lead here. *Sacrifice Your Love: Psychoanalysis, Historicism, Chaucer* (Minneapolis: University of Minnesota Press, 2002).

16. See *Piacere e dolore: Materiali per una storia delle passion nel Medioevo*, ed. Carla Casagrande and Silvia Vecchio, Micrologus' Library 29 (Firenze: Sismel Edizioni del Galluzzo, 2009).

17. Sylvia Huot, *The Romance of the Rose and Its Medieval Readers: Interpretation, Reception, Manuscript Transmission* (Cambridge: Cambridge University Press, 1993), 74. On ethics and enjoyment as it pertains to texts of that period as well as our own, see Sarah Kay, *Courtly Contradictions: The Emergence of the Literary Object in the Twelfth Century* (Stanford, Calif.: Stanford University Press, 2001); Fradenburg, *Sacrifice Your Love*; Jessica Rosenfeld, *Ethics and Enjoyment in Late-Medieval Poetry: Love After Aristotle* (Cambridge: Cambridge University Press, 2011).

18. Influential Marxist historian of technology Edgar Zilsel wrongly argued that this usage of *ingenium* was unknown in the Middle Ages. *Die Entstehung des Geniebegriffs: Ein Beitrag zur Ideengeschichte der Antike und des Fruhkapitalisms* (Tubingen: Mohr, 1926), 251ff. But see Robert Hanning, *The Individual in the Twelfth Century* (New Haven, Conn.: Yale University Press, 1977).

19. *De oratore* 1. xxiii.

20. Paul Guyer, ed., *The Cambridge Edition of the Writings of Immanuel Kant, Critique of the Power of Judgment*, trans. Guyer and Matthews (Cambridge: Cambridge University Press, 2000), 186.

21. I am grateful to Michel Chaouli for helpful clarifications. Ken Freiden argues that

Kant deploys *ingenium* as inborn talent to emphasize his genius as a "mental capacity" rather than mythological visitation, but also "introjects" mythological aspects by way of the Latin *genius*. *Genius and Monologue* (Ithaca, N.Y.: Cornell University Press, 1985).

22. Guyer, ed., *The Writings of Immanuel Kant*, 186–87.

23. Unsurprisingly, Blumenberg's argument for the legitimacy of the epochal break has been widely criticized by medievalists for the reasons and in the manner one might expect. Newhauser and Peters, to whom I am greatly indebted, each critique the inaccuracies of Blumenberg's reading of medieval *vitium curiositatis*, as we shall see. Kathleen Biddick argues that *Legitimacy* founders on German historiography concerning medieval gnostic heresies from the period after World War II; it cannot escape, she argues, "the Jewish question of the 1920's and 30's" which function, she suggests, as "the ghost in Blumenberg's legitimacy machine," *Medieval Review* (TMR 10.09.12). For more on this point see, Benjamin Lazier, *God Interrupted: Heresy and the European Imagination Between the World Wars* (Princeton, N.J.: Princeton University Press, 2008). The most thorough-going analysis of Blumenberg's unhappy influence from the perspective of a medievalist, and making clear Blumenberg's part in the particularly problematic association of the medieval (and sacred) precisely *as* the residual or "not-new," can be found in the collection of essays edited by Andrew Cole and D. Vance Smith, *The Legitimacy of the Middle Ages: On the Unwritten History of Theory* (Durham, N.C.: Duke University Press, 2010), including the editors' "Introduction: Outside Modernity," 1–36. The often erudite analyses in this volume, however, often downplay the degree to which Blumenberg's *Legitimacy* also makes legible certain dependencies between modern and premodern thought. His work seems notable, particularly when considered alongside projects appearing at the same time, such as Kuhn's 1962 *Structure of Scientific Revolutions*, and Foucault's 1966 *Les Mots et les choses*. For my own critiques and admittedly perverse uses of Blumenberg, see Chapter 6.

24. Christian Zacher, *Curiosity and Pilgrimage: The Literature of Discovery in Fourteenth-Century England* (Baltimore: Johns Hopkins University Press, 1976), 23.

25. Zacher asserts that such distinctions, important to Classical thinkers, were revived in the Renaissance. Newhauser has shown the various ways that medieval intellectuals and moralists situated excessive curiosity, but not all curiosity, in terms of vice. See "Towards a History of Human Curiosity: A Prolegomenon to its Medieval Phase," *Deutsche Vierteljahrschift fur Literaturwissenschaft und Geistesgeschichte* 52 (1982): 569–75; "Augustinian vitium curiositatis and its reception," in *Saint Augustine and His Influence in the Middle Ages*, ed. Edward B. King and Jacqueline T. Schaefer, Sewanee Mediaeval Studies 3 (Sewanee, Tenn.: Press of the University of the South, 1988), 99–124.

26. Newhauser, "Towards a History," 568.

27. On Aquinas's use of necessity in the context of debates over creation ex nihilo, see Chapter 1.

28. As Blumenberg beautifully puts it, *Legitimacy of the Modern Age*, 344.

29. Edward Peters, "*Libertas Inquierendi* and the *Vitium Curiositatis* in Medieval Thought," in *La notion de liberté au Moyen Age: Islam, Byzance, Occident*, ed. George Makdisi et al. (Paris: Belles Lettres, 1985), 89–98, 95.

30. Peter of Limoges, *The Moral Treatise on the Eye*, ed. and trans. Richard Newhauser, Medieval Sources in Translation (Toronto: Pontifical Institute of Medieval Studies, 2012), "The Costliness of the Eyes in Respect to Other Members of the Human Body," 108–10, 110.

31. In addition to Cole and Smith's *Legitimacy of the Middle Ages*, see Kathleen Davis, *Periodization and Sovereignty: How Ideas of Feudalism and Secularization Govern the Politics of Time* (Philadelphia: University of Pennsylvania Press, 2008).

32. Peters, "Vitium Curiositatis in Medieval Thought," 89.

33. Newhauser, "History of Human Curiosity," 563.

34. Cole and Smith, *Legitimacy of the Middle Ages*. I do find legitimacy a strangely overdetermined category for such engagement, particularly given the degree to which it emerges in debates over human creativity in the medieval period. But I would also agree with a recent review that the volume at times seems uninterested in the differences of value across time. It can feel as if "nothing seems interestingly different from anything else." Fradenburg, *The Legitimacy of the Middle Ages: On the Unwritten History of Theory* (review). *SAC* 33 (2011): 306–311, 310.

35. Joseph A. Schumpeter popularized the term in *Capitalism, Socialism and Democracy*, 3rd ed. (New York: HarperCollins, 2008).

36. Schumpeter's notion is taken to an absurd extreme in recent work on innovation in management culture, as in Peter A. Drucker, *Managing in a Time of Great Change* (New York: Truman Talley, 1995), cited here.

37. David Edgerton, "Innovation, Technology, or History: What Is the Historiography of Technology About?" *Technology and Culture* 51, 3 (July 2010): 680–97, 681.

38. Ibid., 681. Edgerton's popular *The Shock of the Old* dismantles the apparent opposition between old and new in a call to rethink the place of invention and innovation within technological histories. Edgerton himself, however, duplicates features of the condescension toward novelty. Here, too, the medieval case will prove instructive.

39. The emphasis on innovation seems especially disabling to scholars of premodern technology like Pamela O. Long, who suggests that today's preoccupation with innovation has, despite medievalist Lynn White's important legacy as a founder of the field of the history of technology, worked against a continued interest in premodern histories. Long, "The Craft of Premodern European History of Technology, Past and Future Practice," *Technology and Culture* 51, 3 (July 2010): 698–714, 713.

40. Joel Mokyr, *The Lever of Riches: Technological Creativity and Economic Progress* (New York: Oxford University Press, 1992), where creative innovations from the period register primarily as a driver of economic development in the West, with little attention to the complexities of interaction across the range of cultures and societies. Mokyr's account seems, in crucial ways, to overstate the case of the West and underanalyze the facts of cross-cultural interaction and borrowing. Edgerton similarly notes the Schumpeterian impulse legible in Mokyr's work: "In economic history, the dominant tradition of thinking about technology has been Schumpeterian in inclination, and thus very innovation-centric, as is evident in the work of David Landes and Joel Mokyr," "Innovation, Technology, or History," 689.

41. Rather than recommend that we avoid, or strictly curtail, a consideration of innovation as a cultural-historical category (like Edgerton), or ventriloquize its current usage in the corporate University (like Liu), Latour's work radically recasts its terms, about which more below.

42. On the medieval distinction between *ingenium, usus,* and *consuetudo,* see Chapter 1, pp. 36–40.

43. Alan Liu, *The Laws of Cool: Knowledge Work and the Culture of Information* (Chicago: University of Chicago Press, 2004). Liu's emphasis on the putatively derivative—as opposed to creative—force of copying is not surprising. The notion that creative innovation requires a radical break from all that has come before traces its history to Romantic-era notions of authorship and poetic genius, ideas indebted to Kantian accounts of the genius as radical innovator with the vision and power outmatching—and not at all indebted to—his predecessors. Geniuses don't copy.

44. Ibid., 3.

45. N. Katherine Hayles expresses a similar reservation in a largely favorable review of Liu's book: "In adopting a strategy of ventriloquizing that which he resists, Liu risks overstating the scope of business culture, or at least understating what remains outside its arena of operation" (237). I am thus in sympathy with Hayles's larger point: "surely it is an exaggeration to claim, as Liu says, ventriloquizing the voice of diversity management, that 'pure business culture remains definitive of all culture' (54). Although the ethos of the unknown may indeed be significant as a site of resistance, by no stretch of the imagination is it the only, or even the primary, possibility for participating in cultures very different from the culture of corporate knowledge work." "The Achievement of the *Laws of Cool,*" *Criticism* 47, 2 (2005): 235–39, 237.

46. I use the term "sciences" advisedly, since medieval "sciences" were not identical to modern notions of science; indeed, this is part of Blumenberg's point. Scholars in History and Philosophy of Science continue to debate whether the term can even be used with reference to the early period. As plural, "sciences" here refers to a range of endeavors—philosophical as well as technical—not a part of modern science; the term remains useful for my project in historical rereading.

47. This may be one reason Latour's ground-breaking account of networks of innovation has been so useful and important to medievalists and early modernists. In place of standard accounts of either "creativity" or "economic progress," he offers the dynamic power of networks as interplays of creativity and bureaucracy (the latter, often at its most banal), retrenchment and promotion, stagnation, or torpidity. See "Irreductions," addendum to English edition of *The Pasteurization of France,* trans. John Law (Cambridge, Mass.: Harvard University Press, 1998), 153–236.

48. Innovation is not a synonym for "newness" in Latour's account so much as a set of sociocultural, bureaucratic, technical, artistic, and libidinal networks of affiliation and antagonism among human and nonhuman actants. In *Aramis, or the Love of Technology,* for instance, he offers a moving narrative of the cultural power of an ingenious invention never finally implemented, an innovative electric train that never made it past the prototype

stage. That kind of story—told via an imaginative assemblage of bureaucratic memos, technical blueprints, newspaper records, even the ventriloquization of the train's own dashed hopes—resonates with fictionalizing features of medieval romance, replete with "manmade marvels" that act, move, or demand response. Formally, too, *Aramis* gestures in insightful ways to the complex productivity of desire. Blending an archive of technological, political, and bureaucratic texts with the imaginary diary of the train that never was—merging, that is, the science-fictional with the documentary—Latour speculates persuasively on both the emotive affinities for new things, and the drive for and against innovation at its most vulgar and instrumental. *Aramis, or The Love of Technology* (Cambridge, Mass.: Harvard University Press, 1996).

49. Even as Blumenberg "reoccupies" medieval questions, he remains committed to intellectual and cultural change, after the manner of Kuhn's notion of the paradigm shift.

50. Andrew Ladis and Carolyn Wood, Introduction to *The Craft of Art: Originality and Industry in the Italian Renaissance and Baroque Workshop*, ed. Andrew Landis and Carolyn Wood (Athens: University of Georgia Press, 1995), 1–4, 2.

51. Deleuze, *Difference and Repetition*, 90.

52. Hans W. Loewald, "Some Considerations on Repetition and the Repetition Compulsion," *International Journal of Psychoanalysis* 52 (1971): 59–66, 59. Loewald argues that "re-creation" constitutes the "reactivation on a higher level of organizing potential which makes possible novel configurations and novel resolutions" (59). Loewald's coordination of "passive repetition" with "reproduction" as distinct from re-creation begs a number of questions regarding the "new." Similar oppositions were important to the gender politics of medieval accounts of human creativity and human corruption, as recent rereadings of Alain de Lille's *Complaint of Nature* have made clear, although in more equivocal ways, as we shall see.

53. Profoundly in Jean Laplanche, *Nouveaux fondements pour la psychanalyse* (Paris: Presses Universitaires de France, 1987), 6–7. Here and throughout, I cite Laplanche's work in a new translation by Robert M. Stein, and forthcoming in The Unconscious in Translation Series from International Psychoanalytical Books. I am grateful to Stein for sharing his work-in-progress with me. See also Françoise Davoine and Jean-Max Gaudilliere, *History Beyond Trauma*, trans. Susan Fairfield (New York: Other Press, 2004). The point has been powerfully made by scholars of both medieval and Renaissance literatures. See Fradenburg, *Sacrifice*, but also Linda Charnes, *Hamlet's Heirs: Shakespeare and the Politics of a New Millennium*, Accents on Shakespeare (New York: Routledge, 2006).

54. As cited by Laplanche, *Nouveaux fondements pour la psychanalyse*, 7. Stein's translation, as he notes, "follows Laplanche who appears to be quoting from memory" (typescript, n.1).

55. Psychoanalytic approaches to invention and novelty are, in other words, illuminating for the medieval case on account of this fundamental assumption, sharing certain features with medieval theological, aesthetic, and technological understanding even as it diverges in some key ways.

56. Jacqueline Cerquiglini-Toulet, *A New History of Medieval French Literature*, trans. Sara Preisig (Baltimore: Johns Hopkins University Press, 2011), 132.

57. In his essay on the "Rat Man," Freud explains how ambivalence for a particular object could explain the particular features of obsessive thought. Sigmund Freud, "Notes upon a case of Obsessional Neurosis," *SE*, X: 151–318. One might consider scholasticism as this kind of obsessional process of thought. On scholasticism as obsessive, see Aranye Fradenburg, "Amorous Scholasticism," in *Speaking Images: Essays in Honor of V. A. Kolve*, ed. Charlotte Morse and Robert F. Yeager (Chapel Hill, N.C.: Pegasus, 2001.)

58. As Fradenburg puts it, "The Real's return always generates the effect of the stunningly new," "Simply Marvelous," 16.

CHAPTER I. SCHOLASTIC NOVELTIES

Epigraphs: Henry Adams, *Mont-Saint-Michel and Chartres* (1905; New York: Houghton Mifflin, 1935), 377; Michael Colacurcio, "The Dynamo and the Angelic Doctor: The Bias of Henry Adams' Medievalism," *American Quarterly* 17, 4 (1965): 696–712.

1. Henry Adams, *Mont-Saint-Michel and Chartres*, 377. Hereafter *Chartres*.

2. Ibid., 345.

3. Jennifer Fleissner, "The Ordering Power of Disorder: Henry Adams and the Return of the Darwinian Era," *American Literature* 84 (2012): 31–60, 53.

4. William Courtney, "The Virgin and the Dynamo: The Growth of Medieval Studies in North America (1870–1930)," in *Medieval Studies in North America: Past, Present, and Future*, ed. Francis G. Gentry and Christopher Kleinhenz (Kalamazoo, Mich.: Medieval Institute Publications, 1982), 5–22, 21. This profoundly influential view, according to Courtney, was especially important to the founders of medieval studies in America. He continues, "The contrast of the Virgin and dynamo, of the society of 1200 over against the society of 1900, was the ultimate vision of Henry Adams's education and the one that influenced the attitudes of Ralph Adams Cram and several of the founders of the Medieval Academy of America, as well as Marshall McLuhan, in his *The Mechanical Bride* and *The Gutenberg Galaxy*," 21n8.

5. Adams, *Chartres*, 368–69.

6. Ibid., 370.

7. I am indebted to Colacurcio's nuanced account of Adams's "very peculiar treatment of Saint Thomas Aquinas" in "The Dynamo and the Angelic Doctor."

8. Adams, *Chartres*, 359–60. "Science has to deal . . . with scores of chemical energies which it knows little about except that they always seem to be constant to the same conditions; but every one knows that in the particular relation of mind to matter the battle is as furious as ever. . . . The dispute was—and is—far from trifling. Mind would rather ignore matter altogether. In the thirteenth century mind did, indeed, admit that matter was something—which it quite refuses to admit in the twentieth—but treated it as a nuisance to be abated. . . . Schoolmen as well as mystics would not believe that matter was what it seemed—if, indeed, it existed;—unsubstantial, shifty, shadowy; changing with incredible

swiftness into dust, gas, flame; vanishing in mysterious lines of force into space beyond hope of recovery; whirled about in eternity and infinity by that mind, form, energy, or thought which guides and rules and tyrannizes and is the universe."

9. J. C. Levenson, *The Mind and Art of Henry Adams* (Cambridge, Mass.: Harvard University Press, 1957), 284.

10. As, for example, in this telling addition to the "authorized" English translation of Gilson's *Heloise and Abelard*, trans. L. K. Shook (Chicago: Henry Regnery, 1953), 87. "If this demands further testimony, we have the word of Henry Adams, *whose perspicacity borders on genius*," emphasis added. (Shook was at Toronto at the same time as Gilson, suggesting Gilson's approval of her translation.)

11. Colacurcio, "Dynamo and the Angelic Doctor," 708.

12. See many of the essays, but particularly Stephen Nichols's account of "romantic" medievalism and teleology, in *Medievalism and the Modernist Temper*, ed. R. Howard Bloch and Stephen G. Nichols (Baltimore: Johns Hopkins University Press, 1996).

13. The term is borrowed from Deleuze.

14. Kathleen Biddick, *The Typological Imaginary: Circumcision, Technology, History* (Philadelphia: University of Pennsylvania Press, 2003).

15. The condemnations of 1277 were aimed to large degree at the theology faculty in Paris and elsewhere, so that not all masters were implicated in the suspicion of Aristotle. See Jan A. Aertsen, Kent Emery, Jr., and Andreas Speer, eds., *Nach der Verurteilung von 1277: Philosophie und Theologie an der Universität von Paris im letzten Viertel des 13. Jahrhunderts. Studien und Texte / After the Condemnations of 1277: Philosophy and Theology at the University of Paris in the Last Quarter of the Thirteenth Century. Studies and Texts*, Miscellanea Mediaevalia 28 (Berlin: De Gruyter, 2001).

16. Not, however, to universal acclaim. Wood writes, "Richard Rufus was the earliest Western teacher of the new Aristotle whom we know. He taught Aristotelian physics and metaphysics as a Master of Arts at the University of Paris before 1238. His lectures are the earliest known surviving Western lectures on these subjects. . . . Rufus flourished between 1230 and 1255, teaching philosophy and theology at Oxford and Paris in this crucial period. His philosophical career ended and his theological career began in 1238 when he became a Franciscan friar and left the Arts faculty at Paris" (2). "Introduction" to Richard Rufus of Cornwall, in Rega Wood, ed., *Richard Rufus of Cornwall: In Physicam Aristotelis*, Auctores Britannici Medii Aevi XVI (Oxford: Oxford University Press, 2004). See also "Richard Rufus: Physics at Paris before 1240," *Documenti e Studi sulla Tradizione Filosofica Medieval* 5 (1994): 87–96.

17. Alain De Libera, *Penser au Moyen Âge* (Paris: Éditions du Seuil, 1991): "la crise de la scolastique, le conflit de la foi and de la raison, de la théologie et de la philosophie, ont commencés en Islam avant d'être importés (avec le modèle de l'intellectuel lui-même) en Occident," 20–21. My translation.

18. III S. 37. Dub 1., as cited by E. J. M. Spargo, *The Category of the Aesthetic in the Philosophy of Saint Bonaventure* (New York: Franciscan Institute, 1953), 111.

19. Bonaventure and Aquinas will depend on the distinction between two definitions of things, "res" and "ens," a distinction also important to Aristotle.

20. *Didascalion* I, chap. 9, as cited by Michael Camille, *The Gothic Idol: Ideology and Image-making in Medieval Art* (Cambridge: Cambridge University Press, 1989), 35.

21. Ibid. Camille argues that the proliferation of idols, whether in (Christian) images or (Saracen, pagan, and Jewish) idols, was necessary to make real the very distinction between licit and illicit representations so important to Christian theology. On the one hand, he demonstrates the massive productivity of image-making during a time of "new iconographies, . . . linked to new institutions, laws and prohibitions" (9). On the other, he positions medieval creative production as explicitly dedicated to old figures and forms: artisans "clung" to "the safe cycle of duplication and secondariness, adapting and altering compositions but rarely creating new ones" (39). Hints of this emphasis continue on the next few pages, as in the following: "[Bonaventure] lists chimeras and other fanciful creations of composite art as emblems not of creativity but of mere synthesis" (40).

22. On the use of logic to suggest that truth was grasped through the formal structure of demonstration (*per se*), not through methods of rhetorical or dialectical persuasion (*per accidens*). In the famous response to al-Ghazali's *Incoherence of the Philosophers, The Incoherence of the Incoherence*, Averroës would further suggest that while the latter could be simultaneously untrue and persuasive, the former was persuasive on account of its truth.

23. Richard C. Taylor, "Averroës," in *The Cambridge Companion to Arabic Philosophy* (Cambridge: Cambridge University Press, 2004), 187.

24. Ibid., 186.

25. Averroës argues against allegorical interpretation and for the literal account of creation in scripture since "it is not stated in scripture that God was existing with absolutely nothing else: a text to this effect is nowhere to be found." Cited and translated by Taylor, "Averroës," 186.

26. The question of creation ex nihilo will be debated by Jewish philosophers, with Moses Maimonides being the first to arrive at a philosophical solution. He takes the position that while the Torah articulates such a view of creation, "there is no philosophical proof available to demonstrate this doctrine." As we will see, this will be Aquinas's position as well. On these debates, see Seymour Feldman, *Philosophy in a Time of Crisis* (New York: Routledge, 2003). See particularly chap. 5, "Creation of the World," 40–43.

27. He is here, according to editor Anton C. Pegis, disagreeing with both Avicenna and Peter Lombard. See the *Summa Theologica*, trans. Frs. of the English Dominican Province (N.P. Benziger, 1947, rpt. 1981).

28. As Joshua Kates has helpfully pointed out.

29. On the complex question of equivocal, univocal, and analogy, see the work of E. J. Ashworth, "Signification and Modes of Signifying in Thirteenth-Century Logic: A Preface to Aquinas on Analogy," *Medieval Philosophy and Theology* 1 (1991): 39–67; "Analogy and Equivocation in Thirteenth-Century Logic: Aquinas in Context," *Mediaeval Studies* 54 (1992): 94–135; "Analogy, Univocation, and Equivocation in Some Early Fourteenth-Century Authors," in *Aristotle in Britain During the Middle Ages*, ed. John Marenbon (Turnhout: Brepols, 1996), 233–47. For a reading of the cultural power of equivocation for the contemporaneous poetry of the troubadours, see Sarah Kay, *Courtly Contradictions: The*

Emergence of the Literary Object in the Twelfth Century (Stanford, Calif.: Stanford University Press, 2001).

30. On Hegel's observation, see C. D. Blanton, "Medieval Currencies: Nominalism and Art," in *The Legitimacy of the Middle Ages*, ed. Andrew Cole and D. Vance Smith (Durham, N.C.: Duke University Press, 2010), 194–232, 202–3. With regard to the later period, Joel Kaye's brilliant *Economy and Nature in the Fourteenth Century* (Cambridge: Cambridge University Press, 1998) makes the case that philosophical innovations—the shifts toward multiplication, probability, and equilibrium, among others—were "grounded in" an increasingly monetized society.

31. Lacan obliquely observes: "no one can think except in creationist terms," 126. "On creation ex nihilo," in *The Ethics of Psychoanalysis: The Seminar of Jacques Lacan, Book VII*, ed. Jacques-Alain Miller, trans. Dennis Porter (New York: Norton, 1992), 115–27.

32. This group of masters at Paris were led by Siger of Brabant (c. 1240–c. 1281) and condemned for holding certain views regarding Aristotle's work.

33. I am grateful to Nicholas Ingham, O.P. for crucial assistance on these points.

34. On this, see F. J. A. de Grijs, "The Theological Character of Aquinas' *De Aeternitate Mundi*," in *The Eternity of the World in the Thought of Thomas Aquinas and His Contemporaries*, ed. J. B. M. Wissink (Leiden: Brill, 1990), 1–8.

35. The schoolmen were equally committed to the notion of human freedom as, for one thing, necessary for the possibility of any ethics. The point is emphasized by the fact that the Latin Averroists were condemned in part on the grounds of a putatively overly necessitarian—and hence deterministic—cosmology, a point that examined a bit further in Chapter 2.

36. The uncaused cause is emphatically not a historical origin, the beginning of a series or sequence—such a view would lead back to the problem of multiplicity that Aquinas seeks to solve.

37. *Didascalion*, I, chap. 9.

38. For a summary on the debate over art and nature, see William Newman, *Promethean Ambitions: Alchemy and the Quest to Perfect Nature* (Chicago: University of Chicago Press, 2004), esp. chap. 2.

39. Ibid. Newman shows that the practice of alchemy played a central role in such debates; Camille details the proliferation of nonnatural image-making amid metaphysical concerns over the problems of human creation. Discourses of alchemy produced a range of debate that would affect the understanding of human technology as well as art. Indeed, as Newman argues, much of the debate concerning alchemy had to do with its claims to do more than perfect nature, but to generate an utterly new substance out of natural materials. A number of claims gained for alchemy could be interpreted as claims for perfecting nature.

40. Camille, *Gothic Idol*, esp. chap. 2.

41. It is this long tradition that interferes when Camille concludes that in "clinging" (like children? out of desperation?) to older forms, medieval artists and artisans played it safe. In repeating the old, so the argument goes, medievals repudiated the very possibility that something could be newly made by human activity.

42. Camille, *Gothic Idol,* 35

43. David Luscombe, "The Sense of Innovation in the Writings of Peter Abelard," in *Tradition, Innovation, Invention: Fortschrittsverweigerung und Fortschrittsbewusstsein im Mittelalter,* ed. Hans-Joachim Schmidt (Berlin: De Gruyter, 2005), 181–94.

44. Robert Hanning, *The Individual in Twelfth Century Romance* (New Haven, Conn.: Yale University Press, 1977), 21.

45. As pointed out in the introduction, Kant first stipulates in the Third Critique that genius in art is the capacity to produce *new* rules and models of artistic practice (thereby denying that there are any truly fixed standards). Interestingly, scholars have long argued for the existence of an approach to art for art's sake in the Italian Renaissance. Gombrich deploys historical evidence to argue that a move from a self-understanding as craftsman to the institution of the very conception of Art as such takes place in the very early fifteenth century in Florence, in particular as documented in Ghilberti's stance toward his own successive production of the doors for the baptistry. "The Renaissance Conception of Artistic Progress and Its Consequences," in *Gombrich on the Renaissance* (New York: Phaidon, 1985), 1: 1–10.

46. *Du Cange* or the *Medieval Lexica,* in *The Database of Latin Dictionaries,* s.v. "usus." I am grateful to Bridget Balint for her assistance.

47. Abelard's text is taken from *Historia calamitatum: Texte critique avec une introduction,* ed. J. Monfrin (Paris: J. Vrin, 1962), 69 (also cited by Hanning, *The Individual,* 29).

48. Hanning, *The Individual,* 29.

49. Luscombe cites Letter 10 in *Peter Abelard: Letters IX-XIV,* ed. Smits (Groningen: Bouma, 1983), 243, lines 123–24.: "nec usum rationi nec consuetudinem praeferendam esse ueritati."

50. Bridges, ed., *The "Opus Majus" of Roger Bacon* (London: Williams and Norgate, 1990; rpt. Frankfurt: Druck, 1964): "Quatuor vero sunt maxima comprehendendae veritatis offendicula, quae omnem quemcumque sapientem impediunt et vix aliquen permittunt ad verum titulum sapientiae pervenire, videlicet fragilis et indignae auctoritatis exemplum, consuetudinis diuturnitas, vulgi sensus imperiti, et propriae ignorantiae occultatio cum ostentation sapientiae apprentis," (I, 2).

51. And thus its pertinence, in Hanning's account, to the question of the individual subject in the twelfth century. Hanning may be operating, at least in part, under the influence of Kant's account of "genius." *The Individual.* See esp. 17–24, 28–30.

52. Olivier Boulnois, *Au delà de l'image: Une archéologie du visuel au moyen âge, Ve–XVIe siècle* (Paris: Éditions du Seuil, 2008), 352. For full discussion, see 351–62. Translations are my own.

53. On the questions of divine and human freedom and Scotus's ethics, see Mary Beth Ingham, C.S.J. and Mechthild Dreyer, *The Philosophical Vision of John Duns Scotus* (Washington, D.C.: Catholic University of America Press, 2004); Allan B. Wolter, *Duns Scotus on the Will and Morality* (Washington, D.C.: Catholic University of America Press, 1986).

54. Jacques Le Goff, "Antique (Ancient)/Modern," in *History and Memory,* trans. Steven Rendall and Elizabeth Claman (New York: Columbia University Press, 1992), 26.

55. Nancy Frelick, "Lacan, Courtly Love and Anamorphosis," in *The Court Reconvenes: International Courtly Literature Society, 1998*, ed. B. K. Altman and C. W. Carroll (Cambridge: Brewer, 2003), 107–14, 111.

56. De Libera, *Penser*, 346 ff. Scholars as diverse as De Libera and Kay have noted the resonances between Lacan's formulations and the preoccupations of medieval scholastics and intellectuals. Kay, *Courtly Contradictions*, offers a sustained reading of Lacan's "scholasticism" and its usefulness for reading the paradoxes of troubadour poetry.

57. Kay, *Courtly Contradictions*; Jessica Rosenfeld, *Ethics and Enjoyment in Late-Medieval Poetry: Love After Aristotle* (Cambridge: Cambridge University Press, 2011); Erin Labbie, *Lacan's Medievalism* (Minneapolis: University of Minnesota Press, 2006).

58. Lacan, *Ethics of Psychoanalysis*, 115–27.

59. Ibid., 119.

60. Jeremiah 18:6. In Isaiah, the link to God's preeminence as source of all created matter is more explicitly at issue (see, for instance, Isaiah 45:8–11), a point also, if more obliquely, taken up elsewhere in the wisdom literature. The image of God as artisan, as potter, will be important to Christian theology in the post-Reformation period as well. Citations are taken from *The New English Bible*.

61. Courtly Love elaborates a cultural value that signifies desire beyond its own limits or productions; desire, always pursuing the impossibility of its own permanent satisfaction (the desiring subject prostrate before the Thing as "cruel and inhuman partner" who coldly refuses to be "won"), and thus always alluding to something more, something beyond, something impossible of representation or achievement. There is, at the heart of this transaction, a little bit of nothing; the impossible and/or prohibited love object occupies the space of the Thing, a void, a vacuole, an absence (mis)recognized as cold, inhuman refusal. The signifier comes then to the rescue, headed for the Thing but detouring around the void, preserving the empty space of the Thing sublimed. Creative production comes out of, even as it circles, this nothing at the heart of the Thing. Medieval traditions of courtly love, like the notion of creation ex nihilo, make clear that the Thing cannot be approached directly; "fundamentally veiled," we can only draw near by way of detour, encircling, or bypass. A means of approaching the love object yet never attaining her, courtly love makes "the domain of the vacuole stand out" (152) "at the center of the signifiers" (150) of its discourse.

62. Labbie reads Lacan's work precisely as tracking the complex dynamic of the "universal" with the "particular" by way of the structuring principle of the Real, a universal mode capable of crossing and accommodating various particular changes and shifts in signification over time. Her account makes clear the myriad ways in which Lacan's theorization of an apparently "universal" subject takes considerable inspiration from the "quarrel of the universals" of the scholastics, and is thus particularly indebted to Thomistic and Boethian philosophical traditions, traditions which, Labbie argues, Lacan "turns on their head." *Lacan's Medievalism*, 18.

63. Examining a different archive altogether, Andrew Cole comes to a similar conclusion. Attending to the dynamics of orthodoxy and heresy in age of Wycliff, Cole argues that censure could function not only as inhibiting but also as an unintended spur to innovative

developments in literature and intellectual history. *Literature and Heresy in the Age of Chaucer* (Cambridge: Cambridge University Press, 2008).

64. Kay, *Courtly Contradictions*, 313.

65. Ibid., 26.

66. Lacan, *Ethics of Psychoanalysis*, 145. See the chapter "Courtly Love as Anamorphosis."

67. Ibid., 145.

68. Luke Sunderland, *Old French Narrative Cycles: Heroism Between Ethics and Morality* (Cambridge: Brewer, 2010), 14.

69. On the one hand, this combination grounds one of the main arguments for the deployment of psychoanalysis *for* historicism. On the other, as I am also arguing, the epistemological structure implied by Lacan's work diverges quite significantly from an epistemological investment in an "accurate" recovery of the true story about the absent past, a fact signaled symptomatically by his use of Gaston Paris's "courtly love," a term now judged to be inaccurate by historicist experts.

70. Courtly Love, as Fradenburg puts it, constitutes "a breakaway moment in the history of the signifier," which nonetheless shows the recurring, "universal" structure of subjectivity. *Sacrifice Your Love: Psychoanalysis, Historicism, Chaucer* (Minneapolis: University of Minnesota Press, 2002), 20.

71. Bill Brown, "Thing Theory," *Critical Inquiry* 28, 1 (2001): 1–22.

72. For a summary of the debates on the relation of the one and the many, see Sarah Kay, Introduction, "Another and More Perfect World," in *The Place of Thought: The Complexity of One in Late Medieval French Didactic Poetry* (Philadelphia: University of Pennsylvania Press, 2007), esp. 8–15.

73. Sunderland, *Old French Narrative Cycles*, 16.

CHAPTER 2. CONJURING ROGER BACON

Epigraphs: Roger Bacon, "Epistola Fr. Rogerii Baconis de secretis operibus artis et naturae, et de nullitate magiae," in *Fr. Rogeri Bacon Opera quaedam hactenus inedita*, ed. J. S. Brewer (London: Longman, Green, Longman and Roberts, 1859); John Mathews Manly, "Roger Bacon and the Voynich Manuscript," *Speculum* 6, 3 (July 1931): 345–91, 347.

1. Lawrence and Nancy Goldstone, *The Friar and the Cipher: Roger Bacon and the Unsolved Mystery of the Most Unusual Manuscript in the World* (New York: Doubleday, 2005), 297.

2. William Newman, "An Overview of Roger Bacon's Alchemy," in *Roger Bacon and the Sciences: Commemorative Essays*, ed. Jeremiah Hackett (Leiden: Brill, 1997), 317–36, 335.

3. See Amanda Power, "A Mirror for Every Age: The Reputation of Roger Bacon," *English Historical Review* 121, 492 (2006): 657–92. Evaluations mirror the particular biases of the day: Whig historians see Bacon as a courageous bastion of scientific truth and progress; for others, his story exemplifies the infelicity of pseudo-science in a benighted Catholic

medieval era. As Power shows, the overdetermined nature of the issue has characterized accounts of Bacon since at least the seventeenth century. As she puts it, "Bacon scholarship remains in the mode that it entered in the course of the seventeenth century: it is preoccupied with the question of Bacon's originality" (691). She argues that a myopic preoccupation with Bacon's status as innovator has hindered an understanding of him and his work, particularly as both relate to his identity as a Franciscan. Anxieties about overstating Bacon's importance and influence continue today, as in the repeated reminders that he was a man of his time. This is the aim of Jeremiah Hackett's *Roger Bacon and the Sciences*, where David C. Lindberg puts the question in its most recent version: "Must [Bacon] be condemned to insignificance by his failure to complete the mathematicization of perspectiva and by his limited application of experimental methodology to perspectival matters?" "Roger Bacon on Light, Vision, and the Universal Emanation of Force," in Hackett, 243. On the state of the question, see Hackett's own essay, "Roger Bacon on *Sciencia Experimentalis*," in the same volume, 277–315.

4. That said, Bacon's writings circulated among scholars and scientists in some unrecognized textual forms: a long passage in the *Opus Majus* on the distance between the extreme east and west of the habitable globe was cited without attribution in the *Imago Mundi* of Pierre d'Ailly; it would later be quoted by Columbus as one inspiration for his early modern voyages. Bacon's major works can be found in John Henry Bridges, ed., *The "Opus Majus" of Roger Bacon*, 3 vols., (Oxford: Clarendon, 1897–1900; rpt., Frankfurt: Minerva, 1964). The third (supplementary) volume includes corrections and emendations. I have also relied on Burke's English edition, Robert Belle Burke, trans., *The Opus Majus of Roger Bacon* (Philadelphia: University of Pennsylvania Press, 1928).

5. Hackett, "Roger Bacon: His Life, Career, and Works," and Lindberg, "Light, Vision, and the Universal Emanation of Force," 244, in *Bacon*, ed. Hackett, 20; also Lindberg, *Roger Bacon and the Origins of Perspectiva in the Middle Ages* (Oxford: Clarendon, 1996).

6. The story of this cipher manuscript has been the subject of two recent histories published in the trade press. The Voynich manuscript is currently housed in Yale's Beineke Library.

7. Newbold's findings would be published posthumously: W. R. Newbold, *The Cipher of Roger Bacon*, ed. R. G. Kent (Philadelphia: University of Pennsylvania Press, 1928).

8. The *New York Times*, Sunday March 27, 1921, sec. 2, bore the headline, "Bacon 700 Years Ahead in Science."

9. Goldstone, *Friar and the Cipher*, 248.

10. The bibliography is increasingly long. Most important to my thinking are Kathleen Biddick, *The Shock of Medievalism* (Durham, N.C.: Duke University Press, 1998); John Ganim, *Medievalism and Orientalism* (New York: Palgrave, 2004).

11. We now know that oppositions between scholars and popularizers were crucial to the development of professional medieval studies, a field that benefited from popular interest in the early periods while endeavoring to circumscribe the apparent excesses of the amateur medievalist. For the most recent work on this question, and a full bibliography, see Carolyn Dinshaw, *How Soon Is Now? Medieval Texts, Amateur Readers, and the Queerness of*

Time (Durham, N.C.: Duke University Press, 2012). Dinshaw's account of the amateur is persuasive, although at times it casts a somewhat striated opposition between professional and amateur. The dynamics of affection and attachment among professionals are readily evident in the case of Voynich.

12. Newbold, *The Cipher of Roger Bacon*. For Manly's early support, see his essay, "The Most Mysterious Manuscript in the World: Did Roger Bacon Write It and Has the Key Been Found?" *Harper's Monthly Magazine* 143 (1921): 186–97.

13. Manly, "Roger Bacon and the Voynich Manuscript," 345.

14. Ibid., 355.

15. Lynn Thorndike, *A History of Magic and Experimental Science During the First Thirteen Centuries of our Era*, 8 vols. (vols. 1–2 New York: Macmillan; vols. 3–8 New York: Columbia University Press, 1923–58).

16. Power, "Reputation of Roger Bacon," 692.

17. As Madeleine Akrich, Michel Callon, and Bruno Latour argue, "the fate of innovation . . . rests entirely on the choice of the representatives or spokespersons." See Akrich, Callon, and Latour, "The Key to Success in Innovation, Part II: The Art of Choosing Good Spokespersons," trans. Adrian Monaghan, *International Journal of Innovation Management* 6, 2 (June 2002): 207–25, 217.

18. Ibid., 222.

19. At least since he first reminded us that we have never been modern, Latour has been complicating progressive narratives of history on which stories of the development of empirical science so regularly depend. And his particular account of the contemporary uses of the opposition of "magic" to "science" can help to dislodge the continuing assumption that premodern technical theory and practice was experimentation as a version of "occult" (read illegitimate) science. See Latour, "Irreductions," addendum to the English edition of *The Pasteurization of France*, trans. John Law (Cambridge, Mass.: Harvard University Press), 153–236.

20. Fredric Jameson, *The Political Unconscious: Narrative as a Socially Symbolic Act* (Ithaca, N.Y.: Cornell University Press, 1981).

21. Translations are my own. This text will appear in an important early modern printing. "An excellent discourse of the admirable force and effcacie of Art and Nature, written by the famous Frier Roger Bachon, sometime fellow of Merton Colledge, and afterward of Brasen-nose in Oxford," in Stanton Linden, ed., *The Mirror of Alchimy, Composed by the Thrice-Famous and Learned Fryer, Roger Bachon* (New York: Garland, 1992). For an account of the publishing history, see Linden's introduction, xxiv–xxv. While scholars disagree as to whether the later chapters of the Art and Nature are genuinely Bacon's work, the early sections, quoted here, are uncontroversial. Here is the relevant passage from that edition:

> But as for those things that are contained in the Magicians books, we must utterly reject them, though they bee not altogether devoyde of truth, because they be so stuffed with fables, that the truth cannot be discerned from falsehood. So that we must give no credit to such as say, that Solomon and

other learned men made them: for these bookes are not received by the author-
itie of the Church nor of wise men, but by Seducers, that take the bare letter
and make newe bookes themselves, and fill the world with their new inventions, as daily experience teacheth us. And to the ende men might be the more
throughly [sic] allured, they give glorious titles to their works, and foolishly
ascribe them to such and such Authors, as though they spake nothing of themselves: and write base matters in a loftie stile, and with the cloke of a text do
hide their own forgeries. (51–52)

22. The text is taken from Appendix I, "Epistola Fr Rogeri Baconis De Secretis Operibus Artis et Naturae," in *Fr. Rogeri Bacon opera quadeam hactenus inedita*, ed. J. S. Brewer,
RS 15, v. 1 (London: Longman, 1859), 526.

23. *Opus Majus*, 88.

24. See T. S. Maloney, "Roger Bacon on Equivocation," *Vivarium* 22, 2 (1984): 85–112.
Bacon's systematic theory of signs is concentrated in Part III of the *Opus Majus* and in his
final treatise, *A Compendium of the Study of Theology*. Bacon writes in the *Opus Majus*, part
3: "The sign is in the predicament of relation and is spoken of essentially in reference to the
one for whom it signifies. For it posits that thing in act when the sign itself is in act and in
potency when the sign itself is in potency. But unless some were able to conceive by means
of this sign, it would be void and vain. Indeed, it would not be a sign, but would have remained a sign only according to the substance of a sign. But it would not be a definition of
the sign, just as the substance of the father remains when the son is dead, but the relation
of paternity is lost" (81).

25. *Opus Majus*, 112, 111. His work was particularly innovative, Jan Pinborg argues,
with regard to his articulation of the diverse equivocations wrought by new impositions.
Such concerns resulted in, as Pinborg puts it, "an original systematization of possible
changes [in language] or equivocations that [had] no medieval parallels," "Roger Bacon on
Signs: A Newly Recovered Part of the *Opus Majus*," 403–12. *Sprache und Erkenntnis im
Mittelalter: Akten des VI. Internationalen Kongresses für Mittelalterliche Philosophie der Société
internationale pour l'étude de la philosophie médiévale, 29. August–3. September 1977 in Bonn*,
ed. Von Jan. P. Beckmann [et al.], Hbd. 1, Miscellanea Mediaevalia 13 (Berlin: 1981), 410.

26. Kay has demonstrated the productive power of philosophical contradictions (between, for instance, high and low, subject and object, law and counterlaw, combat and argument, abject and sublime) for the "emergence of the literary object" in the twelfth
century. See Kay, *Courtly Contradictions*. I read Bacon's equivocation as related to, yet also
distinct from, these earlier forms.

27. As Umberto Eco notes, "Bacon definitely destroys the semiotic triangle that was
formulated since Plato, by which the relationship between words and referents is mediated
by the idea, or by the concept, or by the definition." "Denotation," *On the Medieval Theory
of Signs*, ed. Umberto Eco and Constantine Marmo (Amsterdam: Benjamins, 1989), 61.

28. The "equivocation of appellation" was the case in which "a term was used equivocally when its reference was extended from present existents to past or future non-existents."

See E. J. Ashworth, "Analogy and Equivocation in Thirteenth-Century Logic: Aquinas in Context," *Mediaeval Studies* 54 (1992), 94–135, 111.

29. Maloney, "Equivocation," 93.

30. Ibid., 95.

31. "Epistola Fr Rogeri Baconis de secretis operibus artis et naturae," 533.

32. Ibid.

33. Ibid.

34. Ibid., 538.

35. Ibid., 533.

36. Ibid., 537.

37. As Daston and Park note; see *Wonders and the Order of Nature* (New York: Zone, 1998), 94.

38. Proverbial, found in Ibn al-Hajj, Madkhal al-Sharif, i. 79, as cited by J. Berkey, "Tradition, Innovation and the Social Construction of Knowledge in the Medieval Islamic Near East," *Past and Present* 148 (1995): 38–65.

39. John H. Mundy, *Europe in the High Middle Ages, 1150–1309* (New York: Basic, 1973), 492.

40. The condemnation took place sometime between November 1277 and Pentecost 1279, according to Hackett, "Roger Bacon: Life," 19. The surviving record in the Franciscan Chronicle of the XXIV Generals was written some 100 years after the presumed event. On the charge, see *Chronica XXIV Generalium Ordinis Minorum*, in Anal. Franc. iii., 360: "Hic Generalis frater Hieronymous de multorum fratrum consilio condemnavit et reprobavit doctrinam Fratris Rogerii Bachonis Anglici, sacrae theologiae magistri, continens aliquas novitates suspectas, propter quas fuit idem Rogerius carceri condemnatus, praecipiendo omnibus fratribus ut nullus illam teneret, sed ipsam vitaret, ut per Odrinem reprobatum. Super hoc etiam scripset Domino Papae Nicolao praefato, ut per eius auctoritatem doctrina illa periculosa totaliter sopiretur." As cited by A. G. Little, "Roger Bacon's Life and Works," *Roger Bacon Essays*, ed. Little (New York: Russell and Russell, 1914), 26. The manuscript is also cited in Bridges, vol. 3, "Additional Notes," 158.

41. The considered opinion today is that he would have been held under house arrest, and thus likely still had access to a quite substantial library, the Franciscans being renowned for their book collections. Writing in 1914, Little argues that such novelties refer at least in part to Bacon's "defence and practice of the 'magical sciences,' in magic being included the unknown powers of art and nature" (27). Jeremiah Hackett, offering a more modest assessment, writes that Bacon was "ordered to desist from some of his scientific and linguistic pursuits" ("Roger Bacon: Life," 17). Yet Hackett also notes that the aspect of Bacon's work that was likely most dangerous was "that part of Bacon's thought which related closely to theology," namely, "astrology, alchemy, and *scientia experimentalis,*" as well as his links to the "Spiritual" Franciscans (19).

42. Ibid., 17.

43. Clement's letter is housed in the Vatican library. I cite it here as quoted by Brian Clegg, *The First Scientist: A Life of Roger Bacon* (London: Constable, 2003), 96. While

Clegg's account of Bacon's scholarly work is sensible, his narrative of Bacon's imprisonment mirrors many of the assumptions surrounding the claims of *Voynich*. Even if Bacon had been "imprisoned," he surely was not, as Clegg imagines, "sitting in chains in a dank cell" "day after day" (113).

44. See Neslihan Şenocak, *The Poor and the Perfect: The Rise of Learning in the Franciscan Order, 1209–1310* (Ithaca, N.Y.: Cornell University Press, 2012.)

45. William M. Short, "Francis, the "New" Saint in the Tradition of Christian Hagiography," in *Francis of Assisi, History, Hagiography, and Hermeneutics in the Early Documents* (Hyde Park, N.Y.: New City Press, 2004), 153.

46. Ibid., 154.

47. Ibid., 159. For Celano's *Vita*, see "Thomas of Celano's Life of Saint Francis," in *Francis of Assisi: Early Documents* (Hyde Park, N.Y.: New City Press, 1999). Interestingly, the Celano *Vita* would become a model for subsequent hagiography: Guillaume de Tocco would borrow its terms for his influential *Vita* of Thomas Aquinas. On this point, see Luca Bianchi, "*Prophanae novitates et doctrinae peregrinae*: La méfiance à l'égard des innovations théoriques aux XIIIe et XIVe siècles," in *Tradition, Innovation, Invention*, ed. Hans-Joachim Schmidt (Berlin: de Gruyter, 2005), 211–29.

48. Richard Lemay, "Roger Bacon's Attitudes Toward the Latin Translations and Translators of the Twelfth and Thirteenth Centuries," in *Roger Bacon and the Sciences*, ed. Hackett, 25–48, 46.

49. See Paul Sidelko, "The Condemnation of Roger Bacon," *Journal of Medieval History* 22 (1996): 69–81.

50. On this point, see Paolo Zambelli, *The "Speculum Astronomiae" and Its Enigma: Astrology, Theology, and Science in Albertus Magnus and His Contemporaries* (Dordrecht: Kluwer, 1992).

51. He argued, that is, for the possibility of astrological influence on bodies, although not on souls. See Smoller's lucid summary of the scholastic solutions: Laura Smoller, *History, Prophecy and the Stars: The Christian Astrology of Pierre d'Ailly, 1350–1420* (Princeton, N.J.: Princeton University Press, 1994), 30–31.

52. Smoller describes the problems and proposed solutions cogently (36–42).

53. Lemay, "Attitudes," 47. He will continue, just two pages later: "The strictures Bacon placed upon the kind of Aristotelian interpretation favored by the younger generation of friar-scholars may very well have been meant as a retort to the suspicion of 'heresy' felt by 'orthodox' philosophers, including Albertus Magnus and Thomas Aquinas, toward the 'arabic' orientation of Aristotelianism rooted at Oxford since the late 12th century and now carried to Paris in the midst of the Averroistic flourishing" (49).

54. *Études sur le vocabulaire philosophique du Moyen Âge* (Rome: Edizioni dell'Ateneo, 1970), as cited (and translated) by Cerquiglini-Toulet, *A New History*, trans. Preisig, 134.

55. For a concise summary of Joachite teachings and their controversies, Gordon Leff remains useful. *Paris and Oxford Universities in the Thirteenth and Fourteenth Centuries: An Institutional and Intellectual History* (New York: Wiley, 1968), esp. 256–59. While prophetic histories seem to be utterly different from "modern" notions of history, Brian Stock points

to a way of reading in Joachim "the first intimations of a Hegelian type of dialectic, which foresees that different 'spirits' dominate the revolutionary passage from one historical period to another." See "Rationality, Tradition, and the Scientific Outlook: Reflections on Max Weber and the Middle Ages," *Annals of the New York Academy of Science* 441, 1 (2006): 7–19, 16.

56. Hilary M. Carey, "Astrology and Anti-Christ in the Later Middle Ages," in *Time and Eternity: The Medieval Discourse*, ed. Jaritz and Moreno-Riaño (Turnhout: Brepols, 2003), 515–35, 519. See particularly her cogent summary of Bacon's relation to the controversies surrounding the Western use of "conjunctivism."

57. See, for instance, his remarks on Astrology and the coming of the Antichrist, *Opus Majus*, vol. 1, pt. 4, 268–69.

58. Religious debates over the power of heavenly bodies on humans were complex and nuanced. For an account of the larger questions, as well as an excellent summary of Bacon's influence on D'Ailly, see Smoller, *History, Prophecy, and the Stars.*

59. Jeremiah Hackett, "Roger Bacon and the Classification of the Sciences," in *Roger Bacon and the Sciences*, ed. Hackett, 49–66, 53.

60. Carey, "Astrology," 520.

61. *Opus Majus*, 112. "Magis requirit vias sapientiae quam bellicum laborem." Ed. Bridges, *Opus Majus, supplemental volume*, 122.

62. For example: "What makes the situation as bad as possible is the fact that the foundation of our faith began with them, and we should bear in mind that they are of the seed of the patriarch and prophets and, what is more, from their stock the Lord sprang and the glorious Virgin and the Apostles and innumerable sacred authors have descended from them from the beginning of the Church. . . . and the Saracens likewise and the Pagans and the Tartars, and the other unbelievers throughout the whole world. Nor does war avail against them, since the Church is sometimes brought to confusion in the wars of Christians, as often happens beyond sea and especially in the last army, namely, that of the king of France, as all the world knows; and if Christians do conquer other lands, there is no one to defend the lands occupied. . . . The survivors of wars and their sons are angered more and more against the Christian faith because of those wars, and are infinitely removed from the faith of Christ, and are inflamed to do Christians all possible evils. Hence the Saracens for this reason in many parts of the world cannot be converted; and especially is this the case beyond the sea and in Prussia and in the lands bordering on Germany, because the Templars and Hospitallers and Teutonic Knights hinder greatly the conversion of unbelievers, owing to the wars that they are always stirring up and because they wish to have complete sway. . . . For there is no doubt but that all nations of unbelievers beyond Germany would have been converted long since but for the violence of the Teutonic Knights, because the race of pagans was frequently ready to receive the faith in peace after preaching. But the Teutonic Knights are unwilling to keep the peace, because they wish to subdue those peoples and reduce them to slavery, and with subtile [sic] arguments many years ago deceived the Roman Church. The former fact is known, otherwise I should not state the latter." *Opus Majus*, ed. Burke, 111–12. See also *Opus Majus, supplemental volume*, ed. Bridges, 122–23.

63. *Opus Majus*, ed. Burke, 112.

64. Carey's metaphor, in this regard, seems wrong because it cannot accommodate the equivocal nature of Bacon's relations to all parties. This may owe to her association of Bacon's interest in the secrets of art and nature with what she calls the "practical arts of magic," a phrase that seems to her to suggest a stable set of nefarious practices. "Astrology," 529.

65. I adopt here the politico-theological sense of that term, as developed by Slavoj Žižek, and Kenneth Reinhard particularly. See Reinhard, Žižek, and Erik Santner, *The Neighbor: Three Inquiries into Political Theology* (Chicago: University of Chicago Press, 2005). This is the register of Freud's *Nebenmensch* (the "next man"), who is at once strange and familiar, threatening and comforting, radically distant and close at hand.

66. *Opus Maius*, ed. Burke, 77.

67. In Part III (on "Grammar and Tongues") he writes, "It is impossible that the peculiar quality of one language should be preserved in another. For even dialects of the same tongue vary among different sections, as is clear from the Gallic language, which is divided into many dialects among the Gauls, Picards, Normans, Burgundians, and others. . . . Therefore, an excellent piece of work in one language cannot be transferred into another as regard the peculiar quality that it possessed in the former." This leads to the following conclusion: "Therefore, no Latin (reader) will be able to understand as he should the wisdom of sacred Scripture and of philosophy, unless he understands the languages from which they were translated." *Opus Maius*, ed. Burke, 75–76.

68. Scholars generally accept the text as authorial; the early sections (from which this is taken) are particularly uncontroversial. For an account of the relevant manuscripts and publishing history of this text, see Stanton's introduction, xxiv–xxv.

69. Linden, ed., *Mirror of Alchimy*, 51.

70. "Epistola Fr. Rogeri Baconis" 532.

71. Ibid., 525.

72. Linden, ed., *Mirror of Alchimy*, 50.

73. Ibid., 50.

74. *The Magical Letter of Roger Bacon* (Sequim, Wash.: Holmes, 1988; rpt. 2001), 7. The title, obviously a marketing ploy, signals the unnamed editor's own enthusiasms.

75. "Epistola Fr. Rogeri Baconis," 527.

76. Ibid., 52.

77. The point is not original. Bacon relies here on Qusta ben Luca's "De physicis ligaturis," which describes the effect engendered by belief in the efficacy of amulets. I am grateful to Bill Newman for pointing this out to me.

78. One finds other evidence as to Bacon's interest in the linguistic properties of fictionalizing. Alastair Minnis marks him as "one among many schoolmen who furthered the tradition of . . . highlighting the affective, imaginative, figurative, and even fictive properties" of scripture. *Medieval Theory of Authorship: Scholastic Literary Attitudes in the Later Middle Ages*, 2nd ed. with a New Preface (Philadelphia: University of Pennsylvania Press, 2010), xix.

79. On this point, see Linden, *Mirror of Alchimy*, 49.

80. My account of Bacon's alchemy is everywhere indebted to the work of William R. Newman. For relevant material, see his *Promethean Ambitions: Alchemy and the Quest to Perfect Nature* (Chicago: University of Chicago Press), 34–114, and "Technology and Alchemical Debate in the Late Middle Ages," *Isis* 80 (September 1989): 423–45.

81. Bacon's account of creation ex nihilo was, however, entirely orthodox. As he writes in the *Opus Majus*, "God produces forces out of nothing, which he multiplies in things; created agents do not do so, but in another way about which we need not concern ourselves at the present time." *Opus Maius*, ed. Burke, 130.

82. Newman, "Alchemy" in *Roger Bacon and the Sciences*, ed. Hackett, 335.

83. William Eamon, "Technology as Magic in the Late Middle Ages and the Renaissance," *Janus* 70 (1983): 171–212, 181.

84. "So that you shall confess all Magicke power to be *inferior* to these [strange things performed by Arte and Nature] and unworthy to be compared with them." Linden, ed., "Art and Nature," 56.

85. Bacon's distinction seems, that is, akin to the contemporary difference between powerful "innovations" and mere "novelties." And, indeed, Aquinas's accounts of curiosity (specifically, his critiques of *vitium curiositatis*) will rely on a related distinction, as noted in the introduction to this study; Aquinas legitimates curiosity when it is focused on the putatively sober concerns of "necessity," defining the *vice* of curiosity as an interest in superfluous things.

86. On the difficulties that the category of "magic" poses for the historiography of science, see Latour, "Irreductions."

87. Newman has argued that the appendices to Bacon's translation of the pseudo-Aristotelian *Secret of Secrets*, particularly the account of the Philosopher's Stone, suggest that the friar's interest in alchemy was not only theoretical (as Dorothea W. Singer argued) but practical. Newman's astute decoding of those texts suggests what he calls Bacon's "microbial" program of science. Singer, "Alchemical Writings Attributed to Roger Bacon," *Speculum* 7, 1 (1932): 80–86; Newman, "The Philosopher's Egg" and "An Overview of Roger Bacon's Alchemy," in *Roger Bacon and the Sciences*, ed. Hackett, 335. If Bacon was both practically and theoretically inclined, he may have both bridged and policed this institutional, class, and methodological divide.

88. Jacques Le Goff and Jean-Claude Schmitt, "Au XIIIe siècle: Une parole nouvelle." In *Histoire vécue du peuple chrétien*, ed. Jean Delumeau (Toulouse: Privat, 1979), 257–79. See also Kay, *Courtly Contradictions*.

89. Rita Copeland, *Rhetoric, Hermeneutics, and Translations in the Middle Ages: Academic Translations and Vernacular Texts* (Cambridge: Cambridge University Press, 1991).

90. Susan Smith, *The Power of Women: A Topos in Medieval Art and Literature* (Philadelphia: University of Pennsylvania Press, 1995).

91. Sarah Kay, *The Chanson de Geste in the Age of Romance: Political Fictions* (London: Clarendon, 1995); Robert M. Stein, *Reality Fictions: Romance, History, and Governmental Authority* (South Bend, Ind.: University of Notre Dame Press, 2006).

CHAPTER 3. INGENIOUS YOUTH

1. Richard Kieckhefer, *Magic in the Middle Ages* (Cambridge: Cambridge University Press, 2000), 107.

2. Philippe Ariès, *Centuries of Childhood: A Social History of Family Life*, trans. Robert Baldick (New York: Knopf, 1962).

3. The bibliography disputing Ariès's claim is increasingly vast. See in particular Nicholas Orme, *Medieval Childhood* (New Haven, Conn.: Yale University Press, 2001). Recent scholarship suggests a wide range of ways that the child was legible throughout the record. For an extensive bibliography relevant to the question of the toy, see James Schultz, "History and Knowledge of Childhood," in *The Knowledge of Childhood in the German Middle Ages, 1100–1350* (Philadelphia: University of Pennsylvania Press, 1995), 1–20; Seth Lerer, *Children's Literature: A Reader's History from Aesop to Harry Potter* (Chicago: University of Chicago Press, 2008). Phyllis Gaffney's bibliography is the most up to date: *Constructions of Childhood and Youth in Old French Narrative* (Burlington, Vt.: Ashgate, 2011), 3–21. Lynn White similarly linked the history of technology with historiography on medieval childhood. See his presidential address to the American Historical Society "Technology Assessment from the Stance of a Medieval Historian," *American Historical Review* 79, 1 (1974): 1–13.

4. Here, quoting Geoff Egan, in Hazel Forsyth with Geoff Egan, *Toys, Trifles, and Trinkets: Base Metal Miniatures from London 1200 to 1800* (London: Museum of London Unicorn Press, 2006), 142.

5. Ibid., 143.

6. Ibid., 59. Egan continues, "The best of the latest work on medieval childhood now fully acknowledges playthings in the sense used in this volume as a reality. There remain others who are skeptical or simply uninformed from archaeological sources." And, on the question of the mass market: "Of course, those without any spare money would not have been able to afford such trifles, but within towns there would have been many families for whom the occasional indulgence of a few pence on their children would have been easily expendable."

7. Ibid., 58. As Egan and Forsyth point out, an earlier inability to recognize these artifacts as, in fact, toys has much to do with assumptions made about the absence of childhood during the time.

8. In addition to Kieckhefer's *Magic*, see Scott Lightsey, "Chaucer's Secular Marvels and the Medieval Economy of Wonder," *SAC* 23 (2001): 289–316, and *Manmade Marvels in Medieval Culture and Literature* (New York: Palgrave, 2007); William Eamon, "Technology as Magic in the Late Middle Ages and Renaissance," *Janus* 70 (1983): 171–212.

9. Gaffney describes three "innovations" with regard to childhood in Old French texts of romance, beginning in the twelfth century: the increased prominence of young females; the past emerging as an important aspect of the hero's identity; and childhood figuring as a time, she argues, of "ignorance." *Constructions of Childhood and Youth*, 99.

10. *Middle English Dictionary*, s.v., "child," doi: 27105528.

11. Lerer, *Children's Literature*, 44.

12. Ibid., 48.

13. *Le Chevalier au Lion ou Le Roman D'Yvain*, ed. and trans. David F. Hult (Paris: Lettres Gothiques, 1994), 120–23.

14. William Kibler, trans., *Chretien de Troyes, Arthurian Romances* (London: Penguin, 1991), 306.

15. Ibid.

16. Zrinka Stahuljak, Virginie Greene, Sarah Kay, Sharon Kinoshita, and Peggy McCracken, *Thinking Through Chrétien de Troyes* (Cambridge: Brewer, 2011), 82. For an interesting discussion of the adventure as the "time of the future perfect," see 83–86.

17. See White, "Technology Assessment," 4–6.

18. On horse and rider as comprising a knightly "identity machine," see Jeffrey Jerome Cohen, *Medieval Identity Machines* (Minneapolis: University of Minnesota Press, 2003).

19. See Frances Gies and Joseph Gies, *Cathedral, Forge, and Waterwheel: Technology and Invention in the Middle Ages* (New York: Harper Collins, 1994); Elizabeth Hallam, ed., *Chronicles of the Age of Chivalry* (London: Penguin, 1987); Joel Mokyr, *The Lever of Riches: Technological Creativity and Economic Progress.* (New York: Oxford University Press, 1990). See also Lynn White, Jr., *Medieval Technology and Social Change* (New York: Oxford University Press, 1966); although no longer standard, Jean Gimpel, *The Medieval Machine: The Industrial Revolution of the Middle Ages* (London: Penguin, 1977) remains useful.

20. Hanning, *The Individual in Twelfth Century Romance*, 105.

21. Ibid., 111.

22. Ibid., 112.

23. Ibid., 235.

24. In addition to the French and Middle English versions, texts survive in Spanish, Italian, German, Icelandic, Dutch, Norwegian, Flemish, Swedish, and Danish. Boccaccio includes the story in his *Decameron*. Textual issues are complex, and scholars continue to unravel the relations among the various versions. The longstanding dominant view, established in the late nineteenth century, held for the primacy of two French story traditions, the first "roman idyllique," and the second, later, "roman d'aventure." The two vary in plot detail, in person and place names, and, most important, in the explicit role given to Christian providence. The Middle English version is an adaptation of the first of these. Patricia Grieve's groundbreaking and exhaustive account of the importance of the Spanish chronicle traditions has transformed our understanding of the larger European scene—particularly the transmission and diffusion of a third variant of the tale by way of Spain's relations to Scandinavia. Grieve, *Floire and Blancheflor and the European Romance* (Cambridge: Cambridge University Press, 1997). The ME versions survive in four MSS: MS Advocates 19.2.1, National Library of Scotland (the Auchinleck MS); Cambridge University Library, MS Gg. iv. 27.2; British Museum Egerton 2862; and British Museum MS Cotton Vitellius Diii. De Vries uses Egerton as his base text, since it preserves hundreds of lines lost in other recensions. See F. C. De Vries, introduction to *Floris and Blauncheflur: A Middle English Romance edited with Introduction, Notes, and Glossary* (Gronigen: Druk. V.R.B., 1966), 1–12.

Although the earliest Middle English manuscript that contains the romance (the Auchin-leck MS) dates from the first third of the fourteenth century, De Vries provides a reasonable dating of the composition of the ME romance in the mid- to late thirteenth century. There are many adaptations of the French "roman idyllique" version, in a host of European lan-guages. See De Vries's introduction.

25. Geraldine Barnes, "Cunning and Ingenuity in the Middle English *Floris and Blauncheflour*," *Medium Aevum* 53 (1984): 10–25, 12.

26. Throughout this chapter, I will preserve the spelling of names particular to the two versions I examine; thus the names *Floire and Blancheflor* signal the OF version, while *Floris and Blauncheflour*, the ME. In the ME critical tradition spelling is inconsistent, although "Blauncheflour" is generally preferred.

27. Lillian Hornstein, "Romances," in *Manual of Writings in Middle English, 1050–1500*, vol. 1 (Hamden: Connecticut Academy of Arts and Sciences, 1967), 146.

28. Ibid.

29. Although two early fourteenth-century versions (Auchinleck MS and Cambridge Library MS Gg. 4.27) make a token gesture toward Floris's conversion to Christianity, mention of conversion is entirely absent in the other two recensions (Egerton 2862 and Cotton Vittellius D. iii), both very late.

30. Jennifer Fellows, introduction to *Of Love and Chivalry: An Anthology of Middle English Romance* (London: J.M. Dent, 1993), vii–xxxi, xiii.

31. See, for instance, Susan Schibanoff, "Worlds Apart: Orientalism, Antifeminism, and Heresy in Chaucer's Man of Law's Tale," *Exemplaria* 8, 1 (1996), 59–96; Geraldine Heng, *Empire of Magic: Medieval Romance and the Politics of Cultural Fantasy* (New York: Columbia University Press, 2003).

32. Kathleen Coyne Kelly, "The Bartering of Blauncheflur in the Middle English *Floris and Blauncheflur*," *Studies in Philology* 91, 2 (1994): 101–10, 110. Kelly's reconsideration of these concerns took place as part of a larger critical trend in which the pleasures of an ori-entalizing enchantment found in romance are opposed to the scholar's ethical concern with the exploitative, colonizing, aggressive, and commodifying nature of such pleasures.

33. With notable recent exceptions. Aranye Fradenburg has productively analyzed the opposition of ethics to pleasure. See *Sacrifice Your Love: Psychoanalysis, Historicism, Chaucer* (Minneapolis: University of Minnesota Press, 2002); with regard to the pleasures of romance in particular, see Nicola McDonald, "A Polemical Introduction" to *Pulp Fictions of Medieval England: Essays in Popular Romance* (Manchester: Manchester University Press, 2004), 1–21. On this question, see also my "Discipline and Romance," in *Critical Contexts in Medieval Literature*, ed. Holly Crocker and D. Vance Smith (New York: Routledge, 2013), 276–82.

34. Writing on the scene of intercultural foment in the later period, Sheila Delany opposes what she calls the "rational scholarly approach" (the respect for Islamic intellectuals evinced by the indebtedness of scholasticism to Arabic texts and traditions, or by the work of the School of Toledo), against what she understands to be an older "mythic" "patristic and popular orientalism . . . embodied in stories of sexual desire," Sheila Delany, *The Naked Text: Chaucer's Legend of Good Women* (Berkeley: University of California Press, 1994), 186.

35. Alain de Lille, *The Complaint of Nature*, trans. from Latin by Douglas M. Moffat, Yale Studies in English (New Haven, Conn.: Yale University Press, 1908; rpt. 1972), 26.

36. Sylvia Huot, *The Romance of the Rose and Its Medieval Readers: Interpretation, Reception, Manuscript Transmission* (Cambridge: Cambridge University Press, 1993), 74.

37. Julianne Bruneau, "Truth, Sex, and Divine Poetics in Alan of Lille's *De Planctu Naturae*," in *Women and the Divine in Literature Before 1700: Essays in Memory of Margot Louis*, ed. Kathryn Kirby-Fulton (Victoria, British Columbia: ELS Editions, 2009), 65–86, 65.

38. Jessica Rosenfeld, *Ethics and Enjoyment in Late-Medieval Poetry* (Cambridge: Cambridge University Press, 2011), 34–35. As I argued in Chapter 1, the ethical discourse regarding human invention was generated not by the blind appeal of tradition in a religiously conservative age, but as a response to radical expansions of possibility in the realms of art and science. Accounts of the "medieval new" entail this structure of submission in two ways: first, in the ethical demand enacted so as to disavow (that is, both to deny and to preserve) the creative production of human poets and artisans as new; and, secondly, in the traces of perversity that are legible in the ambivalent nature of the gadgets, gizmos, contrivances, and poems thereby produced.

39. Susan Smith, "Chapter 3: Tales of the Mounted Aristotle," in *The Power of Women: A Topos in Medieval Art and Literature* (Philadelphia: University of Pennsylvania Press, 1995), 66.

40. Smith, *Power of Women*. See also Marilynn Desmond, *Ovid's Art and The Wife of Bath: The Ethics of Erotic Violence* (Ithaca, N.Y.: Cornell University Press, 2006). On the *Ethics*, see Joachim Storost, "Femme Chevalchat Aristotte." *Zeitschrift fur französische Sprache und Literatur* 66 (1956): 186–201, as cited by Smith, 69–70.While taking Storost's point on the question, Smith assesses the remarkable, and various, circulation of the trope: "[Some] versions . . . pressed the tale into service to persuade their listeners that women are a danger to men's souls and to induce them to act on that conviction." "Any contrary interpretation of the tale," she continues, "not only holds out an alternative interpretive model but, implicitly, an alternative behavioral model," 102.

41. Rosenfeld, *Ethics and Enjoyment*, 113.

42. Smith, *Power of Women*, 136.

43. Rosenfeld, *Ethics and Enjoyment*, 115.

44. Ibid., 115.

45. Smith, *Power of Women*, 136.

46. This imitation of nature is not, of course, what we will later recognize as the Aristotelian notion of art's capacity to imitate nature in verisimilitude. See Thomas J. Hatton, "Nature as Poet: Alanus de Insulis' *The Complaint of Nature* and the Medieval Concept of Artistic Creation," *Language and Style: An International Journal* 2 (1969): 85–91.

47. Kay, *Courtly Contradictions*, 264. Imaging the ethical subject as submitting passions to the reins of right reason shows that, as Sarah Kay puts it, glossing Lacan's account of Kantian ethics, "desire and law are inseparable." She goes on, "Lacan pursues the implication of the sublime and perverse to the point of contending that they are reverse forms of the same structure." The trope of horse and rider makes explicit the importance of

submission to this structure. Submission is a complex matter, where discipline and amorousness entwine in diffuse and changeable ways. Traditions of the "mounted Aristotle" and, later, the "mounted Virgil" make this clear, suggesting that this structure is not only persistent, but also equivocal. The rider can easily, as here, become the ridden.

48. Susan Schibanoff, "Sodomy's Mark: Alan of Lille, Jean de Meun, and the Medieval Theory of Authorship," in *Queering the Middle Ages*, ed. Glenn Burger and Steven F. Kruger (Minneapolis: University of Minnesota Press, 2001), 28–56, 34, referring here to the *Plaint*.

49. Alexandre Leupin, *Barbarolexis: Medieval Writing and Sexuality*, trans. Kate M. Cooper (Cambridge, Mass.: Harvard University Press, 1989), 68.

50. Ibid.

51. See Rollo's brilliant reading for an assessment of the debates. David Rollo, "Nature's Pharmaceuticals: Sanctioned Desires in Alain de Lille's *De planctu Naturae*," *Exemplaria* 25, 2 (2013): 152–72, 153.

52. There are crucial examples. See Gregory Stone, *The Ethics of Nature in the Middle Ages: On Boccaccio's Poetaphysics* (New York: St. Martin's [Palgrave Macmillan], 1998). John V. Tolan's work has been an important exception; see *Saracens: Islam in the European Imagination* (New York: Columbia University Press, 2002).

53. Greg Stone describes this view, attributed to both Alain de Libera and Ernst Bloch, as "anachronis[tic], but not without justification," Review of Jessica Rosenfeld, *Ethics and Enjoyment in Late Medieval Poetry: Love After Aristotle*, Cambridge Studies in Medieval Literature (Cambridge: Cambridge University Press, 2011), *Medieval Review* 11.09.11.

54. The French text, following the *roman idyllique* sometimes known as the "aristocratic" version, is taken from Margaret M. Pelan, ed., *Floire et Blancheflor*, 2nd ed. (1937; Paris: Belles Lettres, 1956).

55. Noah D. Guynn, "Eternal Flame: State Formation, Deviant Architecture and the Monumentality of Same-Sex Eroticism in the Roman d'Eneas," *GLQ: A Journal of Lesbian and Gay Studies* 6, 2 (2000): 287–319, 292.

56. Ibid., 307.

57. Ibid., 301–2.

58. On milk kinship and the incest prohibitions in a modern context, see Soraya Altorki, "Milk-Kinship in Arab Society: An Unexplored Problem in the Ethnography of Marriage," *Ethnography* 19, 2 (1980): 233–44, who was the first to raise the question. For a fuller history, see Françoise Héritier-Augé, "Identité de substance et parenté de lait dans le monde arabe," in *Épouser au plus proche: Inceste, prohibitions et stratégies matrimoniales autour de la Méditerranée*, ed. Pierre Bonte (Paris: École des Hautes Études en Sciences Sociales, 1994), 149–64. Also Peter Parkes, "Milk Kinship in Islam: Substance, Structure, History," *Social Anthropology* 13, 3 (2005): 307–9. Thanks to Peggy McCracken for assistance on this point.

59. Barnes, "Cunning and Ingenuity," 12.

60. The Middle English poem begins at approximately line 193 of the "aristocratic" French version. Scholars have yet to ascertain whether the preliminary material was intentionally excised by the poet, or lost in manuscript transmission. In either case, the Middle English poem draws greater attention to the schoolroom scene, which now inaugurates the

plot. Furthermore, the adaptations the Middle English poet makes to the "aristocratic" version, which appears to be his source, suggest a special interest in the implications of this scene for the rest of the romance.

61. Text from F. C. De Vries, *Floris and Blauncheflur: A Middle English Romance edited with Introduction, Notes, and Glossary* (Groningen: Druk. V.R.B., 1966) with close comparison to the Everyman edition, ed. Jennifer Fellows and found in *Of Love and Chivalry: An Anthology of Middle English Romance* (London: J.M. Dent, 1993), and A. B. Taylor, *Floris and Blauncheflour: A Middle English Romance, edited from the Trenthan and Auchinleck MSS* (Oxford: Clarendon, 1927), ll. 7–14. For ease of reading, some spelling has been updated and regularized following Fellows's practice. All subsequent line numbers will be cited parenthetically in the text.

62. I have regularized the spelling of proper names in this and subsequent citations.

63. This kind of repetition will occur at similar moments throughout the romance, a rhetorical flourish that constitutes one of the persistent additions the Middle English poet makes to his French source.

64. Text from Pelan, ed., *Floire et Blancheflor*.

65. Sharon Kinoshita, *Medieval Boundaries: Rethinking Difference in Old French Literature* (Philadelphia: University of Pennsylvania Press, 2006), 85.

66. There is, however, no direct evidence of the Persian story as a source for the French. Given the limits of our knowledge of the medieval circulation of these traditions, it is impossible to assess any links definitively.

67. And as María Rosa Menocal points out, as a direct source for Eric Clapton's "Layla." Menocal, *Shards of Love: Exile and the Origins of the Lyric* (Durham, N.C.: Duke University Press, 1994).

68. Barnes, "Cunning and Ingenuity," 13. Barnes preserves the opposition of reason to passion that the romance, I am arguing, implicitly dismantles. Rather than oppose wit and love, the poet makes the two sufficiently useful to each other.

69. Nicholas Orme, *Education and Society in Medieval and Renaissance England* (London: Hambledon, 1989), 9.

70. Ranulph Higden, *Polychronicon*, ed. C. Babington, vol. 2, RS (London: Longmans, Green, 1869), 158–61.

71. Orme, *Education and Society*, 11–21. See also Rita Copeland, *Pedagogy, Intellectuals and Dissent in the Later Middle Ages* (Cambridge: Cambridge University Press, 2001), who notes that the level of instruction in grammar and literacy could be quite diverse: "'elementary' instruction may have many meanings" (17).

72. Roland Barthes, *The Pleasure of the Text*, trans. Richard Miller (New York: Hill and Wang, 1975). In her analysis of the variety of pleasures available in texts of medieval romance, Nicola McDonald has similarly invoked Barthes's distinction between *plaisir* and *jouissance*: "I want to propose," she writes, "that [Barthes's] two kinds of pleasures can be found in the same text and are not incompatible." "A Polemical Introduction," 21.

73. Thomas G. Duncan, Introduction to *Medieval English Lyrics*, 1200–1400, ed. Thomas G. Duncan (London: Penguin, 1995), xlv.

74. Duncan, ed., *Medieval English Lyrics*, 171. This lyric is found only in MS. London BL Sloan 2593, dated to the first half of the fifteenth century, although the language suggests an earlier origin. The ME manuscripts for *FB* are somewhat earlier than Sloan 2593, dated by De Vries to the last quarter of the fourteenth century. Note that the "new" here, according to the editor, relates to puberty. Associations of the springtime garden with sexual awakening are, of course, conventional.

75. Ibid., 247.

76. It alludes as well to other limitations to do with creative production. The eleventh-century scholar Peter Damian will famously address the question of God's omnipotence by way of a disquisition on female virginity: "utrum deus possit reparare virginen post ruinam?" Is it possible for God to restore the virginity of a woman who has lost it?

77. The basket trick circulates widely in a variety of literary guises. One in particular seems notable in the context of the issues I have been examining. John Spargo long ago noted the repeated use of the figure of "Virgil in the basket," a tradition that appears as a version of the "mounted Aristotle" in the European tradition of Virgil the Necromancer. See J. W. Spargo, *Virgil, the Necromancer* (Cambridge, Mass.: Harvard University Press, 1934), especially 136–97.

78. Medieval cooperation between East and West has long been identified not with romance, but with what Delany has called the "rational scholarly approach" evinced by the work of the School of Toledo, and by the intellectual indebtedness of scholasticism to Arabic texts and traditions. Delany sets the respect for Islam within theological and political treatises against an older "mythic" "patristic and popular orientalism . . . embodied in stories of sexual desire." Delany, *Naked Text*, 186.

79. By the 1340s and after—the period during which all four Middle English manuscripts of this romance were inscribed—Cairo's Mamluk empire, the monopoly to which the emir in Floris and Blauncheflour would have belonged, was engaged in a newly vibrant set of economic relations with Europe and Africa, amounting to, in the words of Janet Abu-Lughod, "the integration of Egypt with the world economy" such that textiles from Europe "flooded" Egyptian markets. Janet Abu-Lughod, *Before European Hegemony: The World System A.D. 1250–1350* (New York: Oxford University Press, 1989), 235.

80. Raymond Williams, *The Country and the City* (Oxford: Oxford University Press, 1973).

CHAPTER 4. LITTLE NOTHINGS

1. Frances Gies and Joseph Gies, *Cathedral, Forge, and Waterwheel: Technology and Invention in the Middle Ages* (New York: HarperCollins, 1994), 238. For an interesting account of Renaissance originality as it relates to imitation in the baroque workshop, see Andrew Ladis and Carolyn Wood, eds., *The Craft of Art: Originality and Industry in the Italian Renaissance and Baroque Worksho*p (Athens: University of Georgia Press, 1995).

2. As, for example, in Stephen Greenblatt's overstated claims about the advent of

modernity, in *The Swerve: How the World Became Modern* (New York: Norton, 2011). Greenblatt himself knows better, having written compellingly about the continuities between medieval and Renaissance intellectual cultures. For a set of provocative critical responses to Greenblatt's periodizing history, see the short essays, "Book Review Forum: Responses to *The Swerve: How the World Became Modern*," *Exemplaria: A Journal of Theory in Medieval and Renaissance Studies* 25, 4 (2013): 313–70. See also Kellie Robertson, "Medieval Materialism: A Manifesto," *Exemplaria* 22, 2 (2010): 99–120.

3. White's essay would constitute the basis of his famous book *Medieval Technology and Social Change* (Oxford: Oxford University Press, 1962).

4. In the chapter "Technology and Invention in the Middle Ages," in Gies and Gies, *Cathedral, Forge, and Waterwheel*, 238.

5. The bibliography is increasingly long. On the relation of romance as a genre to developments at the Garden at Hesdin, see Anne Hagopain van Buren, "Reality and Literary Romance in the Park of Hesdin," in *Medieval Gardens*, ed. Elisabeth B. MacDougall (Washington, D.C.: Dumbarton Oaks, 1986), 115–34.

6. E. R. Truitt, "Trei poëte, sages dotors, qui mout sorent di nigromance": Knowledge and Automata in Twelfth-Century French Literature," *Configurations*, 12 no.2 (Spring 2004): 167–93; Scott Lightsey, "Chaucer's Secular Marvels and the Medieval Economy of Wonder," *SAC* 23 (2001): 289–316, and *Man-Made Marvels in Medieval Culture and Literature* (New York: Palgrave, 2007).

7. This is, in large part, a presupposition supported by Marx's theory of the commodity—with its view of the object saturated with thought, ideas, ideology all dependent on yet reaching beyond its status as "thing"; haunted by the relations of production and consumption that constitute its "social life." Marxist analysis, of course, remains importantly committed to disentangling the real relations of production from the ideologies of commodity fetishism that saturate objects of exchange.

8. To borrow from Bertrand Russell. Tiffany writes, "the foundation of material substance is intelligible to us, and therefore appears to be real, only if we credit the imaginary pictures we have composed of it." . . . . This is because "At present we have no way of reconciling the nature of quantum materiality (the physics of subatomic matter) with the experience of ordinary bodies. . . . Real bodies appear to be made of unreal substance." Daniel Tiffany, *Toy Medium: Materialism and the Modern Lyric* (Stanford, Calif.: Stanford University Press, 2000), 3–4.

9. Ibid., 32.

10. Ibid., 15.

11. Truitt, "Trei poëte, sages dotors, qui mout sorent di nigromance," 170. See also the bibliography, 170n13, and see Truitt's forthcoming book, *Medieval Robots* (Philadelphia: University of Pennsylvania Press).

12. Truitt, "Trei poëte, sages dotors, qui mout sorent di nigromance," 172.

13. On Machaut's links to Hesdin, see the introduction and notes to Guillaume de Machaut, "*Le jugement du roy de behaigne" and "Remède de fortune*," ed. James I. Wimsatt and William W. Kibler, Chaucer Library (Athens: University of Georgia Press, 1988), 35–37.

Gardeners and engineers who designed Hesdin took inspiration from al-Jazari's *Book of Knowledge of Ingenious Mechanical Devices*. For a summary of the current opinion, see Van Buren, "Park at Hesdin," 118–19.

14. Van Buren, "Park at Hesdin," 128.

15. D. Vance Smith, *Arts of Possession: The Middle English Household Imaginary* (Minneapolis: University of Minnesota Press, 2003), 77.

16. Ibid. Smith persistently notes the problems that surplus makes for household "arts of possession."

17. Sarah Stanbury, *The Visual Object of Desire in Late Medieval England* (Philadelphia: University of Pennsylvania Press, 2008), 29.

18. Ibid., 28; 27.

19. Umberto Eco, *Art and Beauty in the Middle Ages*, trans. Hugh Bredin (New Haven, Conn.: Yale University Press, 1986).

20. Joel Kaye, *Economy and Nature in the Fourteenth Century: Money, Market Exchange, and the Emergence of Scientific Thought* (Cambridge: Cambridge University Press, 1998), 3.

21. Andrea Denny-Brown reads "Chaucer's broader use of the word 'newe'" in the *Canterbury Tales* as a "focus on the seductive powers of material novelty and its link to changefulness." *Fashioning Change: The Trope of Clothing in High- and Late-Medieval England* (Columbus: Ohio State University Press, 2012), 127. Her primary text is the *Clerk's Tale*. While Denny-Brown's reading of the Clerk is astute, the notion of the new rendered via the Clerk is, I argue, only part of a more ambivalent story.

22. If, as Marshall Leicester has compellingly shown, Chaucer's poetry regularly places the disenchanted self on full display, the *Squire's Tale* reveals the poet's interest in the uses of fascination and delight for compassionate engagement with the world. In a deservedly influential reading of Chaucer's poetry, Leicester deploys a nuanced version of Weber's notion—one directed at social rather than technical registers—to argue convincingly for that poet's disenchanted account of the agency of the subject in the fourteenth century. Leicester cites Chaucer's corpus as historical evidence of disenchanted sensibilities, arguing that it clearly depicts the fourteenth century as an era "in which not only the structures of the Church . . . , but gender roles, and estates (such as wives and knighthood, and, more generally, subjectivity itself) [were] deeply affected by a pervasive disenchanted scrutiny." He thus casts Chaucer as a "disenchanted agent," the pilgrims from his *Canterbury Tales* as the "sufferers and agents of a culture whose cover is blown." Leicester, *The Disenchanted Self: Representing the Subject in the Canterbury Tales* (Berkeley: University of California Press, 1990), all on 28.

23. Lightsey, "Chaucer's Secular Marvels." Morton Bloomfield identifies the *Squire's Tale's* ingenuity not with things medieval but with the "new spirit of the Renaissance." "Chaucer's *Squire's Tale* and the Renaissance," *Poetica* 12 (1979): 28–35, 28. Many critics have remarked on the attractions of the tale's own ingenuity, linked to a range of discourses about its marvels: a composite romance with influences traceable to French, Arabian, and classical Greek sources and analogues.

24. John Fyler, "Domesticating the Exotic in the *Squire's Tale*," *ELH* 55 (1988): 1–26. "But the sword, capable of both healing mayhem and wreaking it, epitomizes the problematic quality of the others as innocent gifts in a world of experience," 3.

25. Alan S. Ambrisco, "'It lyth nat in my tonge': Occupatio and Otherness in the *Squire's Tale*," *Chaucer Review* 38 (2004): 205–28.

26. All references to Chaucer's poem are taken from *The Riverside Chaucer*, 3rd ed., gen. ed. Larry D. Benson (Boston: Houghton Mifflin, 1987). Of course, as we will see, the first narrative is instrumental with regard to the second. The second, that is, is made possible by the technological and magical technologies described in the first: Cambyuskan's daughter Canacee can, with the magic ring and mirror, now understand the wounded bird's tale of unhappy love.

27. Among the discontents of culture registered here may be the limiting boundaries of class the falcon recommends. According to the logic of courtly love, of course, the falcon should be sublimed, set apart and irreplaceable; she is shown to be one elevated object in a set of signifiers that are exchanged and commodified.

28. I am grateful to Frank Grady for the reminder of these similarities.

29. This is not how we are accustomed to thinking about it: "the intimacy between desire and the law is not one we readily acknowledge. We are so accustomed to pitting morality against desire that it is simply hard to believe that morality is a form of desire, or desire is what morality is." Aranye Fradenburg, *Sacrifice Your Love: Psychoanalysis, Historicism, Chaucer* (Minneapolis: University of Minnesota Press, 2002), all on 7.

30. The gendered roles are reversed here to some degree: for Lacan, the "nothing" sublimed in courtly love, the "hole," is sexual as well: indeed, much of Lacan's interest has to do with the erotics of the structure. The constraints of space prohibit a more detailed consideration of this point.

31. *Courtly Contradictions: The Emergence of the Literary Object in the Twelfth Century* (Stanford, Calif.: Stanford University Press, 2001).

32. Alfred David delightfully referred to the peregrine's story as Anelida "with feathers." "Recycling *Anelida and Arcite*: Chaucer as a Source for Chaucer," *Studies in the Age of Chaucer* 1 (1984): 105–15, at 110.

33. At the level of the word, Chaucer was less innovative than has long been thought, as Christopher Cannon has shown. See *The Making of Chaucer's English: A Study of Words* (Cambridge: Cambridge University Press, 1998).

34. "Rara avis in terris nigroque simillima cycno" (Juvenal, *Satires*, 6.165).

35. James I. Wimsatt, *Chaucer and His French Contemporaries: Natural Music in the Fourteenth Century* (Toronto: University of Toronto Press, 1991), 321n59.

36. Alexandre Leupin notes Machaut's repetitive collocation of birds with poetry, linking birdsong to poetic work: "as Machaut declares, at the beginning of the *Remède de fortune*: 'Mes oeuvres estoient volages' ['My works were flighty,' v. 49]." "The attribute," Leupin continues, "applies not only to his so-called early works but also to the flight of the pen on any white page." Alexandre Leupin, "The Powerlessness of Writing: Guillaume de Machaut, the Gorgon, and *Ordenance*," trans. Peggy McCracken, *Yale French Studies* 70 (1986): 127–49.

37. These were distinctive, though not unique. John Gower's dedication of his *Confessio Amantis* to Richard II casts the long poem as the answer to the sovereign's request for "som newe thing"; he wrote in the wake (and, arguably, after the style) of Machaut. On Gower's imitation of Machaut's innovative form, see Peter Nicholson, *Love and Ethics in Gower's* "Confessio Amantis" (Ann Arbor: University of Michigan Press, 2005).

38. See Sylvia Huot, *From Song to Book: The Poetics of Writing in Old French Lyric and Lyrical Narrative Poetry* (Ithaca, N.Y.: Cornell University Press, 1987); Ardis Butterfield, *Poetry and Music in Medieval France* (Cambridge: Cambridge University Press, 2002). The development of these novel technologies have been beautifully analyzed by Butterfield, who argues convincingly for a newly innovating force of the use of *contrafacta* composition, and what she calls "refrain-citation" in texts that combine song and narrative poetry or prose. On *contrafacta* composition, 103–4; on refrain, 89–94.

39. Butterfield, *Poetry and Music*, 1.

40. Ibid., 9. For the "infiltration" of song and narrative, see Butterfield's introduction. A more fully developed treatment of this point must be deferred. For an exciting review of developments in our understanding of medieval song traditions, see Emma Dillon, *The Sense of Sound: Musical Meaning in France, 1260–1330* (Oxford: Oxford University Press, 2012). For a review of relevant scholarship, see Dillon, 8–15.

41. Kevin Brownlee, *Poetic Identity in Guillaume de Machaut* (Madison: University of Wisconsin Press, 1984). 85.

42. Guillaume de Machaut, "Le Dit de l'alerion," *Oeuvres de Guillaume de Machaut*, ed. Ernest Hoepffner, vol. 2. Société des Anciens Textes Français (Paris: Firmin-Didot, 1911), lines 312–14. The translation is taken from Guillaume de Machaut, *The Tale of the Alerion*, ed. and trans. Minnette Gaudet and C. B. Hieatt (Toronto: University of Toronto Press, 1994). Hereafter cited parenthetically.

43. Jacques Boogaart notes Machaut's discussion of the "new" in this poem, linking it to the author's interest in "compositional dissonances" and artistic license: "[Machaut's] pleasure in novelty and the unheard is attested by a passage from the *Dit de l'Alerion* (generally dated before 1349), where a fabulous hunting-bird Alerion is praised for its rareness; its difficult training serves as a metaphor for learning the arts of love and poetry." He does not, however, seem to recognize the full complexity of the discussion of newness undertaken here. "Thought-Provoking Dissonances: Remarks about Machaut's Compositional Licences [sic] in Relation to his Texts," *Dutch Journal of Music Theory*, volume 12, number 3 (2007), 273–292, 273.

44. I cite the translation by Gaudet and Hieatt; I will be qualifying it considerably.

45. It is certainly true that, as Gaudet argues, "in Machaut's poem, the bird is portrayed as merchandise which can be bought, traded, and exchanged." Yet the question of value is no simple matter, and the poem regularly hints at a disjunction between economic transactions and true value. For an alternative reading to mine, see Minnette Gaudet, "Machaut's Dit de l'alerion and the Sexual Politics of Courtly Love," *Romance Languages Annual* (1993): 55–63, 56.

46. Shlomith Rimmon-Kenan, "The Paradoxical Status of Repetition," *Poetics Today* 1, 4, *Narratology II: The Fictional Text and the Reader* (Summer 1980): 151–59.

47. Robert Deschaux noted the degree to which these birds "fournissent des symboles et des schémas nouveaux." "Le bestiaire de Guillaume de Machaut d'après les dits," *Cahiers de l'Association Internationale des Études Françaises* 31 (1979): 7–16, 16.

48. Philip Fisher writes, "the moment of pure presence within wonder lies in the object's difference and uniqueness being so striking to the mind that it does not remind us of anything . . . in which the mind does not move on by association to something else." The set-apart quality of the object, for Fisher, startles and stops us—marked by newness as utter discontinuity, a thing associated with nothing else. (Fisher's is an entirely modern wonder, though Machaut's concatenation of the strange and the novel suggests an earlier iteration of the point.) Fisher, *Wonder, the Rainbow, and the Aesthetic of Rare Experiences* (Cambridge, Mass.: Harvard University Press, 2003), 131.

49. Deleuze, *Difference and Repetition*, 90.

50. On the tradition of Juvenal, and the Stoic tradition more generally, in the Middle Ages, see Marcia L. Colish, *The Stoic Tradition from Antiquity to the Early Middle Ages: Stoicism in Classical Latin Literature* (Leiden: Brill, 1985).

51. Deschaux puts it thus: "L'alérion est un oiseau de prix, difficile à acquérir: il se mérite et ne s'achète pas." "Le bestiaire de Guillaume de Machaut d'après les dits," 13.

52. Leupin, "Powerlessness of Writing," 131.

53. Jean-Joseph Goux, *Symbolic Economies: After Marx and Freud*, trans. Jennifer Curtiss Guge (Ithaca, N.Y.: Cornell University Press, 1990).

54. Andrew Galloway, "The Making of a Social Ethic in Late-Medieval England: From Gratitudo to 'Kyndnesse,'" *Journal of the History of Ideas*, 55, 3 (July 1994): 365–83, 373.

55. Ibid. Galloway notes this usage in texts from the *South English Legendary* to the first Wyclif Bible (372). He asserts that Chaucer "avoids applying 'kynde' and 'kyndenesse' altogether to general social ethics" (381). In the context he means, Galloway's claim is technically correct. I suggest, however, that Chaucer nonetheless engages these larger ethical issues in this tale.

56. Ibid., 374.

57. In *Animal Encounters: Contracts and Concepts in Medieval Britain* (Philadelphia: University of Pennsylvania, 2013), Susan Crane emphasizes compassion as crucial to the "cross-species affinity" depicted in the relations between the peregrine and Canacee. Canacee's "natural compassion," Crane argues, "opposes the tercel's natural disposition for 'newfangelelnesse'" (132). While I find Crane's attention to the poem's complex rendering of species compelling, I am not entirely convinced by the reading of compassion here. For if the tale opposes a "natural" disposition toward the new to a "natural" compassion, why are the salves Canacee compassionately uses to heal the peregrine's wounds also explicitly designated as "new"?

58. Arjun Appadurai, ed., *The Social Life of Things: Commodities in Cultural Perspective* (Cambridge: Cambridge University Press, 1988). And "Courtly Love discourse enacts the economy of 'feudal' subsistence 'seen from the perspective of the Thing'—meaning among other things seen as a matter of life and death, as counting absolutely. As a corollary it performs in the theaters of exchange the loss of the artifact that is interdependent with its

creation, true whether the artifact in question is an abstract instrument (the euro) or the recollected subject" (Fradenburg, *Sacrifice Your Love*, 20).

59. Tiffany remarks, following Krauss, that such a toy serves as "a spectacular device that discloses, in the name of science, the immaterial foundation of the object—the invisibility of the real." Tiffany, *Toy Medium*, 82. See also Lacan, "The Network of Signifier" "Tuché" (usually translated as "fate") and Automaton" and "The Split Between the Eye and the Gaze," in *The Four Fundamental Concepts of Psychoanalysis: The Seminar of Jacques Lacan, Book XI*, ed. Jacques-Alain Miller, ed. and trans. Alan Sheridan (1978; New York: Norton, 1998). My thinking is indebted to Rosalind Krauss, *The Optical Unconscious* (Cambridge, Mass.: MIT Press, 1993), esp. 71–72.

60. Lightsey, "Chaucer's Secular Marvels." He writes: "Chaucer merges the awe inspired by the literary mirabilia of romance with curiosity about the mechanical marvels that were a part of late-medieval court life. The text not only confronts the reader with a romance marvel but also depicts this supposedly supernatural motif as an object of rational inquiry. Chaucer often appears to invite readers to experience marvels as products of human artifice rather than as supernatural phenomena." In his book *Man-Made Marvels*, Lightsey deemphasizes this question of what we might call the tale's investment in "disenchantment" (see 74–80).

61. While I do not have time to address this here, the automaton also alludes to late medieval thinking about the animation of idols, where one also finds concern about the vivacity of matter. Recent work on iconoclasm is pertinent here, particularly Nicolette Zeeman's reading of the Temples in Chaucer's *House of Fame* and *Knight's Tale*. These descriptions offer, she argues, the "naked body of poetry" as pointing, like the image of the idol, "to an anxious fascination with textual reification. " Such images figure the "dangerous matter of the imaginative text" (62). Nicolette Zeeman, "The Idol of the Text," in *Images, Idolatry and Iconoclasm in Late Medieval England*, ed. Jeremy Dimick, James Simpson, and Nicolette Zeeman (Oxford: Oxford University Press, 2002).

62. With regard to Baudelaire, Tiffany concludes, "[he] shrewdly abducts the toy from the sphere of childhood, appropriating it for the uncertain fate of poetry" (*Toy Medium*, 72–75).

63. On fables of Virgil the Necromancer, see John W. Spargo, *Virgil the Necromancer: Studies in Virgilian Legends* (Cambridge, Mass.: Harvard University Press, 1934).

64. Craig Berry, "Flying Sources: Classical Authority in Chaucer's Squire's Tale," *ELH* 68, no.2 (2001): 287–313, 292. If Lightsey positions poetry as a contributing cause to mechanical productions, Berry emphasizes the similarities—not the differences here—between the making of things and the making of poetry.

65. Marijane Osborne, "The Squire's 'Steed of Brass' as Astrolabe: Some Implications for the Canterbury Tales," *Hermeneutics and Medieval Culture*, ed. Patrick J. Gallacher and Helen Damico (Albany: State University Press of New York, 1989), 121–31.

66. From the *Astrolabe*: "Thyn Astrolabe hat a ring to putten on the thombe of thy right hond in taking the height of thinges" (Astr. 1.1); "Than is there a large pyne in manere of an extre [axle tree], that goth thorugh the hole that half the tables of the clymates and

the riet in the wombe of the moder; thorugh which pyn ther goth a litel wegge, which that is clepd the horse, that steynth allthese parties to-hepe" (Astr. 1.14). Further assessment of the implications of this connection must be deferred at present. I am grateful to Peter Travis for drawing my attention to Osborne's work.

67. Descartes, *Passions of the Soul*, §53. See also §70–78 for elaboration.

68. As Lorraine Daston and Katharine Park have demonstrated, *Wonders and the Order of Nature, 1150–1750* (New York: Zone, 1998), 15. I rely regularly here on Daston and Park's magisterial study, which rewrites wonder's periodizing history.

69. Ibid., 316–17. On the medieval history of wonder that Descartes inherits, see Caroline Walker Bynum, "Wonder," *American Historical Review* 102, 1 (Feb. 1997): 1–17. On the limitations of such careful distinctions see Ingham, "'In Contrayez Straunge': Colonial Relations, British Identity and *Sir Gawain and the Green Knight*," *New Medieval Literatures* 4 (2001): 61–93.

70. Daston and Park, *Wonders*, 318.

71. As cited in ibid., 317.

72. Such surplus of objects also works to maintain the royal household as "privileged . . . as a space of surplus." Smith, *Arts of Possession*, 51.

73. Taleb, *The Black Swan*, xviii. Taleb's Black Swan is not associated with the new as such. His work has nonetheless been important to my thinking on the new as a reframing of the unexpected or improbable occurrence.

CHAPTER 5. SUSPECT ECONOMIES

1. Perhaps through no fault of Weber's. See, for example, Max Weber, "Science as Vocation," in Weber, *From Max Weber: Essays in Sociology*, ed. H. H. Gerth and C. Wright Mills (New York: Oxford University Press, 1981). Brian Stock noted the importance of revised accounts of Weber's notion of rationality for accounts of medieval technology. As he put it over thirty years ago, "As curious as it may seem to a generation of historians reared on the notion of unidirectional progress, medieval rationality and rationalization, to use Weber's favorite terms, were actually byproducts of the intensification of tradition." "Rationality, Tradition and the Scientific Outlook: Reflections on Max Weber and the Middle Ages," *Annals of the New York Academy of Sciences* 441, 1 (1985): 7–19, 12. This essay would be developed further in Brian Stock, *Listening for the Text* (Baltimore: Johns Hopkins University Press, 1990), esp. 124–28, 126. On Weber's larger indebtedness to medieval historiography, see Wolfgang Schlueter, *Paradoxes of Modernity: Culture and Conduct in the Theory of Max Weber* (Stanford, Calif.: Stanford University Press, 1996), and, most recently, Lutz Kaelber, "Introduction" to Max Weber, *The History of Commercial Partnerships in the Middle Ages*, trans. Kaelber (Lantham, Md.: Rowman and Littlefield, 2002), 1–47. Weber's work, and its larger relation to notions of enchantment and disenchantment, are currently undergoing important revision. See the following: Jane Bennett, *The Enchantment of Modern Life* (Princeton, N.J.: Princeton University Press, 2001; Alan Sica, *Weber, Irrationality*,

and Social Order (Berkeley: University of California Press, 1988); Thomas Carlson, "Modernity and the Mystical: Science, Technology, and the Task of Human Self-Creation," in *Science, Religion, and the Human Experience*, ed. James Proctor (Oxford: Oxford University Press, 2005); Toby E. Huff and Wolfgang Schlueter, eds., *Max Weber and Islam* (New Brunswick, N.J.: Transaction Publishers, 1999). But "re-enchantment" has its darker sides. See also Jane O. Newman, "Enchantment in Times of War: Aby Warburg, Walter Benjamin, and the Secularization Thesis," *Representations* 105 (Winter 2009): 133–67. For a summary of some issues related to this question, see Patricia Clare Ingham, "Little Nothings: The Squire's Tale and the Ambition of Gadgets," *Studies in the Age of Chaucer* 31 (2009): 53–80.

2. Following the work of Jane Jacobs, Fradenburg reads romance as that medieval genre most attuned to the productive power of the ornamental, the frivolous, and the ludic. Fradenburg, "Simply Marvelous," *Studies in the Age of Chaucer* 26 (2004), 1–26. See also idem, "Needful Things," in *Medieval Crime and Social Control*, ed. Barbara Hanawalt and David Wallace (Minneapolis: University of Minnesota Press, 1999), 49–69.

3. Ibid. It is, Fradenburg insists, "interest[ed] in the *jouissance* of the encounter with the new" (8). It is the *jouissance* of the new to which Roland Barthes refers when, in *The Pleasure of the Text*, he implies that we need to do better than dismiss desire for the "new" as mere whim: "the new is not a fashion, it is a value."

4. Fradenburg, "Simply Marvelous," 26.

5. Leupin, *Barbarolexis: Medieval Writing and Sexuality* (Cambridge, Mass.: Harvard University Press, 1989), here describing the radical effect of Geoffrey of Vinsauf's *Poetria nova*. See esp. chap. 3, "Absolute Reflexivity: Geoffrey of Vinsauf's *Poetria nova*," 17–38, 38.

6. Jacqueline Cerquiglini-Toulet, *A New History of Medieval French Literature*, trans. Sara Preisig (Baltimore: Johns Hopkins University Press, 2011), 133–34.

7. Michael Camille, *The Gothic Idol: Ideology and Image-Making in Medieval Art* (Cambridge: Cambridge University Press, 1989), 35.

8. Carolyn Dinshaw's remarkable *How Soon Is Now? Medieval Texts, Amateur Readers, and the Queerness of Time* (Durham, N.C.: Duke University Press, 2012) leverages this kind of asynchrony for a striking new account of the affective possibilities of such time travel. My interest in the medieval new as the medieval now resonates with her concerns.

9. On this point, see Laura Hodges, "Sartorial Signs in Troilus and Criseyde," *Chaucer Review* 35, 3 (2001): 223–59.

10. For an account of the libidinal vectors of such ambivalent medieval creative productions, George Edmondson's *The Neighboring Text: Chaucer, Boccaccio, Henryson* (South Bend, Ind.: University of Notre Dame Press, 2011) is crucial.

11. The translation and text is taken from Ernest Gallo, *The Poetria Nova and Its Sources in Early Rhetorical Doctrine* (The Hague: Mouton, 1981), lines 802–3. Here is the original: "Talis transsumptio verbi / Est tibi pro speculo: qui ate spcularis in illo." Leupin makes a compelling case for the radical novelty of Vinsauf's method as well as his claims. *Barbarolexis*, 34–37.

12. Both offer, to paraphrase A. B. Taylor, an introduction to "the home-life of the

East." Taylor, ed., *Floris and Blancheflour: A Middle English Romance* (Oxford: Clarendon, 1927), as cited by Smith, 52.

13. *The Etymologies of Isidore of Seville*, Stephen A. Barney et al., trans. with the collaboration of Muriel Hall (Cambridge: Cambridge University Press, 2006).

14. Newhauser and Peters's collaborative project to assess the enormous discursive field that *curiositas* occupied in medieval and early modern times is ongoing.

15. Richard Newhauser, "Curiosity," in Karla Pollmann, ed., *The Oxford Guide to the Historical Reception of Augustine*, vol. 2 (Oxford: Oxford University Press, 2013), 849–52, 849.

16. Zacher asserts that such distinctions were important to Classical thinkers, but fell into disuse in the Middle Ages, only to be revived in the Renaissance. Newhauser has shown the various ways that medieval intellectuals and moralists situated excessive curiosity, but not all curiosity, in terms of vice. See Newhauser, "Towards a History of Human Curiosity: A Prolegomenon to Its Medieval Phase," *Deutsche Vierteljahrschrift fur Literaturwissenschaft und Geistesgeschichte* 52 (1982): 569–75. Also "Augustinian vitium curiositatis and its reception," in *Saint Augustine and His Influence in the Middle Ages*, ed. Edward B. King and Jacqueline T. Schaefer, Sewanee Mediaeval Studies 3 (Sewanee, Tenn. 1988), 99–124; "Curiosity," in Karla Pollmann, ed., *The Oxford Guide to the Historical Reception of Augustine*, vol. 2 (Oxford: Oxford University Press, 2013), 849–52.

17. Peters, "*Libertas Inquierendi* and the *Vitium Curiositatis* in Medieval Thought," *in La notion de liberté au Moyen Âge: Islam, Byzance, Occident*, eds., George Makdisi, et. al. (Paris: Belles Lettres, 1985), 89–98, 95. Peters refers here to the title page of the 1587 *Historia* of Faust, printed in Frankfurt.

18. Newhauser, "Curiosity," 850.

19. Peter of Limoges, *The Moral Treatise on the Eye*, ed. and trans. Richard Newhauser, Medieval Sources in Translation. (Toronto: Pontifical Institute of Medieval Studies, 2012), xi.

20. Newhauser, "Augustinian vitium curiositatis and its reception," 121. Newhauser contests Blumenberg on this point.

21. Joel Kaye, *Economy and Nature in the Fourteenth Century: Money, Market Exchange, and the Emergence of Scientific Thought* (Cambridge: Cambridge University Press, 1998), 168.

22. Blanton, "Medieval Currencies." It was, "in some sense . . .the operation of money that was lurking in the trope of secularization all along" (209).

23. Newhauser, "Curiosity," *Oxford Guide*, 850.

24. Viz.: "videlicet nolle communicare scientia suum." John Bromyard, *Summa Praedicantium, Pars Prima*, see the full chapter on "Avaritiae."

25. Sheila Delany, "Run Silent, Run Deep: Heresy and Alchemy as Medieval Versions of Utopia," in *Medieval Literary Politics: Shapes of Ideology* (Manchester: Manchester University Press, 1990).

26. William R. Newman, *Promethean Ambitions: Alchemy and the Quest to Perfect Nature* (Chicago: University of Chicago Press, 2004), 52–53.

27. Linden, ed., "Art and Nature," 45. Chemical processes held deeper allegorical/

ethical meanings. See Linden's introduction, which outlines alchemical allegory by way of Ripley's twelve stages or gates of the alchemical "castle." Stages include: calcination (reduction of a substance to ashy powder), conjunction (union of opposites/heterosexual), putrefaction (death leading to rebirth—cf. seeds, but also resurrection), sublimation (distillation process, derived from the notion of "elevation"), multiplication (augmentation, or geometric increase in amount/size), projection (calcination of the philosophers stone), 17–18. On the need for a reconsideration of the medieval and early modern discourse of necromancy, see also Richard Kieckhefer's introduction to *Forbidden Rites: A Necromancer's Manual of the Fifteenth Century* (State College: Pennsylvania State University Press, 1998), 10–17. This work is ongoing.

28. As Linden puts it, "The position of serious alchemical experimenters and writers, as opposed to the charlatans, on the relationship between Art and Nature is especially subtle and wide-ranging" (*Alchemy Reader*, 15

29. Sarah Stanbury cites this anxious remark from the eighth-century John of Damascus as influential: "I do not worship matter; I worship the creator of matter." *The Visual Object of Desire in Late Medieval England* (Philadelphia: University of Pennsylvania Press, 2008).

30. William Newman and Lawrence Principe, "Some Problems with the Historiography of Alchemy," in *Secrets of Nature: Astrology and Alchemy in Early Modern Europe*, ed. William Newman and Anthony Grafton (Cambridge, Mass.: MIT Press, 2001), 385–431.

31. Mark Pegg and R. I. Moore have each argued that the picture of Cathars as dualistic Manicheans that emerged in the nineteenth century is a fiction. They argue that the Albigensians were in fact dissenters, and that their persecutors exaggerated the charges against them. See R. I. Moore, *The War on Heresy: Faith and Power in Medieval Europe* (Cambridge, Mass.: Harvard University Press, 2012); Mark G. Pegg, *A Most Holy War: The Albigensian Crusade and the Battle for Christendom* (New York: Oxford University Press, 2007).

32. These debates emerged in philosophy and literature alike, and they continued into Chaucer's day. While Langland would condemn alchemy by linking it with necromancy, "moral" Gower seems to have found the science to be a legitimate, if arduous, undertaking (*Confessio Amantis*, 4). On this point, see Patterson, "Perpetual Motion: Alchemy and the Technology of the Self," *Studies in the Age of Chaucer* 15 (1993): 25–57, 29n13.

33. Jonathan Hsy, "Curiosity, Mars/Venus, and Chaucer," notes the ambiguities. *In the Middle*, Tuesday, August 7, 2012, http://www.inthemedievalmiddle.com.

34. All quotations from Chaucer's texts are taken from Benson, ed., *The Riverside Chaucer*, 3rd ed. (Boston: Houghton Mifflin, 1987).

35. Richard Firth Green makes this too confident statement: "the alchemical project was studiously regressive, not progressive, and its goal at least in terms of its own discourse seemed far from attainable." Richard Firth Green, "Changing Chaucer," *Studies in the Age of Chaucer* 25 (2003): 27–52, 49. Charles Muscatine, *Chaucer and the French Tradition* (Berkeley: University of California Press, 1960), 213–21; Patterson, "Perpetual Motion."

36. Peggy Knapp and Britton Harwood have linked the tale's disenchanting strategies

to the historical transition from feudal to mercantile production. They argue that descriptions of the alchemical laboratory, the false Canon's monetary trickery, and the Canon's Yeoman's critique of his experience of alienated labor reveal the dark secrets of power and exploitation. Britton J. Harwood, "Chaucer and the Silences of History: Situating the Canon's Yeoman's Tale," *PMLA* 102 (1987): 338–42; Peggy Knapp, "The Work of Alchemy," *Journal of Medieval and Early Modern Studies* 30 (2000): 575–99.

37. Most recently Jennifer Sisk identifies what she sees as a type of "idealizing nostalgia" shared by the *Second Nun's Tale* and the *Canon's Yeoman's Tale*. See Sisk, "Religion, Alchemy, and Nostalgic Idealism in Fragment VIII," *Studies in the Age of Chaucer* 32 (2010): 151–77.

38. Nor do I agree with Sisk's assessment of the "esoteric" and "occult" resonances of alchemy; as the citation of Carl Jung suggests, much of this is a nineteenth-century invention.

39. Carolyn Collette, "Reading Chaucer Through Philippe de Mézières: Alchemy, the Individual, and the Good Society," in *Courtly Literature and Clerical Culture*, ed. Christopher Huber and Henrike Lahnemann (Tubingen: Attempto Verlag, 2002), 177–94.

40. Linden argues that linguistic issues are crucial to the development of alchemy, particularly in the English context. *Dark Hieroglyphicks: Alchemy in English Literature from Chaucer to the Restoration* (Lexington: University Press of Kentucky, 1996).

41. Patterson, "Perpetual Motion," 55; David Raybin, "And Pave It Al of Silver and of Gold: The Humane Artistry of the *Canon's Yeoman's Tale*," in *Rebels and Rivals: The Contested Spirit in the Canterbury Tales*, ed. Susana Greer Fein, David Raybin, and Peter C. Braeger (Kalamazoo: Western Michigan Press, 1991), 189–212.

42. The variation of "nyce" as either "foolish" or "wise" is attested in Manly-Rickert's critical edition, *Chaucer: The Text of the Canterbury Tales*, ed. John Matthews Manly and E. Rickert, vol 3: 3–37. On the semantic range, see *Middle English Dictionary*, s.v. "nice," (adv.), where the line is cited as pertinent to the third usage, "strange" and "remarkable."

43. Trinity College, Cambridge MS. R. 14.44 and entitled "The Right Path Albertus Bears Witness" ("Semita Recta Albertus peribet testimoniam"). The text is taken from Peter Grund, "Albertus Magnus and the Queen of the Elves: A 15th Century English Verse Dialogue on Alchemy," *Anglia: Zeitschrift für englische Philologie* 122 (2004): 640–62.

44. Grund (648) notes the possibility of Albert's elevation when he suggests that the dialogue could have been "interpreted as yet another example of [Albert's] connection with the supernatural, thus adding to Albertus's already mythical status."

45. The continuation of alchemy has recently been proven with regard to Boyle's early modern work; see William R. Newman, *Atoms and Alchemy: Chymestry and the Experimental Origins of the Scientific Revolution* (Chicago: University of Chicago Press, 2006).

46. Green, "Changing Chaucer," 33.

47. MED defines "resistance" here as "hindrance," grouping Chaucer's usage with examples of resistant things, like battlements, where the connotation seems stalwart passivity.

48. William Eamon, "Technology as Magic in the Late Middle Ages and Renaissance," *Janus* 70 (1983): 171–212, 173.

49. Pamela O. Long, *Openness, Secrecy, Authorship: Technical Arts and the Culture of Knowledge from Antiquity to the Renaissance* (Baltimore: Johns Hopkins University Press, 2001), 89. Such proprietary claims may involve labor practices.

50. Sisk, "Nostalgic Idealism," 173.

51. Ibid., 176.

52. Ibid., 165.

53. See Kaye, *Economy and Nature in the Fourteenth Century*.

54. Sisk, "Nostalgic Idealism," 167. While I appreciate the equivocal combination, I am not entirely sure why "trial and error" constitutes a "relentless cycle" in which the alchemist is "trapped." The repetitions of trial and error constitute the practice of science to this day, and they are certainly a feature of all scholarly work. When Sisk implies that repetition moves toward an intellectual dead end, she follows the long line of thinking that I have been at some pains to reconsider in my account of the medieval new.

55. Readers pursuing Marxist interpretations (Knapp, Harwood) read here a critique of the future of wage laboring, the exploitation of the worker's body, the destructive force of a cash economy, or the problem of capital as barren and unproductive.

56. Lisa Cooper, *Artisans and Narrative Craft in Late Medieval England* (Cambridge: Cambridge University Press, 2011), 14.

57. On this development, see Hall Bjørnstad, ed., *Borrowed Feathers: Plagiarism and the Limits of Imitation in Early Modern Europe* (Paris: Unipub, 2009).

58. For an account of the "necromancy" of early print, see Elizabeth L. Eisenstein, *Divine Art, Infernal Machine: The Reception of Printing in the West from First Impressions to the Sense of an Ending* (Philadelphia: University of Pennsylvania Press, 2011).

CHAPTER 6. OLD WORLDS AND NEW

Epigraph: Anthony Grafton (with April Shelford and Nancy Siraisi), *New Worlds, Ancient Texts: The Power of Tradition and the Shock of Discovery* (Cambridge, Mass.: Harvard University Press, 1992), 5.

1. Alain Badiou understands the event as a tear in the fabric of the normal. Philosophical interest in the new as radical event, as in Badiou's work, concerns the formal features of the disorienting power of radical rupture. The event functions formally for Badiou, a singular, shattering occurrence emblematized by the narrative of Paul on the road to Damascus—where the former Pharisee becomes a new man, rendering Christianity as the new law capable of dissolving the former identities and loyalties, of slave or free, Greek or Jew, woman or man. To be sure, the status of the new in Pauline Christianity, as Badiou acknowledges, is paradoxical, regularly serving hopes for a new and better universal, if also founding Christian supersessionism, as in Paul's notion that the new and living law of

Christ supersedes the old, apparently dead law of Moses and the Prophets. Certainly Badiou makes legible the revolutionary potential of the (singular) event as a destabilizing formalization capable of demanding that we abandon old forms and old pieties. Yet, as a number of critics of Badiou have pointed out, the radical rupture of a universal Christianity is twinned, in Paul, with residual features of Jewish community and identity, a question of obvious concern to the new world rhetorics of early modernity. Such debates, which fundamentally concern the meaning of repetition, chime with debates over epochal history such as those examined in this chapter. Alain Badiou, *Saint Paul: The Foundation of Universalism*, trans. Ray Brassier (Stanford, Calif.: Stanford University Press, 2003). See particularly Badiou's comments on Paul's role as "inventor" (5–6) and on the "event" (16–30).

2. In this regard Grafton here ventriloquizes an account that seems to rely on Blumenbergian notions of the new age. Blumenberg deploys modernity's new ideas as a means to *legitimate* the epochal break. The narrative value of the new *for* modernity—a claim that, even more than secularization, constitutes the ultimate payoff for Blumenberg—circulates thus as a story of legitimation. Grafton's own erudite work acknowledges many of the dependencies that I am tracing here.

3. Roland Barthes, *The Pleasure of the Text*, trans. Richard Miller (New York: Hill and Wang, 1975), 40.

4. Joseph A. Schumpeter popularized the term. See *Capitalism, Socialism and Democracy*, 3rd ed. (New York: HarperCollins, 2008). It is taken too far in recent work on innovation in management culture, as in Peter A. Drucker, *Managing in a Time of Great Change* (New York: Truman Talley/Dutton, 1995).

5. Jonathan Goldberg, "The History That Will Be," in *Premodern Sexualities*, ed. Louise O. Fradenburg and Carla Freccero (New York: Routledge, 1995), 3–21.

6. Mary Baine Campbell, *Wonder and Science: Imagining Worlds in Early Modern Europe* (Ithaca, N.Y.: Cornell University Press, 1999), 1.

7. Ibid., 285.

8. Also informative is Delano C. West and August Kling, eds., *The "Libro de las profecias" of Christopher Columbus, an en face edition* (Gainesville: University Press of Florida, 1991).

9. Felipe Fernandez-Armesto, *Columbus on Himself* (Indianapolis: Hackett, 2010), 12.

10. See P. M. Watts, "Prophecy and Discovery: on the Spiritual Origins of Christopher Columbus's 'Enterprise of the Indies,'" *American Historical Review* 90 (1985): 73–102; on d'Ailly's context and work, see Francis Oakley, *The Political Thought of Pierre d'Ailly* (New Haven, Conn.: Yale University Press, 1964); for an overview of the annotations, see Fernandez-Armesto, *Columbus*, 11.

11. This is why Northrup Frye calls the New Jerusalem an "undisplaced form . . . of the telos" (34), insisting that "a Christian utopia, in the sense of an ideal state to be attained in human life, is impossible: if it were possible it would be the kingdom of heaven." "Varieties of Literary Utopia," in *Utopias and Utopian Thought*, ed. Frank Manuel (Boston: Houghton Mifflin, 1966), 25–49, 36.

12. Though not most persuasively in terms of "secularity," as commonly understood.

For an account of secularity as a type of relation to religion rather than freedom from it, see Thomas Carlson, "Modernity and the Mystical: Science, Technology, and the Task of Human Self-Creation," in *Science, Religion, and the Human Experience*, ed. James Proctor (Oxford: Oxford University Press, 2005).

13. Karl Löwith, *Meaning in History: The Theological Implications of the Philosophy of History* (Chicago: University of Chicago Press, 1949). His work has been compelling to scholars of early periods, not least because accounts of secular progress converge on developmental rhetorics of colony and empire, and historically served to underwrite the colonial civilizing mission. Increasing interest in the politics of periodization, in the light of postcolonial analyses of the uses of time, have helped us here. See Kathleen Davis, *Periodization and Sovereignty: How Ideas of Feudalism and Secularization Govern the Politics of Time* (Philadelphia: University of Pennsylvania Press, 2008), who notes the importance of Löwith's work, "for its insistence that conceptions of historical time must be understood as political strategy—and in the case of periodized, progressive history, as a means of aggression" (83).

14. Julia Lupton, *Afterlives of the Saints: Hagiography, Typology, and Renaissance Literature* (Stanford, Calif.: Stanford University Press, 1996), 23.

15. Kathleen Biddick, *The Typological Imaginary: Circumcision, Technology, History* (Philadelphia: University of Pennsylvania Press, 2003), 4–8.

16. A good example is Dipesh Chakrabarty, *Provincializing Europe: Postcolonial Thought and Historical Difference* (Princeton, N.J.: Princeton University Press, 2009).

17. Hans Blumenberg, *The Legitimacy of the Modern Age,* trans. Robert M. Wallace (Cambridge, Mass.: MIT Press, 1983). Martin Jay views Blumenberg's account as a "weak" "secularization" thesis, Review of *The Legitimacy of the Modern Age* by Hans Blumenberg, trans. Robert M. Wallace, *History and Theory* 24, 2 (1985): 183–96.

18. "The modern age found it impossible to decline to answer [Christian] questions about the totality of history." Modern claims for progress constitute, thus, not a secularization so much as a category mistake: modern thought "easily . . . discredited the Christian answers," but "was unable to neutralize" the sweeping critical questions about world history "inherited from Christianity." Blumenberg, *Legitimacy*, 48.

19. Jay, Review of Blumenberg, *Legitimacy*, 196.

20. Blumenberg, *Legitimacy*, 62–71. There were, Blumenberg argues, considerable formal distinctions between eschatology and progress: the former transcendent while the latter imminent; the former the consummation of history from the outside, the latter a consummation evolving from the internal logic of human striving; the former dependent upon divine freedom and agency while the latter the result of "human self-assertion." See also Robert M. Wallace, "Progress, Secularization, and Modernity: The Lowith-Blumenberg Debate," *New German Critique* 22 (Winter 1981): 63–79, 75. Emphasis on the reoccupation, rather than secularization, of religious notions seems to some to be a distinction without a difference. See David Ingram, "Blumenberg and the Philosophical Grounds of Historiography," *History and Theory* 29, 1 (1990): 1–15, esp. 3–5.

21. Michel Foucault, *Le Mots et les choses: Une archéologie des sciences humaines* (Paris: Èditions Gallimard, 1966; Thomas Kuhn, *The Structure of Scientific Revolutions* (Chicago:

University of Chicago Press, 1962). Given Kuhn's own rejection of "Whiggish" accounts of the history of science, it would be too simplistic to see his position as predicated on a pro-gressivist notion of history. As Nick Jardine points out, "By the mid-1970s, it had become commonplace among historians of science to employ the terms 'Whig' and 'Whiggish,' often accompanied by one or more of 'hagiographic,' 'internalist,' 'triumphalist,' even 'pos-itivist,' to denigrate grand narratives of scientific progress. . . . In particular, they were sus-picious of the grand celebratory and didactic narratives of scientific discovery and progress that had proliferated in the inter-war years." See Jardine, "Whigs and Stories: Herbert Butterfield and the Historiography of Science," *History of Science* 41 (2003): 125–40, 127–28. The notion of whiggish history was defined by Herbert Butterfield as "the study of the past with direct and perpetual reference to the present." Herbert Butterfield, *The Whig Interpre-tation of History* (New York: Norton, 1931), 11–12.

22. Blumenberg, *Legitimacy*, 345.

23. It would be going too far to say that Blumenberg himself supported such utopia-nism. But the implications of his account of self-assertion would be read (and to some de-gree misread) in such terms in the years after *Legitimacy* appeared.

24. Davis, *Periodization and Sovereignty*, argues that Blumenberg's modern age gains a "self-assertive" claim to sovereignty over time.

25. Sigmund Freud, "Creative Writers and Day-Dreaming," *SE* IX: 148. For an ac-count of fantasy as a version of history writing, see Joan Wallach Scott, *The Fantasy of Feminist History* (Durham, N.C.: Duke University Press, 2011).

26. For an account of the problems with Blumenberg's picture of medieval thought, see the essays in *The Legitimacy of the Middle Ages: On the Unwritten History of Theory*, ed. Cole and Smith, (Durham, N.C.: Duke University Press, 2010), and the editors' introduc-tion, Andrew Cole and D. Vance Smith, "Introduction: Outside Modernity," 1–36. Cole and Smith helpfully draw attention to the crucial place of futurity in Blumenberg's under-standing of both medieval and modern: where modernity sees the future in radically open terms, as itself the very horizon of possibility for new things and ideas, medieval thinkers, like their classical ancestors, remain preoccupied with the limitations to what could be, and thus with the problem of necessity. This astute account offers the clearest explanation of why, at least since Blumenberg, the medieval "new" occupies the space of the impossible, the oxymoronic: unlike the brave new world of modern curiosity, medieval *theoria* (and *curiositas*) is understood to be a closed system, severed from future possibility. And yet the problem of fate, specifically as it pertains to the advent of possible futures, remains. It is this problem that haunts the epoch as such.

27. C. D. Blanton, "Medieval Currencies: Nominalism and Art," in *Legitimacy of the Middle Ages*, ed. Cole and Smith, 194–232, 219. And, of course, speculation has its own links to economies of value. Blanton's brilliant essay has been crucially helpful to me on this point. He writes, "For Blumenberg, the legitimacy of the modern age rests on the reoccu-pation of a structure of 'theoretical curiosity' that drives the scale of scientific knowledge beyond the comprehension of the individual, rendering the totality of the world abstract but immanent. Knowledge, as a variation on method or (as Adorno would insist)

administration, functions as a real abstraction, a cumulative project impelled by collective and continuous intellectual inquiry" (208). Following Marxist epistemologies of Alfred Sohn-Rethel, Blanton describes the relation of theoretical abstraction to commodity exchange, speculation in all its senses. Alfred Sohn-Rethel, *Intellectual and Manual Labor: A Critique of Epistemology* (Atlantic Highlands, N.J.: Humanities Press, 1977). I am, in contrast, interested in the means whereby the functioning of necessity, inherited from the scholastics, converged on definitions of human happiness.

28. On this point, see Anthony Pagden, *European Encounters with the New World: from Renaissance to Romanticism* (New Haven, Conn.: Yale University Press, 1993), 96.

29. As Pagden's study makes clear, Bert Roest argues that the Humanists were at their most innovative not only in what they read, but in the ways they did so: "Rhetoric of Innovation and Recourse to Tradition in Humanist Pedagogical Discourse," in *Medieval and Renaissance Humanism: Rhetoric, Representation, and Reform*, ed. Stephen Gersh and Bert Roest (Leiden: Brill, 2003), 115–48. As Roest remarks, the pedagogical innovations that "brought language itself to the forefront of education" (137) "show an uncanny resemblance with the visionary educational programme put forward in the 1260's by Roger Bacon" (136). He nonetheless distinguishes Bacon's brand of linguistic precision from later versions, since Bacon did not "reject the scholastic method in itself" (136).

30. The phrase is Blumenberg's, *Legitimacy*, 309–15.

31. Over twenty-five years ago, Peter Hulme drew attention to the linguistic and conceptual slide between the supposed "new world cannibals" in Columban texts and "the people of the Great Khan," a reference to the Mongols described in detail by thirteenth-century William of Rubruk, referenced by both Marco Polo and the writer known to us as John Mandeville. William's writing would influence medieval discourses of innovation directly: his confrère Roger Bacon attributes his interest in gunpowder and fireworks to William's descriptions of technological developments observed in Asia. Yet no claim is made, in either William's narrative or Bacon's, for cosmological rupture. William's often-cited remark that his experience of the kingdom of Cathay was like "entering another world" sits alongside his clear awareness that Europeans share with Mongols what today's anthropologists would call a coeval status: the two cultures coexist in time; their differences are spatial and cultural, not temporal. For a reading of William of Rubruck's project as an innovating ethnography, see Shirin Khanmohamadi, *In the Light of Another's Word: European Ethnography in the Middle Ages* (Philadelphia: University of Pennsylvania Press, 2013).

32. Edward Peters, "The Desire to Know the Secrets of the World," *Journal of the History of Ideas* 62, 4 (2001): 593–610, 599.

33. Ibid., 593–610. "Zacher paints [*curiositas*] with too broad a brush and Blumenberg a brush too narrow" (599). Peters revises the overly optimistic view of curiosity first advanced by J. H. Elliott, whereby knowledge was, Elliott wrote, "subordinated to a higher purpose and fitted into a providential design." *The Old World and the New, 1492–1650* (Cambridge: Cambridge University Press, 1970), 31.

34. In fact, the range of topics and registers included in the medieval category of *vitium curiositatis* offers one clue as to the overly simplified nature of the story that

Blumenberg tells. Peters, "Secrets," 595. Newhauser emphasizes critiques of *vitiam curiositas* as fundamental questions of misplaced *cura*, or care. See Richard Newhauser, "Towards a History of Human Curiosity: A Prolegomenon to Its Medieval Phase," *Deutsche Vierteljahrschift für Literaturwissenschaft und Geistesgeschichte* 52 (1982): 559–75. Also "Augustinian vitium curiositatis and its reception," in *Saint Augustine and His Influence in the Middle Ages*, ed. Edward B. King and Jacqueline T. Schaefer, Sewanee Mediaeval Studies 3 (Sewanee, Tenn.: Press of the University of the South, 1988), 99–124.

35. Such evangelism had been, of course, a feature of Christian discourse since the letters of Paul. Newhauser notes the particular way *curiositas* was encouraged in the service of Christian conversion, an issue noted in Roger Bacon's work treated in Chapter 2. See esp. Newhauser's summary of its use in Hermannus Judaeus's account of his conversion to Christianity. Newhauser, "Towards a History," 570.

36. For an account of *curiositas* with modern implications, see Paul J. Griffiths, *Intellectual Appetite: A Theological Grammar* (Washington, D.C.: Catholic University of America Press, 2009).

37. Christian contexts took up both sides of the question, in pilgrimage but also because, as Mary Campbell notes, Christianity's sacred lands are "located emphatically Elsewhere," *The Witness and the Other World* (Ithaca, N.Y.: Cornell University Press, 1988), 18.

38. Peters, "Desire to Know," 600–601.

39. As, for instance, in the Alliterative *Morte Arthure* (c. 1380), a text arguably concerned with the ethics of Arthur's pursuit of the conquest of Rome as "the ends of the earth." On this point, see my *Sovereign Fantasies: Arthurian Romance and the Making of Britain* (Philadelphia: University of Pennsylvania Press, 2001), chap. 3.

40. Paul J. Griffiths argues that this association of *vitium curiositatis* with an understanding of knowledge as property ready to be owned or taken is the crucial feature of what he terms the "Christian" tradition, beginning with Augustine. *Intellectual Appetite*, 19–30.

41. As Peters, "Desire to Know," also points out, 606.

42. Walter of Châtillon, *The "Alexandreis": A Twelfth-Century Epic*, a verse translation by David Townsend (Peterborough, Ont.: Broadview Press, 2007), lines 435b–38. Not surprisingly, they will urge moderation: "Remember, then, to grasp your Fortune closely, / . . . / Pursue the healthful counsel of the moment: / while still your hand can throw a lucky cast, / before you've cause to chide swift-moving Fortune, / impose a limit" (lines 524, 527–30a). In considering questions of history, it is also important to remember that anti-Jewishness was integral to Walter of Châtillon's cosmology. To borrow the words of Anna Sapir Abulafia, "Not only did [the historical relation of Christianity and Judaism] matter so much to him that he wrote a treatise against the Jews, he returned to the subject over and over again in his literary output. He needed language which was anti-Jewish in order to express his deeply held religious convictions. Or to put it differently, anti-Jewish ideas were an integral part of his religiosity." "Walter of Châtillon: A twelfth-century poet's engagement with Jews," *Journal of Medieval History*, 31.3 (2005): 265–86, 284.

43. Peter of Limoges, *The Moral Treatise on the Eye*, trans. Richard Newhauser (Toronto: Pontifical Institute, 2012), 70. Newhauser cites the corroborating primary text as

Epistola Alexandri regis ad Dindimum regem, ed. Friedrich Pfister, in *Kleine Texte zum Alexanderroman*, Sammlung vulgarlateinischer Texte, 4 (Heidelberg: C. Winter, 1910), 10.

44. Peter of Limoges, *The Moral Treatise on the Eye*, 69.

45. Bacon cited the *Secret of Secrets* frequently. In Book 7 of Gower's *Confessio*, Genius explains Aristotle's instruction of Alexander. See John Gower, *Confessio Amantis*, vol. 3., ed. Russell A. Peck, Latin trans. by Andrew Galloway, TEAMS edition (Kalamazoo, Mich.: Medieval Institute Publications, 2004). The introduction of Aristotle's instruction marks a crucial turn in Gower's work: "the device enables the poet to shelve his confessional drama in order to focus on ethics, bringing the educational substructure to its culmination." "Introduction," 5. For a reading of the medieval text linked to accounts of ethics and confession, see Karma Lochrie, *Covert Operations: The Medieval Uses of Secrecy* (Philadelphia: University of Pennsylvania Press, 1999).

46. *Alexandreis*, ll. 436–39.

47. Ibid., 156n1, 157n2.

48. Fernandez-Armesto, ed., *Columbus*, 148.

49. Djelal Kadir, *Columbus and the Ends of the Earth* (Berkeley: University of California Press, 1992).

50. Mario Klarer, "Woman and Arcadia: The Impact of Ancient Utopian Thought on the Early Image of America," *Journal of American Studies* 27 (1993): 1, 1–17, 16.

51. Peters, "Desire to Know," 599.

52. And, as Peters, ibid., points out, in the Old Norse saga, *The Greenlanders*, "Bjarni Herjolfsson is criticized for lacking curiosity and having too little to say about the new lands he has found" (599). On the links between utopian new world thinking and "a tradition of ancient and medieval utopian projections," see Mario Klarer, "Cannibalism and Carnivalesque: Incorporation as Utopia in the Early Image of America," *New Literary History* 30 (1999): 389–410, 389.

53. I do not mean to suggest a radical break between preprint and postprint technologies. On such questions, see William Kuskin, "Caxton's Worthies," and my essay, "Losing French: Translation, Nation, and Caxton's English Statues," in the edited collection, *Caxton's Trace: Studies in the History of English Printing*, ed. William Kuskin (Notre Dame, Ind.: Notre Dame University Press, 2006), 275–98. Iain Higgins's award-winning study of the manuscripts of the *Book of John Mandeville* suggests that the diversity and multiplicity of surviving materials testify to a set of cultural disagreements over such things as medieval belief in the place of Jerusalem, or the geographies of the world. Julia Crick's analysis of surviving manuscripts of Geoffrey of Monmouth's *Historia regum Britanniae* similarly displays the ways attention to the multiplicities and contradictions in a manuscript tradition can open dynamic accounts of reception, contestation, and circulation, obscured by traditional stemmata models, and the search for an "authoritative" or authorial version. Higgins jettisons such arborescent models of descent in favor of the "rhizomatic" multitext; see his "Defining the Earth's Center in a Medieval 'Multi-Text' Jerusalem in the *Book of John Mandeville*," in *Text and Territory: Geographical Imagination in the European Middle Ages*, ed. Sylvia Tomasch and Sealy Gilles (Philadelphia: University of Pennsylvania Press, 1998),

29–53. While not explicitly "rhizomatic," Julia Crick offers a similarly horizontal view in *The "Historia regum Britanniae" of Geoffrey of Monmouth: Dissemination and Reception in the Later Middle Ages* (Cambridge: Brewer, 1991).

54. Campbell, *Wonder and Science*, 9–12.

55. José Rabasa, *Inventing America: Spanish Historiography and the Formation of Eurocentrism* (Norman: University of Oklahoma Press, 1993), 82.

56. To be sure, scholars increasingly suggest various commonalities between cultures, pre- and postprint. And recently medievalists have compellingly argued that genealogical models of medieval textuality significantly mis- or underrepresent a more broadly horizontal, unpredictable, rhizomatic circulation of medieval texts precisely as manuscripts. David Greetham recommends such a revision, critiquing in detail "the classical taxonomies of phylum and tree [which have] tried to produce unambiguous maps on which [a manuscript's] authority could be directly related to [hierarchical] position and level." David Greetham, "Phylum-Tree-Rhizome," in *Reading from the Margins: Textual Studies, Chaucer, and Medieval Literature,* ed. Seth Lerer (San Marino, Calif.: Huntington Library, 1996), 106. The relevant bibliography is long; for a good review see Greetham, above. G. Thomas Tanselle has long since taught us of the insufficiencies of a notion like authorial intention for textual editing. See particularly "The Editorial Problem of Authorial Final Intention," *Studies in Bibliography* 29 (1976): 167–211.

57. Cecil Jane, ed., *Select Documents Illustrating the Life of Columbus,* 2 vols. (London: Hakluyt Society, 1930–33), 2:48.

58. Such opinions were shared by Bartolomé de Las Casas, Columbus's first editor, who shared with Columbus "a providential conception of history according to which the discovery of the New World was ordained at a propitious moment for the salvation of the natives' souls, and Columbus was divinely elected as the instrument of it." Fernandez-Armesto, *Columbus on Himself,* 12.

59. The Fall of Granada meant the end to tributes of gold on which the Aragonese monarch depended; the monarchs hoped, it seems, that Columbus's activity would result in new sources of income. Ibid., 32–33.

60. Ibid., 12.

61. Ibid., 12–14. Fernández-Armesto argues, in contrast to a longstanding view of the Admiral as religiously devout, that his religious interests "grew on him," coming to the fore during the period of the third voyage (14).

62. Margarita Zamora, *Reading Columbus* (Berkeley: University of California Press, 1993).

63. Ibid., 20.

64. Fernández-Armesto prints the text of the Santageal letter in *Columbus on Himself,* his edited collection of Columbus's words; he acknowledges the "significant scruples" that have raised "suspicion" among historians as to its authenticity. *Columbus on Himself,* 101–3. He writes, "It is proper to read the document with those considerations in mind. There is no reason, however, not to see it as wholly or substantially Columbus's work" (103). My point, following Zamora, is not that Columbus had nothing to do with the text, but that

the fame that redounded to the admiral as a result of this letter was the work of many different parties, in many different stages.

65. As Fernández-Armesto points out, "Columbus's portrait of the background to his voyage highlights his patrons' role as champions of Christendom: conquerors of the Moors, potential evangelisers of the Great Kahn, and expellers of the Jews. This was calculated to match the propaganda-image which Ferdinand and Isabella projected of themselves during the Granada war." *Columbus on Himself*, 33.

66. Fernández-Armesto reproduces some of these woodcuts without mentioning their source.

67. By 1498, some four years after the Basel publication of Columbus's letter in Latin, Dutch and Spanish editions of Breydenbach's work would also appear. The similarities were noted by Hugh Davies as early as 1911; they have not registered broadly in contemporary Columban scholarship. See Hugh Davies, *Bernhard von Breydenbach and His Journey to the Holy Land 1483–4: A Bibliography* (London: J.J. Leighton, 1911): "The most noteworthy instance of plagiarism from Revwich's cuts (hitherto unnoticed, so far as the present writer knows) is that in the famous letter of Christopher Columbus translated in 1493. The Basle [*sic*] edition of 1494 has four woodcuts, the first and last of which contain figures of ships, generally considered to be, as is natural, virtually authentic pictures of the Admiral's own vessels. It is obvious, however, on comparison with the figures in the Breydenbach views that the first Columbus cut is directly copied (and reduced) from the Pilgrims' vessel seen in the view of Rhodes and the fourth cut, from that in the Modon view. Both are reversed in copying as regards left and right, but the details are the same, even (in the case of the first cut) down to the Lion of Venice on the awning, and the two flags at stern, which are now turned towards the head of the vessel so as save space laterally. The Jerusalem cross at the head, the copyist had sense enough to omit: even the cattle in the pens are retained." Introduction, xxix.

68. Shannon Miller notes the continued afterlife of Columbus's caravel as reproduced in later versions of More's *Utopia*. Miller's larger argument involves the ways in which "the new world identity of the commonwealth of the Utopia is established through accounts of making and publishing books." "Idleness, Human Industry, and English Colonial Activity in Thomas More's 'fruitfull, pleasant,' 'wittie' and 'profitable' Utopia, in *Laureations: Essays in Memory of Richard Helgerson*, ed. Roze Henschell and Kathy Lavezzo (Lantham, Md.: Rowman and Littlefield, 2011), 19–50, 27. As she puts it, "The humanist circulation of texts that frames our entrance into the Utopia narrative is consequently linked to the activities of, and publications of, new world exploration" (26). But the woodcuts themselves engage traditions of old world pilgrimage as well; and the Columban usage, as we have seen, was itself copied from Breydenbach's earlier text.

69. See Elizabeth Eisenstein, *The Printing Press as an Agent of Change* (Cambridge: Cambridge University Press, 1980), 1:85.

70. William Kuskin, *Recursive Origins: Writing at the Transition to Modernity* (South Bend, Ind.: University of Notre Dame Press, 2013), 16. Kuskin undermines the association of originality with Modernity, demonstrating how, in the transitionary sixteenth century,

literary origins were "recursive." While a useful new account of literary history, his study also begs the question represented by its own intervention into literary history: the question of the new idea, story, or invention.

71. We should also recall, along with Rabasa, that Bartholomé de Las Casas, the primary intermediary through whom Columbus's *Diario* comes to us and a harsh critic of certain aspects of European conquest, will rigorously contest the rhetoric of conquest as an utterly "new" creation. Las Casas will demand that all such events be described as a "discovery" of lands already made, insistently noting that these lands are, like Europe, lands made by God.

72. I rely here on the notion of "reverse causality" as articulated by Gilles Deleuze and Felix Guattari, *A Thousand Plateaus: Capitalism and Schizophrenia*, trans. Brian Massumi (Minneapolis: University of Minnesota Press, 1987), 431–32.

73. Such complex temporalities of event and linguistic description will repeat in the narratives of discovery that follow upon Columbus. Amerigo Vespucci's 1497 encounter offers another story of how the "new world" came to be recognized, one that is well documented and likewise linked to the copying culture of early print. Described in the *Nova Reperto*, it circulated in visual form in Theodor Galle's engraving of *America* (taken from a drawing by Jan van der Straet and printed as plate 1 in the 1580 edition). On this engraving and its theoretical relation to medieval colonial encounter, see Michelle R. Warren, *History on the Edge: Excalibur and the Borders of Britain, 1100–1300* (Minneapolis: University of Minnesota Press, 2000), 248–51.

74. In *The Discoverie of Guiana*, Sir Walter Raleigh will explicitly link his experience in Guiana as verification of "such things as heretofore were held incredible (Mandeville . . . Herodotus, &c)." Thanks to Holly Crocker for drawing my attention to this passage.

75. *Alexandreis*, Prologue, 29.

76. The *Book of Mandeville* is precisely the kind of textual tradition that has helped us to revise our understanding of the circulation of influential texts preprint. For one thing, the text survives in a wide range of versions and languages, particularly Middle English, French, and Anglo-French. For an account of the *mouvance* of the textual tradition, see Iain M. Higgins, "Jerusalem in the *Book of John Mandeville*," 29–53; for a modern English translation of the Anglo-French version, see Iain M. Higgins, ed. and trans., *The Book of John Mandeville with Related Texts* (Indianapolis: Hackett, 2011). On the question of the Middle English tradition, see Ralph Hanna, "Mandeville," in *Middle English Prose: A Critical Guide*, ed. A. S. G. Edwards (New Brunswick, N.J.: Rutgers University Press, 1984), 121–32. For a recent review of the textual situation, see Anthony Bale, "Introduction," to *Sir John Mandeville: The Book of Travels and Marvels*, Oxford World's Classics (Oxford: Oxford University Press, 2012), ix–xxxii.

77. Certainly, as Tamarah Kohanski and C. David Benson put it, "the textual instability of *The Book of John Mandeville* should never be forgotten," "Introduction" to *The Book of John Mandeville*, ed., Kohanski and Benson, TEAMS Middle English Text Series (Kalamazoo, Mich.: Medieval Institute Publications, 2007), 5. I gesture here to Mandeville's "author function," for this provocative link of newness and story-telling. I cite the Penguin

edition of *The Travels of Sir John Mandeville*, ed. and trans. C. W. R. D. Moseley (London: Penguin, 1983), 188. Moseley's edition is based on British Library MS Egerton 1982. For alternative English versions of the cited paragraph, see Bale, trans., *Book of Travels and Marvels*, 124; Kohanski and Benson, *Book of John Mandeville*, 94–95. I wish to engage here the extravagance of Mandeville's vision as a circuit of desire for the new, an important aspect of this work that is sometimes overlooked.

78. There is a longstanding medieval tradition of the new as pedagogically instructive precisely because marvels are so memorable. As Bale puts it, "Introduction," to *Book of Marvels and Travels*, "it was a commonplace in medieval learning that what was strange, new, and shocking is what is most memorable, most instructive" (xxvii). This would be one reason why the medieval discourse of the new, as I have been arguing, persistently emphasized ethical features. It was not identical with the marvelous.

79. As, for instance, in More's Prologue, where the narrator, addressing Peter Giles on the question of Hythloday's response to More's text, says: "If he has decided to write out his own story for himself, he may be displeased with me; and I should be sorry, too, if in publicizing Utopia, I had robbed him and his story of the flower of novelty." This worry over authority as authorship is followed by an account of the varied tastes of the reading public (*Norton Anthology*, Vol. B, 8th ed., ed. Logan et al., 523. See Miller, "Idleness, Human Industry, and English Colonial Activity."

80. Peters, "Desire to Know," 605.

81. On the value of the commodity as heightened by its inaccessibility, see Mary Douglas and Baron Isherwood, *The World of Goods* (New York: Basic, 1981); on value as a production of, not a motive for, exchange, see, of course, George Simmel, *The Philosophy of Money* (London: Routledge, 1978). An introduction to interdisciplinary work on "commodities and the politics of value" is the useful introduction to the edited collection, *The Social Life of Things: Commodities in Cultural Perspective*, ed. Arjun Appadurai (Cambridge: Cambridge University Press, 1986), 3–63. The quote here makes more imaginative play with value and inaccessibility, though the manuscript history of "Mandeville" suggests something of the success of the strategy: the text was widely translated, redacted, and circulated.

82. Moseley, ed., *Mandeville's Travels*, 165, 173.

AFTERWORD

Epigraph: Jean Laplanche, *Nouveaux fondements pour la psychoanalyse* (Paris: Presses Universitaires de France, 1987), 6. This new translation by Robert M. Stein, is forthcoming in The Unconscious in Translation Series from International Psychoanalytical Books.

1. Lacan, "The Network of Signifier" "Tuché" (usually translated "fate") and "Automaton" and "The Split Between the Eye and the Gaze," in *The Four Fundamental Concepts of Psychoanalysis: The Seminar of Jacques Lacan, Book XI*, ed. Jacques-Alain Miller, ed. and

trans. Alan Sheridan (1978; New York: Norton, 1998). My thinking here is also indebted to Rosalind Krauss, *The Optical Unconscious* (Cambridge, Mass.: MIT Press, 1993), esp. 71–72.

2. Andrea Denny-Brown, *Fashioning Change: The Trope of Clothing in High- and Late-Medieval England* (Columbus: Ohio State University Press, 2012), see esp. 33–39, 171–73.

3. The term is Alexandre Leupin's, *Barbarolexis: Medieval Writing and Sexuality* (Cambridge, Mass.: Harvard University Press, 1989), 38.

Bibliography

PRIMARY TEXTS

Abelard, Peter. *Historia calamitatum: Texte critique avec une introduction*, ed. J. Monfrin. Paris: J. Vrin, 1978.

———. *Letters IX–XIV: An Edition with an Introduction*. Ed. Edmé Renno Smits. Groningen: Bouma Bookhuis, B.V., 1983.

Al-Jazari. *Book of Knowledge of Ingenious Mechanical Devices: Kitáb fí ma'rifat al-hiyal alhandasiyya.* Trans. Donald R. Hill. Boston: Reidel, 1974.

Aquinas, Thomas. *Summa Theologica*. Trans. Frs. of the Dominican Province. N.P.: Benziger, 1947.

Bacon, Roger. *Fr. Rogeri Bacon Opera quaedam hactenus inedita*. Ed. J. S. Brewer. London: Longman, Green, Longman & Roberts, 1859.

———. *The "Opus Majus" of Roger Bacon*. Ed. John Henry Bridges. 2 vols. London: Williams and Norgate, 1897–1900; rept. Frankfurt: Minerva, G.m.b.H., 1964.

———. *The "Opus Majus" of Roger Bacon, supplementary volume*. Ed. Roger Bridges. Frankfurt: Minerva, G.m.b.H., 1964.

———. *The Opus Majus of Roger Bacon*. Trans. Robert Belle Burke. Philadelphia: University of Pennsylvania Press, 1928.

———. "The Magical Letter of Roger Bacon: Concerning the Marvelous Power of Art and of Nature and Concerning the Nullity of Magic." Sequim, WA: Holmes Publishing Group, 1988. Rpt. 2001.

Bromyard, John. *Summa Praedicantium*, part 1. http://archive.org/details/JohnBromyard SummaPraedicantiumParsPrima1586.

Chaucer, Geoffrey. *The Riverside Chaucer*. 3rd ed. Gen. ed. Larry D. Benson. Boston: Houghton Mifflin, 1987.

———. *The Text of the Canterbury Tales*. Ed. John Matthews Manly and E. Rickert, vol. 3: 3–37. Chicago: University of Chicago Press, 1940. 3: 3–37.

Columbus, Christopher. *The Libro de las profecias of Christopher Columbus, an en face Edition*. Ed. Delano C. West and August Kling. Gainesville: University Press of Florida, 1991.

De Lille, Alain. *The Complaint of Nature*. Trans. Douglas M. Moffat. Yale Studies in English. New Haven, Conn.: Yale University Press, 1908; rpt. 1972.

Descartes, René. *The Passions of the Soul*. Trans. Stephan H. Voss. Indianapolis: Hackett, 1989.

De Troyes, Chretien. *Le Chevalier au Lion ou Le Roman d'Yvain*. Ed. and trans. David F. Hult. Paris: Lettres Gothiques, 1994.

De Vries, F. C. *Floris and Blauncheflur: A Middle English Romance edited with Introduction, Notes, and Glossary*. Gronigen: Druk. V.R.B., 1966.

Du Cange or the *Medieval Lexica*. In *The Database of Latin Dictionaries*.

Duncan, Thomas G., ed. *Medieval English Lyrics*, 1200–1400. London: Penguin, 1995.

Geoffrey of Vinsauf. *The Poetria Nova*. In Ernest Gallo, *The Poetria Nova and Its Sources in Early Rhetorical Doctrine*. The Hague: Mouton, 1981.

Gower, John. *Confessio Amantis*, 7 vols. Ed. Russell A. Peck, Latin trans. Andrew Galloway. TEAMS Middle English Text Series. Kalamazoo, Mich.: Medieval Institute Publications, 2004.

Higden, Ranulph. *Polychronicon*. Ed. Churchill Babington. Vol. 2. RS. London: Longmans, Green, 1869.

Hugh of Saint Victor. *Didascalicon*. Ed. Charles Henry Buttimer. Washington, D.C.: Catholic University of America Press, 1939.

Isidore of Seville. *The Etymologies of Isidore of Seville*. Ed. Stephen A. Barney et al., trans. with Muriel Hall. Cambridge: Cambridge University Press, 2006.

Jane, Cecil, ed. *Select Documents Illustrating the Life of Columbus*. 2 vols. London: Hakluyt Society, 1930–33.

Kant, Immanuel. *The Cambridge Edition of the Writings of Immanuel Kant, Critique of the Power of Judgment*. Ed. Paul Guyer and Eric Matthews. Cambridge: Cambridge University Press, 2000.

Kibler, William, ed. and trans. *Chrétien de Troyes, Arthurian Romances*. London: Penguin, 1991.

Machaut, Guillaume. *Le jugement du roy de behaigne and Remède de fortune*. Ed. James I. Wimsatt and William W. Kibler. Chaucer Library. Athens: University of Georgia Press, 1988.

Oeuvres de Guillaume de Machaut. Ed. Ernest Hoepffner. 2 vols. Société des Anciens Textes Français. Paris: Firmin-Didot, 1911.

———. *The Tale of the Alerion*. Ed. and trans. Minnette Gaudet and C. B. Hieatt. Toronto: University of Toronto Press, 1994.

Pelan, Margaret M., ed. *Floire et Blancheflor*, 1937. 2nd ed. Paris: Belles Lettres, 1956.

Peter of Limoges. *The Moral Treatise on the Eye*. Ed. and trans. Richard Newhauser. Medieval Sources in Translation. Toronto: Pontifical Institute of Medieval Studies, 2012.

Taylor, A. B., ed. *Floris and Blauncheflour: A Middle English Romance, edited from the Trentham and Auchinleck MSS*. Oxford: Clarendon, 1927.

"Thomas of Celano's Life of Saint Francis." In *Francis of Assisi: Early Documents*. Hyde Park, N.Y.: New City Press, 1999.

The Travels of Sir John Mandeville, Ed. and trans. C. W. R. D. Moseley. London: Penguin, 1983.

Walter of Châtillon. *The Alexandreis: A Twelfth-Century Epic*. Verse trans. David Townsend. Peterborough, Ont.: Broadview Press, 2007.

SECONDARY TEXTS

Abu-Lughod, Janet. *Before European Hegemony: The World System A.D. 1250–1350*. New York: Oxford University Press, 1989.

Abulafia, Anna Safir. "Walter of Châtillon: A twelfth-century poet's engagement with Jews." *Journal of Medieval History* 31, 3 (2005): 265–86.

Adams, Henry. *Mont-Saint-Michel and Chartres*. 1905. New York: Houghton Mifflin, 1935.

Aertsen, Jan A., Kent Emery, Jr., and Andreas Speer, eds. *Nach der Verurteilung von 1277: Philosophie und Theologie an der Universität von Paris im letzten Viertel des 13. Jahrhunderts: Studien und Texte/After the Condemnations of 1277: Philosophy and Theology at the University of Paris in the Last Quarter of the Thirteenth Century*. Studies and Texts, Miscellanea Mediaevalia 28. Berlin: De Gruyter, 2001.

Akrich, Madeleine, Michel Callon, and Bruno Latour. "The Key to Success in Innovation, Part II: The Art of Choosing Good Spokespersons." Trans. Adrian Monaghan. *International Journal of Innovation Management* 6, 2 (June 2002): 207–25.

Altorki, Soraya. "Milk-Kinship in Arab Society: An Unexplored Problem in the Ethnography of Marriage." *Ethnography* 19, 2 (1980): 233–44.

Ambrisco, Alan S. "'It lyth nat in my tonge': Occupatio and Otherness in the *Squire's Tale*." *Chaucer Review* 38 (2004): 205–28.

Appadurai, Arjun, ed. *The Social Life of Things: Commodities in Cultural Perspective*. Cambridge: Cambridge University Press, 1988.

Arendt, Hannah. *The Life of the Mind*. New York: Harcourt, 1971, rpt. 1978.

Ariès, Philippe. *Centuries of Childhood: A Social History of Family Life*. Trans. Robert Baldick. New York: Knopf, 1962.

Ashworth, E. J. "Analogy and Equivocation in Thirteenth-Century Logic: Aquinas in Context." *Mediaeval Studies* 54 (1992): 94–135.

———."Analogy, Univocation, and Equivocation in Some Early Fourteenth-Century Authors." In *Aristotle in Britain During the Middle Ages*, ed. John Marenbon. Turnhout: Brepols, 1996. 233–47.

———. "Signification and Modes of Signifying in Thirteenth-Century Logic: A Preface to Aquinas on Analogy." *Medieval Philosophy and Theology* 1 (1991): 39–67.

Badiou, Alain. *Saint Paul: The Foundation of Universalism*. Trans. Ray Brassier. Stanford, Calif.: Stanford University Press, 2003.

Bale, Anthony. "Introduction" to *Sir John Mandeville: The Book of Travels and Marvels*. Oxford World's Classics. Oxford: Oxford University Press, 2012. ix–xxxii.

Barnes, Geraldine. "Cunning and Ingenuity in the Middle English *Floris and Blaunche-flour*." *Medium Aevum* 53 (1984): 10–25.

Barthes, Roland. *The Pleasure of the Text*. Trans. Richard Miller. New York: Hill and Wang, 1975.

Bennett, Jane. *The Enchantment of Modern Life: Attachments, Crossings, and Ethics*. Princeton, N.J.: Princeton University Press, 2001.

Berkey, Jonathan P. "Tradition, Innovation and the Social Construction of Knowledge in the Medieval Islamic Near East." *Past and Present* 148 (1995): 38–65.

Berry, Craig. "Flying Sources: Classical Authority in Chaucer's Squire's Tale." *ELH* 68, 2 (2001): 287–313.

Bianchi, Luca. "*Prophanae novitates et doctrinae peregrinae*: La méfiance à l'égard des innovations théoriques aux XIIIe et XIVe siècles." In *Tradition, Innovation, Invention*, ed. Hans-Joachim Schmidt. Berlin: De Gruyter, 2005. 211–29.

Biddick, Kathleen. *The Shock of Medievalism*. Durham, N.C.: Duke University Press, 1998.

———. *The Typological Imaginary: Circumcision, Technology, and History*. Philadelphia: University of Pennsylvania Press, 2003.

Bjornstad, Hall, ed. *Borrowed Feathers: Plagiarism and the Limits of Imitation in Early Modern Europe*. Paris: Unipub, 2009.

Blanton, C. D. "Medieval Currencies: Nominalism and Art." In *The Legitimacy of the Middle Ages: On the Unwritten History of Theory*, ed. Andrew Cole and D. Vance Smith. Durham, N.C.: Duke University Press, 2010. 194–232.

Bloch, R. Howard, and Stephen G. Nichols, eds. *Medievalism and the Modernist Temper*. Baltimore: Johns Hopkins University Press, 1996.

Bloomfield, Morton. "Chaucer's Squire's Tale and the Renaissance." *Poetica* 12 (1979): 28–35.

Blumenberg, Hans. *The Legitimacy of the Modern Age*. Trans. Robert M. Wallace. Cambridge, Mass.: MIT Press, 1983.

Boogaart, Jacques. "Thought-Provoking Dissonances: Remarks About Machaut's Compositional Licences in Relation to His Texts," *Dutch Journal of Music Theory*, 12, 3 (2007): 273–92.

Boulnois, Olivier. *Au delà de l'image: une archéologie du visuel au moyen âge, Ve–XVIe siècle*. Paris: Éditions du Seuil, 2008.

Brown, Bill. "Thing Theory." *Critical Inquiry* 28, 1 (2001): 1–22.

Brownlee, Kevin. *Poetic Identity in Guillaume de Machaut*. Madison: University of Wisconsin Press, 1984.

Bruneau, Julianne. "Truth, Sex, and Divine Poetics in Alan of Lille's *De Planctu Naturae*." In *Women and the Divine in Literature Before 1700: Essays in Memory of Margot Louis*, ed. Kathryn Kirby-Fulton. Victoria: ELS Editions, 2009. 65–86.

Burckhardt, Jacob. *The Civilization of the Renaissance in Italy*. Ed. Peter Murray, trans. S. C. G. Middlemore. Penguin Classics. London: Penguin, 1990.

Butterfield, Ardis. *Poetry and Music in Medieval France*. Cambridge: Cambridge University Press, 2002.

Butterfield, Herbert. *The Whig Interpretation of History*. New York: Norton, 1931.

Bynum, Caroline Walker, "Wonder." *American Historical Review* 102, 1 (Feb. 1997): 1–17.

Calhoun, Craig. "The Radicalism of Tradition: Community Strength or Venerable Disguise and Borrowed Language?" *American Journal of Sociology* 88, 5 (1989): 886–914.

Calinescu, Matei. "Postmodernism and Some Paradoxes of Periodization." In *Approaching Postmodernism*, ed. Douwe Fokkema and Hans Bertens. Utrecht: John Benjamins,1986. 239–54.

Camille, Michael. *The Gothic Idol: Ideology and Image-Making in Medieval Art.* Cambridge: Cambridge University Press, 1989.

Campbell, Mary Baine. *The Witness and the Other World.* Ithaca, N.Y.: Cornell University Press, 1988.

———. *Wonder and Science: Imagining Worlds in Early Modern Europe.* Ithaca, N.Y.: Cornell University Press, 1999.

Cannon, Christopher. *The Making of Chaucer's English: A Study of Words.* Cambridge: Cambridge University Press, 1998.

Carey, Hilary M. "Astrology and Anti-Christ in the Later Middle Ages." In *Time and Eternity: The Medieval Discourse*, ed. Gerhard Jaritz and Moreno-Riaño Gerson. Turnhout: Brepols, 2003. 515–35.

Carlson, Thomas. "Modernity and the Mystical: Science, Technology, and the Task of Human Self-Creation." In *Science, Religion, and the Human Experience*, ed. James Proctor. Oxford: Oxford University Press, 2005.

Casagrande, Carla and Silvana Vecchio, eds. *Piacere e dolore: Materiali per una storia delle passion nel Medioevo*, ed., Micrologus' Library 29. Firenze: Sismel Edizioni del Galluzzo, 2009.

Cerquiglini-Toulet, Jacqueline. *A New History of Medieval French Literature.* Trans. Sara Preisig. Baltimore: Johns Hopkins University Press, 2011.

Chakrabarty, Dipesh. *Provincializing Europe: Postcolonial Thought and Historical Difference.* Princeton, N.J.: Princeton University Press, 2009.

Charnes, Linda. *Hamlet's Heirs: Shakespeare and the Politics of a New Millennium.* Accents on Shakespeare. New York: Routledge, 2006.

Clegg, Brian. *The First Scientist: A Life of Roger Bacon.* London: Constable, 2003.

Cohen, Jeffrey Jerome. *Medieval Identity Machines.* Minneapolis: University of Minnesota Press, 2003.

Colacurcio, Michael. "The Dynamo and the Angelic Doctor: The Bias of Henry Adams' Medievalism." *American Quarterly* 17, 4 (Winter 1965): 696–712.

Cole, Andrew. *Literature and Heresy in the Age of Chaucer.* Cambridge: Cambridge University Press, 2008.

Cole, Andrew, and D. Vance Smith, "Introduction: Outside Modernity." In *The Legitimacy of the Middle Ages: On the Unwritten History of Theory*, ed. Cole and Smith. Durham, N.C.: Duke University Press, 2010. 1–36.

———, eds. *The Legitimacy of the Middle Ages: On the Unwritten History of Theory.* Durham, N.C.: Duke University Press, 2010.

Colish, Marcia L. *The Stoic Tradition from Antiquity to the Early Middle Ages: Stoicism in Classical Latin Literature.* Leiden: Brill, 1985.

Collette, Carolyn. "Reading Chaucer Through Philippe de Mèzières: Alchemy, the Individual, and the Good Society." In *Courtly Literature and Clerical Culture*, ed. Christopher Huber and Henrike Lahnemann. Tubingen: Attempto Verlag, 2002. 177–94.

Cooper, Lisa. *Artisans and Narrative Craft in Late Medieval England*, Cambridge: Cambridge University Press, 2011.

Copeland, Rita. *Pedagogy, Intellectuals and Dissent in the Later Middle Ages*. Cambridge: Cambridge University Press, 2001.

———. *Rhetoric, Hermeneutics, and Translations in the Middle Ages: Academic Translations and Vernacular Texts*. Cambridge: Cambridge University Press, 1991.

Courtney, William. "The Virgin and the Dynamo: The Growth of Medieval Studies in North America (1870–1930)." In *Medieval Studies in North America: Past, Present, and Future*, ed. Francis G. Gentry and Christopher Kleinhenz. Kalamazoo, Mich.: Medieval Institute Publications, 1982. 5–22.

Crane, Susan. *Animal Encounters: Contacts and Concepts in Medieval Britain*. Philadelphia: University of Pennsylvania Press, 2012.

Crick, Julia. *The Historia regum Britanniae of Geoffrey of Monmouth: Dissemination and Reception in the Later Middle Ages*. Cambridge: Brewer, 1991.

Daston, Lorraine, and Katherine Park. *Wonders and the Order of Nature, 1150–1750*. New York: Zone Books, 1998.

David, Alfred. "Recycling *Anelida and Arcite*: Chaucer as a Source for Chaucer." *Studies in the Age of Chaucer* 1 (1984): 105–15.

Davies, Hugh. *Bernhard von Breydenbach and His Journey to the Holy Land 1483–4: A Bibliography*. London: Leighton, 1911.

Davis, Kathleen. *Periodization and Sovereignty: How Ideas of Feudalism and Secularization Govern the Politics of Time*. Philadelphia: University of Pennsylvania Press, 2008.

Davoine, Françoise, and Jean-Max Gaudilliere. *History Beyond Trauma*. Trans. Susan Fairfield. New York: Other Press, 2004.

De Certeau, Michel. *The Writing of History*. Trans. Tom Conley. New York: Columbia University Press, 1988.

De Grijs, F. J. A. "The Theological Character of Aquinas' *De Aeternitate Mundi*." In *The Eternity of the World in the Thought of Thomas Aquinas and His Contemporaries*, ed. J. B. M. Wissink. Leiden: Brill, 1990. 1–8.

Delany, Sheila. *The Naked Text: Chaucer's Legend of Good Women*. Berkeley: University of California Press, 1994.

———. "Run Silent, Run Deep: Heresy and Alchemy as Medieval Versions of Utopia." In *Medieval Literary Politics: Shapes of Ideology*. Manchester: Manchester University Press, 1990.

Deleuze, Gilles. *Difference and Repetition*. Trans. Paul Patton. New York: Columbia University Press, 1984.

Deleuze, Gilles, and Felix Guattari, *A Thousand Plateaus: Capitalism and Schizophrenia*. Trans. Brian Massumi. Minneapolis: University of Minnesota Press, 1987.

De Libera, Alain. *Penser au Moyen Âge*. Paris: Éditions du Seuil, 1991.

Denny-Brown, Andrea. *Fashioning Change: The Trope of Clothing in High- and Late-Medieval England*. Columbus: Ohio State University Press, 2012.

Deschaux, Robert. "Le bestiaire de Guillaume de Machaut d'après les dits." *Cahiers de l'Association Internationale des Études Françaises* 31 (1979): 7–16.

Desmond, Marilynn. *Ovid's Art and The Wife of Bath: The Ethics of Erotic Violence*. Ithaca, N.Y.: Cornell University Press, 2006.

De Vries, F. C. Introduction to *Floris and Blauncheflur: A Middle English Romance edited with Introduction, Notes, and Glossary*. Gronigen: Druk. V.R.B., 1966.

Dillon, Emma. *The Sense of Sound: Musical Meaning in France, 1260–1330*. Oxford: Oxford University Press, 2012.

Dinshaw, Carolyn. *How Soon Is Now? Medieval Texts, Amateur Readers, and the Queerness of Time*. Durham, N.C.: Duke University Press, 2012.

Douglas, Mary, and Baron Isherwood. *The World of Goods*. New York: Basic, 1981.

Drucker, Peter A. *Managing in a Time of Great Change*. New York: Truman Talley/Dutton, 1995.

Eamon, William. "Technology as Magic in the Late Middle Ages and Renaissance." *Janus* 70 (1983): 171–212.

Eco, Umberto. *Art and Beauty in the Middle Ages*. Trans. Hugh Bredin. New Haven, Conn.: Yale University Press, 1986.

———. "Denotation." In *On the Medieval Theory of Signs*, ed. Umberto Eco and Constantine Marmo. Amsterdam: John Benjamins, 1989.

Edgerton, David. "Innovation, Technology, or History: What Is the Historiography of Technology About?" *Technology and Culture* 51, 3 (July 2010): 680–97.

———. *The Shock of the Old: Technology and Global Culture Since 1900*. New York: Oxford University Press, 2007.

Edmondson, George. *The Neighboring Text: Chaucer, Boccaccio, Henryson*. South Bend, Ind.: University of Notre Dame Press, 2011.

Eisenstein, Elizabeth L. *Divine Art, Infernal Machine: The Reception of Printing in the West from First Impressions to the Sense of an Ending*. Philadelphia: University of Pennsylvania Press, 2011.

———. *The Printing Press as an Agent of Change*. Vol 1. Cambridge: Cambridge University Press, 1980.

Elliott, J. H. *The Old World and the New, 1492–1650*. Cambridge: Cambridge University Press, 1970.

Feldman, Seymour. *Philosophy in a Time of Crisis*. New York: Routledge, 2003.

Fernandez-Armesto, Felipe. *Columbus on Himself*. Indianapolis: Hackett, 2010.

Fellows, Jennifer. Introduction to *Of Love and Chivalry: An Anthology of Middle English Romance*. London: Dent, 1993.

Fisher, Phillip. *Wonder, the Rainbow, and the Aesthetic of Rare Experiences*. Cambridge, Mass.: Harvard University Press, 2003.

Fleissner, Jennifer. "The Ordering Power of Disorder: Henry Adams and the Return of the Darwinian Era." *American Literature* 84 (2012): 31–60.

Forsyth, Hazel with Geoff Egan. *Toys, Trifles, and Trinkets: Base Metal Miniatures from London 1200 to 1800.* London: Museum of London, Unicorn Press, 2006.

Fradenburg, L. O. Aranye. "Amorous Scholasticism." In *Speaking Images: Essays in Honor of V. A. Kolve*, ed. Charlotte Morse and Robert F. Yeager. Chapel Hill, N.C.: Pegasus Press, 2001.

———. "Needful Things." In *Medieval Crime and Social Control*, ed. Barbara Hanawalt and David Wallace. Minneapolis: University of Minnesota Press, 1999. 49–69.

———. *Sacrifice Your Love: Psychoanalysis, Historicism, Chaucer.* Minneapolis: University of Minnesota Press, 2002.

———. "Simply Marvelous." *Studies in the Age of Chaucer* 26 (2004): 1–26.

Freiden, Ken. *Genius and Monologue.* Ithaca, N.Y.: Cornell University Press, 1985.

Frelick, Nancy. "Lacan, Courtly Love and Anamorphosis." In *The Court Reconvenes: International Courtly Literature Society, 1998*, ed. Barbara K. Altman and Carleton W. Carroll. Cambridge: Brewer, 2003. 107–14.

Freud, Sigmund. "Creative Writers and Day-Dreaming." *SE* IX: 148.

———. "Notes upon a Case of Obsessional Neurosis." *SE* X: 151–318.

Frye, Northrup. "Varieties of Literary Utopia." In *Utopias and Utopian Thought*, ed. Frank Manuel. Boston: Houghton Mifflin, 1966.

Fyler, John. "Domesticating the Exotic in the *Squire's Tale*." *ELH* 55 (1988): 1–26.

Gaffney, Phyllis. *Constructions of Childhood and Youth in Old French Narrative.* Burlington, Vt.: Ashgate, 2011.

Galloway, Andrew. "The Making of a Social Ethic in Late-Medieval England: From Gratitudo to "Kyndnesse." *Journal of the History of Ideas* 55, 3 (July 1994) 365–83.

Ganim, John. *Medievalism and Orientalism.* New York: Palgrave, 2004.

Gaudet, Minnette. "Machaut's *Dit de L'alerion* and the Sexual Politics of Courtly Love." *Romance Languages Annual* (1993): 55–63.

Gerth H. H., and C. Wright Mills, eds. "Bureaucracy and Charisma: A Philosophy of History." In *Charisma, History, and Social Structure*, ed. Ronald Glassman and William H. Swatos. New York: Greenwood, 1986. 11–15.

Gies, Frances, and Joseph Gies. *Cathedral, Forge, and Waterwheel: Technology and Invention in the Middle Ages.* New York: HarperCollins, 1994.

Gilson, Étienne. *Heloise and Abelard.* Trans. L. K. Shook. Chicago: Henry Regnery, 1953.

Gimpel, Jean. *The Medieval Machine: The Industrial Revolution of the Middle Ages.* London: Penguin, 1977.

Goldberg, Jonathan. "The History That Will Be." In *Premodern Sexualities*, ed. Louise O. Fradenburg and Carla Freccero. New York: Routledge, 1995. 3–21.

Goldstone, Lawrence, and Nancy Goldstone. *The Friar and the Cipher: Roger Bacon and the Unsolved Mystery of the Most Unusual Manuscript in the World.* New York: Doubleday, 2005.

Gombrich, E. H. "The Renaissance Conception of Artistic Progress and Its Consequences." In *Gombrich on the Renaissance.* New York: Phaidon, 1985. 1–10.

Goux, Jean-Joseph. *Symbolic Economies: After Marx and Freud.* Trans. Jennifer Curtiss Guge. Ithaca, N.Y.: Cornell University Press, 1990.

Grafton, Anthony. *Worlds Made of Words: Scholarship and Community in the Modern West.* Cambridge, Mass.: Harvard University Press, 2009.

Grafton, Anthony, with April Shelford and Nancy Siraisi. *New Worlds, Ancient Texts: The Power of Tradition and the Shock of Discovery.* Cambridge, Mass.: Harvard University Press, 1992.

Green, Richard Firth. "Changing Chaucer." *Studies in the Age of Chaucer* 25 (2003): 27–52.

Greenblatt, Stephen. *The Swerve: How the World Became Modern.* New York: Norton, 2011.

Greetham, David. "Phylum-Tree-Rhizome." In *Reading from the Margins: Textual Studies, Chaucer, and Medieval Literature*, ed. Seth Lerer. San Marino, Calif.: Huntington Library, 1996.

Grieve, Patricia. *Floire and Blancheflor and the European Romance.* Cambridge: Cambridge University Press, 1997.

Griffiths, Paul J. *Intellectual Appetite: A Theological Grammar.* Washington, D.C.: Catholic University of America Press, 2009.

Grund, Peter. "Albertus Magnus and the Queen of the Elves: A 15th Century English Verse Dialogue on Alchemy." *Anglia: Zeitschrift für englische Philologie* 122 (2004): 640–62.

Gumbrecht, H. U. *The Production of Presence: What Meaning Cannot Convey.* Stanford, Calif.: Stanford University Press, 2006.

Guynn, Noah D. "Eternal Flame: State Formation, Deviant Architecture and the Monumentality of Same-Sex Eroticism in the Roman d'Eneas." *GLQ: A Journal of Lesbian and Gay Studies* 6, 2 (2000): 287–319.

Hackett, Jeremiah, ed. "Roger Bacon and the Classification of the Sciences." In Hackett, ed., *Roger Bacon and the Sciences.* 49–66.

———, ed. *Roger Bacon and the Sciences: Commemorative Essays.* Leiden: Brill, 1997.

———. "Roger Bacon: His Life, Career, and Works." In Hackett, ed., *Roger Bacon and the Sciences.* 9–23.

———. "Roger Bacon on *Sciencia Experimentalis*." In Hackett, ed., *Roger Bacon and the Sciences.* 277–315.

Hallam, Elizabeth, ed. *Chronicles of the Age of Chivalry.* London: Penguin, 1987.

Hanna, Ralph. "Mandeville." In *Middle English Prose: A Critical Guide*, ed. A. S. G. Edwards. New Brunswick, N.J.: Rutgers University Press, 1984. 121–32.

Hanning, Robert. *The Individual in the Twelfth Century.* New Haven, Conn.: Yale University Press, 1977.

Harwood, Britton J. "Chaucer and the Silences of History: Situating the Canon's Yeoman's Tale." *PMLA* 102 (1987): 338–42.

Hatton, Thomas J. "Nature as Poet: Alanus de Insulis' *The Complaint of Nature* and the Medieval Concept of Artistic Creation." *Language and Style: An International Journal* 2 (1969): 85–91.

Hayles, N. Katherine. "The Achievement of the *Laws of Cool*." *Criticism* 47, 2 (2005): 235–39.

Heng, Geraldine. *Empire of Magic: Medieval Romance and the Politics of Cultural Fantasy.* New York: Columbia University Press, 2003.

Héritier-Augé, Françoise. "Identité de substance et parenté de lait dans le monde arabe." In *Épouser au plus proche: Inceste, prohibitions et stratégies matrimoniales autour de la Mediterranée*, ed. Pierre Bonte. Paris: École des Hautes Études en Sciences Sociales, 1994. 149–64.

Higgins, Iain M. "Defining the Earth's Center in a Medieval 'Multi-Text' Jerusalem in the *Book of John Mandeville*." In *Text and Territory: Geographical Imagination in the European Middle Ages*, ed. Sylvia Tomasch and Sealy Gilles. Philadelphia: University of Pennsylvania Press, 1998. 29–53.

———, ed. and trans. *The Book of John Mandeville with Related Texts*. Indianapolis: Hackett, 2011.

Hill, Donald R. *A History of Engineering in Classical and Medieval Times*. New York: Routledge, 1996.

Hodges, Laura. "Sartorial Signs in Troilus and Criseyde." *Chaucer Review* 35, 3 (2001): 223–59.

Holsinger, Bruce. *The Premodern Condition: Medievalism and the Making of Theory*. Chicago: University of Chicago Press, 2005.

Hornstein, Lillian. "Romances." in *Manual of Writings in Middle English, 1050–1500*, vol. 1. Hamden: Connecticut Academy of Arts and Sciences, 1967.

Huff, Toby E., and Wolfgang Schlueter, eds. *Max Weber and Islam*. New Brunswick, N.J.: Transaction, 1999.

Huot, Sylvia. *From Song to Book: The Poetics of Writing in Old French Lyric and Lyrical Narrative Poetry*. Ithaca, N.Y.: Cornell University Press, 1987.

———. *The Romance of the Rose and Its Medieval Readers: Interpretation, Reception, Manuscript Transmission*. Cambridge: Cambridge University Press, 1993.

Ingham, Mary Beth, and Mechthild Dreyer. *The Philosophical Vision of John Duns Scotus*. Washington, D.C.: Catholic University of America Press, 2004.

Ingham, Patricia Clare. "Discipline and Romance." In *Critical Contexts in Medieval Literature*, ed. Holly Crocker and D. Vance Smith. New York: Routledge, 2013. 276–82.

———. "'In Contrayez Straunge': Colonial Relations, British Identity and *Sir Gawain and the Green Knight*." *New Medieval Literatures* 4 (2001): 61–93.

———. "Little Nothings: The Squire's Tale and the Ambition of Gadgets." *Studies in the Age of Chaucer* 31 (2009): 53–80.

———. "Losing French: Translation, Nation, and Caxton's English Statutes." In *Caxton's Trace: Studies in the History of English Printing*, ed. William Kuskin. South Bend, Ind.: University of Notre Dame Press, 2006. 275–98.

———. *Sovereign Fantasies: Arthurian Romance and the Making of Britain*. Philadelphia: University of Pennsylvania Press, 2001.

Ingram, David. "Blumenberg and the Philosophical Grounds of Historiography." *History and Theory* 29.1 (1990): 1–15.

Jameson, Fredric. *The Political Unconscious: Narrative as a Socially Symbolic Act*. Ithaca, N.Y.: Cornell University Press, 1981.

Jardine, Nick. "Whigs and Stories: Herbert Butterfield and the Historiography of Science." *History of Science* 41 (2003): 125–40.

Jay, Martin. Review of *The Legitimacy of the Modern Age* by Hans Blumenberg, trans. Robert M. Wallace. *History and Theory* 24, 2 (1985): 183–96.

Justice, Stephen. "Did the Middle Ages Believe in Their Miracles?' *Representations* 103, 1 (Summer 2008): 1–29.

Kadir, Djelal. *Columbus and the Ends of the Earth*. Berkeley: University of California Press, 1992.

Kaelber, Lutz. "Max Weber's Dissertation in the Context of His Early Career and Life." "Introduction" to Max Weber, *The History of Commercial Partnerships in the Middle Ages*, trans. Lutz Kaelber. Lanham, Md.: Rowman and Littlefield, 2003.

Kay, Sarah. *The Chanson de Geste in the Age of Romance: Political Fictions*. London: Clarendon, 1995.

———. *Courtly Contradictions: The Emergence of the Literary Object in the Twelfth Century*. Stanford, Calif.: Stanford University Press, 2001.

———. *The Place of Thought: The Complexity of One in Late Medieval French Didactic Poetry*. Philadelphia: University of Pennsylvania Press, 2007.

Kaye, Joel. *Economy and Nature in the Fourteenth Century: Money, Market Exchange, and the Emergence of Scientific Thought*. Cambridge: Cambridge University Press, 1998.

Kelly, Kathleen Coyne. "The Bartering of Blauncheflur in the Middle English *Floris and Blauncheflur*." *Studies in Philology* 91, 2 (1994): 101–10.

Khanmohamadi, Shirin. *In Light of Another's Word: European Ethnography in the Middle Ages*. Philadelphia: University of Pennsylvania Press, 2013.

Kieckhefer, Richard. *Forbidden Rites: A Necromancer's Manual of the Fifteenth Century*. State College: Pennsylvania State University Press, 1998

———. *Magic in the Middle Ages*. Cambridge: Cambridge University Press, 2000.

Kinoshita, Sharon. *Medieval Boundaries: Rethinking Difference in Old French Literature*. Philadelphia: University of Pennsylvania Press, 2006.

Klarer, Mario. "Cannibalism and Carnivalesque: Incorporation as Utopia in the Early Image of America." *New Literary History* 30 (1999): 389–410.

———. "Woman and Arcadia: The Impact of Ancient Utopian Thought on the Early Image of America." *Journal of American Studies* 27 (1993): 1–17.

Knapp, Peggy. "The Work of Alchemy." *Journal of Medieval and Early Modern Studies* 30 (2000): 575–99.

Kohanski, Tamarah, and D. David Benson, "Introduction" to *The Book of John Mandeville*, ed. Kohanski and Benson. TEAMS Middle English Text Series. Kalamazoo, Mich.: Medieval Institute Publications, 2007.

Krauss, Rosalind. *The Optical Unconscious*. Cambridge, Mass.: MIT Press, 1993.

Kuhn, Thomas. *The Structure of Scientific Revolutions*. Chicago: University of Chicago Press, 1962.

Kuskin, William, ed., *Caxton's Trace: Studies in the History of English Printing*. Notre Dame, Ind.: University of Notre Dame Press, 2006.

———. *Recursive Origins: Writing at the Transition to Modernity*. Notre Dame, Ind.: University of Notre Dame Press, 2013.

Labbie, Erin. *Lacan's Medievalism*. Minneapolis: University of Minnesota Press, 2006.

Lacan, Jacques. *The Ethics of Psychoanalysis, 1959–1960: The Seminar of Jacques Lacan, Book VII*. Ed. Jacques-Alain Miller, trans. Dennis Porter. New York: Norton, 1992.

———. *The Four Fundamental Concepts of Psychoanalysis: The Seminar of Jacques Lacan, Book XI*. Ed. Jacques-Alain Miller, trans. Alan Sheridan. New York: Norton, 1998.

Ladis, Andrew and Carolyn Wood, eds. *The Craft of Art: Originality and Industry in the Italian Renaissance and Baroque Workshop*. Athens: University of Georgia Press, 1995.

Latour, Bruno. *Aramis, or The Love of Technology*. Cambridge, Mass.: Harvard University Press, 1996.

———. "Irreductions." Addendum to English edition of *The Pasteurization of France*, trans. John Law. Cambridge, Mass.: Harvard University Press, 1998. 153–236.

———. *We Have Never Been Modern*. Trans. Catherine Porter. Cambridge, Mass.: Harvard University Press, 1993.

Lawton, David. "History and Legend: the Exile and the Turk." In *Postcolonial Moves, Medieval Through Modern*, ed. Patricia Clare Ingham and Michelle Warren. New York: Palgrave, 2003. 173–94.

Lazier, Benjamin. *God Interrupted: Heresy and the European Imagination Between the World Wars*. Princeton, N.J.: Princeton University Press, 2008.

Leach, Elizabeth Eva. *Sung Birds: Music, Nature, and Poetry in the Later Middle Ages*. Ithaca, N.Y.: Cornell University Press, 2007.

Leff, Gordon. *Paris and Oxford Universities in the Thirteenth and Fourteenth Centuries: An Institutional and Intellectual History*. New York: Wiley, 1968.

Le Goff, Jacques. *History and Memory*. Trans. Steven Rendall and Elizabeth Claman. New York: Columbia University Press, 1992.

Le Goff, Jacques, and Jean-Claude Schmitt. "Au XIIIe siècle: une nouvelle parole." In *Histoire vécue du peuple chrétien*, ed. Jean Delumeau. Toulouse: Privat, 1979. 257–79.

Leicester, Marshall. *The Disenchanted Self: Representing the Subject in the Canterbury Tales*. Berkeley: University of California Press, 1990.

Lemay, Richard. "Roger Bacon's Attitudes Toward the Latin Translations and Translators of the Twelfth and Thirteenth Centuries." In *Roger Bacon and the Sciences: Commemorative Essays*, ed. Jeremiah Hackett. Leiden: Brill, 1997. 25–48.

Lerer, Seth. *Children's Literature: A Reader's History from Aesop to Harry Potter*. Chicago: University of Chicago Press, 2008.

Leupin, Alexandre. *Barbarolexis: Medieval Writing and Sexuality*. Trans. Kate M. Cooper. Cambridge, Mass.: Harvard University Press, 1989.

———. "The Powerlessness of Writing: Guillaume de Machaut, the Gorgon, and Ordenance." Trans. Peggy McCracken. *Yale French Studies* 70 (1986): 127–49.

Levenson, J. C. *The Mind and Art of Henry Adams*. Cambridge, Mass.: Harvard University Press, 1957.

Lightsey, Scott. "Chaucer's Secular Marvels and the Medieval Economy of Wonder." *SAC* 23 (2001): 289–316.

———. *Manmade Marvels in Medieval Culture and Literature*. New York: Palgrave, 2007.

Lindberg, David C. *Roger Bacon and the Origins of Perspectiva in the Middle Ages.* Oxford: Clarendon, 1996.

———. "Roger Bacon on Light, Vision, and the Universal Emanation of Force." In *Roger Bacon and the Sciences: Commemorative Essays*, ed. Jeremiah Hackett. Leiden: Brill, 1997.

Linden, Stanton, J., ed. *Dark Hierogliphicks: Alchemy in English Literature from Chaucer to the Restoration.* Lexington: University Press of Kentucky, 1996.

———. *The Mirror of Alchimy, Composed by the Thrice-Famous and Learned Fryer, Roger Bachon.* New York: Garland, 1992.

———. *The Alchemy Reader: From Hermes Trismegistus to Isaac Newton.* Cambridge: Cambridge University Press, 2003.

Little, A. G. ed. *Roger Bacon: Essays.* New York: Russell and Russell, 1914.

———. "Roger Bacon's Life and Works." In *Roger Bacon: Essays*, ed. Little. New York: Russell and Russell, 1914.

Liu, Alan. *The Laws of Cool: Knowledge Work and the Culture of Information.* Chicago: University of Chicago Press, 2004.

Lochrie, Karma. *Covert Operations: The Medieval Uses of Secrecy.* Philadelphia: University of Pennsylvania Press, 1999.

Loewald, Hans W. "Some Considerations on Repetition and the Repetition Compulsion." *International Journal of Psychoanalysis* 52 (1971): 59–66.

Long, Pamela O. "The Craft of Premodern European History of Technology, Past and Future Practice." *Technology and Culture* 51, 3 (July 2010): 698–714.

———. *Openness, Secrecy, Authorship: Technical Arts and the Culture of Knowledge from Antiquity to the Renaissance.* Baltimore: Johns Hopkins University Press, 2001.

Löwith, Karl. *Meaning in History: The Theological Implications of the Philosophy of History.* Chicago: University of Chicago Press, 1949.

Lupton, Julia. *Afterlives of the Saints: Hagiography, Typology, and Renaissance Literature.* Stanford, Calif.: Stanford University Press, 1996.

Luscombe, David. "Peter Abelard's Carnal Thoughts." In *Medieval Theology and the Natural Body*, ed. Peter Biller, Alastair J. Minnis, and Eamon Duffey, York: York Medieval Press, 1997. 31–60.

———. "The Sense of Innovation in the Writings of Peter Abelard." In *Tradition, Innovation, Invention: Fortschrittsverweigerung und Fortschrittsbewusstsein im Mittelalter*, ed. Hans-Joachim Schmidt. Berlin: De Gruyter, 2001. 181–94.

Maloney, T. S. "Roger Bacon on Equivocation." *Vivarium* 22, 2 (1984): 85–112.

Manly, John Matthews. "The Most Mysterious Manuscript in the World: Did Roger Bacon Write It and Has the Key Been Found?" *Harper's Monthly Magazine* 143 (1921): 186–97.

———. "Roger Bacon and the Voynich Manuscript." *Speculum* 6, 3 (July 1931): 345–91.

Matin-Asgari, Afshin. "Islamic Studies and the Spirit of Max Weber: A Critique of Cultural Essentialism." *Critique: Critical Middle Eastern Studies* 13, 3 (Fall 2004): 293–312.

McDonald, Nicola. "A Polemical Introduction" to *Pulp Fictions of Medieval England: Essays in Popular Romance.* Manchester: Manchester University Press, 2004. 1–21.

Menocal, María Rosa. *Shards of Love: Exile and the Origin of the Lyric*. Durham, N.C.: Duke University Press, 1994.

Miller, Shannon. "Idleness, Human Industry, and English Colonial Activity in Thomas More's 'fruitfull, pleasant,' 'wittie' and 'profitable' Utopia." In *Laureations: Essays in Memory of Richard Helgerson*, ed. Roze Henschell and Kathy Lavezzo. Lantham, Md.: Rowman and Littlefield, 2011. 19–50.

Minnis, Alastair. *Medieval Theory of Authorship: Scholastic Literary Attitudes in the Late Middle Ages*. 2nd ed. with a new Preface. Philadelphia: University of Pennsylvania Press, 2010.

Mokyr, Joel. *The Lever of Riches: Technological Creativity and Economic Progress*. New York: Oxford University Press, 1990.

Moore, R. I. *The War on Heresy: Faith and Power in Medieval Europe*. Cambridge, Mass.: Harvard University Press, 2012.

Mundy, John H. *Europe in the High Middle Ages, 1150–1309*. New York: Basic Books, 1973.

Muscatine, Charles. *Chaucer and the French Tradition*. Berkeley: University of California Press, 1960.

Newbold, W. R. *The Cipher of Roger Bacon*. Ed. R. G. Kent. Philadelphia: University of Pennsylvania Press, 1928.

Newhauser, Richard. "Augustinian vitium curiositatis and its reception." In *Saint Augustine and His Influence in the Middle Ages*, ed. Edward B. King and Jacqueline T. Schaefer. Sewanee Mediaeval Studies 3. Sewanee, Tenn: Press of the University of the South, 1988. 99–124.

———. "Curiosity," in Karla Pollmann, ed., *The Oxford Guide to the Historical Reception of Augustine*, vol. 2. Oxford: Oxford University Press, 2013. 849–52.

———. "Towards a History of Human Curiosity: A Prolegomenon to Its Medieval Phase." *Deutsche Vierteljahrschift für Literaturwissenschaft und Geistesgeschichte* 52 (1982): 569–75.

Newman, Jane O. "Enchantment in Times of War: Aby Warburg, Walter Benjamin, and the Secularization Thesis." *Representations* 105 (Winter 2009): 133–67.

Newman, William R. *Atoms and Alchemy: Chymestry and the Experimental Origins of the Scientific Revolution*. Chicago: University of Chicago Press, 2006.

———. "An Overview of Roger Bacon's Alchemy." In *Roger Bacon and the Sciences: Commemorative Essays*, ed. Jeremiah Hackett. Leiden: Brill, 1997. 317–36.

———. "The Philosophers' Egg: Theory and Practice in the Alchemy of Roger Bacon." *Micrologus*, 3 (1995): 75–101.

———. *Promethean Ambitions: Alchemy and the Quest to Perfect Nature*. Chicago: University of Chicago Press, 2004.

———. "Technology and Alchemical Debate in the Late Middle Ages." *Isis* 80 (September 1989): 423–45.

Newman, William and Lawrence Principe. "Some Problems with the Historiography of Alchemy." In *Secrets of Nature: Astrology and Alchemy in Early Modern Europe*, ed. William Newman and Anthony Grafton. Cambridge, Mass.: MIT Press, 2001. 385–431.

Nicholson, Peter. *Love and Ethics in Gower's* '"Confessio Amantis." Ann Arbor: University of Michigan Press, 2005.

Nolan, Maura. "Making the Aesthetic Turn: Adorno, the Medieval, and the Future of the Past." *Journal of Medieval and Early Modern Studies* 34, 3 (2004): 549–75.

Oakley, Francis. *The Political Thought of Pierre d'Ailly.* New Haven, Conn.: Yale University Press, 1964.

Orme, Nicholas. *Education and Society in Medieval and Renaissance England.* London: Hambledon, 1989.

———. *Medieval Childhood.* New Haven, Conn.: Yale University Press, 2001.

Osborne, Marijane. "The Squire's 'Steed of Brass' as Astrolabe: Some Implications for the Canterbury Tales." In *Hermeneutics and Medieval Culture*, ed. Patrick J. Gallacher and Helen Damico. Albany: State University Press of New York, 1989. 121–31.

Pagden, Anthony. *European Encounters with the New World: From Renaissance to Romanticism.* New Haven, Conn.: Yale University Press, 1993.

Parkes, Peter. "Milk Kinship in Islam: Substance, Structure, History." *Social Anthropology* 13, 3 (2005): 307–9.

Patterson, Lee. "Perpetual Motion: Alchemy and the Technology of the Self." *Studies in the Age of Chaucer* 15 (1993): 25–57.

Pegg, Mark G. *A Most Holy War: The Albigensian Crusade and the Battle for Christendom.* New York: Oxford University Press, 2007.

Peters, Edward. "The Desire to Know the Secrets of the World." *Journal of the History of Ideas* 62, 4 (2001): 593–61.

———. "*Libertas Inquierendi* and the *Vitium Curiositatis* in Medieval Thought." In *La notion de liberté au Moyen Age: Islam, Byzance, Occident*, ed. George Makdisi et al. Paris: Belles Lettres, 1985. 89–98.

Pinborg, Jan. "Roger Bacon on Signs: A Newly Recovered Part of the *Opus Majus*." 403–12. In *Sprache und Erkenntnis im Mittelalter: Akten des VI. Internationalen Kongresses für Mittelalterliche Philosophie der Société internationale pour l'étude de la philosophie médiévale, 29.August–3. September 1977 in Bonn*, ed. Von Jan P. Beckmann et al. Miscellanea Mediaevalia 13. (Berlin: de Gruyter, 1981), Vol 1.

Power, Amanda. "A Mirror for Every Age: The Reputation of Roger Bacon." *English Historical Review* 121, 492 (2006): 657–92.

Pugh, Tison, ed. "Book Review Forum: Responses to *The Swerve: How the World Became Modern*," *Exemplaria: A Journal of Theory in Medieval and Renaissance Studies* 25, 4 (2013): 313–70.

Rabasa, José. *Inventing America: Spanish Historiography and the Formation of Eurocentrism.* Norman: University of Oklahoma Press, 1993.

Raybin, David. "And Pave It Al of Silver and of Gold: The Humane Artistry of the Canon's Yeoman's Tale." In *Rebels and Rivals: The Contested Spirit in the Canterbury Tales*, ed. Susana Greer Fein, David Raybin, and Peter C. Braeger. Kalamazoo: Western Michigan Press, 1991. 189–212.

Reinhard, Kenneth, Slavoj Žižek, and Erik Santner. *The Neighbor: Three Inquiries into Political Theology.* Chicago: University of Chicago Press, 2005.

Rimmon-Kenan, Shlomith. "The Paradoxical Status of Repetition." *Poetics Today* 1, 4, *Narratology II: The Fictional Text and the Reader* (Summer 1980): 151–59.

Robertson, Kellie. "Medieval Materialism: A Manifesto." *Exemplaria* 22, 2 (Summer 2010): 99–120.

Roest, Bert. "Rhetoric of Innovation and Recourse to Tradition in Humanist Pedagogical Discourse." In *Medieval and Renaissance Humanism: Rhetoric, Representation, and Reform,* ed. Stephen Gersh and Bert Roest. Leiden: Brill, 2003. 115–48.

Roland, Alex. "Once More to the Stirrups." *Technology and Culture* 44 (July 2003): 574–85.

Rollo, David. "Nature's Pharmaceuticals: Sanctioned Desires in Alain de Lille's *De planctu Naturae.*" *Exemplaria* 25, 2 (2013): 152–72.

Rosenfeld, Jessica. *Ethics and Enjoyment in Late-Medieval Poetry: Love After Aristotle.* Cambridge: Cambridge University Press, 2011.

Schibanoff, Susan. "Sodomy's Mark: Alan of Lille, Jean de Meun, and the Medieval Theory of Authorship." In *Queering the Middle Ages,* ed. Glenn Burger and Steven F. Kruger. Minneapolis: University of Minnesota Press, 2001. 28–56.

———. "Worlds Apart: Orientalism, Antifeminism, and Heresy in Chaucer's Man of Law's Tale." *Exemplaria* 8, 1 (1996): 59–96.

Schlueter, Wolfgang. *Paradoxes of Modernity: Culture and Conduct in the Theory of Max Weber.* Stanford, Calif.: Stanford University Press, 1996.

Schmidt, Hans-Joachim, ed. *Tradition, Innovation, Invention: Fortschrittsverweigerung und Fortschrittsbewusstsein im Mittelalter.* Berlin: de Gruyter, 2005.

Schultz, James. *The Knowledge of Childhood in the German Middle Ages, 1100–1350.* Philadelphia: University of Pennsylvania Press, 1995.

Schumpeter, Joseph A. *Capitalism, Socialism and Democracy.* 3rd ed. New York: HarperCollins, 2008.

Scott, Joan Wallach. *The Fantasy of Feminist History.* Durham, N.C.: Duke University Press, 2011.

Şenocak, Neslihan. *The Poor and the Perfect: The Rise of Learning in the Franciscan Order, 1209–1310.* Ithaca, N.Y.: Cornell University Press, 2012.

Short, William M. "Francis, the 'New' Saint in the Tradition of Christian Hagiography." In *Francis of Assisi, History, Hagiography, and Hermeneutics in the Early Documents,* ed. Jay M. Hammond. Hyde Park, N.Y.: New City Press, 2004.

Sica, Alan. *Weber, Irrationality, and Social Order.* Berkeley: University of California Press, 1988.

Sidelko, Paul. "The Condemnation of Roger Bacon." *Journal of Medieval History* 22 (1996): 69–81.

Simmel, George. *The Philosophy of Money.* London: Routledge, 1978.

Singer, Dorothea. "Alchemical Writings Attributed to Roger Bacon." *Speculum* 7, 1 (1932): 80–86.

.

Sisk, Jennifer, "Religion, Alchemy, and Nostalgic Idealism in Fragment VIII." *SAC* 32 (2010): 151–77.

Smalley, Beryl. "Ecclesiastical Attitudes to Novelty, c. 1100–1250." In *Church, Society, and Politics,* ed. Derek Baker. Oxford: Oxford University Press, 1975.

Smith, D. Vance. *Arts of Possession: The Middle English Household Imaginary.* Minneapolis: University of Minnesota Press, 2003.

Smith, Susan. *The Power of Women: A Topos in Medieval Art and Literature.* Philadelphia: University of Pennsylvania Press, 1995.

Smoller, Laura. *History, Prophecy and the Stars: The Christian Astrology of Pierre d'Ailly, 1350–1420.* Princeton, N.J.: Princeton University Press, 1994.

Sohn-Rethel, Alfred. *Intellectual and Manual Labor: A Critique of Epistemology.* Atlantic Highlands, N.J.: Humanities Press, 1977.

Spargo, E. J. M. *The Category of the Aesthetic in the Philosophy of St. Bonaventure.* New York: Franciscan Institute, 1953.

Spargo, John W. *Virgil the Necromancer: Studies in Virgilian Legends.* Cambridge, Mass.: Harvard University Press, 1934.

Stahuljak, Zrinka, Virginie Greene, Sarah Kay, Sharon Kinoshita, and Peggy McCracken. *Thinking Through Chrétien de Troyes.* Cambridge: Brewer, 2011.

Stanbury, Sarah. *The Visual Object of Desire in Late Medieval England.* Philadelphia: University of Pennsylvania Press, 2008.

Stein, Robert M. *Reality Fictions: Romance, History, and Governmental Authority.* South Bend, Ind.: University of Notre Dame Press, 2006.

Stock, Brian. *Listening for the Text.* Baltimore: Johns Hopkins University Press, 1990.

———. "Rationality, Tradition, and the Scientific Outlook: Reflections on Max Weber and the Middle Ages." *Annals of the New York Academy of Sciences* 441, 1 (2006): 7–19.

Stone, Gregory. *The Ethics of Nature in the Middle Ages: On Boccaccio's Poetaphysics.* New York: St. Martin's, 1998.

Storost, Joachim. "Femme Chevalchat Aristotte." *Zeitschrift fur französische Sprache und Literatur* 66 (1956): 186–201.

Sunderland, Luke. *Old French Narrative Cycles: Heroism Between Ethics and Morality.* Cambridge: Brewer, 2010.

Taleb, Nicholas N. *The Black Swan: The Impact of the Highly Improbable.* New York: Random House, 2007.

Tanselle, G. Thomas. "The Editorial Problem of Authorial Final Intention." *Studies in Bibliography* 29 (1976): 167–211.

Taylor, Richard C. "Averroës." *The Cambridge Companion to Arabic Philosophy.* Cambridge: Cambridge University Press, 2004.

Tiffany, Daniel. *Toy Medium: Materialism and the Modern Lyric.* Stanford, Calif.: Stanford University Press, 2000.

Thorndike, Lynn. *A History of Magic and Experimental Science During the First Thirteen Centuries of our Era,* 8 vols. Vols. 1–2 New York: Macmillan; Vols. 3–8 New York: Columbia University Press, 1923–58.

Tolan, John V. *Saracens: Islam in the European Imagination*. New York: Columbia University Press, 2002.

Triutt, E. R. "'Trei poëte, sages dotors, qui mout sorent di nigromance': Knowledge and Automata in Twelfth-Century French Literature." *Configurations* 12, 2 (Spring 2004): 167–93.

Van Buren, Anne Hagopain. "Reality and Literary Romance in the Park of Hesdin." In *Medieval Gardens*, ed. Elisabeth B. MacDougall. Washington, D.C.: Dunbarton Oaks, 1986. 115–34.

Wallace, Richard. "Lowith-Blumenberg Debate." *New German Critique* 22 (Winter 1981): 63–79.

Warren, Michelle R. *History on the Edge: Excalibur and the Borders of Britain, 1100–1300*. Minneapolis: University of Minnesota Press, 2000.

Watts, P. M. "Prophecy and Discovery: On the Spiritual Origins of Christopher Columbus's 'Enterprise of the Indies.'" *American Historical Review* 90 (1985): 73–102.

Weber, Max. *From Max Weber: Essays in Sociology*, ed. H. H. Gerth and C. Wright Mills, New York: Oxford University Press, 1981.

———. *The Sociology of Religion*. Trans. Ephraim Fischoff. Boston: Beacon, 1963; repr. 1993.

White, Lynn. "The Historical Roots of Our Current Ecological Crisis" *Science* 155, 3767 (March 10, 1967): 1203–12.

———. *Medieval Technology and Social Change*. Oxford: Oxford University Press, 1962.

———. "Technology Assessment from the Stance of a Medieval Historian." *AHR* 79, 1 (1974): 1–13.

Williams, Raymond. *The Country and the City*. Oxford: Oxford University Press, 1973.

Wimsatt, James I. *Chaucer and His French Contemporaries: Natural Music in the Fourteenth Century*. Toronto: University of Toronto Press, 1991.

Wolter, Allan B. *Duns Scotus on the Will and Morality*, Washington, D.C.: Catholic University of America Press, 1986.

Wood, Rega. Introduction to Richard Rufus of Cornwall, *In Physicam Aristotelis*, ed. Rega Wood. Auctores Britannici Medii Aevi XVI. Oxford: Oxford University Press, 2003.

———. "Richard Rufus: Physics at Paris Before 1240." *Documenti e Studi sulla Tradizione Filosofica Medieval* 5 (1994): 87–96.

Zacher, Christian. *Curiosity and Pilgrimage: The Literature of Discovery in Fourteenth Century England*. Baltimore: Johns Hopkins University Press, 1976.

Zambelli, Paolo. *The "Speculum Astronomiae" and Its Enigma: Astrology, Theology, and Science in Albertus Magnus and His Contemporaries*. Dordrecht: Kluwer, 1992.

Zamora, Margarita. *Reading Columbus*. Berkeley: University of California Press, 1993.

Zeeman, Nicolette. "The Idol of the Text." In *Images, Idolatry, and Iconoclasm in Late Medieval England*, ed. Jeremy Dimick, James Simpson, and Nicolette Zeeman. Oxford: Oxford University Press, 2002.

Zilsel, Edgar. *Die Entstehung des Geniebegriffs: Ein Beitrag zur Ideengeschichte der Antike und des Fruhkapitalismus*. Tubingen: Mohr, 1926.

Index

Abelard, Peter, 10, 84, 210n47; debate with Bernard of Clairvaux, 17, 37, 40–41, 60, 80, 210n49; innovation in *Historia Calamitatum*, 38–39

Adams, Henry, 5, 20, 36, 46, 50, 53; treatment of Aquinas in *Mont-Saint-Michel and Chartres*, 23–28, 206nn4, 8

Adulteration, adulterate: and ethics, 72, 81, 90, 109; and Hugh of St. Victor, 30, 35, 85; and the new 36, 85–86; and sexuality, 85–86

Alain de Lille, 4, 44, 84–85, 205n52, 224nn35, 46, 225n51

Alchemy, 5, 28, 35, 40, 49, 52, 68, 70, 71, 77, 85, 237n32; as a craft practice, 19, 80, 151–52, 160–62, 239n49; and elvishness, 155–59, 165, 238n42; as experimental science, 71–72; and greed, 148–49; 162–63; and historiography, 46, 149–50, 237n30; and linguistic equivocation, 61–62, 153–54, 236n27, 238n40; as utopian, 148–49. *See also* Bacon, Roger; *Canon's Yeoman's Tale*; Utopianism

Alexander the Great, 72, 76, 143, 177–78, 189, 245n45

The Alexandreis, 177–78, 188–89, 244n41

Alighieri, Dante, 5, 29, 54, 86

Ambivalent, ambivalence, 6, 14, 15, 18, 24, 26, 37, 46, 49–51, 53, 68, 103, 105, 121, 131, 134, 152, 165, 169, 176, 191, 224n38, 229n21, 235n10; and ethics, 78–80, 138–40; and Henry Adams, 26–28; and *Floris and Blaunchflour*, 109–11; psychoanalytic sense, 26, 206n57. *See also* Desire

Apocalypse, apocalyptic, 55, 65, 241n20; and Christopher Columbus, 170–72, 175, 178, 180, 188, 192, 240nn10, 11. *See also* Joachim de Fiore

Aquinas, Thomas, 4, 5, 10, 11, 29, 41, 42, 44, 60, 64, 65, 86, 113, 147, 161, 202, 207n19, 208n26, 217n41, 220n85; in Henry Adams, 24–26; and newness, 31–39. *See also* Aristotle

Arabic, 28, 49, 86, 89, 112; astronomical texts, 63–66; commentators of Aristotle, 29, 40, 217n50, 227n79; in *Flore and Blancheflur* tradition, 88, 89, 92, 98, 110; influence in Europe, 86–87, 228n13; and milk-kinship, 89, 225n58; as sources for romance, 83, 84, 107. *See also* Islam

Aristotle, 18, 20–21, 48, 51, 62, 54, 78, 125, 128, 169; Aquinas on, 23–26; "the mounted Aristotle," 44, 76–77, 84–85, 88, 96, 97, 105, 224n40, 225n47, 227n77

Art, 8–9, 12, 28, 35, 42, 85, 88, 128, 149, 200n9, 209n39, 210n45; and Bacon, 67–68, 71, 112, 214n21; and economic exchange, 128–29, 165; and Fortune's Wheel, 194–96; in Lacan, 45–46, 91; and science, 3, 12–15, 19, 27, 48, 54, 224n38; and toys, 132–33. *See also* Science

Artisan, artisanal, 4, 5, 14, 19, 29–30, 35, 42, 43, 116, 133, 153, 161, 211n60, 224n38; and proprietary craft, 163–65, 239n49

Astrolabe, 35, 134, 136, 150, 151, 233nn65, 66

Astronomy, 6, 8, 64–66, 216n41, 218nn56, 57, 219n64

Auctoritas, 6, 55, 68, 70, 72, 151, 164. See also *Textus*

Authority: uses of, 39–40, 51, 71, 72, 186, 245n53, 249n79; used falsely, 54–56, 68–70

Automata, 8, 116, 133–34, 143, 233n61, 249n1

Averroës, 29, 31, 33, 61, 63, 208n25; Latin Averroists, 26, 33, 63, 209n35

Bacon, Roger, 5, 17, 20, 38, 47, 112, 150, 156, 170, 176, 178, 212n3; 213n4; 214n21; 215n21; and alchemy, 70–72, 156, 161; as

Acknowledgments

Many conversations with beloved friends, family, teachers, and colleagues freshened my thinking and renewed my spirit over the many years it took to finish this book. Early encouragement from Aranye Fradenburg, and from my dear woodland friends at Lehigh University (especially Beth Dolan, Alex Doty, and Jan Fergus) set me on my way. Jerry Singerman and the production staff at the University of Pennsylvania Press have taken the project efficiently and elegantly to its end.

Indiana University has offered an unparalleled intellectual community. I could not have written this book without it. Special thanks to Rosemarie Mc-Gerr of the Medieval Studies Institute for an early invitation to present portions of my work, to Bridget Balint, whose expertise in Latin assisted me early on and in an utterly formative way, and to the prolific and learned Bill Newman, who guided me through the currents of scholarship on the medieval history of science, rescuing me from error on more than one occasion. Medievalist colleagues in English, Michael Adams, Rob Fulk, Shannon Gayk, and Karma Lochrie responded generously to every query or request I sent their way. Shannon and Karma each generously read early versions of chapters, regularly providing erudite and wise advice. It's a pleasure to share this little spot of academic earth with them. I also owe thanks to Judith Anderson, Penelope Anderson, Linda Charnes, Michel Chaouli, Ed Comentale, Jonathan Elmer, Mary Favret, Rae Greiner, Susan Gubar, Christoph Irmscher, Joshua Kates, Ivan Kreilkamp, Lara Kriegel (dog to my cat), Adam Leite, Andrew Miller, Ellen MacKay, Diane Reilly, Bret Rothstein, and Dror Wahrman. Lively conversation over steaming bowls of oatmeal (both courtesy of power-couple, Hall Bjørnstad and Sonia Velàzquez) sustained me and this project. Students in my 2008 graduate seminar (Corey Sparks, Kerilyn Harkaway-Kreiger, Elise Lonich, Jessica Tooker, Ben Garceau, Cindy Rogers, and Sos Bagramyan) inspired more than one idea here. Bonnie Erwin, Corey Sparks, and Emilie Cox each provided expert research support at crucial moments. I gratefully acknowledge financial support from the College Arts and Humanities Institute (CAHI) and the New Frontiers Fellowship Program at IU.

I am lucky to call so many smart, funny, and supportive medievalists my friends. This is a better book because Medieval Studies rocks. Thanks are due to Dorrie Armstrong, Jeffery Jerome Cohen, Holly Crocker, Carolyn Dinshaw, George Edmondson, Ruth Evans, Sharon Farmer, John Ganim, the much beloved Noah Guynn, Emily Houlik-Ritchey, Shaun Hughes, Sarah Kay, Miriamne Krummel, Emma Lipton, David Matthews, Mark Miller, Susie Nakley, Megan Palmer-Browne, Tom Prendergast, Tison Pugh, Kellie Robertson, Randy Schiff, Sarah Stanbury, Peter Travis, Stephanie Trigg, Elly Truitt (my new bff), David Wallace, and Michelle Warren. A special word must be reserved for Frank Grady (cracker-jack editor and one of the most astute readers I know), and Tom Goodmann (whose life regularly amazes me). The brilliant and funny Elizabeth Scala has kept me keeping on for more than a decade. She is my best reader, and her generosity and friendship (to say nothing of her superb culinary tastes) regularly bear me up. Peggy McCracken and Richard Newhauser read the entire manuscript, offering wise counsel that improved the book in every instance.

At the National Humanities Center my work and my spirits were improved by the conviviality of the class of 2012–2013 (a banner year for the early periods). Thanks to fellows early and late, but especially to Fred Anderson, Anthony Bale, Sarah Beckwith, Paula Blank, Cynthia Brokaw, Carla Nappi, Bruce Rusk, Dyan Elliott, Marcia Kupfer, Drew Clayton, Susan Wolf, Stefan Collini, and Ruth Morse. Pamela O. Long read everything I wrote on alchemy and was enormously kind and encouraging. The entire staff at the Center (especially Cassie Mansfield, Karen Carroll, Brooke Andrade, Eliza Robertson, and Lois Wittington) enabled us all. I gratefully acknowledge the support of a fellowship made possible by the National Endowment for the Humanities. Any views, findings, conclusions, or recommendations expressed in this book do not necessarily reflect those of the NEH.

A few special debts: Bob Stein, supporter for so many years, aided me from start to finish, asking difficult questions, applauding my answers, generously editing my ragged prose, and providing crucial assistance with language and theory both. My brother Nicholas offered elegant summations of Aquinas, and my sister, Mary Beth, advised me on medieval philosophy (Scotus especially) and cheered me on when I needed it most. In Bloomington, the wise and wonderful Sydney Anderson enabled a different way of thinking about creativity, about repetition, and about the power and promise of fresh-feeling. Linda, David, and Sophie Giedroc put up with my rants about the value of the humanities, and made Bloomington feel more like home. My dearest local *amies*: Judith Brown—the most creative thinker I know—was my port in any storm, dispensing kindness, sharp ideas, and elegant metaphors in equal measure; Jen Fleissner pushed me on modernity, got me interested again in Henry Adams, and never let me forget how important these questions are; Constance Furey—generous interlocutor, stunning reader, and energetic collaborator—inspires me to try to keep faith with my very best self. I lost my beloved Alex Doty too soon, during the final years of writing this book. Alex's wit and wisdom made me happier, and his friendship enriched my life. His memory keeps me on the lookout for unexpected pleasures, but especially for excellent tequila. Thanks to the Misses Ellie, Tillie, and Isabel for all the snuggling and for making me go outside, even when I didn't much feel like it.

By far my greatest debts are to Doug Moore, the kindest and most generous person I know. He who never lets me get too beleaguered, who still makes me laugh, who brings me tea (or wine) and makes me dinner (or pancakes), who refreshes my prose and my thinking, and who is still willing, after all these years, to pull up stakes and take off again on some new adventure. I dedicate this book to him with gratitude for being my unflagging fan, healer of cats with broken bones, adorable and willing partner—my oldest newest friend.